D1563688

Confederate Engineer

Confederate Engineer

>>>

TRAINING AND CAMPAIGNING
WITH JOHN MORRIS WAMPLER

GEORGE G. KUNDAHL

Voices of the Civil War
Frank L. Byrne, Series Editor

THE UNIVERSITY OF TENNESSEE PRESS / KNOXVILLE

Published in cooperation with the United States Civil War Center.

Library of Congress Cataloging-in-Publication Data

Kundahl, George G., 1940-
Confederate engineer : training and campaigning with John
Morris Wampler / George G. Kundahl.—1st ed.
    p. cm.
"Published in cooperation with the United States Civil War Center."
Includes bibliographical references and index.
ISBN 1-57233-073-2 (cl.: alk. paper)
I. Title. II. United States Civil War Center. 1. Wampler, John Morris, 1830–1863. 2. Confederate States of America. Army. Corps of Engineers—Biography. 3. Confederate States of America. Army of Tennessee—Biography. 4. Military engineers—Confederate States of America—Biography. 5. United States—History—Civil War, 1861–1865—Engineering and construction. 6. United States—History—Civil War, 1861–1865—Transportation.
E546.7 .K86 2000
973.7'13'092   99-006871

To My Mother, Adelaide Wampler Kundahl,
the inspiration for it all and the link between
Kate and Morris Wampler and the present

Contents

Illustrations

Foreword

While this book is more a biography than an edited document, its use of extensive quotation from its subject's writings and the use of his maps and drawings make it an authentic Voice of the Civil War. It speaks for the important, though often overlooked, army engineers. In this respect, the volume is a Confederate counterpart to Ed Malles's earlier book in this series entitled *Bridge Building in Wartime*. Neither that work's subject, Union Col. Wesley Brainerd, nor Confederate Engineer Capt. John Morris Wampler was a product of West Point, then the leading American engineering school. Instead they had learned the trade largely by practical apprenticeship—though Wampler had also served with the scientifically oriented United States Coast Survey. His career demonstrated the connection between the prewar and wartime engineering professions.

A man of the Upper South, Wampler enthusiastically tried to carve out a career for himself in the young Confederacy. Since the war came early to his home, he served at its start in the 8th Virginia. Contacts made there, especially with P. G. T. Beauregard, led to his gaining a leading role on the staff of the Armies of the Mississippi and of Tennessee. After leaving his wife and children in the East, he took part in the abortive Confederate invasion of Kentucky in 1862, culminating in the Battle of Perryville. He then was associated with the engineers who attempted to prepare for the defense of the Confederate foothold in Tennessee.

By the summer of 1863, Captain Wampler once again responded to Beauregard's need for engineers, this time to resist the Union siege of Charleston, South Carolina. On the edge of that harbor was Battery Wagner, under attack from land and sea. In the former assault, the black 54th Massachusetts distinguished itself, as the motion picture *Glory* would portray well over a century later. In the latter action, an unprecedentedly heavy naval bombardment, Wampler encountered instant death. Like many other officers on both sides, his first memorial was the sandy earthworks named for him at Charleston Harbor, Battery Wampler. George Kundahl's book is a more enduring monument.

Frank L. Byrne
Kent State University

Acknowledgments

Contemporary scholars cannot thoroughly understand life and events of a century and a half ago without assistance from many people who have dedicated their lives, in whole or in part, to preserving and disseminating knowledge of times, skills, and events now obscure. In my journey along the roads traveled by Morris Wampler, I have been assisted by numerous "good Samaritans," without whose help this endeavor would not have been possible.

First of all, the project could not have begun without the cooperation of my late cousin, Thomas N. Wampler, and his widow Marge. John DePue started me on my way by suggesting the title for the work. I was periodically the beneficiary of insights from Edwin C. Bearss, truly a national historic resource, whose inspiration, encyclopedic knowledge of the war, and unfailing courtesy and helpfulness repeatedly encouraged me. Another friend, Craig Kellermann, served as my Muse, literary sounding board, and informal editor, insisting that Wampler's life be drawn so as to hold relevance, beyond his Civil War experiences, for modern readers. Craig read and commented upon the manuscript repeatedly, for which I am deeply indebted. Brian Pohanka, a civil war editor for *Time/Life* books, among other credentials, was generous with his time, expertise in the vocabulary of the mid-nineteenth century, and extraordinary editing skills. Finally, Martin Gordon at the U.S. Corps of Engineers historian's office provided thoughtful advice at numerous decision points.

Each individual chapter had one or more specific patrons. Many of the thoughts I express are theirs; all of the errors in interpretation and fact are mine alone. Foremost among these friends was the late John Divine, the unofficial historian of Loudoun County, Virginia. John devoted countless days to me, showing and explaining locations described by Wampler, helping to interpret entries in his journals and the writings of his wife, and sharing an extensive personal library and unparalleled knowledge of Leesburg and its environs during the war. John was the epitome of a gracious Southern gentleman, and I am but one of many younger Civil War inquirers who learned from him things that are not written down or accessible in any other way. John Divine's imprint is seen especially in chapters 4 and 5. I regret that he did not live to see the completion of this work in its entirety.

The discussion of Margaret Mercer and Belmont in chapter 1 was enriched by the contributions of Bill Bakken, just as Inez Brown assisted with family references in this chapter and throughout the book. Chapter 2 would have literally been impossible without the explanations of Capt. (Ret.) Albert "Skip" Theberge, who, coincidentally, was compiling a history of the U.S. Coast Survey at the same time I was trying to understand Wampler's service in that under-recognized and misunderstood government dinosaur. Skip also critiqued Wampler's graphodometer, just as Harry Hunter, the Smithsonian Institution armorer, evaluated the significance of Wampler's modifications to breech-loading weapons. These innovations are described in chapter 3. Kim Holien, an authority on Balls Bluff, among other subjects, and Horace Mewborn, John Singleton Mosby's biographer, added their expertise to chapters 4 and 5, respectively.

A different set of guides led me along Wampler's trail in the West. My traveling companion in this quest was an old army buddy, Pat Adams, who pitched in with his typical enthusiasm. At each stop along the way trod by the Army of the Mississippi, and later the Army of Tennessee, different local historians added specialized insight to my understanding: Hugh Horton in Corinth; Alex Morgan in Aberdeen; Charlie Long at Mount Washington; Kurt Holman at Perryville; Milan Hill in Tullahoma; and Bob Duncan in Columbia, Tennessee. Their contributions are evident in chapters 6 and 7. The medical diagnosis in the latter chapter was made after consultations with Dr. John Mather, who has done an extensive analysis of Sir Winston Churchill's health, and Dr. Alfred Jay Bollet, clinical professor of medicine at Yale University. Also in chapter 7, Dale Floyd applied his expertise in nineteenth-century engineering to my narrative, and Jim Ogden, a historian for the National Park Service, offered insights not only related to his home base at Chattanooga, but also regarding the broader Tennessee war as well.

A fuller understanding of the defense of Charleston Harbor in 1863, addressed in the prologue and in chapter 8, was made possible through the generosity and perceptiveness of historian Stephen Wise and preservationist Willis "Skipper" Keith of James Island, South Carolina. Dr. Charles V. Peery was generous with his extensive collection of images from the period. Penetrating Wampler's use of encryption required access to very specialized skills. The discussion in the epilogue could only begin after Rudy Lauer of the National Security Agency broke Wampler's code. Relating Wampler's ciphers to those of the Masons was possible thanks to

Brent Morris, an unusually learned historian of the Masonic Order. Signals historian Dave Gaddy also provided assistance.

Not to be forgotten are a legion of archivists, librarians, and curators, many unknown to me by name. Like many researchers, my list must begin with Mike Musick at the National Archives, who is unfailingly helpful with his unique appreciation of that institution's Civil War treasures. Richard J. Sommers, archivist at the Military History Institute, identified documents to aid my research. Joyce McMullin and George Combs at the Lloyd House in Alexandria, Jane Sullivan at the Balch Library in Leesburg, Rebecca Rose and John Ahladas at the Museum of the Confederacy, and Francis O'Neill at the Maryland Historical Society head a long list of helpful and patient librarians at the many collections identified in the bibliography. I am also indebted to the staffs at the historical societies of the District of Columbia (Columbia Historical Society), Kentucky, Maryland, Missouri, Pennsylvania, South Carolina, and Virginia, and at the state archives in Georgia, Kentucky, Maryland, North Carolina, South Carolina, Tennessee, and Virginia. My sincere thanks go to each of the staffs of these repositories.

Thanks go to the University of Tennessee Press as well. Its director, Jennifer Siler, maintained confidence in this project long after she might have been expected to lose interest. Editor Scot Danforth was invaluable in smoothing grammar, spotting mindless mistakes, and asking simple, penetrating questions caused by imprecise writing no longer obvious to an author blinded by detail. David Madden at the U.S. Civil War center also provided important support at a critical juncture.

I should not forget my computer gurus, John Komoroske and Ken Staples. John repeatedly came to my rescue, day or night, at considerable personal inconvenience. Ken is renowned for his extraordinary patience with novices like myself. Unfortunately, other important contributors must undoubtedly have gone unrecognized, for which I apologize.

Finally, a multiyear undertaking of this kind does not succeed without acceptance, understanding, and succor from one's spouse. My wife, Joy, provided the loving reassurance that accompanied me all the way from Baltimore in the early 1800s to the completion of the final manuscript in Alexandria, Virginia, in the late 1900s. I will never adequately express my appreciation for her support in this endeavor, and for so much more.

A Note on Primary Sources

The foundation for an examination of the life of Morris Wampler is the assortment of eight journals retained by his descendants. These consist of three volumes maintained by Wampler during a portion of his service with the U.S. Coast Survey, from 1849 to 1851, and while pursuing engineering opportunities with the railroads in Texas and Arkansas in 1853 and 1854. Five other notebooks present an almost daily account of his life during the Civil War, beginning in mid-1861 and continuing to 1863. Notations in early 1861 are less frequent. For some days in 1862–63, there are actually two entries in different volumes. The journals also provide a sporadic record of his finances— the cost of purchases, payments for food and lodging, money lent to friends, distances traveled and expenses incurred, and engineer notations, such as supplies drawn from the quartermaster and a list of hands who worked on Sunday. Wampler provides a wealth of additional material in the text and in the margins of these journals, including drawings of conceivable inventions, field sketches of terrain, algebraic theorems, and engineering formulas.

Gaps in the time periods covered by the journals, with the exception of the last half of the 1850s, are filled largely by correspondence. Well over one hundred Confederate Army documents and personal letters are retained by Wampler's descendants. A similar quantity of his correspondence with the superintendent of the U.S. Coast Survey may be found in the National Archives. Maps drawn by Wampler for the Coast Survey are retained by its successor organization, the National Oceanic and Atmospheric Administration. The National Archives also contains official communiqués and documents in Wampler's military service records, as well as some of his correspondence with the Confederate government in Richmond. A handful of other letters has been found scattered in libraries and archives in Maryland, Ohio, Pennsylvania, North Carolina, and California.

Wampler's service during the war is further illuminated by contemporary accounts, official and personal, which make reference to him. While to my knowledge they number fewer than ten, their particular value, of course, lies in their third-person perspective.

Information about Wampler's life in Baltimore must be inferred from contemporary sources other than diaries or letters, such as newspapers, city directories, and court records maintained in the Baltimore City Archives and Maryland State Archives. Descriptions of his inventions are preserved in the civil collection of the National Archives and at the U.S. Patent and Trademark Office. The few known images of Morris and Kate are held by family members.

Kate Wampler's experiences during the Civil War are recorded in two primary sources. The first is her private journal, which begins on May 12, 1863, and ends abruptly three months later on August 21. Kate must have learned of Morris's death the following day. The account resumes suddenly on February 17, 1864, continues with commentaries on February 18 and 22, and terminates on March 3. These latter entries are longer than normal for her diary, each relating a specific episode in some detail. The second narrative, which may be characterized as a remembrance, is an undated reflection on the war, which does not always tie incidents to definite periods of time. Knowledge of the events swirling about her in Loudoun County, Virginia, however, permits the modern reader to relate Kate's commentary to specific dates and occurrences.

In general, Kate's journal, along with her reflections after the war, is more textured than her husband's. He tends to stress facts, noting the wind and weather, recording what he did each day, carefully divided by designating A.M. or P.M., and relating events in a matter-of-fact style, which only occasionally includes his personal observations. At the other extreme, Kate fills her accounts with feelings and impressions of events. Her narrative includes warm passages concerning her children and repeated prayers for Morris and their new nation. A sense of personal caring flows through the commentary, while her husband's notations might be considered the stereotypical male account of what transpired, without the equally stereotypical sensitivity commonly associated with the opposite gender.

Despite any limitations in quantity or coverage, the available source material affords rich detail about the lives of a Confederate engineer and his family, enduring the almost continuous conflict on the perimeter of the new southern nation. When examined with a full understanding of the personalities and occurrences referred to, the extant primary materials concerning Morris and Kate Wampler paint a unique and often poignant portrait of a husband and wife during the Civil War.

Prologue

The sun rose over Charleston harbor at 5:44 A.M. on August 17, 1863, but the soldiers in gray, manning Battery Wagner, had been awakened at 5:00 by the first shells from Parrott guns in Union batteries on the far side of Morris Island. Once again, it had been difficult to get a good night's sleep. Slow, continuous, overnight firing from Wagner's land face had not ceased until 4:30. In turn, it had been answered sporadically by enemy mortars. Thankfully for the Confederates, the barrage ceased for a while just before 6:00, when they confirmed that no one had been wounded and no serious damage had been done to the earthen fortification.[1] On Sunday, enemy batteries had fired infrequently on Battery Wagner, but with this early start, Monday, the thirty-ninth day of the Yankee siege by Gen. Pierre Gustave Toutant Beauregard's count, promised to be more intense.

A Federal fleet soon appeared, consisting of the *Ironsides* and six monitors, supported by one mortar hulk, four gunboats at long range, and a dozen shore batteries as close as 830 yards away. The warships concentrated their fire on Fort Sumter and Batteries Wagner and Gregg. At 6:30, the battery's chief engineer, Capt. John Morris Wampler, known to his fellow officers by his middle name, observed, "[T]he Ironsides & 2 Monitors came close in abt. 600 to 1000 yds. & commenced a terrific fire, our guns returning at abt. 7¼. 1 man wounded. 7½ o'c, another man slightly wounded, two or three more bro't in."[2] In accordance with the commanding general's guidance, the battery permitted the enemy combatants to move near before Lt. J. J. Alston's detachment, manning two 10-inch Columbiads, and a squad directed by Capt. Robert Pringle, serving a rifled 32-pounder, returned the fire. Acting as gunner of the right Columbiad, Alston focused on the left and nearest monitor, about 600 yards away, while a sergeant fired the left Columbiad against the *Ironsides*, 100–200 yards more distant. The monitors replied with canister and shrapnel. At one point Wampler repaired the traverse circle of the 32-pound rifle, enabling Pringle, by his own estimate, to fire over 40 bolts, eventually hitting his target every third round on average.[3]

"Firing terrific after 8:00. 2 or 3 more men horribly wounded," Wampler noted, when an incoming round exploded in the midst of a detachment from the Charleston Battalion under Capt. Francis Miles, wounding or stunning every one of its soldiers. The Rebel guns were also having some effect. Adm. John Dahlgren led the Union monitors while aboard the *Weehawken,* anchored 1,000 yards off Battery Wagner. When the tide rose, he moved his squadron in as close as 450 yards, and Alston was therefore able to depress the right Columbiad sufficiently to hit the turret of the monitor *Catskill.* The explosion drove splinters of iron into the fleet commander and paymaster, killing them instantly, as well as wounding the pilot and quartermaster.[4] Unaware at the time of the exact impact of their shelling, Wampler and his compatriots noticed only that one monitor withdrew, apparently damaged, and thus transferred their fire to the next ship on the right.

During the two-hour period, from 6:30 to 8:30 A.M., the *Ironsides,* monitors, gunboats, mortar hulk, and land batteries hurled 1,068 rounds at the Confederate works.[5] With seven 11-inch guns and one heavy rifle in its starboard battery, the *Ironsides* landed 805 shells inside Wagner that Monday and Tuesday, despite being struck 30 times.[6] By 8:40, the brisk incoming fire caused the battery commander, Col. Lawrence M. Keitt, to withdraw all cannoneers off the sea face and assemble them inside the underground shelter of the bombproof, as the risk far outweighed the benefit from continued service at their duty stations.[7] Forty minutes later, the parapet in front of the left Columbiad was badly damaged, causing Captain Wampler to take immediate action to strengthen it. "9.5 A.M. 2 more men wounded," he recorded. Next, he and Maj. Henry Bryan, assistant adjutant general, examined the magazines and reported them safe.[8]

Since his expertise was not needed for a few moments, the engineer paused to reflect on the apocalypse about him. A Marylander by birth, a Virginian by choice, Captain Wampler had commanded an infantry company at the Battle of First Manassas and had been present at Ball's Bluff. He had served as an engineer officer at Perryville and in several skirmishes in the Western Theater. He had never, however, encountered a barrage with the ferocity of the naval gunfire and artillery shelling his outpost was now receiving. By skipping their rounds across the water, Yankee gunners were able to direct shells into the battery's interior. The precision of Northern fuses ensured that mortar rounds burst just above or within the Confederate earthworks. Rounds exploded as often as every two seconds at the crescendo of the Federal firestorm.[9] Rifled artillery fire increased accuracy beyond anything that Wampler had ever before experienced. "Enemys boats knocking our sand about considerably," Wampler lamented.[10]

Two monitors moved to Wagner's left at about 10:15 A.M. and proceeded to open up a particularly heavy fire upon the fortification. Inside the battery's headquarters, Wampler chatted about his family with Colonel Keitt and Capt. Charles S. Hill, the battery ordnance officer.[11] Overhead, shells screamed and exploded, reverberating throughout the bombproof. Shortly before 11:00, Surgeon Henry Horlbeck graciously vacated his chair for the chief engineer to use while writing home.[12] Wampler sat down and began, "My dear wife and child. . . ." The salutation lay unfinished in the rubble on the ground, the husband and father slaughtered by the fragment of a naval round exploding into the bombproof.

Killed at Battery Wagner was an educated man and talented civil engineer. Wampler's interests and endeavors were broad: he was a surveyor, draftsman, poet, artist, inventor, soldier, and musician. While he did not achieve great success in any field, there is a timeless quality to the application of his talents and energy in an era of dynamic change in virtually every field of endeavor. The biography of Morris Wampler is also the story of many accomplished men who tied their fates to the uncertainty of a new nation.

This is not the chronicle of a celebrated engineer or distinguished general commanding an army. It is, instead, the account of a southern staff officer. Morris Wampler was an individual from a modest background who, after a rather unusual education, had the good fortune to be trained as a topographical engineer, a respected profession in his day. He thereafter attempted, sometimes unsuccessfully, to address the multitude of opportunities and challenges presented to Americans in the mid-nineteenth century—the greatest, of course, being the Civil War. This, then, is the story of an ordinary American—an engineer, soldier, husband, and father—in an extraordinary time. The account of Wampler's preparation for and experiences as a Confederate engineer is unique. His personal struggles to succeed in his career and provide for a family resonate a century and a half later.

Wampler's credentials as a topographical engineer were earned with the United States Coast Survey, the nation's premier scientific organization in the antebellum period, but largely unheralded by modern historians as a training ground for Civil War engineers. The years between his tenure at the U.S. Coast Survey and the outbreak of hostilities were difficult ones for Wampler personally, although they provided opportunities to develop as a civil engineer. Surveying for the railroad on the frontier, practicing engineering in Baltimore, serving a short stint as a public water resources engineer, and exercising his mechanical aptitude through inventions all sharpened skills that would make him valuable to the Confederacy in the war effort ahead.

During the same period, he married and started a family. Long absences from home and repeated disappointments undoubtedly toughened Wampler psychologically for the extended separation from his family and the personal hardships encountered while fighting for the South.

Wampler began the Civil War as a line officer, commanding a company of volunteers in battle. This provided invaluable experience in the art of warfare, helping put him on equal footing with engineer officers who had experienced combat in the Mexican War. His early service also affords a sharp portrait of training and encampment early in the conflict, as civilians, North and South, put on uniforms and began doing things the military way.

The culmination of Wampler's story is his service as an engineer officer in the Provisional Army of the Confederate States. By midway through the Civil War, Wampler had the distinction of having worked on engineering projects in eight of the eleven Confederate states, plus Maryland and Kentucky, either before or during the conflict. Following his footsteps offers a perspective unlike that provided by the generals above him, whose strategic vision and battlefield leadership have already been thoroughly examined in a rich array of biographies. Nor does this account concern the common foot soldier, a point of view that has been the subject of classic treatises. Morris Wampler, Confederate engineer, was a staff officer, called upon to direct and lead on occasion, but far more precious to his army for his professional competence, all too unique in the cause he served. His niche, midway between the general and the private, allowed Wampler to offer thoughtful commentary on each, while providing insight into the terrible conflagration erupting about him.

Wampler's wartime experiences span the range of activities of a nineteenth-century military engineer. His forte was cartography. In addition, the journals, letters, and other sources I rely upon show him building and repairing earthen works and analyzing more permanent fortifications; laying out and preparing hasty defensive positions; conducting reconnaissance and directing pioneers in the vanguard of road marches; reconstructing bridges, including installing pontoon structures; mending rail lines; gathering intelligence on the enemy; and, in more than one assignment, supervising other officers performing these same functions, while tackling the administrative burdens attendant to being a chief engineer. At the same time, Wampler's exploits shed light on the credentials and accomplishments of his peers in the Confederate Corps of Engineers.

While Wampler soldiered, his loved ones at home also suffered the hardships of war. A look at their experiences not only broadens modern understanding of the Confederate engineer—who he was and why he served—but also helps bring closure at the end of the war and paints a fuller picture of Wampler. The story of Kate and Morris Wampler is not unlike that of the families of over half a million other soldiers who perished in the war. It is made more vivid, however, through the accounts they left behind, and more poignant to the author because they were his great-great-grandparents.

CHAPTER ONE

>>>

"The Only Boy Educated at Belmont"

As a child, Morris Wampler was introduced to the misfortunes of life as soon as he was cognizant of his family. His father died fourteen months after Morris's birth on May 3, 1830. This sorrow was compounded when his brother and sister, Jefferson and Virginia, died in childhood, leaving Morris alone with his mother.[1]

Morris's father, Thomas Jefferson Wampler, was born in 1801, a descendant of German immigrants named Wampler, or "Wampfler," who arrived in Maryland, in all likelihood, after first settling in Pennsylvania. Young Jefferson attended the newly established St. Peter's Episcopal Sunday School in Baltimore. Upon attaining manhood, he offered his services as a tinner, or "tin plate maker," fashioning the metal as well as applying it to rooftops. On Sunday evening, May 6, 1827, he was married by Reverend Mr. Morris to twenty-two-year-old Ann B. Johannes. Her father, John, was a jeweler, watchmaker, and silversmith, and his prominence as an artisan may well have accounted for the nuptials being reported in the press, at a time when such matters were not routinely recognized by newspapers in cities of Baltimore's size. The young couple immediately started a family, and Ann was pregnant with their third child when her husband was taken ill. After many weeks, Thomas Jefferson Wampler died on July 1, 1831. Of an estate totaling six hundred dollars, one-fourth was required to meet the burial expenses, pay the house rent due at the time of his death, and resolve the accountings and filings required with the city register. Thomas Wampler's affairs were placed in the hands of George H. Steuart, a veteran of the War of 1812 and father of a boy of Morris's age, who would graduate from West Point and, as a general, be known as "Maryland" Steuart when leading that state's soldiers fighting for the Confederacy.[2]

Ann Wampler must have taken her young brood back to her parents' home to live, as there is an indication that her husband's parents died not long after their son. Most likely through their common affiliation with the Episcopal Church, Ann became acquainted with Margaret Mercer, who had opened a girls' school a few miles northwest of Baltimore City in the community of Franklin. Ann's own education was sufficient to qualify her as an assistant teacher with Miss Mercer, who was recognized as a leader in social and educational reform. She was to be the first of three prominent mentors in Morris Wampler's life.

MARGARET MERCER

Margaret Mercer was a native of Annapolis, a center of culture and prominence with theater, balls, and races to entertain its landed gentry. She was born in 1791 at Strawberry Hill, now the site of the U.S. Naval Academy cemetery. After soldiering as a colonel with Washington, representing Maryland at the Constitutional Convention and serving a term as its governor, her father retired to his estate at Cedar Park, south of Annapolis. A principal occupation became the education of his daughter in Latin, French, and Hebrew literature. Margaret was also schooled in the tenets of the Society of Friends, her mother's faith. Accomplishment in the art of flower painting quite naturally led Margaret to the study of botany.[3] She also took an interest, unusual at that time, in the welfare of the family slaves, teaching herself the rudiments of medicine in order to treat their illnesses.

After the death of her parents, in 1825 Margaret opened a school for young ladies at Cedar Park. Her passion, however, continued to be the freeing and resettling of slaves.[4] Removing blacks to Africa was supported by many northerners as a step toward total emancipation and by some southerners as a means of ridding their region of freed Negroes. The female educator's personal leadership in the movement was so prominent that a schooner built in Baltimore to transport the former slaves was christened the *Margaret Mercer*. Her wealth was eventually exhausted by a penchant for purchasing the freedom of blacks and by the expense of hiring help to replace slaves she had liberated and sent to Africa.[5] At last she was forced to resort to buying an individual's freedom with the understanding that the cost would be repaid by wages earned while working at her school.

When her brother's eighth child was born at Cedar Park in 1834, Miss Mercer decided to turn over the family home to him and relocate her school to Franklin, where she expected to receive more students and incur lower operating expenses. She was sorely disappointed on both accounts. Furthermore, she had difficulty finding competent assistants, an exception being a newly widowed mother, Ann B. Wampler. Upon concluding that her venture would not succeed in Franklin, Miss Mercer began looking for alternate sites for her academy and was fortunate to locate an estate that she could afford to purchase, near Leesburg in Loudoun County, Virginia.[6] Its name was Belmont, and along with Miss Mercer went Mrs. Wampler and her six-year-old son, Morris.

LOUDOUN COUNTY

The mosaic of people, geography, resources, and politics that made up Loudoun County would be the home for Morris Wampler and his family for the next three decades. Loudoun was part of that large tract of land between the Rappahannock and Potomac Rivers known as "the northern neck" of Virginia. Three mountain ranges traverse its area of over five hundred square miles. Serving as the county's western boundary are the Blue Ridge Mountains, appearing from afar as a hazy backdrop for the less-imposing Short Hills four miles to the east, and the Catoctin range, even more gentle, eight miles farther, which constitute a spine down the center of the county. These three ranges run parallel in a southwesterly direction from the Potomac River, separating Maryland from Virginia, and define the fertile Loudoun Valley.

Although iron ore was present, the area was not rich in minerals. The region had other attributes, however. Residents pointed with pride to the pillars on the Capitol building at Washington, made of Loudoun limestone. Timber was abundant. The county was laced with streams and runs, which came down from higher elevations in a northeasterly direction. Goose Creek was the most prominent, draining half the county before emptying into the Potomac a mile or so from Belmont. Indeed, Loudoun's most important natural resource may well have been the water provided by innumerable small springs and the power generated by its waterways, which propelled as many as seventy-five merchant mills, gristmills, and sawmills. Plentiful water and predominately good soil contributed directly to the richness of Loudoun agriculture, which reportedly ranked first in the state in bushels of wheat and corn harvested, second in numbers of farming implements and machinery, and third in the value of its orchards. Cultivation and grazing took place on gently rolling fields, bottomland meadows, and green upland pastures. As many as ten thousand head of beef were traded every year. Cattle, sheep, and swine each numbered about twenty thousand.[7] Coincidentally, this approximated the county's steady population figures throughout the nineteenth century, with one-quarter of the antebellum number consisting of slaves. Fewer than a thousand Loudoun residents were chattel holders, however, and well over half of these owned fewer than five slaves.[8]

Villages were generally small and well kept. Residents otherwise fit largely into three patterns. The northwestern corner of the county was settled by German Americans, mostly from Pennsylvania, living in modest log homes on small, well-cultivated farms. In the central county were found prosperous Quakers in masonry homes on larger tracts of productive farmland. Finally, in the southern and eastern parts of the county, including the Belmont area, lived well-to-do residents of English ancestry on large estates cultivated by slaves.[9] Leesburg was the county's largest community with five hundred houses and seventeen hundred inhabitants. The "paved" Little River Turnpike and the Alexandria-to-Leesburg Pike in front of Belmont tied the county's agriculture with markets to the east, the most accessible being Alexandria, Georgetown, and Washington City, all a distance of thirty miles or so.

Two dimensions of Loudoun culture would have appealed to Margaret Mercer. The first was a vibrant opposition to slavery, tied closely to its Quaker community. While not necessarily the position of a majority of county residents, the antislavery movement was nonetheless strong enough to support two colonization associations: the Loudoun Auxiliary of the American Colonization Society and the Loudoun Manumission and Emigration Society.

While there were pockets where education was not a priority, the second noteworthy characteristic was that the concern for education in Loudoun exceeded that of most other Virginia counties, even if it may have paled in comparison with academic development in many communities of the North. In the mid-1830s, Leesburg alone could boast of one classical and two English schools for males and three for females. Private academies, boarding schools, and family-sponsored schoolhouses were common throughout the county, in addition to seventy-five schools for the poor, attended by an estimated nine hundred indigent pupils.[10]

BELMONT

Margaret Mercer established her academy on one of the largest tracts in eastern Loudoun County. Situated on a ridge south of the Alexandria Pike, five miles from Leesburg, Belmont had been the estate of Ludwell Lee, a lawyer and planter who was the son of Richard Henry Lee, the continental army

officer and signer of the Declaration of Independence. The house was constructed in a Georgian style of colonial brick imported from England and set
amidst a stand of oaks and cedars. The central two-story structure was extended on both sides by covered corridors connecting to kitchen and pan-
tries on one side and an outbuilding later converted into classrooms on the
other. The Marquis de Lafayette, President John Quincy Adams, and former
President James Monroe had attended a grand ball at Belmont in 1825, culminating a triumphal visit to Loudoun County. When Margaret Mercer acquired the property from heirs to the Lees in 1836, however, it had fallen into
decay, causing her to characterize Belmont as "rundown."

Miss Mercer's first winter at Belmont was especially trying. Even with
tuition and board of $250 per year, the population of ten paying (plus five
indigent) students could not support the employment of seven teachers.[11]
Belmont was isolated from the culture and society to which Margaret Mercer had grown accustomed in Annapolis. Many of the surrounding inhabitants were former slaves or sharecroppers, all terribly poor. Primitive sanitary
practices, shallow wells, and bogs served as breeding grounds for frequent
outbreaks of pestilence.[12] The last advantage this depressed section of Loudoun
County seemed to need was a girls boarding school, and so the nearby residents were initially hostile to the new entrepreneur. In a rare reflection of
despair, Miss Mercer lamented, "[T]his most uncultivated corner of the lord's
vineyard. I never saw such people. The Sabbath profaned, and no church in
the neighborhood."[13]

One of those non-paying pupils was "the only boy educated at Belmont,"
the son of Margaret Mercer's assistant, Ann Wampler.[14] Young Morris was
exposed to a curriculum that included botany and chemistry, French and
Latin, English grammar and literature, natural and political history, geography, mathematics, and rhetoric. These subjects were comparable to those
offered at private schools throughout the antebellum South. At Belmont,
music was practiced with great enthusiasm.[15] Artistic undertakings were enriched by use of a camera obscura located in the library. Before the advent of
sensitized plates and film, this enclosure projected an image onto a surface
where it could be viewed and studied for drawing.

The core of a Belmont Academy education was Miss Mercer's lectures,
collected under the rubric "Ethics, or Moral Obligations." Believing it "the
first duty" of teachers to imbue young minds with sound moral principles
and finding no appropriate text available to other educators, she published
her lectures in 1841.[16] The forty subjects ran the gamut from religion to personal behavior, covering philosophy, metaphysics, ethics, temperance, the

senses, intellectual power, cultivation of the mind, the attributes of God, the origins of evil, the Scriptures, prayer, prudence, charity, and benevolence. To preserve one's health, the author prescribed regular warm baths, frequent change of clothes suitable to the climate, sleep not to exceed eight hours, warm feet, staying out of drafts, and regular exercise. Patriotism received special emphasis, as the lecturer feared that freedom and individual rights won at great cost against cruel oppressors were in danger of being forgotten. This latter message may have struck a particularly responsive note in an impressionable youth like Morris.

Miss Mercer required her students to master a bookshelf of classical literature. Among the thirty-three histories were Gibbon's *Decline and Fall of the Roman Empire,* Washington Irving's *Conquest of Granada,* and the writings of Josephus, Livy, and Tacitus. Science was learned from works like Silliman's *Elements of Chemistry,* Herschel's *Treatise on Astronomy,* Mrs. Lincoln's *Botany for Beginners,* and Lyell's *Principles of Geology.* Religious and moral instruction was drawn from fifty-four tomes, including Doddridge's *Rise and Progress of Religion in the Soul,* Lyttleton on St. Paul, Scougal's *Life of God in the Soul of Man,* and Watts on the conduct of the mind.[17]

While Morris lived separately with his mother, the female boarders slept on the second floor of the main house in large rooms converted into dormitories, each furnished with five double beds, accommodating ten girls. A round table in the middle of each room held five basins arrayed around a central bucket of water equipped with a dipper. Dancing and playing shuttlecock, a variation of badminton, in the covered corridors took the place of outdoor recreation on rainy days. Meals were taken together, but despite the appetites associated with growing youngsters, the young ladies of Belmont Academy were expected to exhibit polite restraint in their eating habits. Requesting a second helping was considered in bad taste (and, no doubt, threatening to the parsimonious Mercer larder). Consequently, food from home was treasured. Boarders from New Orleans received shipments of oranges, pecans, and syrup, which their schoolmates contrived to enjoy in their rooms.[18]

Belmont Academy soon earned a reputation throughout the South for academic excellence and for strong religious and ethical instruction. It was not long before Miss Mercer's enrollment numbered forty-six paying children.[19] Consequently, the neighborhood became enriched, as the school was able to employ more laborers and procure added produce in the markets. Local children were invited for instruction in agricultural techniques and domestic economy, as well as tutoring by the full-time students in personal hygiene and virtue.[20] Most important to Miss Mercer, on Sundays her house was opened for family worship, with services held in the large hall. Thus began her last consuming cause, bringing God to a people "but a grade above the children of the mist."[21]

Morality was taught at Belmont Academy with a decidedly Episcopalian slant, but the nearest church was St. James in Leesburg. Shelburne Parish to the east charged pew rents to its congregation, which, when combined with the cost and difficulty of the commute, made organized religion inaccessible to the poor residents around Belmont. This assumes that they wanted to be Episcopalians, which is unlikely, since the denomination retained a stigma from its association with the Church of England and the landed aristocracy. Nevertheless, Miss Mercer persevered and began accumulating funds to build a sanctuary, using the profits from a collective farming arrangement she had established.[22] By the late 1830s, she was ready to begin work. For a design, Miss Mercer wrote to her Baltimore friend, John H. B. Latrobe, elder son of Benjamin Latrobe, America's first professional architect and engineer, and a draftsman in his own right, requesting a "*simple* but *tasteful* plan, the very *cheapest* that can be constructed. . . . The site is a slight elevation in a skirt of wood near the road."[23]

Located a half-mile east of the mansion at the northeast corner of the estate, Belmont Chapel was ready for worship in 1840. A fieldstone facade in the Gothic style rose forty feet above the ground, protecting three other walls of wood with clear glass windows and a steep roof. The interior was white with Georgian board trim. At the front on a raised platform stood a simple altar table. The communion rail surrounding it and the railing in the gallery were Morris Wampler's contributions, designed and fashioned by him in the small upstairs workshop at nearby Mavin's Mill.[24] The remainder of the interior was built by local craftsmen.[25]

As an ardent Episcopalian, Miss Mercer naturally enlisted George Adie, the rector at St. James, to conduct services at the chapel, generally on Sunday afternoons. Before breakfast, the students recited verses, sang hymns, and studied Bible lessons under the personal tutelage of Miss Mercer. Sunday School involved the academy's students, including Morris, as both learners and teachers of the young. Evening prayers took the place of formal worship, if Reverend Adie or another clergyman were unavailable. Prior to nighttime prayers, a final Bible lesson was recited.[26] With this strong religious grounding, it is not surprising that, just shy of his sixteenth birthday, Morris was confirmed as a member of the Episcopal Church by Bishop William Whitingham of Maryland on March 18, 1846.

Miss Mercer had long been a firm believer in the importance of Sunday

Portrait of Margaret Mercer by Thomas Sully, 1848, from a daguerreotype.
The Historical Society of Pennsylvania.

Watercolor of Belmont Chapel by A. Bernisen, 1887.
St. David's Episcopal Church, Ashburn, Virginia.

Sketch of Belmont House by Yardley Taylor, 1853.

School, in an age when it was still something of a novelty and not always well regarded. She utilized the Sabbath to extend Belmont's educational opportunities to everyone in the local area. While Biblical and religious studies were paramount, Sunday School provided her an occasion to teach basic reading and writing skills. Seeking to eliminate illiteracy among the black laborers on her lands and neighboring properties, she welcomed them heartily on Sundays.[27] Sabbath worship was by no means the week's only devotion to Christian precepts. In addition to the strong religious content of the curriculum, each day began and ended with prayer, which, in the evening, featured Miss Mercer's reading from a Biblical chapter or text on morality.[28]

The headmistress naturally preferred that her pupils concentrate on their studies, free from the distractions of the world outside Belmont. She resisted the introduction of newspapers into her school, for example.[29] Young minds opened to the intellectual stimulus at Belmont Academy could not have been oblivious to what was taking place in the world outside their plantation's fences, however, either within Loudoun County or in the nation beyond. A majority of the residents of Loudoun County supported Whig candidates for national office throughout the 1830s and 1840s.[30] A torchlight procession through the streets of Leesburg in support of William Henry Harrison during the 1840 campaign included a band of schoolgirls, but it is doubtful that Miss Mercer permitted any Belmont Academy students to participate.[31] Beyond the confines of Belmont, few of the books being written or scientific discoveries being made were by Virginians, as the state's best intellects were channeled into law and politics, traditionally the callings of prominence.[32] How much more extraordinary does that make the direction in life taken by young Wampler.[33]

YOUTH ASCENDING

Morris Wampler emerged from Miss Mercer's tutelage as a cultured individual by the standards of any century. Denied a masculine role model by his father's death in early childhood, Morris had been reared solely by his mother. As the only surviving child, this bond must have been exceptionally strong. His sensitivity was undoubtedly cultivated by living and learning in a world of women, presided over by a renowned educator who instilled in all her pupils an appreciation of life's spiritual, sensual, and aesthetic dimensions.

Morris's keen awareness of the beauty in nature, apparent in his personal journals, is therefore understandable. At the same time, he had a refined literary sense that appreciated beauty in the written word. An avid reader as a young man, he devoured James Fenimore Cooper's *Sea Tales,* the novels of Sir Walter Scott, Maxwell's *Border Sketches,* and assorted poetry, among other fare. It is not surprising, therefore, that he tried his hand at verse in later life, addressing a variety of subjects, to include his wife, the timelessness of Freemasonry, and, at the apex of the Confederacy in May 1863, "A Prayer for the Times." His facility with written expression is also evident in his journals, which constituted not merely accounts of daily events, as a diarist might record, but reflections on what he saw about him. Crossed-out words, incomplete thoughts, and erasures are noticeable by their infrequency, as are misspellings, usually reserved for proper names which, in all likelihood, were phonetically derived, as Wampler had not seen them in writing. It would naturally follow that Morris was articulate in speech as he was with the pen. He had a sense of humor as well, as evidenced by simple pranks played on comrades while campaigning in the Western Theater.

In appearance, Morris was diminutive in stature, compensating for his slight build with energy and decisiveness. A thick crop of dark brown hair swept up in a pompadour atop the left side of his high forehead, before continuing downward in long sideburns. As an adult, the oval shape of his face was accentuated by a short beard with accompanying mustache. Dark, penetrating eyes and a straight, prominent nose conveyed the impression of a man who was self-assured, if not determined, and inclined to be direct and forthright in dealing with other members of his own sex. Morris was also known to enjoy a good smoke. The combination of his pleasing appearance and courtly manners acquired at Belmont Academy no doubt created a handsome image, attractive to women.

Morris Wampler was prepared to make his way in a nation expanding its influence across the North American continent, developing sophistication in science and engineering, while its political institutions struggled to fashion a peaceful resolution to the increasingly debilitating issue of slavery. At Belmont, Morris acquired a solid grounding in religion and ethics, obtained an appreciation for literature and the arts, and, most important to his ability to make a living in the industrial age ahead, learned the rudiments of mathematics and science and perfected his artistic talents to enable him to represent graphically the world that lay ahead.

CHAPTER TWO

>>>

Alexander Dallas Bache and the Coast Survey

The year 1846 was a turning point in the life of Morris Wampler. His first mentor, Margaret Mercer, died on September 17. Burdened with frail health most of her life, Miss Mercer passed away in her Virginia home, apparently a victim of tuberculosis.[1] She was buried beneath the chancel of her beloved Belmont Chapel at a service conducted by the Rev. George Adie. Wampler's mother married an English immigrant, William Mavin, in the schoolroom at Belmont on December 20 and took up residence at his mill on nearby Goose Creek. In what must have been, in part, a reaction to these changes, Wampler secured an appointment with the U.S. Coast Survey, an experience that would mold a career for the remainder of his life.

In 1846, the United States had a population of twenty million people. President James K. Polk presided over a nation from a capital that had scarcely forty thousand inhabitants, and where Wampler would reside while working as a draftsman at the Coast Survey office. The country had suffered a severe depression in the earlier 1840s but was recovering to enjoy a surge of economic growth by the end of the decade. Having grown up with his widowed mother, struggling to make ends meet, the seventeen-year-old must have been pleased to obtain a "situation," especially with a most prestigious employer.

A SURVEY TO BE TAKEN OF COASTS

The Coast Survey has been described as "the largest and most important institution supporting science in antebellum America."[2] The modern university had not yet evolved in the United States. Only the U.S. Military Academy at West Point offered education in science, mathematics, and engineering until 1835, when Rensselaer Polytechnic Institute graduated its first class. Institutions like the Yale Scientific School were just beginning to offer courses on nature and the physical sciences. Throughout the nation, one young man in a hundred went to college, and certainly not someone with the humble origins of Wampler. As it did so often, America patterned its pursuits on the British model, which looked to government to fuel the engine of scientific discovery. As a counterpart to the British Ordnance Survey, the U.S. Coast Survey provided the foremost institutional support of science in a land that had relied heretofore on individual scientific inquiries—the most notable being, of course, those of the incomparable Franklin and Jefferson.

By an act of February 10, 1807, Congress authorized the president "to cause a survey to be taken of the coasts of the United States, in which shall be designated the islands and shoals, with the roads or places of anchorage, within twenty leagues of any part of the shores."[3] The reasons for such an undertaking were manifold. The young nation relied heavily on waterways and coastal shipping for its commerce. Travel time between ports could be reduced and shipwrecks avoided with accurate knowledge of the location of underwater obstacles. As the Coast Survey matured, reports on the discovery and delineation of channels and bars, changing depths, and obstructions blocking rivers and harbors became invaluable to the ports of Boston and New York, Charleston and New Orleans. It was said with pride that, in even its most prolific prewar years, the annual cost of the Coast Survey was no more than that of a single first-class steamship.[4]

Consequently, insurance companies, chambers of commerce, and shipping concerns were unified in support of the Coast Survey's work. Nor was its military significance overlooked. A nation that intended to defend itself from adversaries most likely to approach from the sea had best have a precise knowledge of its coastlines, particularly when two of its rivals, Great Britain and France, had patrolled the same waters in colonial times and knew them far better than their former colonists at the outset of the American Republic. Surveying would lead to the erection of navigational signals and the establishment of private map-making firms, both thought to be beneficial. The Coast Survey was also viewed as a chance to engage in applied science. Surveying and mapping provided employment and field opportunities for a coterie of inquisitive minds and adventuresome youth. To pure scientists, however, the Coast Survey's unstated purpose was geodesy, determining the magnitude and shape of the earth. They would extend the function of surveying to encompass research into the related disciplines of meteorology, oceanography, and natural history in their ongoing effort to promote the advancement of science.

The Coast Survey was initially entrusted to Ferdinand Hassler, a Swiss geodesist, whose greatest legacy was his insistence that precise measurement never be sacrificed for the sake of speedy results sought to obtain political favor. This eccentric traveled to early field sites in a huge yellow traveling carriage, which transported his wardrobe, scientific gear, and cooking equipment, as he often ate and slept in the conveyance.[5] Hassler died in 1843, and so when Wampler joined the Coast Survey, its new superintendent was just beginning to flex his muscle, burning his personal imprint onto its operations. He would become the second important mentor in Morris Wampler's life.

Professor Bache

The first credential invariably used to introduce Alexander Dallas Bache is that he was the great-grandson of Benjamin Franklin. Bache's father was one of eight children of Sarah, Franklin's only daughter. On his mother's side were prominent names as well. Sophia Bache was the daughter of Alexander J. Dallas, appointed by President James Madison to be the sixth secretary of the treasury, and the sister of George M. Dallas, vice president of the United States under James K. Polk. Born in 1806, their namesake, Alexander Dallas Bache, was something of a child prodigy, graduating from West Point at the top of his class at age eighteen. His introduction to the military would serve Bache well in later life. Bache taught in the engineering department at the U.S. Military Academy and worked as an assistant to Joseph G. Totten in the construction of Fort Adams at Newport, Rhode Island. Not to be overlooked was Bache's exposure to army culture, its obedience and discipline, its leadership imperatives and management style. These were also characteristics of the Coast Survey under Bache's tutelage, as Morris Wampler would quickly learn.

After his selection as superintendent of the Coast Survey by President John Tyler, Bache undertook to improve its management and political support. One tactic was to appoint a military officer to serve as assistant in charge of the Coast Survey's office in Washington. A succession of extraordinary men held this title in the prewar years—Andrew A. Humphreys, who later became the revered chief of engineers, Isaac I. Stevens, and Henry W. Benham, each destined to become general officers in the Union Army. With

Alexander Dallas Bache. Smithsonian Institution Archives,
Photograph Collection, Record Unit 95.

the formation of the Corps of Topographical Engineers, an increasing number of army officers brought interest, training, and expertise to the Coast Survey's work.[6] The agency served as a graduate school for Professor Dennis Hart Mahan's engineering curriculum at the U.S. Military Academy. The navy was not as fortunate. Its professional school had only recently been established in 1845, and the naval cadre assigned to the Coast Survey appeared to be motivated both by the opportunity of avoiding the half-pay commensurate with shore duty, as well as by the prospect of honing engineering skills or advancing scientific learning. If for no other reason, Superintendent Bache must have appreciated the military presence on the staff as a source of personnel not funded out of his limited appropriation. In addition, he could count on military personnel as a pool of disciplined labor not unaccustomed to remote survey sites or rough waters where their work often took them.

When adding to the civilian complement of his staff, Bache often looked to what few centers of scientific learning existed in the United States, namely, Boston, New York, and his native Philadelphia. Members of his own family were not excluded by any serious public outcry against nepotism, although wags of the day liked to remark that there was "always a Bache or a son of a Bache" in the Coast Survey. Political referrals were favorably received by Bache, as he persisted in trying to build support for his agency. Not many years after Wampler's appointment, the superintendent was testing applicants without political connections in algebra, geometry, plain and spherical trigonometry, analytical geometry, differential and integral calculus, theoretical astronomy, and analytical mechanics.[7] Obtaining an appointment did not guarantee indefinite employment, however, as employees were promoted (and fired) based on merit.

What was it, therefore, that could have attracted the erudite Alexander Dallas Bache to hire Morris Wampler? He was an untried product of a girls' school in rural Virginia, was not known for scientific achievement, and was the son of a widowed mother of humble means, rather than the scion of a family of wealth or prominence. With their common ties to Philadelphia, Margaret Mercer could easily have known Bache and, before her demise, may have recommended her protégé to him. Shared qualities in the two men would certainly have facilitated a rapport. Wampler's artistic talent was of paramount importance; samples of applicants' drawing skills were always carefully scrutinized by the superintendent. It is also possible that Bache saw something of himself in the applicant from Virginia. Wampler's father had died when he was an infant. Similarly, Bache's father, the postmaster of Philadelphia, had abandoned his family, leaving "Dallas," as he was known at home, as the means of support for his eight brothers and sisters. Wampler's education at the foot of Margaret Mercer had inculcated in him an artistic appreciation and social refinement uncommon for boys of his age. Wampler had proved that he could flourish in an environment populated by the genteel sex. Bache was equally adept. A friend wrote to Bache in 1855: "No one who saw you for the first time, without knowing you, among a party of ladies, joining in their conversation and talking of painting and poetry and music and all the elegance of female society as if you were in your favorite element would ever imagine that you are the Alexander D. Bache whose admirable direction of our noble coast survey is calling forth the praise and rivalry of the commercial world."[8]

Like Wampler, Bache was an Episcopalian. Furthermore, he was described by the first secretary of the Smithsonian Institution as being predisposed to "high moral principles."[9] It was the promise of moral, as well as intellectual, discipline that attracted many young people to Bache. His education at Belmont Academy gave Wampler a similar disposition. Furthermore, Bache held a long-standing interest in developing young minds, as well as considerable experience in educational reform. For a period of time while serving as president of Girard College, created by a large endowment to educate orphans from their earliest years through puberty, Bache also served as superintendent of Philadelphia's Central High School, where he revamped the curriculum, injecting more science and mathematics to reflect his own formal education. A young man with Wampler's background would have most likely been the recipient of Bache's genuine interest and concern. Finally, Bache was supportive of social mobility, which would buttress the notion of a young fellow of modest southern background joining the progeny of patrician society in the Northeast.

With the artistic talent evidenced by his contributions to the interior design of Belmont Chapel, Wampler joined the Coast Survey as a draftsman in 1847, at a monthly salary of fifteen dollars, plus three dollars per week for board, an amount persistently complained about by all who received it. By the next year, his base pay would rise to twenty dollars, but the subsistence allowance would remain the same.

A City of Magnificent Intentions

Moving from the Loudoun countryside into the national capital presented a startling contrast to Wampler. Antebellum Washington was a "city of magnificent intentions," as yet unfulfilled, as Charles Dickens had observed when visiting earlier in the decade.[10] Pierre L'Enfant's vision provided for a network of broad avenues that remained unpaved and underpopulated. The boulevard that served as the city's showcase was Pennsylvania Avenue, 160 feet wide, stretching between the Capitol and the White House, and lined with shops, businesses, and hotels, to include the prominent hostelry of the Willard brothers. Frock coats and crinolines helped create the impression of a southern county seat. The city's dominant structure, the Capitol building, was still under construction, covered with scaffolding, and surrounded by granite blocks and other building materials. Down the Mall, the monument to the country's "father" was likewise a work in progress. It was not uncommon to see cows, geese, and pigs on city streets, commuting to and from nearby fields. Game birds, frogs, and mosquitoes were prevalent as well—especially mosquitoes. Their favorite breeding place, the Washington Canal, divided the city as it wandered from the Potomac past the White House and the Washington Monument and around Capitol Hill, before emptying into the East Branch, or Anacostia River.

The Coast Survey was located on the "island," the area bound by the canal and river. The office consisted of three adjacent buildings on New Jersey Avenue, south of the Capitol, where a House office building now stands. Known as the "castle," the complex more readily resembled an "anthill, honeycombed with complex ins and outs" and was "appointed with 'plain pine tables, common wooden chairs, [and] uncarpeted floors.'"[11] During Wampler's tenure, a system of wires and bells enabled the assistant in charge to summon any of his staff with a precise jingle.

The size of the office staff grew markedly during the 1840s, from a dozen or so at the outset to fifty individuals by the end of the decade. Organized into departments, personnel bore a variety of designations. "Computers" refined calculations made in the field; engravers specialized in printing, symbols, navigational lines, etc.; instrument makers repaired devices bought elsewhere or fashioned new gadgets, such as self-registering tide gauges, unavailable from commercial vendors; "draughtsmen" drew maps to a smaller scale, based on working charts provided at the end of each season by assistants who led field parties. Wampler's artistic facility made him well-suited for this last position, although he was not as gifted as a draftsman later employed for a few months in 1854, the artist James McNeill Whistler. Following completion of the office drafting, sheets were passed along to engravers. A copperplate printing press accurately reproduced the precision of the Coast Survey's hand-drawn charts.

Wampler's contributions to the work of the drawing department were many and varied. They included reducing to a smaller scale sheets representing Black Rock and Bridgeport, the Patapsco River, and the south shore of Long Island Sound; making projections and plotting triangulation points for several topographical parties; drawing the hydrography of Nantucket; doing sketches for the superintendent's 1848 annual report to Congress; and tracing a copy of the map portraying Key West harbor.[12]

INTO THE FIELD

Wampler perfected the art of drawing maps in the Coast Survey office until April 27, 1849, when he was given the opportunity to begin learning the science of topographical engineering. Superintendent Bache directed him to report to the field party headed by Assistant Richard D. Cutts, working from the schooner *Meredith* along the eastern and western shores of the Chesapeake Bay between the Potomac and Rappahannock Rivers. A month later, when informed that Wampler was being reassigned to the party of Henry L. Whiting in Massachusetts, Cutts reported that Wampler had "learned rapidly. . . . I shall be very sorry to part with him."[13] Whiting's party took to the field in July, and by October had completed 26 square miles of area with 27 1/2 miles of shoreline and 54 1/2 miles of roads in the vicinity of Lynn, Marblehead, and Salem.[14] Wampler must have exhibited exceptional qualities that impressed Whiting, one of Bache's most trusted assistants, for in the fall the young man was selected to lead a field party in Texas.

Upon taking charge of the Coast Survey, Bache had divided the Atlantic and Gulf coastlines into nine sections, where work proceeded simultaneously.[15] With the admission of Texas as a state in 1845, the expanse to be mapped increased by 3,359 miles of tidal coastline.[16] After the war with Mexico, the Pacific Coast was opened to surveying. Indeed, upon being asked by members of Congress when the seemingly endless survey would finally be completed, Professor Bache was fond of responding, "When will you cease annexing territory?"[17] Bache sought to establish a presence in as many states as possible, both for the purpose of charting and to build a foundation of political support for his agency's program. Yet, there was not a large pool from which to select knowledgeable field supervisors, and so Wampler, at age nineteen, was thrust into the breach to help fill vacancies created by staffing new field parties on the West Coast.

Bache's reputation as a superior administrator rested on the discipline he instilled in the Coast Survey as an outgrowth of his own military upbringing and on the tight control he exercised over every facet of agency operations.

Oversight of a field party began with submission by the team leader of a project prospectus, accompanied by an estimate of expenses, always of concern to the budget-minded superintendent. Bache would then issue a letter of instruction, outlining his expectations and the schedule for commencing and terminating work. Periodic reporting and close accounting for funds were made from the field to the Coast Survey office. In turn, Bache transmitted an annual report to the Congress, based upon input of a standard quality and format from his assistants and sub-assistants. Requisitions for supplies and equipment, to include surveying and drawing instruments, required the superintendent's personal approval. Communications outside the Coast Survey also needed his permission, as Bache orchestrated all external relations, including one of his innovations: private dinners with influential political figures, such as the senator from Mississippi and later secretary of war, Jefferson Davis. Bache's control was so absolute that he begrudged employees getting married, as it divided their loyalties, complicating and disrupting their service, especially in the field, as Wampler would eventually experience.[18]

Bache learned that he could generate better productivity, with less sickness and workdays lost due to extreme weather conditions, by dispatching field parties to the north in the warmer months and south during the winter. While stationed at Salem, Massachusetts, Wampler received his first letter of instruction from Bache regarding the coming season in Texas. By the end of November, Wampler had arranged for tents to be made in Philadelphia and engaged an auxiliary boat in Baltimore for his party's use. After finalizing arrangements at the Washington office, Wampler left for Belmont to visit his mother before traveling to Texas. His inexperience in preparing for fieldwork was evident, however, as Wampler admitted to his superintendent in a letter from home on December 4 that he had miscalculated the scale of the drawings in his work plan, thereby showing only one-fourth the area intended. Four days later, Wampler was sheepishly asking Bache to resign a copy of the estimate of expenses in order to satisfy a requirement of the Coast Survey's disbursing officer, for Wampler had already packed and sent off the original. Overcoming these lapses, Wampler departed for Texas on December 10.

Little is known of his trip west, other than a snippet written the day after Christmas at Natchez, Mississippi: "I was struck with the singular grandeur & abruptness of scenery that presents itself here, more pleasurable to the sight on acct. of its strong contrast with the rest of the Miss. R. that we have passed with only the exception of Vicksburg. The Hills have no slope towards the River but are quite perpendicular of a yellow clay. A road leads up the side making a section like a step to the city proper. The city not at all visible from the river or lower town."[19] Wampler's recent training in topographical surveying is obvious, as is an aesthetic sense inspired by Margaret Mercer.

THE SCIENCE OF ENGINEERING

Wampler was engaged in the United States' most ambitious scientific undertaking of the antebellum period, the mapping of its coastline. This feat involved the observation and calculation of an interlocking series of triangles. The initial triangulation took place between Fire Island and Long Island, New York, and Kent Island, Maryland. A later check measured an error of only 4 inches over a distance of 300 miles. A subsequent series of triangulations northward from Long Island was completed with an error of 8 millimeters over 350 miles, recording an astonishing accuracy of one part per million. Astronomical checks were also performed to ascertain precise latitude and longitude. At any one point in time, during its peak under Alexander Dallas Bache, the Coast Survey had at least 2 to 3 crews in the field doing first-order triangulation and as many as 6 or 7 teams engaged in second-order triangulation, tied to the first. The average margin of error was 1:250,000 or $2\frac{1}{2}$ inches for 10 miles. The challenge of absolute accuracy was further complicated by the curvature of the earth, thus necessitating a "geodetic survey" to locate points exactly upon an irregular, curved surface. When the entire triangulation project was completed in the early twentieth century, over 400,000 fixed markers had been erected across the United States. Among numerous other applications, these reference points were utilized for every property survey done throughout the country.

A baseline measurement of 6 miles or so generally took 2 months to complete. Bache's apparatus for measuring distance was 6 meters long. It consisted of 2 bars, 1 iron and the other brass, coated with a substance to retard distortions caused by variations in temperature and humidity, thus insuring an accurate measurement of invariable length. A team of 20 men was required to perform on-line measurement by positioning the bars so that they were level and straight. Line of sight was used to relate to fixed markers already erected, using, of course, the surveyor's theodolite. On occasion, these primary triangulation markers were visible from as far away as 40 or 50 miles. Once a fixed distance and an azimuth between two known points had been determined, a primary triangle was formed, from which additional triangles could be established. Smaller secondary triangles were used to help fix prominent features on the landscape.

A surveyor employed a plane table on a tripod. A mechanical device was used to level the table, upon which sat the alidade (or "alhidade" in the old spelling). The alidade was a telescope that rotated vertically as well as horizontally. The surveyor would draw the direction to a fixed marker on paper atop the plane table, annotating the measured angle. By shooting more than one marker, a relatively precise latitude and longitude could be determined graphically by the intersection of the drawn lines. Distances could be derived as well. Sextants were also employed, horizontally to measure the angle between points and, while at sea, vertically to orient with the stars. Sheets on the order of 1:10,000 or 1:20,000 were drawn by the assistant or sub-assistant in charge of the party from these plane table sketches while still in the field, in the Coast Survey headquarters in Washington, or at home after returning from a deployment. These drawings were then reduced in scale at the Coast Survey office, so that maps of 1:40,000 or 1:80,000 could be printed and disseminated to interested parties, both government and private.

Topographers built their maps with detail extending as far as five miles inland. They represented natural objects, streets, houses, and other observable features on these field sheets, in addition to the shape of the terrain and coastline. Very little surveying and mapping was being done in the interior of the United States at the time Wampler worked for the Coast Survey.

Reconnaissance parties generally preceded all other field parties, since their mission was to identify prominent high points, which could be incorporated into the superintendent's approved project plan for a triangulation project. Field parties performed primary triangulation, the most exacting measurement upon which all other surveying depended. Ideally placed twenty to thirty miles apart, primary triangulation markers were the reference points for the secondary surveys that followed. Field parties, like Wampler's, with the mission of conducting secondary triangulation, sited an adequate number of known points for topographic mapping. This entailed the erection of secondary markers five or ten miles apart, tied to the primary stations, and sometimes another generation of tertiary markers. Topographic mapping required orientation to fixed points in order to draw accurately the curvatures of coastlines, riverbanks, hills, etc., as well as to position man-made structures and other conspicuous landmarks accurately on a map. The counterpart of a topographical survey on the water was the hydrographic survey, which involved charting currents, depths, and obstacles, and locating and erecting navigational signals, using coastal features and markers provided by the topographical party as points of orientation and reference.

The pecking order in the field was assistant, sub-assistant, aide (or deputy

to the party leader), laborer, and cook. Assistants had considerable experience and were usually assigned only to primary triangulations. Sub-assistants,
like Wampler, possessed only enough knowledge to direct secondary triangulations. They might head separate field teams or work under the immediate supervision of an assistant. Both assistants and sub-assistants took direction from and communicated with the superintendent. An aide might be
assigned to a field party, depending upon the complexity of the project and
the wishes of the team leader. Laborers were retained locally to transport
equipment and help position the surveying devices. The cook obtained and
prepared the food and handled a variety of other miscellaneous chores as
specified by the field team leader. His competence was vital to the men's
morale and well-being.

Surveying Galveston Bay, 1850

The city of Galveston that greeted Wampler encompassed a population of
five thousand inhabitants. Recently established in 1838, its streets, public
squares, and residential areas had been carefully plotted. The homes were
almost all of frame construction, the more affluent prefabricated in a classical style in New England, before being shipped to Texas. Along the water-
front were wharves and warehouses stuffed with cotton. Indeed, Galveston
was considered "the great commercial emporium of Texas," since it was the
state's largest city, trading center, and primary Gulf port. To future president
Rutherford B. Hayes, who visited in December 1848, it appeared to be a
"neat fine town on a sand beach and apparently healthy.—A glorious contrast to the filth of New Orleans."[20] In 1839, however, an Irish visitor described the panorama as Wampler first saw it.

> The appearance of Galveston from the Harbour is singularly dreary. It is
> a low flat sandy Island about 30 miles in length & ranging in breadth from 1
> to 2. There is hardly a shrub visible, & in short it looks like a piece of prairie
> that had quarrelled with the main land & dissolved partnership. There is also
> another small Island in the Bay of a similar hideousness and called Pelican I.
> by reason of its being colonised by nobody but the Pelicans.
> The town is very irregularly built & extends or rather straggles for
> about half a mile along the coast the Houses being of wood entirely with a
> few exceptions of the better class & these only boast of a brick foundation
> of a few feet.[21]

Wampler commenced topographical work at the eastern end of Galveston
Island, heading a team of four men and a cook. He soon encountered the

kind of problems that would become all too common. The tidal marshland along the coast was "without a bottom," that is, the work party could not stand on it. Visibility was impaired by grass and reeds growing to heights of eight to twelve feet. Even more disconcerting was the presence of alligators and a variety of snakes. Not surprisingly, perhaps, Wampler reported to the superintendent on March 4, 1850, that his men had gone on strike, causing him to increase their pay after losing two workers. All of this seemed inconsequential, however, in comparison to difficulties arising with the schooner *Nymph,* problems that would plague the remainder of Wampler's tenure with the Coast Survey.

Wampler initially announced that the *Nymph* exceeded his expectations, and he "could manage to live as comfortably on her as on *any boat* the most fastidious could wish."[22] Originally built as a naval vessel, the *Nymph* weighed twenty tons, small by comparison with other Coast Survey schooners, and had been refitted within the past year to convert her from warfare to surveying purposes. She was in terrible condition upon arriving in Galveston on January 24, 1850, after a five-day sail from Pensacola. To the distress of the frugal Bache, Wampler reported the need for an array of additional repairs, estimated to cost one thousand dollars. She had lost her main gaffe, fore gaffe, and boom. Sitting on an entirely new bottom, she leaked about the centerboard. While tolerable, the rigging needed some new lines. Nor was she adequately outfitted, except for gear transferred from a sister vessel. The windlass was broken, as was the anchor. Service on an expedition to Round Island had caused the *Nymph* to lose her dinghy, which Wampler was intent on replacing, as it was indispensable to the work ahead. Once the *Nymph* was shipshape, however, Wampler's problems with her were far from over.

Richard Cutts, who had trained Wampler during the spring, was the senior assistant in Galveston Bay that winter, heading a primary triangulation party. He was assigned the schooner *George M. Bache,* named for the superintendent's brother, who had drowned during a hurricane while studying the Gulf Stream on Coast Survey duty in 1846. Upon arriving on February 11, Cutts concluded that the *Nymph* would be better utilized by Samuel A. Gilbert, another assistant engaged in erecting signals in the West Bay. In the interim, Wampler was expected to camp on the edge of Galveston City, where he was surveying and mapping, street by street, house by house. This change in plans took away Wampler's flexibility in accomplishing his project plan. Furthermore, it denied quarters on board a vessel, considered preferable to tents, since this arrangement removed the crew from the unhealthy marshland. He was justifiably unhappy about being usurped by his seniors,

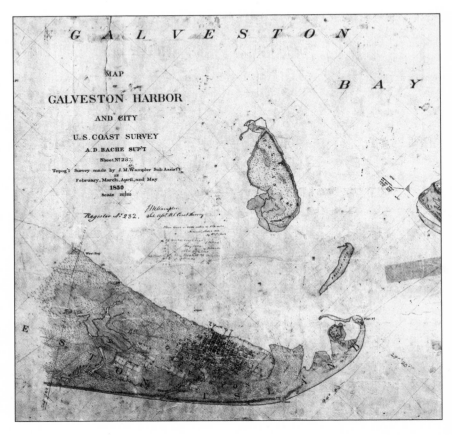

Galveston Harbor and City, J. M. Wampler, U.S. Coast Survey, 1850.

but after several weeks was permitted use of the schooner *Bache,* while Cutts continued his work from a camp at Virginia Point.

Months passed, and the superintendent directed that, for budgetary reasons, work should terminate by the first of June, when the *Nymph* would be laid up in Galveston and the *Bache* sailed north for another survey project. Local employees were to be discharged, gear stored in town, horses transported aboard the *Bache,* and instruments requiring repair sent back by freight to Washington. Wampler fretted about the effect on the *Nymph* of a summer in Galveston, writing Bache of the deterioration likely from "the *burning sun,*" gales, and worms, "the great enemy of Southern shipping."[23] Dutifully suspending operations on May 26, Wampler could rightfully take pride in the quantity of work completed in his first season heading a field party. His crew had surveyed 166 miles of shoreline and 5 miles of roads, within 997 square miles of area, much of it requiring fine detail to portray the streets and individual buildings that made up the city of Galveston. On June 1, Wampler boarded ship to begin the journey home.

The Romance of Antebellum Travel

His trip home would take him, first, to New Orleans by schooner, then up the Mississippi and Ohio Rivers by steamer, and finally overland by rail and stagecoach to Washington. Wampler's record of this twenty-seven-day odyssey contains some of his best descriptive writing, revealing at the same time the romanticism of a young man who had just celebrated his twentieth birthday.

The jewel in this account is his stop in St. Louis. Wampler arose early, at 5:30 A.M. on Thursday, June 13, to view the approaches to the city. He wrote warmly of seeing Jefferson Barracks, "where triumphantly waved, the flag of flags, the glorious Star 'Spangled Banner'." This outburst of patriotism would be repeated ten years hence, albeit for a different arrangement of stars and bars. "Oh how excited were my feelings as we approached this great City when I thought of my proximity to, & the probability of seeing that same day, the dearest being on this Wide Spread Earth. I mean My 'J. S.'" How Wampler knew this young lady is unknown. It is possible that she attended Belmont Academy, although there are no extant enrollment records to verify this hypothesis.

Upon docking, Wampler and a traveling companion, J. B. Heylin, went to the Planters House hotel, where they obtained rooms across from one another. After the midday dinner, Wampler dressed in his finest and drove to the Convent of Visitation, where he presented his card to the veiled atten-

dant who received him. He asked to see the Stettinius sisters, but was refused, despite "telling falsities," for only a father or brother was permitted to
see the young ladies in residence. The nun did allow, however, that permission from their father would permit him to be admitted, so Wampler and
Heylin hurried off to find Joseph Stettinius, a prominent merchant and civic
leader, who entertained the proposition. "I left him fully persuaded that as
far as he was concerned, I would be his son-in-law, but he gave me to understand that he thought Julia had changed her mind, but he promised to call at
the Convent on Sunday & speak with her seriously, & if she would see me,
he would give a letter etc. & I could go on Monday A.M. This is an eventful
trip and one on which depends a great deal of my future. But God's will be
done, if my prayers are answered and it is his will, then I Shall be Happy."[24]

The following day, Wampler met the girls' brother, John, and had a
pleasant visit with both the senior and junior Stettinius, during which the
father directed his son to take Wampler to see his sisters at the convent the
following evening.

> John went in and after waiting 15 long minutes he came out for me. I was
> delighted to meet the girls, though, notwithstanding Helen's smiling wel-
> come, Julia's mournful face & their Black mourning dresses cast a gloom
> over me that was terrible indeed. I saw by her repulsive look & short an-
> swers that my case was a hopeless one. Helen was delightful, pleasant &
> agreable [sic]. They had neither of them changed in appearance, since I last
> saw them. Julia hastened us off, refused to let me speak with her alone, and
> then oh then, I with beating heart bade her before, poor girl she wished
> not to be considered engaged while so young but said if the *same* feelings
> existed two or three years hence it would then be time to think of engage-
> ments etc. I guess the same have existed all the time on her part. Poor girl!
> She is either entirely devoid of any feeling for me, or else full of the most
> sacred & refined. I can't tell which & it would puzzle the best judge of
> human nature to devine. We left, I with the deepest misery loading down
> my already too much tried heart. Oh! God! Can those feelings be appreci-
> ated by any but those who have sadly experienced them.[25]

Wampler and John Stettinius walked around the city, talking until midnight, and did the same the following evening. On Monday, Wampler bid
John farewell, thanking him for his compassion and companionship. As he
boarded the steamer *Fashion,* the forlorn suitor strained for one last look at
the site of his rejection.

> The Convent! Oh! What numberless Hells do the contents of your walls
> create in the warm constant Boson [sic] of man. Oh! Women, you say we

are a more wicked & a sex more addicted to vice, but what vice can compare, what wickedness is so great as yours. You win the affections of some warm hearted & highminded young man. You promise an everlasting return of his love. You declare even that his pure feelings are but shaddows [*sic*] of those you entertain for him, in time you are engaged to him and when he comes to claim his cherished bride, when his happiness should have reached its summit, then with the slightest effort on your part you tumble him headlong into a Hell of Misery.[26]

The paddle-wheeler entered the Ohio River the following morning, stopping briefly at Cairo, which Wampler hastily sketched. Next came Paducah and then Shawnee Town. Wampler awoke the following morning, "feeling much better." He admired the Indiana countryside on the portside, "beautifully undulating & quite hilly & wooded," and regretted not having the descriptive powers to do it justice. At Portland, Kentucky, he disembarked, taking an omnibus into Louisville, where he enjoyed breakfast. Wampler then boarded steamer *Telegraph No.2,* where he met, to his delight, three friends from the Coast Survey—Augustus Rodgers and William E. Greenwell, who would subsequently survey in California, and Samuel Gilbert, who only months before had taken the *Nymph* from Wampler on Galveston Bay. At Cincinnati, Wampler again changed steamers, this time boarding the *Hindoo,* bound for Wheeling. He continued to be impressed with the beauty of the rolling landscape as the vessel proceeded up the Ohio River. On June 23, the steamer made a brief, unscheduled stop.

About 9 o'c we (the Steamer) ran close into an Island called Williamson's Id. to "bring the dead," which consisted of one of the firemen (free Coloured), who died early this A.M. of the Cholera. It was Melancholly to see how little thought or attention was paid during such solemn rites, but 5 men got into the yawl and a oblong box was passed in, the men cracking jokes occasionally. They pulled ashore, about 30 yds, & in a sand bank well shaded with bushs they dug a hole somewhat below high water mark, Laughing & Joking the while. After this was completed the box containing the body was let down & the hole filled as expeditiously as possible. When the boat was brought back & we were soon underweigh [*sic*] for Wheeling where we arrived at 3 o'c P.M.[27]

Wampler had traveled almost eleven hundred miles from St. Louis when he reached Wheeling, Virginia. After spending the night at "the dirty hole" known as the United States Hotel, Wampler climbed aboard a Concord-type stagecoach, which traveled by his calculation at a rate of ten knots over the National Road to Washington, Pennsylvania. His St. Louis woes far behind him, but his technique still firmly in place, Wampler checked into another "dirty" hotel, changed his clothes, and set off in search of "Lizzie G.," who, in turn introduced the traveler to a number of "pretty girls" at a party, including "a little charmer," Miss Mary Dawson. "What fine cut about the bows this little craft has, & nicely rounded timbers well set fore & aft, aloft & below, & she is hard to beat with all canvass set going free her top rigging & *figure head* cut water all of nicest mold & taper ends of the foretop arms were the nicest little fixtures."[28] Clearly, Wampler had been around sailing vessels for too long since leaving Miss Mercer's cultured femininity. After two more days of socializing, Wampler was back in a stagecoach, rattling over the dusty pike. The following morning, he arrived at Cumberland, the western terminus of the Baltimore and Ohio, where he switched to rail. The train took him first to Harper's Ferry, then to the Relay House outside Baltimore, where he transferred to different cars, and finally arrived at Washington, D.C., at 7:00 P.M. on June 27, almost four full weeks after leaving Galveston. At his destination, the weary Wampler noted that he still retained the bouquet given to him by Annie G., one of his new lady acquaintances in Pennsylvania.[29]

THE SUMMER OF 1850

Wampler wasted no time in reporting to the Coast Survey office. He was accorded a warm reception and immediately set about writing his progress report to the superintendent, as required of field party leaders at the close of each surveying season. Since this was Wampler's first such account, he was apprehensive about its form and content and so apologized to Bache, rationalizing that he had no example to follow. His fears proved groundless, however, as his report was quickly approved. At this time, the superintendent was working at a primary triangulation station at nearby Beltsville, Maryland. The following day, Wampler took the cars to see him. To meet him at the station, Bache sent the "Arc," the large yellow carriage introduced by Bache's predecessor, Ferdinand Hassler. The professor was in an affable mood, dining with his young guest and showing him the state-of-the-art instruments in the observation and astronomical tents. Consequently, Wampler returned to Washington in good spirits and spent the next day, a Sunday, calling on two more female friends.

The following ten days mixed business and pleasure. Wampler began the sub-assistant's ritual of redrawing his field maps to a smaller scale suitable for the superintendent's annual report to Congress. He made time for social calls, as well as two trips to Alexandria to see if Capt. Andrew Hussey, a civilian who piloted boats back and forth to Texas for the Coast Survey, had arrived with the schooner *Bache*. The two finally renewed acquaintance on July 6, in a reunion which included "serial rounds of dissipation," causing Wampler to complain the next morning of a "horrid bad head ache."

A historic event took place on July 9: "President [Zachary] Taylor extremely ill. Doctors with him all day. P.M. 10 h[ours] 35 m[inutes]. He breathed his last, when a great nation overflowed with tears, and wept a bitter grief. Singularly awful [*sic*] and what changes! What Changes! will be made in our government. Many for the worse, but few for the better."[30]

The president had participated in ceremonies laying the cornerstone for the Washington Monument on a typically steamy Independence Day and had taken ill that evening with what his physician described as "a bilious remittent fever, following an attack of serious cholera morbus."[31] He never recovered. Washington offices closed, and crape hung throughout the city, as Wampler packed his trunks the following day for the stage to Belmont. The coach deposited him with his baggage on the Leesburg Pike, in front of the Belmont plantation. Leaving his belongings to be picked up by carriage, Wampler walked through fields alive with men harvesting, down the ridge and into a frame house, where he found his mother and half-brother Bobby.

During his sojourn at Belmont, the sub-assistant devoted himself to preparing finished drawings of the surveys made by his party in the vicinity of Galveston. It was not at all uncommon for Professor Bache to permit his subordinates to return home to finish their drawings after a long stint in the field. While farmers cut and stacked wheat outside, Wampler spent eight hours each day at the drawing table. The only exceptions were Sundays or when a special visitor happened by, as in the case of an academician who operated a seminary in Madras, East India, and visited the academy to examine its curriculum. On August 19, Wampler finished the inking, printing, and cleaning of his sheets and received a brief recess before rejoining Whiting in Massachusetts.

A week later, Wampler complained of "a bilious attack," which would prevent him from undertaking the journey north. This tested Bache's patience, and he immediately replied from New Haven that Wampler was needed immediately to assist in Whiting's plane table work, and, as an inducement, he offered to meet with the young sub-assistant in New York or Boston to discuss his duties during the winter season. They met at Manhattan's elegant Irving Hotel on September 6. Bache offered Wampler an opportunity to work in South Carolina. He refused. Would his career in the Coast Survey have progressed further and longer had Wampler accepted the superintendent's offer? At least he would have escaped further adventures with the schooner *Nymph.* The mentorship remained intact, however, as his subordinate accompanied Bache downtown to visit the firm of George W. and Edmund G. Blunt, private chartmakers and sellers, which benefited from Edmund's simultaneous position on the Coast Survey staff as a senior assistant.

Mapping Marblehead

Continuing on to Massachusetts, Wampler found that the Survey party had established a camp within walking distance of Salem, which they named for Whiting. Arriving there on September 9, the sub-assistant discovered Spencer C. McCorkle, a fellow surveyor whose career path was destined to intertwine with Wampler and William E. Greenwell, another topographer who had steamed up the Ohio with him. Wampler immediately set to work tracing an additional copy of one map and inking a sheet depicting the nearby town of Lynn. When Whiting departed for ten days, Wampler returned to Marblehead to resume the surveying and drawing begun the previous season.

His work party, consisting of A. M. Harrison and Richard M. Bache, one of the superintendent's nephews, commuted by sailboat across Marblehead Harbor, which separated the community from Marblehead Neck. Some days, the breeze would produce a smooth voyage, requiring only a single canvas; on others, the short trip would entail tacking back and forth. Wampler lamented that someone stole a "declinator" from his boat, an instrument used on the plane table to determine the variation of the compass reading from true north. While on the mainland near Fort Sewall at the southeast corner of the Marblehead peninsula, young boys played "devilishly" around the plane table, hindering his work. When the table broke, Wampler dispatched Moses, a free black or personal servant brought from Virginia, to transport the instrument to Salem for repair. After initially setting up at the lighthouse on the northeast tip of the neck, the field party proceeded toward the western shore, surveying and drawing. All the while, Wampler was aware of sailing parties and vessels around him on the water, and, when he was confined to camp by bad weather, would sketch passing schooners to amuse himself. He took particular note of a Cunard steamer. Finally, on September 24, Wampler completed his rough field sketch and outline of Marblehead Neck, which on his finished map resembled an island connected to the peninsula by only a thin strip of beach.

As a bachelor raised in the company of young women, Wampler was not inclined to neglect his social life. Immediately upon arriving in the Salem

Marblehead detail of U.S. Coast Survey map, N.W. Shore of Massachusetts Bay,
J. M. Wampler et al., 1849–50.

area, he reestablished contact with George Whipple, his chum from the year
before, and the two were soon picnicking, dancing, playing cards, and enjoying piano music and singing with various female companions, including
Martha Chase, Lizy Webb, and the Goodhue sisters, Martha and Lucy. Some
guests were uninvited, however. "Got to camp Sun set. After Supper Mr.
Whiting & McCorkle arrived, had some ladie visitors. I got a fine Shot at the
troublesome Skunk and wounded him. He left his *Card*."[32]

Having finished on the Neck, Wampler moved his base of operations
from Camp Whiting to Marblehead itself, where he would now concentrate
his work. Wampler hired two local men as laborers and baggage carriers to
assist his crew as they engaged in the tedious work of chaining and mapping
the streets. Chaining entailed using links of precise length to measure distances. It enabled the men to move about and thereby stay warm, not an
inconsequential consideration to a field party at this time of year. While
standing still, sketching at the plane table, Wampler was more likely to be
affected by the wind and cold. When driven indoors by the elements, he
worked on finishing his sheets in ink. One day, McCorkle drove over from
Salem by buggy to ask Wampler to make a tracing of the shoreline he was
mapping for use by the hydrographic party, which had just arrived with the
Coast Survey steamer *Bibb*. Perhaps remembering all too well the schooner
Nymph, Wampler made note of the *Bibb*'s "fine accommodations" when he
accompanied McCorkle and Whiting aboard the vessel.[33]

As was frequently the case, Wampler's account of what transpired is of
interest as much for its personal dimension as for its record of the Coast
Survey. In the fall of 1850, Jenny Lind arrived in America, fresh from a series
of triumphal European performances. P. T. Barnum had paid her $150,000
for a series of 150 concerts booked across the country.[34] After winning the
adulation of New York, she moved on to Boston, where it was reported that
her appearances each generated from eight to twelve thousand dollars in
receipts. Swept up in the euphoria, Wampler took the train into Boston to
hear "the Swedish nightingale" at Fitchburg railroad station. Surprisingly, he
later characterized his reaction as "somewhat disappointed," despite having
what he described as a good seat.[35] Perhaps his feelings were tempered by
over-subscription of as many as one thousand tickets, or by ladies fainting, as
the doors were shut to limit overcrowding.[36] Wampler might also have been
in a bad mood after being denied entry to his rooms in Salem when he
returned late that night.

Not long thereafter, however, Wampler was buoyant about a European
act known as the Kilmistes, whom he heard perform in Marblehead, and

consequently he returned the following evening for a second concert. They were a family ensemble that performed songs and dances accompanied by harp, violin, and guitar.[37] The crew enjoyed its own recreation, as illustrated by a young girl at their boarding house, who begged Wampler to let the men remain one last night for a dance, after finishing their work at the end of the season. He promptly agreed, not wanting to "break up their fun" by denying the fiddler. Nor was Wampler's affair of the heart in St. Louis completely forgotten, as he received a letter from John Stettinius in New Orleans and, in turn, wrote to J. B. Heylin, his traveling companion at that time.

As October turned into November, the surveying season in Massachusetts gradually drew to a close. Wampler concluded his work at the drafting table in Camp Whiting, inking finished sheets from the pencil drawings done at the plane table in the field. Rowing himself back to Marblehead Rock, presumably to recheck some points, he encountered heavy seas in a boisterous wind from the north-northwest. His thoughts turned to the upcoming season in Texas. The steamer *Bibb* departed for her moorings in Boston to be laid up for the winter. Whiting and R. M. Bache went to Boston as well, although they would return to close up the camp. Wampler settled his bills and departed Massachusetts for the last time, bound for Coast Survey headquarters in Washington.

PREPARING TO TAKE TO THE FIELD AGAIN

In the capital city, Wampler readied himself for the winter surveying season. On November 11, the superintendent and his sub-assistant wrote to each other, Wampler from the office in Washington, and Bache from Webb's hill, a primary triangulation station in Anne Arundel County, Maryland, which served as his personal headquarters for a short period. Professor Bache's training at West Point had impressed upon him the importance of spending time with troops on the ground. In contrast to his predecessor, Hassler, Bache liked to be among his subordinates, helping with the most difficult geodetic operations, spending by one estimate as much as half of each year in the field.[38]

Bache's communiqué was another in a series of precise letters of instruction. He directed Wampler to take care to protect the government's interest in the event of extraordinary damage to the *Nymph* during summer storage in Galveston. Wampler had to be prepared for the possibility that he might once again be asked to exchange the *Nymph* with Cutts, should its shallow draft be better suited to the locations scheduled for primary triangulation. Further, he was reminded of the standard requirement to submit monthly reports to Washington, along with a journal. Finally, Wampler was told to prepare a sketch of his proposed work for personal approval by the superintendent. Wampler would "be allowed the usual field party" and expected to commence work as early in December as possible. Leaving nothing to chance, Bache went on to specify June 15 as the season's closing date and repeated what Wampler already knew from his report-writing experience six months earlier, namely, the requirements for a sketch of a particular scale, commentary on the progress achieved, estimates of the square miles mapped, and the length of shoreline and roads, along with any other points of interest.[39] Attention to detail had earned Alexander Dallas Bache a reputation in scientific and government circles of being an able administrator.[40]

At the same time, Wampler was setting forth his estimate of the cost of operations. He reminded Bache of the *Nymph*'s need for new rigging and a replacement windlass. The sub-assistant intended to hire his men in New Orleans and required five in all to accomplish the chaining proposed for the extreme north and east shores of Galveston Bay. Wampler planned to take a Negro cook all the way from Washington. He pointed out that unless assigned a vessel larger than the *Nymph,* he could scarcely store more than two weeks of provisions, necessitating supplementary transportation back and forth across the forty or fifty miles between his field sites and Galveston City. Finally, Wampler asked if he might not receive an increase in salary, especially considering the crude living conditions aboard the *Nymph* and the difficulty of the terrain where he would be working.[41] The superintendent approved the estimate of expenses the same day, with the exception of extra boats for transporting the men and cook, and hedged on the size of the field party. He agreed to take the matter of Wampler's compensation under consideration.

With the determination and self-righteousness of youth, Wampler would not accept anything short of unqualified approval. His rebuttal explained the necessity of having an extra boat when the primary vessel ran aground, as frequently occurred in the tidal areas in which he planned to work, when the main vessel was being maintained or repaired, and when it was necessary to carry fresh water, wood, and provisions. He described the small dimensions of the *Nymph* with its undersized berth deck for the complement of men and gear to be transported. Finally, Wampler defended his intention to accompany the cook personally on the trip from Washington, as being economical as well as necessary to facilitate clearance through the port of New Orleans, where persons of color, traveling alone, would undoubtedly have been unusual. Wampler was concerned that the cook might not receive expeditious passage.[42]

Wampler defined the specific areas he intended to survey, predicting that, by the close of the season, he would catch up with the primary triangulation party. He cited the need for a special topographical symbol to depict the palmetto, a prominent feature on the Galveston landscape. Lecturing the professor, he pointed out to Bache the various factors that would affect the productivity of a topographical party—experienced workers (using Henry Whiting as an example), the character of the terrain, and the skill of the individual inking the final sheets.[43] In a later letter, Wampler estimated that inking required three-fourths of the time actually engaged in surveying. He characterized a day inking at home as averaging two or three more productive hours than its counterpart in the Coast Survey headquarters, influenced, perhaps, by his preference for being at Belmont or maybe by the realization that office hours in Washington were normally 9:00 A.M. to 3:00 P.M.[44] Thoroughly accustomed to the brashness of youth, Bache patiently wrote a simple three-line response, approving the project plan and observing that it appeared ambitious, and, consequently, he would not be disappointed if it were not completed in full.

LIVING AND WORKING AT GALVESTON

Arriving in Galveston on December 19, Wampler encountered an all-too-familiar problem: the poor condition of the schooner *Nymph*. He reported to Superintendent Bache that the vessel had suffered from the sharp contrast of the torrid Texas summer and the stormy autumn and winter. The rudder casing was torn loose, the centerboard fouled, masts warped and twisted, cleats carried away, topmasts shorn off or sprung, and the foresail and jib were rotten because of the combination of, first, mildew and, then, hot, dry weather. Wampler had recruited four men for his party, and he put them to work on the boat, along with two others lent by Capt. James S. Williams from his crew. Wampler pitched in as well, helping to caulk the dinghy. When his two ship carpenters repeatedly failed to meet their commitments, the sub-assistant discharged them, hiring the only available alternative, a house carpenter, who required continuous supervision, and an old salt, on whose advice Wampler relied. He opined to Bache that the *Nymph* was best suited as a tender or as the second vessel for a double triangulation party, perhaps used to install signals, but would not be dependable for topographical use during the next season.[45] Bache responded with an apology, noting that the *Nymph* had been completely overhauled just a year ago at the Pensacola Navy Yard, while, at the same time, pointedly stating that Wampler should put her in the best condition possible, as it was unlikely another vessel would be acquired to take her place.[46] Repairs completed, on January 9, 1851, the *Nymph* set sail in a northeasterly direction.

Anchoring in the East Bay, the topographical party's first task was to determine the position of a nearby triangulation point, which proved no easy matter. Some signals erected by an earlier primary triangulation party had fallen down or were not visible at every point from which the topographical party sought to observe them. Sometimes they were obscured by stands of trees. Wampler complained of the paucity of signals left for his orientation. Consequently, he and his crew erected additional stations, some on pilings in the water, marking them with distinctively colored cloth. The men then began fixing signals as reference points in mapping the terrain. These were occasionally set higher than the triangulation points for easier observation. Wampler worked his way down the beach with the plane table, to be met four or five miles hence by the schooner, repeating the process the following day. When he moved inland, up a river, for example, Wampler determined the exact location of a prominent object, such as a house, and then began his compass courses to draw the river's curves and outlets into the bay. At one point, he was interrupted by the hydrographic party from the schooner *Morris,* which required a tracing of the coastline to relate its readings to those being taken ashore. When he happened upon a body of water not shown on preliminary sketches done by the primary triangulation team, Wampler promptly gave it the name "Lake Surprise," a designation that has persisted from February 12, 1851, to the present.[47]

The season's work in the East and Upper Bay posed constant challenges, but in two instances, the problems were so egregious as to cause Wampler to write pointed letters to his supervisor. The first was misidentification of the East Bay Bayou triangulation point. When it did not appear to be located as recorded, Wampler rechecked the tables given him of latitudes and longitudes, then recalculated the lengths of triangles and took extra measurements of side distances. He concluded that the primary triangulation party had misplotted the point by 1,274 meters or approximately three-quarters of a statute mile.[48] Bache consulted the charts in the Coast Survey office and acknowledged the error. The second letter addressed what Wampler characterized as "superfluous" signals and the need for additional points of reference in certain terrain. His party had been confused by signals erected earlier

East Galveston Bay,
J. M. Wampler, U.S.
Coast Survey, 1851.

but apparently not required for orientation. Consequently, he requested that triangulation parties be instructed to remove these distracters not previously recorded. He also cited the difficulty in determining locations on straight stretches of coastline without distinguishable features, as encountered on the Galveston marshland. Could the triangulation team erect inland signals in these areas at intervals of two miles or so, visible from the shore? This would save Wampler the extra step of positioning and repositioning floating signal buoys, attached to the shank of an anchor, as tertiary reference points in the water, which he had resorted to as a field expedient.[49] Bache committed only to having superfluous signals removed, if not identified.

This was by no means the full extent of the problems encountered by the topographical party. The contrast between the more defined terrain and refined surroundings in the Northeast and what he faced in Texas was continually evident to Wampler. He was not reluctant to describe these hardships to Bache, who had not ventured far enough from the seat of political power for a firsthand look at the Texas coast. It was sometimes difficult for Wampler's party to approach land by wading or by boat. He wrote to Bache: "I found the delta of the Trinity River an extremely disagreeable place to work in. Not being able to land, I was compelled to make my stations on the bars at the mouths of the several Bayous, thigh deep in Mud & Water, and upon bedded drift logs, etc. etc."[50]

At another low point off Hannah's Reef, the work party was fortunate to complete surveying and chaining before the land went underwater at high tide. The winter season did not deter mosquitoes, and when a crew member fell sick, as the captain, Wampler took on the duty of ministering to him. On another occasion, Wampler noted that a drunk brandished a loaded pistol, threatening to shoot his compatriots. The challenges of Galveston Bay presented a sharp contrast to the world of Jenny Lind and the Massachusetts field site.

The weather was a constant source of discomfort. The field party encountered almost daily storms, with wind, often at gale force, and rain, sometimes in the form of thunderstorms, severely limiting work, when not stopping it altogether. "Wind very strong E.S.E. Out to work but could not see, wind shook [plane] table too much."[51] When the rain stopped, fog often appeared: "thick fogg all day." By year's end, the superintendent had taken note of the inhospitable conditions and made mention of them in his annual report to the Congress: "His [Wampler's] duties were made arduous by an inclement season, and by the necessity of often working at stations covered with water."[52]

The adverse conditions affected navigation as well as surveying. When winds were moderate and from the stern, the *Nymph* could fly "wing & wing," sails set out on either side of the mast, resembling a bird. That was not the norm in 1851, however. One trip back to Galveston from the East Bay encountered multiple difficulties: "Cold wet & dense fogg, & rain. I got underweigh [*sic*] A.M. & started for Galveston, beat [zig zag] through fogg & came to Ladies pass, but did not know it on acct of the Barrel & Stake [a buoy possibly marking a sand bar] being washed away, so I hunted about in vain till I saw one of my marks where I knew the pass & beat through it nicely. When off Bolivar Channell, Schr. Drifted so much that I brought up at Millers (tremendous current)."[53] When the current was not against them, the tide often was. "Got underweigh, tide & wind adverse. Got as far as entrance to East Bay, when crossing the Channel that drains E.B., passing between Bolivar Pts. & Pelican Spit, wind so light & tide so very strong that the Schr. was drifting out fast, spite of sails. I came too all standing but Gib, and immediately a dead calm came upon us."[54]

Nor were the party's two vessels always safe from each other in rough weather. Returning in the dinghy to the anchored *Nymph* in increasing wind and rain, the boat smashed into the schooner, breaking the tiller. A week later, Wampler stayed up all night in Galveston harbor, securing the schooner from a "violent norther," which pressed the *Nymph* into the wharf. Wampler's spirits sank as the weather deteriorated.

> It is a down right imposition on a gentlemans feelings to be sent to a far off section, not half provided for. A schooner, that would not make a launch for a small sloop of war, no securities for boats [no davits], going before the wind. Boats are staving into her, have to use a cable to tow with or lose the boat [dinghy]. There is not a dry corner in her berth deck when the weather is rough. How can men be expected to work cheerfully through a varied winter, made up of the severest storms imaginable, & the hotest possible bearable weather, in such a place. Is it not very self evident that such economy, as prompts the Supt. to retain the Schr. Nymph in service is false, utterly [*sic*] false.[55]

During one hard blow from the north, Wampler spotted a vessel bearing down on the *Nymph*. As it came within shouting distance on the port side, the captain inquired as to their present location. When Wampler thought to look back, his dinghy was adrift. The two-and-one-half-inch rope, used to tow it astern, had chafed apart in the rough sea, leaving Wampler fuming over losing his only new hull. Fearing the current would carry it into the treacherous waters of the Gulf and not wanting to risk pursuit in the *Nymph,* he "wrote an advertisement & reward to the finder, put it into an empty bottle & threw said bottle overboard."[56] Three days later, when he next came upon a house, he sent a message to Galveston about the lost boat. Returning to the city later in the week, Wampler hired a horse and sent a man to inquire along the shore about the vessel. The crew member returned with the happy news that the boat was in the hands of a Mr. Bates at Virginia Point. As they sailed east again, two days later to resume surveying, the *Nymph* paused long enough for Wampler to give Bates a ten-dollar reward and reclaim the wayward dinghy.

When not buffeted by storms, the party ran the risk of running aground on uncharted reefs or mud flats that constituted much of the East Bay shoreline: "Got stuck with boat on the mud flats, & could not get within a mile of Shore any way but one & that I did not want to go. Returned with difficulty to Schr. Rowing mud the whole way up to vessel the tide having left the Nymph in 18 inches. Water only. However did some work. . . . Will probably be afloat by morning."[57]

Five months of fieldwork were not without their lighter moments. It was, for example, a pleasant surprise to return to port and discover another Coast Survey vessel tied up at the dock. On one such occasion, the skipper was Andrew Hussey with whom Wampler had caroused in Washington the previous summer. The two friends enjoyed an evening of billiards. Wampler dined with the hydrographic party aboard the schooner *Morris* when it made a port call and, in turn, entertained its captain aboard the *Nymph.* Other old friends like Williams and McCorkle were in town periodically. Wampler also made the acquaintances of G. W. Parish, later to serve as his aide, George W. Stevens, cousin of the Coast Survey's executive officer, and Tunis A. M. Craven.

When prevented by adverse weather from conducting operations, Wampler turned to a variety of activities, such as writing to Coast Survey colleagues or other friends and family at home. Keeping accounts of Coast Survey funds for Samuel Hein, the agency's disbursing officer, consumed more time. Reading was a favorite pastime. Further, it was not uncommon for Wampler to draw for his own pleasure, and at the end of one day's work he amused himself by illustrating a parabolic reflector, an instrument allowing reflection of the sun to be seen a long way off in a specific direction. Bright red clay and sand collected along the shore of the Upper Bay provided the ingredients to make a pipe. As the season drew to a close, Wampler's thoughts naturally turned toward home, and he fashioned a model topsail schooner for his half-brother Bobby.

As the sole port on the bay, Galveston offered the only opportunity for social exchange with women. Wampler never tied up at Galveston without noting his interactions with the eligible young ladies there. Courting in 1851 began very familiarly with a call on New Year's Day to Julia Stettinius, who was staying with Judge Franklin. Exactly one week later, however, the romance was truly over. "Called on Miss Stettinius and from the uncivil treatment I received of her, I have resolved that she be scratched from my books."[58] In her place went the name of "Miss Lizzie Watrons." They attended church, rode on the beach in a buggy, and attended parties together. Wampler gushed, "I'll be darned if I dont *love* her."[59] When the *Nymph* set sail for surveying, Lizzie could be seen waving a handkerchief from her carriage on the shore. A blustery day at the end of January provided an excuse to keep the *Nymph* in port (although the *Belle* was able to get underway for the West Bay) and an opportunity to organize a tea party for the ladies. In addition to Misses Watrons, Jones, and Fontaine, two other local fellows joined the social aboard the *Nymph*. Fruitcake, lemonade, and oyster soup were served, along with wines and brandy. The party merrily left the schooner after sunset and dispersed, Wampler proceeding to another gathering at Mrs. Price's, where he flirted with Mary Sydnor and Eliza Price. The bloom was already off the rose of the Lizzie Watrons affair. By the middle of the following month, Wampler and Lizzie had a lovers' quarrel, and he was calling on the Whitaker sisters, "nice girls," even if they were Yankees. Fewer days were spent in port as the season progressed, and more time was lost on station, waiting for the weather to clear. For the remainder of his stay, when free in Galveston, Wampler seemed to divide his time between Miss Watrons and the Whitaker girls, as well as with a new contender for his affections, "Miss Idy Saltmarsh," undoubtedly a pseudonym for someone Wampler did not wish to identify.[60]

As winter turned to spring, an interesting exchange of correspondence took place between Wampler and Bache, illustrating the superintendent's program of garnering local support for his surveying efforts. Wampler wrote Bache that a local landowner, Gen. Thomas Jefferson Chambers, had requested a tracing of the coastline of Turtle Bay, the Trinity River delta, and Fort Anahuac, the area in which he was laying out a town.[61] General Chambers was a colorful character in early Texas history, organizer and commander of troops to fight Mexicans and Indians, rival of Sam Houston, and murderer of "a ruffian O'Brien," who had taken possession of much of Chambers's land by dubious means.[62] Indeed, Wampler noted seeing the house where Chambers had shot O'Brien. Bache was in the field, inspecting Charleston Harbor, and it was almost a month later before he received the communiqué. Responding in true bureaucratic fashion, the superintendent requested permission from the treasury department to convey the drawing, but at the same time authorized Wampler to make a tracing and "lend" it to Chambers with the Coast Survey's compliments.[63] During the interim, Wampler called upon Chambers to borrow a pocket compass in order to ascertain directions while using the dinghy. Distance on the bayou would be estimated by equating each stroke of the oars to so many meters. To return the favor, and perhaps the compass, Wampler took tea with the general three days later and gave him the requested drawings. The spirit of Bache's political policy had been adhered to, if not the letter of its administrative controls. The approval process worked more smoothly later, when Bache directed Wampler to provide drawings to a Mr. James, who was compiling a map of Galveston Island and Bay and had made application with the treasury department for access to Coast Survey charts.[64]

The season ended with the field party working in the Upper Bay, where the coast was better defined, especially at the mouth of the Trinity River. That did not preclude navigational obstacles. After "kedging" the *Nymph* off a sandbar (that is, freeing the schooner by pulling it toward the anchor, using the chain), Wampler noted three steamers—the *Reliance, Jack Hays,* and *Magnolia*—all aground around him. They were being assisted by eight or nine vessels lightering them off.[65] Wampler went aboard the *Magnolia* to visit with its captain and inquire about any letters addressed to his party. Eight days later, the *Reliance* and *Magnolia* were still grounded.

OTHER DUTIES AS ASSIGNED

In conformance with the superintendent's instructions, Wampler closed down operations in mid-June and returned to Washington, arriving on June 28. He paused at the Coast Survey office only long enough to inform Bache of the termination of work and then went home to Belmont to ink his sheets and draft a final report.[66]

With his April progress report from the field, Wampler had appended a request to be granted leave over the summer months, to which the superintendent had seemed agreeable, barring unforeseen circumstances. It therefore came as a surprise to Wampler to receive instructions from Maj. Isaac I. Stevens, the Coast Survey executive officer, directing him to take temporary supervision of the party of Assistant George D. Wise, who had fallen ill. Wise was in charge of the schooner *Franklin,* named for Bache's great grandfather, operating in the Atlantic off the coast of Chincoteague. The superintendent's letter, dated July 14, from the primary triangulation station at Portland, Maine, did not catch up with Wampler until he was already aboard the *Franklin.* Bache asked Wampler to ascertain whether Mr. Denny, Wise's assistant, was capable of filling in for him on a long-term basis, and, if not, to employ another individual capable of shouldering this responsibility, W. M. Johnson.[67] Wampler's pique over this disruption of his summer respite was reflected in the full month he took to report to Washington and then proceed to the lower Delmarva peninsula. The interruption in inking sheets also provided justification, in his mind, for delaying departure for Texas the following fall.

There was one piece of unfinished business that Wampler tried to resolve while he considered the Coast Survey indebted to him. When first laying eyes on the schooner *Belle* in January, Wampler had written to Bache, requesting that she be assigned to topographical work in Texas the following year. Bache vacillated, asking that the matter be resurfaced "when a proper time comes." Wampler, for his part, calculated that this was the time. In restating his case, the supplicant may well have made a tactical mistake—not surprising, considering his years—by adding other grievances that occurred to him as he bobbed in Chincoteague Inlet, waiting to be relieved. Wampler fretted over the paucity of encouragement offered by his seniors. He complained that he had been permitted to remain home for only two weeks, and much of that time was taken up drawing. He asked for an aide on his next survey to attest to his accounts, pointing out that only his black cook could perform this function in the season just ended. He concluded by assuring Bache that his letter was not intended as a request for a salary increase, nor, by being so frank, should he be considered to have entered upon the "path of discontent."[68]

Writing this time from Ossipee Station in Maine, the superintendent acknowledged receipt of Wampler's petition. Bache considered the schooner *Belle* unsuited to the topographical work to be performed over the next season, because of Captain Williams's problems with her deep draught while doing primary triangulation in the same waters the past year. Bache refused to compliment the quality of work performed by Wampler's field party until he had an opportunity to examine it closely, but did express satisfaction with its quantity. He apologized for having to dispatch Wampler to the field again so quickly and agreed to authorize an aide, if funding remained available after meeting Wampler's other expenses. Taking the bait, Bache closed by stating his intention to seek an increase in salary for Wampler at the earliest opportunity, presumably from pursekeepers in the parent treasury department. Before Wampler received this reply, W. M. Johnson had joined the field party and proven himself to be far abler than Denny. Wampler was thereby free to depart, while complaining of "suffering from indisposition."[69]

The Great Nymph Debate Continues

The cross fire between Maine and Virginia resumed as soon as Wampler returned once more to Belmont. He pointed out that the *Belle* drew only six more inches of water than the *Nymph*. He complained that it was not possible for him to work again from that schooner. The *Belle* seemed a convenient and comfortable alternative, but, of course, he would defer if the superintendent had another vessel in mind.[70] Bache's terse two-sentence reply introduced the prospect of using tents.[71] Wampler's rejoinder played on the superintendent's near obsession with productivity by pointing out the impracticality of moving camp every two days or so, taking valuable time away from surveying. Vessel-based operations were easily relocated. He observed that primary triangulation was inherently more stationary than secondary, due to its rigor and precision, should the superintendent wish to base that party ashore and transfer the schooner *Belle* to his team.[72] Bache reiterated his intention to assign the *Nymph* to the topographical party, wisely causing Wampler to stop, but unfortunately not to end, this discussion. Wampler acquiesced, "Quite *enough* has been said by me of the 'Nymph' and you shall not be further troubled I assure you by more allusions to the unfitness of that vessel."[73]

Despite Wampler's apparent concession, his relationship with Bache continued to deteriorate during the winter over differences of opinion concerning the *Nymph*. Wampler asked for permission to buy a replacement vessel for whatever amount the superintendent could afford out of the Coast Survey's appropriation, which, interestingly, had grown, along with its activities, from $152,000 in 1848 to $456,000 by 1852. Bache replied that he would entertain the prospect of a purchase the following year, but not in the present one. If a *"bargain"* was offered, he would consider it, funds permitting.[74] This was the opening Wampler was looking for, and he soon telegraphed Washington that a schooner had been found in Galveston, "very suitable, well built, sound bottom, nearly zincked right, new set sails & rigging, copper fastened, drawing only two feet [off] water."[75] The asking price was $2,500 with $500 allowed for the *Nymph*. An estimated $350 would be necessary to modify the vessel for topographical use. It was "a rare chance." A month later, Major Stevens sent a negative response on behalf of the superintendent, both telegraphically and in writing, citing the lack of funds.[76] The matter was dropped once again, but not forgotten.

Superintendent Bache eventually issued his letter of instructions for the topographical party with the standard provisions and an allocation of $2,800, excluding Wampler's salary. An aide would be assigned, if the *Nymph*'s accommodations were adequate to house him.[77] The response came back that Wampler "would prefer one of congeniality of feelings, one who evinces a strong interest in the work." There is reason to believe that G. W. Parish, who was selected, did not live up to Wampler's expectations, as he withdrew his request for an aide the following year.

The topographical party was late getting underway. Wampler was delayed two weeks in Louisville by ice on the Ohio and then for several days when his steamer ran aground in the Mississippi. Prolonged northwest winds lowered water levels by as much as three to four feet in West Galveston Bay, where the party's work was to be concentrated in 1852, interfering with the *Nymph*'s arrival and its utilization close to shore.[78] Nevertheless, by mid-April, Wampler's party had completed surveying based on primary triangulation sheets furnished at the season's outset. Assistant James S. Williams, heading the nearest triangulation party, was asked for more fixed reference points west of "Jupiter" station to permit topographical work to continue for three or four weeks longer. Spencer McCorkle, who was doing primary measurements to the west of Williams, agreed to pass these along to Wampler as soon as completed. Williams and McCorkle would both figure prominently in a later adventure involving Wampler.

At about this time, confusion set in as to the date when Texas operations would cease. Bache wrote on April 12 that work should stop by May 15 or earlier, if necessary to achieve a desired saving of four hundred dollars. Before the letter arrived in Galveston, Wampler received a telegram warning that the cancellation would be rescinded. He had already disbanded his party, however, putting up the *Nymph* for the summer and stowing the equipment, in accordance with his original instruction to close operations when work had progressed sufficiently and the allocated monies were near an end.

Wampler's party had surveyed 163.5 miles of shoreline, along with 62.5 square miles of terrain, less than the two previous seasons, which disappointed him, although there is no indication that the superintendent was dissatisfied. Wampler wrote and then telegraphed his leader about the cessation of work, whereupon Bache wired back, "All right. Come to Washington."[79] There was undoubtedly an ulterior motive in the brisk termination of operations in Texas, for on his return trip Wampler stopped at Baton Rouge long enough to be married to Catharine Nugent Cummings, a Louisiana lass he had met earlier.

Wampler was back in the Washington office by the first of June. Working with his aide, he squared accounts, apparently to the satisfaction of the exacting disbursing officer, Samuel Hein. He subsequently retreated to Loudoun County, where on August 20, he reported that he was suffering from dysentery, which was prevalent thereabouts. Wampler was thus delayed in returning to headquarters to assist Major Stevens with register maps and other duties, as the superintendent had requested. This was Wampler's first summer at home with his new wife, which might well have caused him to linger at Belmont. Bache asked again, and inquired about the status of Wampler's final inking of the Texas sheets, now overdue. This time Wampler complained of rheumatism, which, he explained, crippled his fingers and hands. Wampler eventually reported to the office in early September, but his days with the Coast Survey were clearly numbered.

By the end of the month, he had asked for and received a letter of recommendation from Bache to the secretary of the interior, possibly in regard to employment with the General Land Office, the antecedent to the Bureau of Land Management. Bache stated that he would be sorry to see Wampler leave, although pleased to see him succeed. Whatever the career opportunity, it did not materialize as Wampler had expected, and he tried to rebuild his bridges with Bache, if only temporarily, with a letter of thanks for the warm recommendation, along with an expression of "love" for service in the Coast Survey.[80] Wampler was soon launched in a different direction, however, through temporary assignment to the engineer bureau of the war department, where he would work with Lt. Montgomery C. Meigs.

THE WASHINGTON AQUEDUCT

On November 3, 1852, Lieutenant Meigs had been ordered to make "the necessary surveys, projects, and estimates for determining the best means of affording the cities of Washington and Georgetown an unfailing and abundant supply of good and wholesome water."[81] The city's population was estimated to have already grown 25 percent since the 1850 census and now numbered fifty thousand inhabitants. The need for water for drinking and bathing was rapidly outgrowing the supply from the springs and wells upon which the city relied. The prevalence of wood and tar paper used in expanding the Capitol building had impressed upon Congress the reality that two large cisterns containing water from Smith Spring would prove woefully inadequate in the event of a fire. Col. George W. Hughes of the Corps of Engineers had initially been engaged to devise a solution, but he had disappointed Congress by proposing a dam across Rock Creek, which would only provide an additional twelve to twenty-two million gallons daily, depending on the season.[82] Congress then appropriated five thousand dollars for a more exhaustive survey. In three months' time, with only a trio of professional assistants, Meigs completed his assignment and submitted a report to Congress. Wampler's contribution was preparing the topographical map of the Potomac River, for which Meigs commended him to Bache at the project's conclusion.[83]

The solution proposed by Meigs and his team was for a canal to be constructed, one hundred feet wide and six feet deep, to carry water twelve miles from the Great Falls of the Potomac to Georgetown. Two intermittent reservoirs would help settle out the mud. Cast-iron pipes would permit distribution of water throughout the city of Washington. The Washington Aqueduct would include a series of tunnels and conduits, seven feet in diameter. Its most prominent feature was a bridge spanning the valley of Cabin John Creek, one hundred feet high and almost five hundred feet in length. Meigs estimated the total cost at close to two million dollars. This expense would be more than offset, in his view, by reduced insurance rates, higher property values, and the increased comfort of living in the nation's capital. The enormity of the undertaking rested on an aesthetic vision, which Wampler must have helped Meigs to shape, of a series of fountains, pleasing to the eye, to cool the city, and a network of hydrants, readily available to clean the streets of their unsightly and unhealthy offal.[84] The proposal was designed to meet the capital's water requirements for two hundred years by providing thirty-six million gallons of water a day. As it turned out, the population of Washington exceeded the aqueduct's capacity in one-third that time, although it still remains in use.[85]

Congress adopted Meigs's design and enacted an initial appropriation for 1853. Meigs was promoted to captain and selected to take charge of the aqueduct's construction, along with simultaneously being designated superintendent of the building projects at the Capitol and Post Office building.[86] Wampler returned to the drawing department of the Coast Survey, where he reported on February 15, and began drafting, among other projects, a map of the new Washington Territory.

CONCLUDING BUSINESS AT THE COAST SURVEY

By serving on the aqueduct project with Meigs, Wampler forfeited the option of leading a survey party during the winter season. Sub-assistant George W. Dean was allocated Wampler's gear for use in setting up two astronomical stations in Texas. Concerned about the condition of the schooner *Nymph*, as reported to him by Assistant James Williams, the superintendent asked Wampler to enforce the obligations of the arrangement he had made in Galveston for her care over the summer. By March 8, 1853, Wampler believed he finally had the story straight, thanks to a letter from McCorkle in Galveston.

Bache was no doubt upset because the *Nymph* had sunk, not once, but twice. McCorkle reported that the man Wampler left in charge of the *Nymph* over the summer had regularly rinsed her decks, and possibly pumped her out as well, despite not receiving any compensation for doing so from the government. McCorkle believed that water had permeated the hull due to worms, but Wampler could not accept the explanation that a vessel would sink so quickly from an infestation of that sort, and speculated that the schooner had been scuttled. Andrew Hussey raised the *Nymph* the second time and coaxed her to the pier. The vessel's gear was almost worthless: sails and mattresses rotted, copper and iron fastenings rusted, and decks mud-strewn throughout. McCorkle estimated her worth at $280, although he had only received an offer of $150. Oblivious to the strained relationship between the two, he encouraged Wampler to reassure Bache that the blame did not reside with the vessel's caretakers and that the *Nymph* had best be sold expeditiously, before she deteriorated further. Wampler considered this assessment a vindication of his views on the schooner, as well as of his arrangements upon leaving Texas, and he so informed the superintendent. The loss of the *Nymph* was for the best, he wrote, as she would have soon gone down, quite likely with loss of life, had she remained in service and sailed to Matagorda, as surveying extended along the Texas coast.[87]

Not surprisingly, Bache did not agree. Also reporting from Galveston,

McCorkle's supervisor, James Williams, wrote to the superintendent that Wampler's arrangement for upkeep of the *Nymph* had provided only for the custodian's servant to dampen the decks occasionally, not for the conduct of meaningful maintenance. Nor was compensation promised. Consequently, Bache concluded that the damage was due to the faulty agreement entered into by Wampler.[88]

A fortnight later Bache signed a letter of instructions, designating Wampler as assistant in the triangulation party under James Farley on the James River, an assignment Wampler had recently expressed interest in receiving. "I shall be delighted with that station as it is much nearer home," he had written Bache on January 31.[89] Wampler now viewed his circumstances in a different light, however.

On the first of April, Wampler resigned his position with the Coast Survey. The reasons stated were family, lack of opportunities for advancement, and low salary.

> I presumed, the other day, when you asked me, in the omnibus, if I was ready to take the field, that I was to take charge of Some Party, and when I answered you in the affirmative, I reckoned upon the time usually spent in preparing for field duty, as being probably sufficient to restore my wifes health, to enable her to be removed. She having been recently confined, and at present not able to sit up. It is impossible for me to leave at present.
>
> I would furthermore say, that I have certainly expected, and most anxiously looked for, a realization of those hopes that you have from time to time, within the last four years, inspired within me. Judging from the last "instructions" they appear as far in the future as ever, and nothing but inspired hope has kept me so long attached to the Coast Survey, and even in spite of an offer three years ago, of a good situation of $1500 per annum, made me by a friend.
>
> I feel sir, that my services considering their responsibilities & hardships are worth to the government double my salary of $800, that I have been induced thro' "hopes deferred" to work for.
>
> Can you conceive it possible to exist in this city, with a family, upon $800 pr annum, at the most economical rate of living.
>
> I need not say that I have been necessarily sinking pecuniarily during the last year, but such is a fact. And had not the duty devolved upon me to make the Survey for Capt Meigs, for which I received good pay, I really do not know what I would have done.[90]

Wampler's first child had been born in Washington on March 17. Family considerations were obviously foremost on his mind, but this was also a decision that had been building for some time. His resignation letter blamed the Coast Survey and the schooner *Nymph* for "an affliction which will go with me to the grave. I mean Rheumatism." And he resurfaced the controversy of the *Nymph* and McCorkle's assessment, which, apparently, the superintendent had not yet acknowledged.

For Alexander Dallas Bache—scientist, government administrator, and mentor to his young staff—this decision, although hardly unexpected, must have seemed something of a defeat. His response reflected his weariness with the situation.

> I have received with no little surprise your letter of April 1st marked private. You take a very different view of your case from what I have always supposed. You came in the C.S. as draughtsman & went into the field to suit yourself. Had you remained in the office you would have been promoted as your experience & knowledge rendered advisable. But you preferred to go to the field & get experience in a new line. I wished to put you at the head of a triangulation party a few days since but you had not the requisite experience & I assigned you as an assistant to prepare you for a charge. I think you will be throwing away your prospects to leave the C.S. but of course you are the best judge. Until you have been the rounds of the parties & acquired knowledge to take charge in each it must of course depend upon circumstances of vacancies whether you can be put ahead or not. You can hardly expect to be put in charge until qualified to fill a triangulation or astronomical vacancy until you have served in that line. Such is my view of the matter. I will not act upon your letter until I hear that you desire it. Perhaps as you now understand my motives (which I supposed you did before) you may be satisfied with the results. I am willing that any of those who enter the survey should obtain a large experience, at its expense, or by confining themselves to one line as drawing should make progress & be advanced, but they cannot do both.[91]

Wampler was quick to reaffirm his decision in a bitter letter, which was forwarded to the superintendent, again in the field, this time at Charleston, South Carolina. Upon approval of the secretary of the treasury, Wampler's resignation became effective on April 30, 1853.[92] It was a sad ending to an experience that had enriched his life and provided the skills he would use to support his family in the future. Wampler's relationship with Bache would not be the last time he touched greatness, but he would never again work for someone who had his best interests at heart, as the old professor seemed to have exhibited at every turn in a relationship that spanned six years. Service with the Coast Survey had exposed Wampler to far more of the country than most Americans of his day could expect to see in an entire lifetime. He had been blessed with the opportunity of working with some of the brightest minds the nation possessed in the fields of science and engineering.

In eight years' time, many of these same individuals would join Wampler on the battlefields of the Civil War, but in virtually every instance, his former Coast Survey colleagues would be wearing the blue, while Wampler proudly donned the gray. Capt. Andrew A. Humphreys, the assistant in charge of the Coast Survey office when Wampler entered upon duty, would serve as a major general, fighting gallantly at Antietam, Fredericksburg, and Gettysburg, and in subsequent battles until, as a senior Union corps commander at Appomattox, he pursued Lee to the denouement. Other Coast Survey employees had nearly equally stellar careers. Richard D. Cutts and Samuel A. Gilbert were both breveted brigadier generals, Cutts serving on Henry Halleck's staff the entire war and Gilbert in the Army of Kentucky. Isaac I. Stevens would also attain the rank of general officer in the Union army and died leading his division. George Wise served with the Union Quartermaster Corps, at one point as chief of ocean transportation. Some, like Spencer C. McCorkle (who temporarily left government service), worked for the Coast Survey throughout the conflict.[93]

Union warships navigated and northern blockades succeeded by using Coast Survey maps. Coast Survey personnel and alumni were often found on Federal naval vessels. Tunis Craven, Wampler's colleague in Galveston, would be killed by a torpedo in Mobile Bay while accompanying Rear Adm. David Farragut in 1864. Coast surveyors knew the tides and currents, along with the topography, and so were invaluable in helping to design the Union plan of attack. Professor Bache remained in charge of the Coast Survey during the war, positioning his personnel and other resources to maximum advantage for the Federals. Bache died in February 1867, after a series of strokes. Finally, one of Wampler's newest friends, Montgomery C. Meigs, would earn immortality as Grant's logistician.

As a member of the Coast Survey staff, Wampler rightfully considered himself among the nation's engineering elite. The contacts were in place for a long and productive career that would be personally rewarding, if not necessarily one that maximized his earning potential. By this time, however, Wampler had acquired the basic skills of a civil engineer in the mid-nineteenth century and may well have decided that there was little more to be gained by remaining in govern-ment employ. Opportunities to the west must have appeared endless in a country mainly inhabiting the eastern third of its territory. Having just cel-ebrated his twenty-third birthday and with a new family to support, Wampler was full of energy and enthusiasm. He had another, and perhaps better, idea in his own approach to practicing the profession of surveyor and topographer. Thus, as he did later in life, with tragic consequences, Wampler took off in a different direction.

CHAPTER THREE

>>>

The Antebellum Years: Success and Failure

The years immediately after leaving the Coast Survey afforded Morris Wampler a period to grow personally and professionally, before the eruption of civil strife that led to his transformation from civil engineer to Confederate engineer. North America was being unwrapped and shaped through discovery, science, and industry. As one of few Americans trained in a science, Wampler was uniquely qualified to join in his nation's surge into the industrial age. Through his professional training and by dint of personality—his natural inquisitiveness, an ability to see, explore, and record, and an ambition that, at times, led him to visualize an opportunity where, perhaps, none existed—Wampler was prepared and inclined to take part in the expansion of America. As he undertook to do so, however, he had another responsibility common to young men at his age in any society. He had to provide for a wife and growing family.

KATE

Wampler's new wife was Catharine Nugent Cummings of Iberville Parish, Louisiana, known as "Kate." Family legend relates that they met on a steamer headed for New York, where she was going to visit relatives. Certainly, Wampler's repeated passage to and from Texas, via New Orleans, would have placed him on the path of a young woman sent to visit her father's family and acquire the finer culture found in the Northeast. Courting easily could have taken place when Wampler passed through Louisiana.

Kate was born near Plaquemine on June 27, 1833, the daughter of James McNamara Cummings and Eliza Erwin. Theirs was a marriage of only two years' duration, as Kate's father died the following year, most likely in one of the many epidemics that swept across the Mississippi Delta. He may have died of cholera, smallpox, malaria, or yellow fever, known as the "saffron scourge." Kate's mother was therefore a widow and orphan at age nineteen, her own parents preceding her husband to the grave. Eliza's family was prominent in Iberville Parish, descended from her grandfather, Joseph Erwin, a plantation baron in the early nineteenth century. Kate grew up in a community thick with aunts, uncles, and cousins but bordering on destitution. On the verge of bankruptcy, Joseph Erwin committed suicide in 1829. Years passed before his encumbered property was divided. Strapped for money, Eliza sold her rights to one-thirtieth of the inheritance for forty-five hundred dollars in February 1837. When Eliza remarried Benjamin F. Holmes, Kate was provided the protection of a stepfather, but he soon died as well, returning Eliza to a widow's lot.

Two of Joseph Erwin's sons-in-law served as executors of his estate, consisting of houses, land, and slaves. They soon engaged in buying up the interests of the other five siblings and their descendants. By 1849, an aggregation of these heirs, including Eliza, joined to initiate legal action against the executors for fraud, alleging self-dealing, improper accounting, and violation of fiduciary obligations to the minors, like Eliza. The plaintiffs were represented by Louis Janin, a Portuguese nobleman and former general under Frederick the Great, who was a premier land lawyer in the United States, and Judah Benjamin, a New Orleans attorney destined to become successively the Confederate attorney general, secretary of war, and secretary of state. When Eliza died two years after her daughter's marriage, Kate took her place as co-plaintiff in the suit, which was appealed to the U.S. Supreme Court in 1855. The case was remanded to the Louisiana District Court, however, as its decree was deemed not final. It is doubtful that the newlyweds ever gained financially from the matter, although Wampler later referred to the case in correspondence with Secretary of War Benjamin in order to introduce himself and plead his cause.[1]

Having been reared amidst the acrimony of her mother's family, it is not surprising that Kate felt a closer connection with her paternal ancestors. Kate's father was descended from Dr. Donald Cummings, a native of Scotland who came to America as a surgeon for the British Army in 1755. He settled in

John Morris Wampler.

Saco, Maine, just south of Portland, where he married and established a successful medical practice, along with a reputation for cheerfulness and good humor. When he died in 1774, after being thrown from his horse, he left three sons, one of whom, James, was Kate's grandfather. As pleased as she was with the celebrated physician who had planted the Cummings family in the New World, however, Kate was far more proud of her Nugent heritage.

Kate traced her grandmother's lineage back to Sir Gilbert Nugent, the first Earl of Wentworth, in the time of Henry II. The Nugents resided at Castle Ross, their ancestral home in County Kerry, Ireland, until its loss in the seventeenth century, as a consequence of participating in England's own civil wars between its royalists and puritans. This downturn in fortunes led John Nugent to immigrate to the West Indies. He settled in Trinidad, serving for many years as that island's chief judge. The jurist was a Catholic, his wife a Protestant. They had two daughters and agreed to educate one in each faith. The first went to a convent in England, and the other daughter, Catharine, Kate's grandmother for whom she was named, was sent for schooling in Hartford, Connecticut. Not surprisingly, she met and married an American, a physician in New York City, Dr. James Cummings. All her life, Kate treasured silverware used on the Isle of Trinidad bearing the cockatrice, the coat of arms of the Nugent family.[2]

When he stopped on his way back from Galveston to marry Kate on May 12, 1852, in St. James Protestant Episcopal Church in East Baton Rouge, Wampler tied his life to someone in circumstances similar to his own. Kate, like Morris, had never known her father. She was escaping her mother's penury, just as her bridegroom had once left home when his mother's circumstances changed. Approaching her nineteenth birthday, Kate must have shared the same sense of opportunity and excitement Morris had experienced as a teenager, going off to join the Coast Survey and roam the waterways and coastlines of America. Kate's appetite was whetted for the wider world on her visit to New York, and she was now set to embark on an adventure that would take her far from her Louisiana home, to which she was destined never to return. Kate differed from her new husband, however, in her sense of family, both in distaste for the litigious Erwins and pride in her illustrious Nugent forebears.

Kate had certainly seen in her beau a gentility developed at Miss Mercer's academy. For example, throughout their relationship, Morris turned to verse to express his feelings toward Kate. Three months before their wedding, when sitting alone aboard ship in Galveston Bay, he beseeched his betrothed to remember him.

> When in soft twilight's witching hour
> While youths bright dreams around thee hover
> Transported to Love's sunniest bower
> Kate, dearest, think of me!
>
> And when the midnight toll is pulsing
> Thou dearest of Heaven's choicest blessing,
> A friend, protector, rich possesion
> Kate, dost thou dream of me?
>
> When in the busy haunts of men
> And flattered oft by many a friend
> Thine ear to heartless puffs ne'er lend,
> But Kate, then think of me.

Catharine Nugent Cummings Wampler.

Should love's soft dew anoint thy heart
Thy pure affection share a part
With favored friend. Then mine thou art
If thus thou't think of me.

The object of Wampler's affection had dark hair, parted in the middle
and pulled back. She was of average height and build. A face bordering upon
roundness was punctuated with dark eyes and a full nose and mouth. Onto
one finger of her sturdy hands, which would never be strangers to work,
Wampler placed a thin gold band. Not long after the birth of their first child,
James Thomas (called "Tommy" as a youth), and Wampler's subsequent de-

fection from the Coast Survey, he sadly left his wife and son behind and returned to the West in search of fortune that would prove to be elusive.

ROBERT J. WALKER'S TEXAS RAILROAD ADVENTURE

One of the legacies of Alexander Dallas Bache to Morris Wampler may well have been an introduction to his brother-in-law, Robert J. Walker, U.S. senator from Mississippi, 1836–45, and secretary of the treasury under President James K. Polk. It seems more than a coincidence that, upon leaving the Coast Survey, Wampler received a telegram inviting him to New York to meet with the energetic and enigmatic Walker.

"A mere whiffet of a man," Walker made up in schemes and speculations what he lacked in physical bulk.[3] An early advocate of annexing Texas, he was credited with drafting the compromise in the Senate which resolved the congressional deadlock over its admission to the Union in 1845. Appointed treasury secretary that same year, Walker pushed for acquisition of all of Mexico and the purchase of Cuba. After his return to private life in 1849, Walker began to float a variety of speculative ventures. His name was associated for several years with a silver mine in California, advertising annual yields in excess of one million dollars. He planned a Central American canal and negotiated rights of way through El Salvador and Honduras. In another venture, Walker offered to build a southern transcontinental railroad, provided Congress agree to certain stipulations. Walker next launched an effort to finance the Illinois Central Railroad and organized, in succession, two syndicates to finance construction of east–west railroads through Texas. The second railroad syndicate permitted track to be laid from any point in east Texas across the state to El Paso. It was in this last scheme that Wampler became entangled.[4]

Arriving for his appointment in New York City on April 29, 1853, via the cars, Wampler met with Walker the following day and was engaged as first assistant engineer at fifteen hundred dollars per year, plus expenses, to build a railroad in Texas. Wampler took the opportunity to visit his grandmother and uncle and to pay a call on James Dwight Dana, editor of the *American Journal of Science and Arts* and an authority on the natural history and geology of the western United States.

Three weeks later, Wampler was en route to Texas. The separation from his wife and baby weighed heavily on his thoughts, and he sent correspondence to her at every stop. Traveling overland to Wheeling, Virginia, via Cumberland, he boarded a steamer down the Ohio to Cincinnati, where, by chance, he encountered Kate's uncle, Thomas P. Cummings. The next stop was Louisville. Wampler changed boats and headed for Cairo, Illinois, where he took passage on another vessel down the Mississippi. The engineer made note of railroad construction at Cairo. He was also impressed by the introduction of life-preservers in every stateroom and a lifeboat on deck, the result of recent congressional legislation and, apparently, new additions since his river travel the previous June. His keen eye also observed the height of corn in fields lining the riverbanks. Approaching Baton Rouge, Wampler encountered passengers acquainted with his new wife, filling him with pride, while, at the same time, adding to his melancholy.

Wampler contented himself by reading Sir Walter Scott's *Rob Roy* and *Kenilworth* for the five days he remained in New Orleans before embarking on the steamer *Louisiana,* bound for Galveston. In a practice that would be common throughout his wartime separations from Kate, Wampler derived some solace in sociable evenings with the ladies on board. Two full days of sailing brought the vessel to its destination on June 7.

The returning engineer obtained accommodations and began waiting for his supervisor. His joy at finding the crew of the Coast Survey schooner *Morris* ashore was tempered by being subpoenaed to testify in the murder trial of a Coast Survey employee. The case was eventually dismissed and the defendant discharged. The days in Galveston soon exhibited characteristics of earlier tours upon the bay. The weather was invariably sultry. Calling on the ladies and attending church twice on the Sabbath sufficed for diversion, though isolation from his new family weighed heavily upon him.

After a week at Galveston, Wampler encountered two of his former Coast Survey comrades—James S. Williams and Spencer C. McCorkle. Williams had graduated from the U.S. Military Academy in 1831 and fought in the Black Hawk War. Resigning his commission six years later, he began a series of assignments as assistant construction engineer on railroads near Cincinnati, Louisville, and Charleston, S.C. Upon joining the Coast Survey, Williams conducted expeditions in Florida, along the Atlantic and Pacific Coasts, and on the Gulf of Mexico, where he and Wampler became acquainted. McCorkle was Wampler's old comrade from survey parties at both Marblehead and Galveston. The threesome began spending a great deal of time together, strengthening a friendship that would later present another engineering opportunity for Wampler. They acquired technical books, took the boat to Bolivar to measure fluctuations in the tide, and generally enjoyed each other's company.

Weeks went by, while Wampler waited for the arrival of R. J. Walker's supervisory engineer. Through another Coast Survey friend, William S. "Tip"

Walker, the underemployed engineer obtained an opportunity to survey lots in the city and was soon plotting his findings. His map of Galveston City earned Wampler fifteen dollars. It was with special pleasure and pride that he received his first money for work done outside the government, providing reassurance that he was indeed capable of making a living as a private engineer. Galveston was still in the untamed West, and Wampler and Tip Walker were caught up by chance in a scuffle between a Dutch sea captain and a man who alleged that the seafarer had seduced his wife on a voyage. At night, the two friends began studying the stars, using the transit. Kate's birthday passed by, with her husband sitting idle a thousand miles away, and still no word came from Walker or his senior engineer.

Finally, at the end of June, Wampler learned that Walker had received an appointment from President Franklin Pierce as minister to China. The hopelessness of the situation was becoming evident. Wampler wrote to Walker, seeking an explanation, and returned to the tiresome business of waiting. Galveston celebrated the Fourth of July with fireworks, cannon firing, and speeches by candidates for Congress. The lonely engineer attended the Children's Ball, but danced only one cotillion. He was far more excited the next day, when he received a letter from Kate.

Throughout the month of July, Wampler worked on a map of Galveston Island. The steamers regularly passing back and forth to New Orleans carried mail between the Wamplers, which cheered him somewhat. As the heat intensified, he began suffering from headaches and diarrhea. At last, Wampler was convinced to give up his vigil, return to Washington, and file suit against his erstwhile employer. A friend provided money for the passage. Upon saying his goodbyes and paying his bills, on July 24, Wampler boarded the steamer *Perseverance,* aptly characterizing his experience at Galveston, and began the long journey eastward.

His route back took him through New Orleans, beset with yellow fever, Mobile and Montgomery, Alabama, and West Point, Stone Mountain, and Augusta, Georgia.[5] He was terribly disappointed with Robert J. Walker, but not yet discouraged about his own prospects as a civil engineer, as he demonstrated by tendering his name and address to a fellow traveler with purported railroad connections. A final low point in this ten-week exercise in futility occurred when Wampler's train ran over a cow near Stone Mountain, derailing three cars, and injuring two passengers, one fatally.[6]

Robert J. Walker resigned his appointment to the China mission shortly after receiving it, using his wife's fragile health as an excuse, and soon began a new undertaking as governor of Kansas Territory. In the end, his railroad schemes produced no more than twenty-seven miles of track in the middle of the Texas prairie.[7]

CAIRO & FULTON RAILROAD

Wampler's desire to tie his fate to the railroad was hardly unwise in 1850s America. The optimism and prosperity that accompanied western expansion, represented most spectacularly by the 1849 California Gold Rush, was reflected in the growth of railways. The nation's material wealth increased as the value of manufactured goods and farm products doubled and greater access was afforded to natural resources in the West. The evolving rail network furnished the linkage necessary for this economic growth.

Railroads constituted business on a grand scale, attracting broad financial support. They employed vast numbers of men with diverse skills. The distance traversed by track tripled in the 1850s, from less than ten thousand to over thirty thousand miles. The eleven southern states soon to form the Confederacy, plus Missouri, accounted for over half the increase during that decade. This progress is all the more striking when considering that in 1850 the four states west of the Mississippi, which included Texas and Arkansas, were without a single mile of rail.[8]

Robert J. Walker's syndicate in Texas was but one of 115 different railroad companies in operation in the South by 1860. The year before Wampler's initial attempt to become involved in railroading, Congress passed and President Millard Fillmore signed bills that chartered two lines in Arkansas and a third through Missouri and Arkansas.[9] The last of these was the Cairo & Fulton Railroad.[10]

As part of a transcontinental rail system, the chief engineer of the war department, Bvt. Gen. Joseph G. Totten, had been directed to make a survey of the most advantageous route from St. Louis to the Big Bend of the Red River. He identified a line on a Northeast–Southwest axis through Arkansas, upon a plateau above the river's overflow. The route envisioned would not incur the expense of cutting, filling, and bridging. Consequently, on February 9, 1853, Congress approved the necessary right of way through public lands. Grants were made from the head of Lake Michigan in Illinois to Cairo and then through Missouri into Arkansas, a distance of 444 miles. Texas was authorized lines from the Arkansas border to El Paso, 800 miles in length, and to Galveston, affording an outlet to the Gulf of Mexico.

That same winter, the general assembly of the State of Arkansas passed an act incorporating the Cairo & Fulton Railroad Company. The corporation elected Roswell Beebe as its first president. Beebe had helped lay out the town of Fulton, a community no longer in existence near the notch in the Texas boundary at the southwest corner of Arkansas. On October 7, 1853, the new company appointed Wampler's former colleague from the Coast Survey, James S. Williams, to be its chief engineer. He immediately began to purchase instruments and gear necessary for two field parties. Williams was in Washington, D.C., at the time of his appointment, and it is not surprising that he selected his friends, Morris Wampler and Spencer C. McCorkle, as two assistant engineers. The company's instructions to the engineers were "to survey, select and report the most direct, eligible and practicable route for a railroad, all things considered," between the most suitable point on the boundary with Missouri and the Texas line, near Fulton on the Red River, with branches from Little Rock to the Mississippi River and to Fort Smith.[11]

Leaving wife and child with his mother in Loudoun County, Wampler departed for the West on November 11, 1853. He stopped briefly in Washington to conduct business and, again, in Baltimore to visit with relatives and friends. Taking the Susquehanna cars on November 19, he met McCorkle the next morning in Harrisburg. They traveled by train together through Pittsburgh to Cincinnati, where they boarded a new steamboat down the Ohio to Louisville. A second boat carried them to Tennessee, where they paused before entering Arkansas. At Memphis, Wampler viewed a panoramic painting of a voyage down the Rhine River that he considered to be "capital." It would be the closest he would come to experiencing the European landscape and culture he so often read about.

The Arkansas frontier was as revolting to the eastern engineer as the faint suggestion of Europe had been pleasant. "The miserable little steamer Joan D'Arc" sailed at 3:00 P.M. on December 1, heading toward Little Rock. The "Gambling, swearing & drinking" exceeded anything experienced on any of Wampler's many other river voyages. Passengers were forced to sleep in their clothes on the deck. "I pray to God I may never have to come to this forsaken country again," the sullen engineer lamented.[12]

The vessel proceeded with the current down the Mississippi and then steamed slowly northward up the White River into Arkansas. Arriving at De Valls Bluff, due east of Little Rock, Wampler and McCorkle went ashore to try and arrange a conveyance. Wampler played with a pet bear, patting him on the head, while tame deer bounded nearby. Bouncing along fifty-five miles of rough roads the next two days on a chartered wagon, the seven passengers from the steamboat fired regularly at prairie hens, deer, and other game. When the whip lost its effect, the four mules were spurred onward by the shouting and firing behind them. The wayfarers finally reached Little Rock on December 7, just ahead of rain and sleet.

If he were disappointed in the crudeness of his destination, Wampler was pleased to be met by Williams and two fellow engineers, William P. Bowman and Edward F. Campbell. For once, the others went socializing at the Fancy Ball and left Wampler behind, moping and melancholy over his family far away. He quickly immersed himself in engineering, however, making a statistical table for Williams and taking surveying equipment into the streets with Campbell. As he became more comfortable with his new surroundings, the old Wampler emerged. Stopping at the Episcopal Church on December 21, to watch the decorating with evergreens, Wampler and Campbell were introduced to a Miss Buckner who asked for their assistance. Wampler was soon drawing letters on pasteboard and cutting them out to proclaim "Glory to God on high, on earth Peace, good will towards Men." The ladies seemed delighted at this creative addition to the holiday ornamentation. Christmas day arrived, cold and snowy. As he listened to the bishop's sermon, Wampler's thoughts returned to his family.[13]

February 1854 found Wampler at Camp Bettie, fifteen miles outside Little Rock, where he had been staying for nearly three weeks. The survey team had divided into two parties. McCorkle and Bowman were assigned to the northern district. Wampler, Campbell, and another engineer, John J. Halsey, whose wife lent her name to their outpost, worked with the party responsible for the south. Weeks of cold, wet weather had brought progress almost to a standstill. When the skies cleared, the party moved slowly in a southwesterly direction. Initially, it was necessary for Wampler to conduct reconnaissance on foot, as the southern party was without a horse. By mid-month, an ox team, wagon, and horse with "carry all" enabled the surveyors to pick up the pace. The shabby hamlets of Benton, Fairplay, and Rockport all looked the same to Wampler, as his party crossed the Ouachita River and plodded toward Arkadelphia and Fulton, one hundred miles ahead. One night, a pack of rooting hogs would have taken the bedclothes if Wampler and the rodman, George Hughes, had not used their guns. Sleeping in the open air led to illness, and Wampler administered ipecac, a preparation made from dried roots, and applied a plaster to the side of one of the workmen, apparently suffering from a bronchial condition.

Breaking camp on Caddo Creek on February 15, the party was proceeding slowly southward when Campbell's wagon overturned, leaving it in pieces and Wampler's trunk in a mud hole, which ruined his shirts. Mending the wagon as best they could, the surveyors continued on to the Little Missouri

River, where they left the carriage at a blacksmith shop and the black cook at his master's house. The bad roads continued and the horse proved difficult to control, but the travelers prided themselves on eating well, despite the chef's absence. That did not deter them, however, from accepting a kind invitation to take supper and spend the night in any home along the way. Chills and fever continued to diminish their ranks until they arrived at Washington, Arkansas, only thirteen miles northeast of Fulton. Washington was renowned as the birthplace of the famed bowie knife, and the winter residence of Sam Houston before he led his army against Mexico to win freedom for Texas.[14]

So the work continued, through Fulton to the Texas boundary line. Winter turned into spring, and the southern party moved up and down the proposed roadbed, completing the survey. On June 2, Wampler was finally released to return home. Riding an old mule and accompanied by a black slave named Ben, he proceeded to Arkadelphia, sixty-five miles southwest of Little Rock. Along the road, he encountered Campbell, who gave him a little fawn, recently captured, which Wampler tied on the saddle before him. In Arkadelphia, he bought a bear cub to add to his menagerie. After a stage ride to Little Rock, Wampler boarded the steamer *Forest Rose* for Louisville, his pets by his side. He returned by the same route through Cincinnati and Wheeling that he had used to reach Arkansas. The fate of the deer and bear remains a mystery.[15]

At the outbreak of the Civil War, Arkansas boasted a paltry thirty-eight miles of rail line, the fewest of any state. Segments of the Memphis & Little Rock Railroad linked North Little Rock with De Valls Bluff, thereby connecting the Arkansas and White Rivers, and an isolated spur emanated from Hopefield on the Mississippi River to Madison, inside Arkansas.[16] Indeed, even with the high profile of Robert J. Walker, Texas accounted for only 307 miles of track in 1860, primarily radiating from Houston but with no linkage to the rest of the Confederacy through either Arkansas or Louisiana to the east.[17] From the numerous projects underway, Wampler had not chosen major contributors to the expansion of America's railroads.

HANGING OUT THE SHINGLE IN BALTIMORE

Wampler's return from the West reunited him with his wife and son but raised the question of how to support them. Prospects appeared brightest in Baltimore, where Wampler retained family connections. Within months, he packed up his belongings in Loudoun County, moved Kate and the infant Tommy to Baltimore, and opened a practice as civil and mechanical engineer on Second Street in the heart of the city. His business card advertised estimates and contracts for "Buildings, Bridges, Engines, etc." Wampler further offered to conduct "topographical surveys and maps of farms, lots and cemeteries, roads, rail roads, etc." He was prepared to furnish mechanical drawings as well. The engineer listed among his references Prof. A. D. Bache and Isaac I. Stevens (who had become governor of Washington Territory) from his Coast Survey days, militia general George H. Steuart, and John H. B. Latrobe, the designer of Belmont Chapel. Several blocks away on Spring Row, Kate managed the home for their growing family, giving birth to three daughters in four years: Catharine Rochester (the married name of Kate's fraternal aunt) in 1855, Annie Erwin in 1857, and Julia Cummings in 1858.

Baltimore was a vibrant, but often dangerous place during the six years the Wamplers lived there. It was the nation's third-largest city and seaport, serving as a link between the industrializing Northeast and the largely agrarian South. Baltimore was a caldron containing slaveholders and abolitionists; German and Irish immigrants and conservative, old-line Marylanders; Catholics, Episcopalians, Methodists, Presbyterians, and Jews. It was also a center for the Baltimore and Ohio Railroad, but actual construction had moved westward, forcing the city's economy to develop in other directions—manufacturing, mercantile trade, and even trade with Cuba and South America. A burgeoning population also meant expansion in the city's infrastructure, a dimension of growth well-suited to Wampler's capabilities.

There was a darker side to Baltimore as well. A series of fires during the mid-1850s destroyed several city blocks at a time and, in one particularly violent blaze, killed thirteen citizens. Just as threatening were the volunteer fire-fighting companies—inflated organizations with hangers-on who often gave them a political or ethnic dimension. An alarm, real or false, in some cases as a result of arson by the firemen themselves, was a signal for pitched battles between rival units. Elections ignited riots as well, as gangs used firearms at polling places with apparent impunity in 1856 and 1858. In one ward, a cannon was introduced by the Democrats, causing the opposition Know Nothings to wheel out a swivel gun, before police succeeded in ending the melee. Wampler's reaction to this violence is unrecorded, but his choice to remain in the city indicates he found ways of coexisting with it. There is no indication that the lawlessness interfered with his engineering practice.[18]

Civil engineering was uneven in quality during the antebellum period, as some practitioners had little real training and relied instead upon apprentice experience on survey parties. In an era predating formal professional standards and licensing boards, the self-taught engineer might not be immediately discernible from U.S. Military Academy graduates or Coast Survey alumni in private practice. Wampler apparently relied upon friendships to bolster his claim that past experience with coast and railroad surveys guaranteed quality above that of the typical surveyor. By late 1856, however, it appears that Wampler's practice was not proving as lucrative as hoped. He applied to Thomas Swann, Baltimore's Know Nothing mayor, to be an appointed commissioner "for opening streets." Wampler viewed this as an opportunity to make himself known to builders and developers, while at the same time familiarizing himself with the city's expanding periphery. Swann was reminded by Wampler of their acquaintance, dating back to his early childhood in Baltimore, and of his personal support in the mayor's last election campaign. He cited familiar references—Professor Bache and Isaac I. Stevens, adding Col. James D. Graham, Capt. M. C. Meigs, and Capt. Thomas J. Lee from the Coast Survey. Wampler went on to assure the mayor that his business was flourishing but had become somewhat "dull" for him.[19] While he did not receive the commissionership, Wampler's contact with Swann did lead to another opportunity.

On July 23, 1857, Wampler was appointed chief engineer of the Baltimore City Water Works, at an annual salary of twenty-five hundred dollars, the most remuneration of his life. His contract with the city specified a term of one year. Wampler's experience working with Meigs on the Washington aqueduct in 1852–53 was about to pay unexpected dividends. Baltimore had acquired a privately owned water company in 1854, whereupon the length of distributing mains was extended to half of all households in the city, doubling the number of users. Engineer consultants advised the water board to prepare for the needs of 500,000 residents, each consuming an average of 30 gallons a day, as compared with the city's 200,000 inhabitants in the mid-1850s. From the perspective of Meigs's far-reaching study and recommendations on Washington's water supply, Wampler was confident he could meet the challenge. He worked long hours, leading to his asking the water board president—another hat worn by Swann—to authorize extra burners for heating his offices with the new gas system being introduced throughout Baltimore.

Engineers across the city seemed to agree that Gunpowder Falls should be used to provide the greater supply of water, albeit at a large capital cost.[20] Swann and his allies favored expanding the flow from Jones Falls into reservoirs north of the city limits. Wampler must have been caught on the wrong side of this controversy, for, after fewer than three months on the job, he was summarily dismissed on October 19, 1857.[21]

Wampler was distraught. The suddenness of his termination left him without an income. His competence as an engineer would likely be questioned by potential clients, naturally suspicious that he had been fired for incompetence or misconduct. He filed suit for a full year's compensation, per the terms of his contract, plus damages. Attorneys for the city succeeded in obtaining successive delays until September 1862, when the defendants claimed they had never been indebted to Mr. Wampler. He was no longer in the United States to contest their allegation.

During the previous academic year, Wampler had presided over mechanical, architectural and general drawing classes at the prestigious Maryland Institute for the Promotion of the Mechanic Arts. Yet, he could not obtain a reappointment, despite his connections with three of the school's leading lights—co-founder John H. B. Latrobe, vice president Thomas Swann, and Prof. A. D. Bache, an honorary member. The underemployed engineer resorted to buying an annual membership, but even that credential did not return him to the faculty.[22]

Now, any engagement, any possibility, seemed worth pursuing. Despite his want of experience in the field, Wampler expanded his billing as an engineer to add architecture to his credentials.[23] He did not pass up the opportunity to sit on a coroner's board, inquiring into the death of a forty-five-year-old white man.[24] Nor did Wampler overlook the prospect of returning to railroad engineering.

Wampler set his sights on an embryonic railway in central Virginia. That state's legislature had incorporated the Covington & Ohio Railroad company on February 15, 1853, as the vital link in a transportation system connecting the Chesapeake Bay with the Ohio and Mississippi River valleys. Navigation would proceed along the James River past Richmond and then via the Kanawha canal to Covington, Virginia. The company's chief engineer, Charles B. Fisk, issued a report the following year attesting to the feasibility of constructing 150 miles of rail portage through the mountains from Covington to the head of steamboat navigation on the Kanawha River (in what is now West Virginia), which, in turn, would lead to the Ohio.[25]

In correspondence suggesting he practiced in both Washington, D. C. and Baltimore, Wampler introduced himself to Fisk and indicated his interest in bidding for contracts to survey ten miles of the proposed roadbed. His solicitation for information on which to base a bid apparently did Wampler little good, as he was unsuccessful in reaching agreement with the chief engineer.[26]

Fortunately, another opportunity was surfacing. Most likely through the intercession of Maryland Militia Gen. George H. Steuart, administrator of his father's estate, Wampler's services were solicited by Brig. Gen. Henry Mankin, another militiaman, to survey and map property being developed north of Baltimore by the Hampden Improvement Association. The owner of a flourishing shipping and trading firm, Mankin conceived of a building society patterned on successful entities sprouting up in England, to provide housing for workers in Baltimore's foundries and mills.[27] The association engaged Wampler to survey the new development in October 1856. He employed a chief assistant, George W. Martinet, and two sub-assistants, who functioned as chainmen or axmen to clear away brush and set stakes for the rodman.[28]

On April 30, 1857, the association's board of directors requested Wampler to lay off the property into specific lots. Progress was slow, reputedly due to bad weather and the distance of the property from the central city, causing loss of time in reaching it. Wampler's survey party completed its work by the end of the year, and he submitted a final bill on January 21, 1858. By then, however, his relationship with the association had soured. Its directors alleged that "the work was done imperfectly & unsatisfactorily" and that the delay in staking out the lots had constituted a serious problem for their business venture. Once again, Wampler found himself in the role of plaintiff in a civil action, which, in this case, was decided by an arbitrator, Benjamin H. Latrobe Jr., whose older brother was one of Wampler's references.

The son of the planner for the nation's capital city and an engineer in his own right, Latrobe agreed to decide the matters in dispute—the date when Wampler's service commenced, the rates charged, how Wampler used his time, and the manner in which his work was performed. Latrobe found in the plaintiff's favor on two of the issues and delivered a mixed opinion on the remainder. He placed considerable weight on the fact that the association had never fixed Wampler's compensation or that of his subordinates and continued to retain him, and even add to his tasks, while possessing the power to discharge him at any time. Consequently, the arbitrator agreed with the date that Wampler stated he began work and accepted his billing rates, except when the combined hourly charge for Wampler and Martinet exceeded ten dollars. Wampler was entitled to $7.50 per day, Martinet $2.50 or $5.00, depending upon his duties, and a dollar a day was appropriate for the hands, assuming they were not mere boys. The association had objected to the time charged by Wampler, complaining that he arrived in the field too late in the day. Latrobe disallowed their claim. While failing to find fault with Wampler's maps, Latrobe did conclude that "the time occupied in the execution of the work appears to have been unreasonably long."[29] This may have been so, if Wampler's practice had become as stagnant (and his other income as scant) as it appeared and he had intentionally stretched out his engagement.

Over a period of time, Wampler had written a series of twenty notes to the association, due from 1857 through 1861, thereby collecting almost $1,100. He had also contracted to purchase one of the lots. When tallying the results of his findings, the arbitrator found that the plaintiff owed the Hampden Improvement Association a net of $202. The decision was rendered on March 7, 1861, however, and by then the debtor was out of state and only months away from becoming a military engineer.

INNOVATION

As Wampler's civil engineering practice glided into dormancy, he was free to turn his ingenuity to the technological challenges he observed about him. In two instances, his speculation evolved into concrete inventions, which he submitted to Washington for formal recognition and acceptance. There is reason to believe he also designed a loom, although he never patented it. On another occasion, he referred the inventor of a new lifeboat to A. D. Bache, in hopes that the government in Washington would adopt the design.[30] It can only be speculated as to what interest, financial or otherwise, Wampler might have had in this venture. The timing was bad, however, as the Coast Survey was fighting with the navy for its survival, while struggling under a tightly constricted budget. It is therefore unlikely that the superintendent took Wampler's bait.

Wampler's first patented invention was a response to the laborious process of surveying and drawing topography by hand. Certainly, technologically advanced scientists in the 1850s could perform this task in a more efficient manner, he reasoned, using a recorder attached to the common horse-drawn chassis. Four centuries earlier, Leonardo da Vinci had conceived of a similar device. Leonardo had envisioned a horizontal wheel, connected by gears to a wagon axle, recording distance by dropping balls into a collecting box. The Italian's scientific genius had not been rediscovered in the America of Wampler's day, so he had no way of knowing of this antecedent to his own "graphodometer."

The graphodometer measured two parameters—the distance traveled and the grade or slope of the ground traversed.[31] To accomplish this, the instrument was attached to a carriage with its mounting plate parallel to the plane formed by the contact points of the carriage's four wheels on flat ground. The instrument was also coupled to a carriage wheel in order to determine the total distance traveled, which was accomplished by a gear that translated every revolution of the wheel into a proportional movement on the graphodometer. The gearing system drove a pencil plotter along a paper chart at a rate determined by the carriage speed. By knowing the wheel's diameter, the linear distance along the ground was easily calculated.

Changing elevation was figured as the hypotenuse of a triangle. A pendulum was incorporated into the design to sense the divergence from true horizontal as the instrument (and carriage) progressed up or down a slope. The gearing arrangement was modified to reflect the trigonometric relationship between the hypotenuse and its horizontal and vertical components, i.e., the horizontal distance traveled was the cosine of the slope's angle multiplied by the hypotenuse. The modified gearing arrangement represented a profile of the ground traversed on an exaggerated vertical scale, 5:1 being the ratio indicated on Wampler's description of the invention. This overrepresentation was thought to better illustrate changes in elevation.

A similar machine, called an "orograph," had been devised in 1853.[32] Thus Wampler was not working on an original idea, but rather perfecting a related design. The objectives were the same—to record an accurate topographic profile of a particular route, along with a precise measurement of its length. The instrument was not intended to specify the route's direction, which, presumably, could be manually annotated onto the chart from compass readings taken along the way.

Wampler obtained Patent Number 20,908 for his mechanism on July 13, 1858. He then attempted to market the device to the largest, most prestigious topographical exponent in the country, the United States Government. He submitted his invention to the War Department's Office of Explorations and Surveys for evaluation, with the intention of selling the instrument for military surveys. In January 1859, its topographical engineer in charge, Capt. Andrew A. Humphreys, who was serving in a comparable position in the Coast Survey when Wampler began working there in 1847, appointed a board, consisting of Lts. Gouverneur K. Warren and Henry L. Abbot, to examine and report upon the machine.[33]

It soon became evident that the graphodometer contained a fatal flaw, producing vibration in the instrument as it recorded the distance traveled. Presumably, the gearing mechanism introduced periodic oscillation, which caused the instrument, first, to infer an accelerated rate of movement from what was actually occurring, then misjudging the speed in the opposite direction

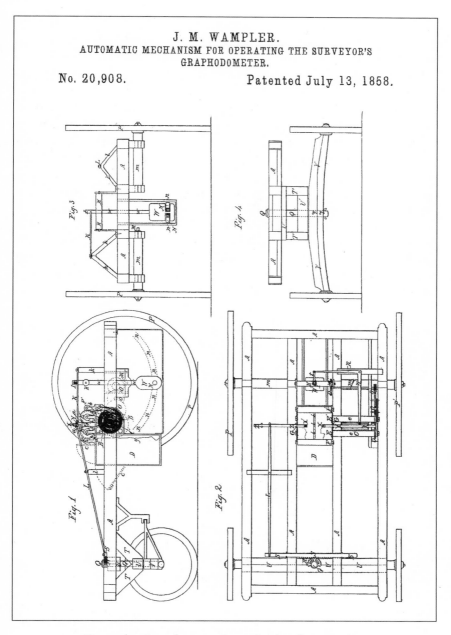

J. M. WAMPLER.
AUTOMATIC MECHANISM FOR OPERATING THE SURVEYOR'S
GRAPHODOMETER.
No. 20,908.   Patented July 13, 1858.

Patent drawing of automatic mechanism for operating
the surveyor's graphodometer.

as too slow, and repeating the cycle. Consequently, the distance traveled would be shown as longer or shorter than actual. Slopes were also misrecorded when the machine vibrated.[34]

Thus began a series of unsuccessful efforts by the board over the next four months to give the graphodometer a field test in the presence of its inventor. In January, Wampler was confined to his bed by sickness; in March, he was away from Baltimore, quite possible in Philadelphia, where he reported having investors interested in the future patent rights; and in April, a matter in Loudoun County court precluded his cooperation with the board in Washington. All the while, he maintained regular correspondence with the two army officers, providing assurances of his good intentions and urging them not to reply to any third-party queries concerning the mechanics of his innovation.

At the same time, Wampler continued experimentation with the graphodometer in Baltimore. It gradually became obvious to him that vibrations were causing inaccuracies in profile and course. He blamed the poor construction of his model, but confided that he was not at that time financially able to produce an improved version of his concept. Pressed to make a report of some kind, the board suggested that Wampler withdraw his design, which he did with reluctance on May 20. Lieutenants Warren and Abbot so informed their supervisor, and Wampler suffered another personal defeat.[35]

Wampler's second patent grew out of his familiarity with firearms, combined with inventiveness and mechanical aptitude, which coalesced in improvements in the design of breech-loading weapons. Patent Number 27,399 was awarded on March 6, 1860. His apt attention to breech-loading actions recognized their superiority over the traditional muzzle-loading firearm, the standard shoulder weapon being issued to the military at that time. He also appreciated the advantages of the new metal cartridge over its cruder, more time-consuming, and less-reliable predecessors made of paper, skin, rubber, and other material. His focus on a single-shot weapon, however, was not state-of-the art in 1860.

The application for a patent claimed four unique features. The first was an L-shaped spring catch, which served the double purpose of suppressing the breech while holding up the trigger-guard. Its advantage was that both could be disengaged simultaneously by pushing down on the guard with a single finger. The second purported improvement was the location of the locking and release mechanism for the breech inside the stock cavity, instead of on the exterior at the hammer, as featured, for example, on the 1854 Volcanic and 1860 Henry rifle. When the breech was open, a safety catch locked the firing mechanism at half-cock. Once fully cocked, the lever freed the safety, Wampler's third perfection. He cited as a fourth innovation, the mounting of the back sight atop the rear of the breech with two screws, which permitted the sight to be moved back and forth in order to remove an exploded cartridge.

Provision for extracting the copper cartridge was the latest in firearm technology, if not original with Wampler. More impressive is Wampler's concept of cocking the piece inside the stock, where it would be protected from unintentional interference, an approach not featured on other firearms of the day. His advocacy of a metal stock is puzzling, if not an outright drawback of the proposed design. Iron and brass were the only conceivable candidates for a metal stock, and either one posed a serious weight problem.

Wampler's improvements were never incorporated into the design of breech-loading weapons in production. The military market determined what was produced for soldiers and civilians alike. The high cost of independently manufactured designs or special-purpose firearms could not compete with models mass-produced for the military market. Literally dozens of patents were granted for firearm modifications during the decade ending in 1865. Most were destined to become only ordnance oddities. One of the few Civil War officers born in the eighteenth century, Brig. Gen. James Ripley, head of the Federal Ordnance Department from 1861 until 1863, was unbending in advocating muzzle-loading musketry, to the exclusion of any interest in perfecting breech-loaders. After his tenure, multiloading weapons offered by Spencer, Sharps, Henry, and their competitors made Wampler's patent obsolete. His inventiveness failed to make an impact on the manufacture of firearms in the North or South, at a time when arsenals on both sides were taxed to their limits, and the frantic search for more efficient and lethal weapons captivated the ingenuity of many of the continent's inventors and would-be entrepreneurs.

THE POLITICS OF THE DAY

As the decade of the fifties drew to a close, the forces of decency, law, and order began to assert themselves in Baltimore. Maryland Gov. Thomas W. Ligon ordered General Steuart to ready the 1st Light Division of Maryland Volunteers for duty, so it could be called on to preserve peace in the municipal elections of 1857. There was, however, no repetition of the violence experienced the previous year. By 1860, Baltimore was an attractive convention site for two national political parties. The Constitutional Union Party nominated John Bell for president. Both factions of the Democratic Party convened in Baltimore, one putting forth Vice President John C. Breckinridge from Kentucky, and the other choosing Sen. Stephen A. Douglas of Illinois.

Having been introduced to the political issues of the 1840s in Whig-dominated Virginia, it is not surprising that, upon reaching his majority, Wampler considered himself a Whig and supported that party's policies and candidates. As proponents of westward expansion and internal improvements, Whigs in the South would have had natural appeal to a topographical engineer who was trained, experienced, and ready to map new territory for purposes of government or to extend the railroads.[36] The party of Henry Clay and Daniel Webster had turned in a different direction for a standard-bearer in 1848, nominating "Old Rough and Ready," the apolitical frontier military hero, Zachary Taylor. Although not yet enfranchised, Wampler's anguish over President Taylor's sudden death in 1850 is therefore understandable. Decisive defeat in the 1852 presidential election behind Gen. Winfield Scott left the Whig Party in tatters. Wampler presumably was disappointed as well and, as the decade continued, must have become increasingly disillusioned by the party's bifurcation on the issue of slavery, reflecting the division taking place in the nation's body politic.

At the same time, a new political movement was sweeping the country in the wake of unprecedented immigration following the Mexican War. The introduction of Irish and German Catholics was disquieting in the northeastern cities where they congregated. A demonstration in Baltimore's Monument Square in August 1853 promoted Americanism and separation of church and state, among other issues. Along with millions of other native-born Americans, Wampler became intrigued with the American or "Know Nothing" Party, which elected 104 of its candidates to the 234 seats in the U.S. House of Representatives in 1854, while barely losing the Virginia governor's race the following year. Absorption of the Whigs into the American Party in Maryland, which took the name Union Party, and the alliance of southern Know Nothings and Whigs behind Millard Fillmore in 1856 made it easy for Wampler to support the former president in his unsuccessful contest against victorious James Buchanan, the Democratic candidate, and Republican John C. Frémont. His predilection may have been reinforced by the rump convention of the remnants of the Whig Party in Baltimore in September of that year, which coalesced behind Fillmore as the best hope for preserving national unity.[37]

Wampler's personal political orientation conformed with that of his native Loudoun County. During the 1850s, the county's Whiggery reflected its loyalty to the Union and a rejection of both extremes on the slavery issue—abolition and southern secession. A gathering of Whigs and Democrats in Leesburg in 1850 underscored this position by echoing the standard southern rallying cry that the laws of the land, including the Fugitive Slave Act, be duly enforced.[38] Late in the decade, when national unity was further threatened by an abolitionist's raid on Harper's Ferry, the county reacted feverishly by forming and drilling militia companies. Wampler responded to John Brown as well, by joining the Maryland Militia in Baltimore. Once the tide began to turn against the South, however—and Abraham Lincoln's election in November 1860 was seen as a sign of the shift—Wampler's allegiance, like those of many Loudoun County loyalists, began to swing from the Stars and Stripes to the state of Virginia and its perceived best interests.

Wampler's practice as a civil engineer had not prospered as he had envisioned upon leaving the Coast Survey in 1853, or when he hung out his shingle in Baltimore the following year. The creation of a Southern nation with a new government held the promise of opportunity for someone with training and experience beyond that of most Americans. The prospect of returning to Loudoun offered the chance to participate in this new order. It was decidedly a gamble, but he had little to lose with his engineering practice stalled.

There is no reason to believe that the issue of slavery played a part in Wampler's decision. His written views on slavery, if any existed, are lost to contemporary readers. If anything, the strong influence exerted by Margaret Mercer early in his life would have weighed against returning to the most populous state in the slaveholding South. No evidence exists that Wampler ever owned a slave. Admittedly, he employed black workers while engaged in fieldwork for the Coast Survey and when serving as an engineer for the Confederacy, prior to and during the war. Slaves were owned and utilized by his stepfather, William Mavin, at the family mill and by Miss Mercer's successors at Belmont, the Kephart family. Loudoun County personal property assessments for 1860 reported that the Mavins owned two slaves, an adult and a teenager under seventeen years of age, while the Kepharts were taxed for four adult slaves and six others under the age of seventeen years. From these associations, Wampler must have felt comfortable in the presence of slavery, as well as from residing in two basically southern cities, Baltimore and Washington, where slaveholding was commonplace.

Thus, it is unlikely that Wampler held strong views on the slavery issue. Instead, his decision to resettle in what would become the Confederate States of America was motivated by the career possibilities opening for him.

Wampler's ties by marriage and work experience were predominantly south-ern. Perhaps, too, his business failures had jaundiced him somewhat on the pragmatic, industrial North. The South was attractive as an idealistic "finer society," in contrast to the combative, diverse ethnicity increasingly encoun-tered in Baltimore. What is clear is the exhilaration with which he cast his fortune with the seceding states.

CHAPTER FOUR

>>>

The 8th Virginia

"Dec 20 1860. Left Washington, and South Carolina seceded. Got home same day & once more breathed free Southern air."[1] Wampler's enthusiasm was representative of the national excitement in the wake of Abraham Lincoln's election, followed by the provocative action of the South Carolinians. He was far ahead of Virginia, however, as the convention called to decide its course was not to meet in Richmond until February 13, 1861, with John Janney of Leesburg, a leader of the old Whig Party, as its president. Not waiting for an announcement from Richmond, Wampler proceeded in January to write a "Declaration of Independence for a Southern Confederacy." What became of his initiative is not known.

Wampler was clearly unsuccessful in raising a company of volunteers at this time. The men of southeastern Loudoun were not yet eager to join the militia company that Wampler would have named the "Lee Guards." His "Constitution and By Laws" for the unit provided for election of officers as prescribed by the state's militia laws, Tuesday drills, monthly meetings for company business, a system of military justice for such infractions as disrespectful language to an officer and drunkenness in uniform, and designation of honorary members. A gray uniform trimmed with red and black shoulder knots would have been set off by a shako adorned with blue pompon and gilt buttons bearing the state's coat of arms. But, alas, it was not to be. Instead, Wampler was forced to be content drilling militia troops already organized, as an unpaid volunteer. Wampler's enthusiasm reached new highs as the number of seceding states increased, a Confederate government was established with

Jefferson Davis as its provisional president, and Federal troops surrendered forts in Texas. On March 19, 1861, he exclaimed, *"Virginia must go out. Yankees arming & organizing to enslave us. South arming etc too."*[2]

His wish came true on April 17, when the convention in Richmond voted eighty-eight to fifty-five for secession after the fall of Fort Sumter and Lincoln's call for troops to fight for the Union. A statewide referendum was scheduled for May 23 to ratify the decision. Wampler raised what he believed to be the first secession flag in Loudoun County, a distinction subsequently claimed by others as well. By the first of May, four hundred volunteers had enrolled in the Loudoun Guard, Loudoun Artillery, Loudoun Cavalry, and Hillsboro Border Guards.[3] Rabid secessionist leaders traveled throughout Virginia, including Leesburg, to coalesce public sentiment. Wampler supported this cause by writing articles on its behalf.

Wampler's military expectations were soon realized by the formation of the 8th Virginia Infantry at Leesburg with Col. Eppa Hunton as its commander. Hunton was a thirty-eight-year-old former schoolteacher, brigadier general in the militia, and lawyer, then serving as commonwealth's attorney in Prince William County. Appointed a delegate to the Richmond convention, he proved to be an ardent secessionist. He and Wampler were of one mind politically, for in the subsequent Virginia plebiscite, the latter was recorded as favoring secession, along with 1,625 other Loudoun residents. The 726 opposed were mainly in the northwestern portion of the county, heavy with non-slaveholding Germans and Quakers. The statewide vote was 128,884 to 32,134, a ratio of four to one in favor of secession. It appeared almost a formality, as Virginia had already been admitted into the Confederate states on May 7, agreed to access by southern troops, and offered Richmond to the new national government as its capital.[4]

Engineer Activities in Preparation for War

Wampler's significant military involvement in the southern cause began with Hunton's arrival in Leesburg. On May 15, Wampler received appointment as a special civilian aide and engineer for Hunton, based upon his rank as captain in the state militia and his credentials as a civil engineer. His first assignment, conveyed on May 16 before the final secession vote, was to inspect the trestle over Goose Creek and other nearby bridges of the Alexandria, Loudoun & Hampshire Railroad to determine the most suitable means for their destruction "in case of necessity."[5] A week later, Wampler was in-

volved in arranging transportation for eighty percussion muskets and three
boxes of cartridges and caps with the railroad superintendent.[6] He was also
employed by Hunton in establishing a line of signal stations along the railroad.[7] Once Federal troops moved into northern Virginia on the day after
the referendum favoring secession, Wampler began gathering intelligence
on their movements.[8] He later participated in cavalry incursions into Maryland, skirmishing with Union troops, "destroying the [Chesapeake & Ohio]
canal locks, and capturing hundreds of sacks of salt from the U.S. Govt."[9]
Sabotage of the canal was undertaken in accordance with instructions from
Maj. Gen. Robert E. Lee, commanding Virginia forces from Richmond,
who specified "cutting the dams at Seneca and Edwards Ferry, and blowing
up the Monocacy Aqueduct."[10]

Hunton also dispatched Wampler to Richmond during this period. The
commander of the new regiment at Leesburg believed that the Federals intended
to occupy Loudoun County in order to isolate Harper's Ferry from the south.
The methodical attorney drafted a justification for bolstering defense forces and
sent Wampler first to Manassas Junction for Brig. Gen. P. G. T. Beauregard's
endorsement and then on to Leroy Walker, the secretary of war in the Confederate capital. Referred from Walker to Davis, Wampler was then shuffled to the
president's private secretary. He, in turn, sent the envoy to Brig. Gen. Samuel
Cooper, the army's senior ranking officer and adjutant general. Cooper directed
Wampler to Lee, who knew nothing of the matter and returned Hunton's surrogate to Walker's office. Finally, Wampler was dismissed with assurances that the
president would reinforce the Loudoun outpost at the earliest opportunity. (Davis
would later add a note to his secretary of war on Wampler's fervent appeal for
help in defending Loudoun County, asking, "What does it mean?") A dejected
subaltern returned home after receiving the classic bureaucratic runaround.[11]

Meanwhile, at Manassas, General Beauregard, the Confederate hero of
the confrontation at Fort Sumter, had assumed command of the southern
troops arrayed opposite Washington. Beauregard prided himself on being a
strategist and military engineer, and he was rightfully concerned about the
vulnerability of his left flank at Leesburg. On June 9, secessionists destroyed
the bridges at Shepherdstown, Harper's Ferry, Berlin (now Brunswick), and
Point of Rocks. On June 15, they burned the turnpike bridge across Goose
Creek, connecting Alexandria and Leesburg. Loudoun County was nonetheless vulnerable to invasion from Maryland by means of ferries and fords,
thirteen in total, plus other places shallow enough to wade across when the
Potomac was low.

As a stranger to northern Virginia and unfamiliar with the terrain, Beauregard soon directed a reconnaissance of the entire area to identify his opportunities for offense and his vulnerabilities on defense. He enlisted the talents of Col. William G. Williamson, Capts. David B. Harris and Walter H. Stevens, and Morris Wampler.[12] Williamson and Harris were members of the Virginia State Engineer Corps, and Stevens, a West Point graduate, was one of fourteen members of the newly formed Confederate Regular Army's Corps of Engineers. Harris was also a West Pointer, having graduated seventh in the class of 1833. A businessman in the tobacco trade in the 1840s and 1850s, he had been commissioned a captain in the Virginia Volunteers and assigned to duty with Brig. Gen. Philip St. George Cocke. Sixteen years Wampler's senior, Harris's service to the South would closely parallel the Marylander's.

Harris made a detailed drawing of the road network in western Fairfax County, while, on orders from Beauregard, Wampler mapped routes farther west, in eastern Loudoun, as well as other portions of that county.[13] This contribution as a topographical engineer first brought Wampler to the general's attention; it was the beginning of a relationship with his third mentor. Not only was Beauregard impressed by Wampler's precision as a cartographer, but he must have also valued the engineer's knowledge of the local area, which was rooted in his boyhood. This knowledge enabled Wampler to add detail to maps, such as mills and other commissary resources, obscure water crossings, backroads and trails, and the names of residents, which would facilitate troops finding their way over unfamiliar terrain. Wampler was mapping when a twelve-pounder Howitzer fired at him across the Potomac at the mouth of Goose Creek, to his knowledge the first cannon shot over the river above Washington.[14]

The Alexandria, Loudoun & Hampshire Railroad posed a particular problem for the Confederates. Completed as far as Leesburg within the preceding year, it offered a direct avenue into Confederate Virginia for Union troops stationed at Alexandria. When that town was occupied on May 24, most of the railroad's rolling stock was seized by the Federals, with the exception of a fine locomotive and a large number of freight cars, which happened to be at the Leesburg depot.[15] On June 8, Lee ordered Hunton to destroy the railroad's bridges, according to the specifications Wampler had earlier been instructed to prepare, and transfer any rolling stock not demolished to the Orange or Manassas Gap Railroads. Hunton's initial reaction was to inquire whether General Lee intended him to stop drilling raw troops, which was important to them, and cut back on picket duty in order to accomplish this mission.[16] Instead, Hunton gave the assignment to Wampler, who employed a party of men to tear up rails and burn ties, utilizing the engine to move up the line.[17] He left the locomotive at Leesburg in a condition that he considered worthless to the enemy, if not dangerous:

> The slide valves are all removed, and steam chests placed in condition as tho' all was right, the valve rods remaining in position as tho' in proper connection with the slides.
> The valve rod connecting Rods have been removed.
> The Pump valves have been removed & the pumps placed in condition to appear as tho' in perfect working order. This disarrangement of itself will insure an explosion should the enemy repair the other parts and attempt to run the Engines. They will not discover the absence of the pump valves until the consequences, too late. betray it.
> The hand gear is also removed in part & in part disarranged.[18]

Hunton sent some of the rolling stock into the mountains. When the Federal Army threatened Leesburg, he directed that the cars be set afire. Then Hunton executed a novel idea.[19] By hitching up twelve yoke of oxen, he had the engine itself moved along the roadways to Piedmont Station (now Delaplane), for use by the army on the rail line passing through Manassas Gap.[20] It is not difficult to imagine the surprise of Mrs. Ida Dulaney at Oakley Plantation in Upperville, when she glanced out her window one day and saw a locomotive passing her gate.[21]

Wampler's remuneration for his service to Colonel Hunton was calculated on two separate bases. From May 15 until June 23, he was to be paid as a special aide at the rate of $100 per month. From June 23 until July 13, he was considered a topographical engineer, due $150 a month. Although he immediately made claim for the compensation due him, payment was delayed by transfer of military responsibility from Virginia to the Confederate states and exacerbated by bureaucratic interference from an auditing board and, then, the second auditor's office and comptroller. As a result, Wampler was not paid in full until April 1862. He did, however, receive recognition in his capacity as a militia officer, for by the end of June 1861, he had been promoted to the rank of major.

During the spring, construction began on three forts to guard the approaches to Leesburg—Fort Johnston, on the east slope of the Catoctin range, a mile north of town; Fort Evans, a mile east, toward the river; and Fort Beauregard, on high ground to the south. There is reason to believe that Wampler was responsible for Fort Evans, and, as the only engineer available to Hunton at the time, it is likely that he was instrumental in the design and construction of the other fortifications as well.[22]

Perched on the highest point of the ridge overlooking Leesburg, Fort Johnston was the most intricately designed of the three earthworks. Its shape was that of a four-sided star, with each arm extending 110 feet from base to point in a slight curve. Twenty-foot embrasures midway on each side provided placement of up to eight cannon in all. A ditch, conforming to the standard of not less than 6 feet in depth and at least 12 feet wide, separated the parapet from the glacis.[23] In the middle of the star was a bombproof, 50 feet in width.

Situated on a strategic elevation overlooking the Potomac River, Fort Evans was shaped like a trapezoid, with its east and west walls measuring close to 350 feet, and the north and south parapets spanning 204 and 286 feet, respectively. Gun emplacements, 30 feet in diameter, were positioned at the four corners. Apertures for three barrels in the salients at either end of the northern parapet provided protection toward the water, while those on the back wall housed fewer artillery pieces. Embrasures were spaced as well along all four walls. Entrance into the spacious interior was permitted at the southern end of the east wall, the corner of the redoubt in the direction of Leesburg.

At an elevation of 430 feet, rectangular Fort Beauregard covered two roadways, the Alexandria Pike to the east and the Sycolin Road to Gum Spring (today Arcola) and eventually Manassas to the south. Its location, only 1,000 yards, as the crow flies, from Mavin's Mill on Goose Creek, was the most accessible of the earthworks to Wampler's home, and yet Fort Beauregard appeared to have been the least finished. Perhaps its position farthest from the river made this defensive position seem less urgent to complete.

Work on the three fortifications continued throughout 1861 into 1862, yet only Fort Johnston appears to have approached completion. Loudoun County men loyal to the southern cause had not volunteered for military service to labor with picks and shovels like common fieldhands. More than one male resident crossed the Potomac to join the Union army in protest over the prospect of excavating trenches for the Confederacy. It was only after they had tasted battle that Civil War soldiers began to appreciate the life-saving importance of digging in. Beauregard also recognized that constructing earthworks with raw troops took them away from the drill and military instruction essential to young soldiers. In early June, he requested that patriotic citizens send such slaves as could be spared, along with spades and pick axes, to perform this task.[24] Faced with a northern invasion, Brig. Gen. Daniel Harvey Hill made a similar call from Leesburg the following February, and yet he found that even though slaves were running off every night, wealthy owners would not agree to their working on the forts, unless paid two dollars a day for their services.[25] With insufficient laborers, the Leesburg fortifications were never finished.

RECRUITING AND ORGANIZING

While Wampler was performing engineering duties, Eppa Hunton's 8th Virginia Infantry was gradually taking shape. Immediately after the convention's vote for secession, the Hillsboro Border Guards had been accepted into state service for one year and would soon be designated Company A. In May, four more companies were added—the Piedmont Rifles, Evergreen Guards, Champe Rifles, and Hampton's Company—as companies B, C, D, and E. Another company, the Blue Mountain Boys, enlisted as Company F in June. While Company A had converted from militia service, a majority of the soldiers filling the ranks of the other companies were raw recruits without prior military training. Consequently, they assembled for instruction at a camp on the fairgrounds at the north end of King Street in Leesburg. The bivouac site on the edge of town permitted the ladies to visit regularly, often bringing homemade delicacies for the hungry trainees.[26] Before long, the fledgling assemblage had acquired the nickname of the "Cornstalk Regiment," not necessarily a term of respect, from the town's impertinent young people.[27]

Much of the leadership during the regiment's formative period was provided by the Berkeleys, four brothers of a well-to-do, local landowning family. Norborne held the rank of major and was the regiment's third in command, after Hunton and Charles B. Tebbs, a Leesburg attorney appointed lieutenant colonel. Edmund and William served as commanders of companies C and D, respectively. The youngest Berkeley, Charles, was a lieutenant in William's unit. The solid reputation of the Berkeleys was said to have enhanced the regiment's ability to recruit good men.[28]

Company H and James Simpson's Company I joined the 8th Virginia on July 13. The regiment would subsequently add James Thrift's Company G and Robert Scott's Company K, bringing the total to ten, the number authorized for a regiment of infantry—six from Loudoun County, two from Fauquier, and one each from Fairfax and Prince William Counties. The members consisted mainly of farmers, with a few clerks and tradesmen, "rough, uncouth-looking, shaggy-bearded men," in the observation of one of its soldiers.[29] Sworn in by Colonel Hunton of Leesburg to command Company H, known as the Potomac Grays, was Morris Wampler, with the rank of captain and a rate of pay of $130 per month.

Forty-eight men, mostly residents of Loudoun County, stepped forward with Wampler for induction into Company H. A dozen or more were teenagers, while a forty-four-year-old was sent home for being overage. Interestingly, at least seven of the unit members, in addition to their company commander, came from Maryland. That number included Festus Griffith, who would succeed Wampler, and Albert E. Matthews, Griffith's successor as commander. Both served Wampler as lieutenants during the company's formative months, indicating a Maryland clique in the unit's leadership. The definitive work on the 8th Virginia Infantry, the regimental history by John Divine, names 114 soldiers who served in Company H at some point during the Civil War.[30] Of that number, seventy-five men were assigned while Wampler was its commander. From uniform records and other sources, another six soldiers may be identified as members during his tenure.[31]

BATTLE OF BULL RUN (OR FIRST MANASSAS)

By mid-July, General Beauregard's Army of the Potomac was centered at Manassas, the junction of the Manassas Gap Railroad and the Orange & Alexandria line. The town's strategic value lay in its direct access to the Shenandoah Valley through the Bull Run Mountains at Thoroughfare Gap and the Blue Ridge Mountains at Manassas Gap. Beauregard had been quick to recognize that his proximity to Brig. Gen. Joseph E. Johnston's Army of the Shenandoah would enable the two to reinforce each other, concentrating the largest available southern force in opposition to whatever the Federals had to offer.

On July 16, the Federal commander in the field, Brig. Gen. Irvin McDowell, began marching his troops westward toward Centreville and Manassas. Beauregard received word of the movement from Rose Greenhow, a Confederate spy in Washington. Having a smaller force than his adversary, Beauregard telegraphed Jefferson Davis for reinforcements. The Confederate president reacted immediately, and the 8th Virginia Infantry was one of the regiments ordered to report to Manassas.[32] Early the next morning, a mere five days after swearing in many of its soldiers, Colonel Hunton led eight of the ten companies under his command out of Leesburg. Company G from Dranesville and Company K from Fauquier, not yet fully formed, were left behind. The regiment covered eighteen miles the first day to Aris Buckner's Auburn Farm on Sudley Road in southern Loudoun County. They bivouacked in an open field, which Wampler described as "very hot & exposed—water, horrid & scarce, food (the same), sleeping on bare ground."[33]

Arriving at Bull Run early the next afternoon, after a ten-mile tramp, the 8th Virginia was assigned to the 5th Brigade, commanded by Col. Philip St. George Cocke, a West Point graduate from an old Virginia family. Cocke was assigned responsibility for that portion of the stream at Lewis's and Ball's Fords. At the mouth of Holkums Branch, where Wampler's company was stationed, Bull Run was about fifty feet in width, its banks steep, and the bottom soft. Col. Nathan G. "Shanks" Evans's 7th Brigade guarded the Confederate flank to their left at the Stone Bridge, which carried the Warrenton Turnpike over Bull Run. In support of the 5th Brigade were five companies of cavalry, the battery of Capt. H. Gray Latham, and Capt. Arthur L. Rogers's Loudoun Artillery, in positions selected by David B. Harris, now assigned to Beauregard's staff, while retaining his commission in the Virginia Corps of Engineers.[34]

The confrontation at Bull Run had begun on July 18, when a Federal reconnaissance party was repulsed by Brig. Gen. James Longstreet's 4th Brigade at Blackburn's Ford. During the following two days, as Union forces concentrated at Centreville, McDowell's engineer, Maj. John G. Barnard, searched for a crossing above the Stone Bridge to enable the Federals to envelop the Confederates' left flank. At the same time, General Johnston was making the first strategic use of a railroad in the history of warfare to unite his troops with Beauregard. The two opposing generals soon had equal numbers of troops available for combat, at approximately thirty-five thousand per side. Arriving himself on July 20, Johnston, as senior to Beauregard, published orders assuming command of the Army of the Potomac. The two would work in tandem to direct the disposition of troops during the ensuing battle.

While McDowell was exploring the route around the Confederate left, Beauregard was developing a plan to envelop the Federal left. With the main thrust coming from a force attacking and rolling up the left side, Beauregard's concept envisioned Cocke's unit as one of two or three brigades that would conduct a frontal attack on McDowell's army at Centreville. This plan was not to be, however, for in the early hours of Sunday, July 21, the Union army began to move against the southerners' left flank. Wampler recorded, "The early booming of cannon announced that the battle had actually begun." Instead of advancing, Cocke's men were now directed to remain in place, alert to any forces confronting them. If attacked, they were to maintain their position at all cost.[35] The 8th Virginia stood its ground, despite being subjected to fire from a battery across the creek. The Confederate artillery soon responded, and it was not long before shots were falling in front and screaming over the heads of Hunton's soldiers.[36]

The Yankee flanking movement was spotted from Signal Hill by Capt. Edward Porter Alexander, who noticed sunlight gleaming from the bayonets and cannon. He notified Evans near Stone Bridge, who recognized it for what it was, the main Federal force.[37] Notifying Cocke on his right of what he intended to do, Evans shifted the bulk of his undersized brigade to the left onto, first, Buck's and, then, Matthews Hill to block the Union advance. Additional northern troops were also moving onto the battlefield, and it was not long before the Confederates executed a strategic retreat back across Warrenton Turnpike onto Henry Hill.

McDowell mistakenly thought the withdrawal was a rout, and the Federals took two hours to congratulate themselves, rest, and reorganize before completing their apparent victory. The southern commanders made good use of this time. Arriving on Henry Hill about noon, General Beauregard concentrated on reconstituting, inspiring, and employing units in the vicinity of the Henry House, a one-and-a-half-story frame structure overlooking the battlefield.

For soldiers who had never tasted combat and subscribed to the popular notion that this was to be a short conflict, ripe with glory for their side as the obvious victors, the sounds of battle were tantalizing and frustrating. The ready reserve behind the battle lines saw the wounded, the exhausted, and the fearful fleeing from the confrontation. Units out of sight, but not out of hearing, while guarding the flanks, were anxious to become directly involved. Eppa Hunton expressed his frustration at not being called up by Col. William "Extra Billy" Smith, the former and future governor of Virginia, leading his small battalion to Henry Hill. Smith conveyed the message to Beauregard, who immediately summoned the 8th Virginia.[38] About the same time, General Johnston rode the half mile from his headquarters to Lewis Ford to direct Cocke to the front. The brigade commander's caution in withdrawing contributed to his unit being employed piecemeal, as individual regiments, instead of as a unified command. Marching via a farm lane from its position at the mouth of Holkums Branch to Henry Hill, the 8th Virginia was initially deployed by Beauregard as a reserve to protect the right flank in the direction of Young's Branch and the Stone Bridge.[39] In that position, they supported Smith's 49th Battalion.[40]

Beauregard had now assembled a strong line of infantry on Henry Hill, bolstered by artillery. Before the 8th Virginia entered the fray, Chaplain Charles Linthicum, only twenty-two years old, moved to the front of the regiment to lead its men in prayer.[41] For the next two hours, intense fighting revolved around two batteries of Federal artillery, which McDowell had ordered to the crest of the hill. Now, for the first time, the infantrymen of Loudoun County were exposed to troops retreating in disorder, and Hunton was challenged to hold his soldiers in place, while trying to rally the stragglers. The smoke and confusion of close combat was further compounded by the variety of uniforms in this first battle of the war. Men on each side wore blue and gray, and both armies had regiments of Zouaves.[42] Furthermore, the flags of the opposing forces were so similar in color and design as to be easily misidentified, when laying limp against their staffs, the Confederate Stars and Bars being mistaken for the Union Stars and Stripes, and vice versa.

Shortly before 3:00 P.M., Beauregard called up his reserves to sweep across the hilltop, capturing the northern guns in the most intense fighting of the day.[43] Led by Colonel Hunton, the 8th Virginia charged, first with the 18th Virginia against the 38th New York, and then driving back the 69th New York and seizing terrain around the Henry House.[44] Beauregard was reported to have observed "that he never witnessed a charge more gallantly or more *awkwardly* made," the latter no doubt a reference to the rawness of Hunton's troops.[45] Both sides regrouped, Hunton withdrawing his men to the shelter of a ravine on the east side of the house.[46] The fighting shifted across Sudley Road to Chinn Ridge, where uncoordinated attacks by successive Union regiments were repulsed. As the tide turned, Beauregard ordered forward the right flank of his line, including the 8th Virginia, but the pursuit did not continue for long.[47] The Federals were in full retreat, recrossing Bull Run by the same routes taken to the battlefield. The false report of a new threat at Manassas Junction caused Hunton to move his troops to Camp Pickens, near where the Prince William County courthouse stands today. Bleeding, exhausted, and hungry, having eaten only a single meal that day, the men of the 8th Virginia finally staggered back into their own camp at Bull Run long after dark.[48]

Wampler tersely characterized the next two days as "suffering." Heavy rain contributed to the misery. Hunton's regiment was quickly ordered back to Leesburg, however, along with the three companies of cavalry that had accompanied it to Manassas. Departing on July 24, they took two full days to reach Camp Berkeley at Ball's Mill in southern Loudoun County. Citizens along the way hailed the fledgling soldiers as conquering heroes. The next day, Colonel Hunton submitted his official report, listing 33 casualties: 6 killed, 23 wounded, and 1 missing. The Leesburg *Democratic Mirror* had already published an unofficial list of losses, tendered by the Rev. C. H. Nourse, a local boarding school proprietor, who rushed home from the battlefield. It cited three wounded, but no one killed in Wampler's Company H.[49]

Eppa Hunton in a brigadier general's uniform.
Valentine Museum, Richmond, Virginia.

Gen. Pierre Gustave Toutant Beauregard, April 13, 1861, about two months before Wampler met him at Manassas. Peery Southern Maritime Collection at the South Carolina Historical Society.

The men of the 8th Virginia now entered upon a new phase in the school of the soldier, enduring the boredom, trials, and tribulations of life in bivouac.

SUMMER SOLDIERING

Special Orders No. 169, published four days after the Battle of Bull Run by the Army of the Potomac, listed Col. Eppa Hunton's 8th Virginia Volunteers as a separate command in Leesburg. On August 8, however, General Beauregard issued new instructions, sending Colonel Evans to Leesburg to assume command of all Confederate forces in Loudoun County with the mission of protecting the corps' left flank. To the three Mississippi regiments he brought from Manassas—the 13th, 17th, and 18th—Evans added Hunton's Virginians.[50]

After resting at Camp Berkeley for almost three weeks, the 8th Virginia relocated to a site just south of Leesburg called Camp Carolina. Rumors of a Yankee foray into the northern county caused the soldiers to pack a full load of ammunition and move again on August 18. The threat did not materialize, however, and so the regiment established another base near Waterford, in a large meadow on a hillside beside a forest. This encampment was named for the newly designated commanding general of the Confederate Army of the Potomac, Joseph E. Johnston. They would remain there for almost two full months.

It was at Camp Johnston that Company H was transformed from a collection of individuals, who had "seen the elephant" at Bull Run, into a cohesive military unit. The daily routine consisted of morning roll call, breakfast, guard mount, company and squad drill, and midday meal, followed by regimental drill, dress parade, supper, evening roll call, and, finally, tattoo and taps.[51] The men of Company H learned the school of the soldier—the manual of arms, cleaning weapons, policing the area of debris, and serving on various camp details. Each company had two baggage wagons loaded with cooking stove, camp stools, mattresses, and assorted gear. Enlisted personnel lined their tent floors with straw; officers and more affluent volunteers enjoyed the comfort of cots. The rank-and-file endured coarse food, dirty blankets, and unwashed clothes, while everyone despised the ever-present camp vermin.

Basking in the warm sun and glow of their glorious victory over the northern invaders, this was a time of summer soldiering. Visitors to the 8th Virginia encampment were not uncommon, especially when the regiment was posted near the homes of unit members. Baskets of food and sweethearts in their finery accompanied families visiting their soldier boys. For those farther from home, mail call was the day's highlight.

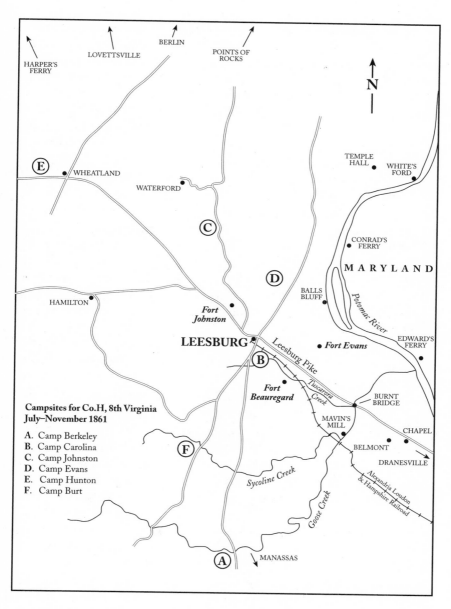

Loudoun County locations prominent in the lives of Morris and Kate Wampler.

Soldiering was not for everyone, however. Many farm boys lacked natural immunities to protect them from disease, when crowded together for the first time. At one point, only 22,291 of the 32,655 men in Beauregard's corps were fit for duty, causing him to complain to President Davis about the subsistence being provided and to urge subordinate commanders to give more attention to field sanitation.[52] The bimonthly muster of the 8th Virginia on August 31 showed 53 sick, of whom 41 required treatment at a military hospital.[53] For example, 2nd Lt. Arthur Follin, twenty-two years old, died of typhoid, prompting Company H to march to Hamilton to give him a soldier's burial in the Harmony Methodist Church cemetery. Wampler lamented, "Poor fellow, his affectionate little wife has made her sacrifice to the cause of the South."[54] Pvt. George Stewart was another Company H fatality. Many were incapacitated, at least temporarily, by measles and mumps.[55] Some attributed the problems to poor camp hygiene, although Wampler placed the blame on "the exposure & hard fare since leaving home." During early September, he too fell ill and went home on sick leave for ten days.[56] Even Eppa Hunton was put out of action by a fistula or abscess on his posterior, which prevented him from riding a horse and compelled him to command his regiment from a wagon bed.[57]

While not covered as prominently or enthusiastically, reports of defections from the Southern cause and increasing realism concerning the state of affairs began to appear on the pages of Leesburg's *Democratic Mirror*. About the time of the Bull Run engagement, Loudoun County's 56th militia regiment, from west of the Catoctin Mountains, reported that 400 of its 850 members had deserted into Maryland, including three or four captains.[58] General Beauregard published notice that arms, horses, and wagons, supplies, and munitions of war had been removed from the Manassas battlefield by civilians, and should this bounty not be turned in to the proper Confederate authorities, the culprits would be dealt with according to military law.[59] Not long thereafter, the arrests of several local citizens for providing aid and comfort to enemies of the Commonwealth were announced. Wampler himself was dispatched to apprehend "a Union man," Mr. Davis, who was released the same day, upon taking the oath of allegiance to the Confederacy at Camp Johnston.[60] Finally, as the nights began to turn chilly, the county newspaper acknowledged that the conflict would not be over by winter and urged its readers to collect warm clothing and blankets for the men in uniform.

The ranks of the 8th Virginia were far from full. In the optimistic weeks following Bull Run, Wampler enlisted five more volunteers for Company H. Albert Bean, age fourteen, was soon released, however, as the South was not yet ready to sacrifice its young. Aware of what was being said in Washington, through reprints of articles from other periodicals in the *Democratic Mirror,* it is likely that many residents of Loudoun County, along with its soldiers, initially believed that the ninety-day war promised by Lincoln must soon be over. By autumn, the demands of soldiering and the horror of battle were more obvious, which dampened recruiting.

Even without a large influx of new soldiers, there was a need for uniforms. The men enlisted in early July had insufficient time to be issued Confederate gray before being dispatched to Bull Run. From July 27 through the end of November, therefore, Wampler accumulated a sizable account, totaling $813.68, in cloth and accouterments with the Leesburg merchant, L. W. S. Hough. Eight yards of cottonade, costing $2.25, was necessary for the trimmings on a jacket and trousers. Brass buttons, socks, and shoes were also purchased. Wampler assigned Pvt. George Hanes to cut the material into uniform patterns. Then, one of a number of town ladies was paid $1.75 to make an enlistee's jacket and pants (and more for an officer's). One of these seamstresses was Mrs. John Orr, the mayor's wife. Wampler consequently combined the task of contracting for uniforms with the pleasure of dining with the prefect, a civil engineer, and kindred spirit, at their home on East Cornwell Street in Leesburg.

The resulting uniform was not always admired by its recipient. Pvt. Randolph A. Shotwell complained that the short jacket design left six inches of torso uncovered, while the pants resembled a coffee sack. A forage cap with floppy crown, coarse brogan shoes with a single shape for either foot, cartridge box, cap pouch, canteen, flintlock musket altered to percussion, bayonet, and canvas haversack completed the military issue.[61]

Trained, clad, and equipped as soldiers, the men of Company H needed only someone to fight. Rumors of Yankee incursions into Loudoun County and skirmishes with Southern defenders were not uncommon, and sometimes proved to be true. On August 2, a northern party crossed at Edwards Ferry, where Goose Creek empties into the Potomac, and burned the ferryman's house and an old warehouse.[62] Firing across the river had ceased being a novelty: the Daley house near the water served as a favorite target for Union artillerists. A cavalry skirmish at Harper's Ferry attracted attention. Confederates were reported to be constructing batteries along the west shore of the Potomac, south of Alexandria. Union engineers peered into Loudoun County from elevations across the river in Maryland, studying the topography and gathering intelligence on troop dispositions for their maps of northern Virginia.[63] Federal soldiers were also seen all along the Maryland shore opposite Loudoun County. On some Sundays, an informal truce permitted pickets to converse and even exchange mail, newspapers, and tobacco in the middle of the current.[64]

On September 21, Wampler's company and four others were suddenly dispatched to Lovettsville. Arriving after a fatiguing march, they discovered that the Yankees had withdrawn across the Potomac. Three days later, Company C went to nearby Point of Rocks and exchanged fire with the enemy. Orders were issued to be ready to march at a moment's notice. The anxiety was heightened on the afternoon of the twenty-sixth, when a dispatch from Beauregard alerted the 8th Virginia that they would be attacked that night. Pickets were doubled, cartridges distributed, knapsacks packed, and horses outfitted for immediate use. Severe rain and heavy winds heightened the tension, but nothing happened. The regiment remained under arms the following day, the rain and wind continued, but the enemy never came.[65] The soldiers at Camp Johnston quickly fell back into their familiar regimen. Before breaking camp, Company H elected a third lieutenant and orderly (or first) sergeant.

BATTLE OF BALL'S BLUFF (OR LEESBURG)

Three months after the Union embarrassment at Manassas, Radical Republicans in Washington were once again clamoring for movement toward the Confederate capital at Richmond.[66] Southern defenses were concentrated in forts and batteries down the Potomac River and at Centreville, opposite the Union army in Alexandria. Farther to the north, however, the southerners were less entrenched. The three forts ringing Leesburg remained the only fortifications on the Confederate's left flank. The town was situated at a crossroads, important as the connector between Centreville and Winchester in the fertile Shenandoah Valley and as the terminus of the Alexandria, Loudoun & Hampshire Railroad. By dislodging Evans's brigade, the Federals might influence the main body of Beauregard's force to withdraw to its next logical defensive line on the Rappahannock River, thereby beginning the push toward Richmond demanded by the politicians.

In mid-October, Maj. Gen. George B. McClellan, who had replaced McDowell, received indications that Rebel forces were ready to pull out of Loudoun County. McClellan decided to draw the Confederates' attention by sending Brig. Gen. George McCall's division of 12,000 Pennsylvania Reserves along the Georgetown Pike to its intersection with the Alexandria–Leesburg Pike at Dranesville Tavern, twelve miles east of Leesburg. To intensify the pressure, McClellan ordered Brig. Gen. Charles P. Stone's division, headquartered at Poolesville, Maryland, to conduct a demonstration, keeping close watch on the reaction in Leesburg. On October 20, Stone ordered Brig. Gen. Willis Gorman to stage a feint across the Potomac at Edward's Ferry, landing his brigade at the mouth of Goose Creek, four short miles from Leesburg. Stone's main thrust, however, would come from another task force crossing farther up the river at Smart's Mill Ford.

Beauregard's instructions to Evans were to maintain possession of Leesburg "against odds."[67] The 8th Virginia departed Waterford on October 12, marched to Thomas Swann's farm, the summer residence of Baltimore's former mayor just north of Leesburg, and set up what Wampler dubbed Camp Evans on the slopes of the Catoctin Mountains facing the Potomac. Two days later, in unison with the Richmond Howitzers and two Mississippi companies, Wampler's company moved again, this time to Wheatland plantation, where they bivouacked on a clear cold night. The following day, Company H stopped at Hillsboro, northwest from Leesburg in the Short Hills, where they pitched "*Camp Hunton* in a most beautiful spot, with lovely panoramic view."[68] Fearful that he would be isolated from Beauregard's main body by a Union flanking movement up the Aldie Turnpike, Evans began massing his troops in strong positions at Carter's Mill, south of Leesburg in the direction of Centreville, some twenty-five miles away. On October 17, en route to join the main body of the 7th Brigade, Wampler's task force was diverted to its old campground, Camp Carolina. From that vantage point, they were able to watch Yankee signals from the strategic elevation of Sugar Loaf Mountain, across the Potomac in Frederick County, Maryland. While the Federals were gathering intelligence through direct observation, the Confederates were fortunate to capture one of McCall's couriers, carrying dispatches that revealed the position and purpose of his force at Dranesville. In response to Evans's request for help, Beauregard sent word that Leesburg would not be reinforced from Centreville.[69] Consequently, the 8th Virginia received orders at 1:00 A.M. on October 20, to block westward movement into Loudoun County by Federal troops along the Alexandria–Leesburg Pike.

The regiment broke camp before daybreak. As it passed through Leesburg on that Sunday morning, the whole town turned out to cheer what, in light of the success at Manassas, was thought certain to be another victory. One member of Company H remembered the scene: "Several practical housewives are dispensing hot coffee, buttermilk, cider, and sandwiches gratis to those nimble enough to dash out of the ranks and gulp them down before ordered back by their officers. Dozens of young misses flutter from doorstep to doorstep—from one point of observation to another—to see the troops pass. . . . Handkerchiefs are waving from every window and portico."[70]

The 8th Virginia reoccupied a line of entrenchments along Goose Creek.

Hunton deployed his troops to cover the shallow fords beside the abutments of the bridge burned by southern sympathizers. With wooded bluffs on either side, the stream provided a natural line of defense. Wampler found himself positioned near his mother's home, not far from his wife and children. He posted pickets across the creek on the ridge to the east. That night, the soldiers of Company H slept on the ground, weapons by their sides, expecting a fight to erupt at any moment.

While the Confederates rested, General Stone sent a scouting party across the Potomac to determine the enemy disposition at Leesburg. Misidentifying a stand of trees as a southern encampment, the scouts caused Stone to dispatch four companies of the 15th Massachusetts to attack this position. Instead, the Federals were surprised by Capt. William Duff's company of the 17th Mississippi Regiment, which fired several volleys into the Yankee ranks, causing them to scatter. While the invaders were reforming, Duff received reinforcements. Directing the disposition of southern forces from the earthworks at Fort Evans, centrally located east of Leesburg, "Shanks" Evans monitored the movements of Gorman's division at the river two miles to his front. Retaining the main body of three Mississippi regiments at Fort Evans to counter the growing Yankee presence at Edwards Ferry, he dispatched four companies of Mississippi infantry, plus three skeletal troops of Virginia cavalry, to aid Duff.[71] For a short time the horsemen fought alongside the infantry, to include Lt. George Baxter of the Loudoun Cavalry, who earned praise for leading a dismounted charge.[72] Southern reinforcements soon included the 8th Virginia, less Company H, which was sent back to the Burnt Bridge over Goose Creek to protect against the introduction of McCall's sizable force from Dranesville. "Wampler was dreadfully mortified at not being allowed to go with us to the fight," Hunton recalled later.[73]

Colonel Hunton's selection of Wampler's unit to guard the Confederate flank must be viewed as a compliment, in light of the thousands of Northern troops assembled just down the pike. As local boys, the soldiers of Company H were familiar with the terrain, and certainly their commander knew Goose Creek, having grown up on its banks. The choice of Company H also reflected Hunton's confidence in these soldiers and their commander to act effectively on their own, delaying the overwhelming enemy force, if challenged, until receiving reinforcement. Indeed, Hunton's report of the engagement at Ball's Bluff singled out "the gallant Wampler's company" for special recognition.[74]

Hunton rushed his 8th Virginia soldiers, 375 in number, via Fort Evans to Ball's Bluff at double-quick, canteens jingling, and, when fighting resumed, his regiment pressed the Yankee left sufficiently to seize the critical terrain along a ridge line. More reinforcements were added on both sides, this time consisting of the remainder of the 17th and 18th Mississippi for the southerners, leaving only the 13th Mississippi below Fort Evans to oppose the Union force at Edwards Ferry. Almost out of ammunition, the last assault by the 8th Virginia relied primarily on the bayonet and succeeded in capturing two Federal howitzers.[75] The Confederates then pushed forward to the edge of the bluff, forcing the Yankees down the hundred-foot embankment to the water. Panic ensued among the defeated Federals, who were trapped without sufficient boats to carry them back to the safety of Harrison's Island, or all the way to the Maryland shore. Terrified soldiers jumped into the water, overloaded the few available bateaux, causing them to sink, or congregated along the beach, presenting inviting targets for the pursuing riflemen. After nightfall, Elijah V. White, a resident of the area on leave from Ashby's Cavalry, led a band of 52 volunteers, by his own count, all from the 8th Virginia, back to the river's edge, where they rounded up 325 prisoners, along with their arms and ammunition.[76]

Here is how the commander of Company H summarized the day's dramatic events:

> Oct. 21. Monday A.M. Heard the Enemy were coming in another direction, i.e. back of Leesburg. Brigade ordered to meet them. When near them, My Co. was sent back to hold & defend, as pickets, the ford at the Bridge. My Regt, with slight assistance achieved a glorious victory over abt. 4 thousand. The fight commenced in morning bet. Capt. Duff's Co. Miss. & 4 Cos. Yankees. Capt. Duff fell back, when Lt. Baxter with 10 men of Loudoun Cavalry charged on two Yankee Cos. & put them to flight. The 8th (My Regt) then came up & engaged the Enemy, assisted by three Cos. Miss, the Enemy vastly superior in numbers. Later abt. 3 o'clk the 8th advanced driving the Enemy back & had sharp engagement for abt 2 hours when abt. time our ammunition was out, the Miss 17th & 18th came up. At this juncture the 8th charged on the Yankee Cannons. When the Miss. Regt. followed & ended the fight in short order, taking abt. 700 prisoners, drowning abt. 250, & killing & wounding 3 or 4 hundred. About 40 of our men took 320 of the Yankee prisoners unaided. At night we slept on ground, or rather, laid awake, but not I. I heard the Yankees working & crossing all night at the Ferry. We lost abt 150 killed & wounded.[77]

So, when he wrote in his journal at the Burnt Bridge, Wampler recorded the names and basic story of Ball's Bluff just about right. His casualty figures for the Confederates were remarkably accurate, as they reported 36 killed, 117 wounded, and 2 missing.[78] While inflated, his estimate of Union losses was not completely out of line with the actual figures of 49 killed, 158 wounded, 553 taken prisoner, and 161 missing, most drowned in the Potomac.[79] The real distortions occurred in numbers of soldiers reported to have been engaged in the battle. It is always advantageous to portray an opponent as far larger than one's own force. If the battle is lost, the vanquished are the victims of overwhelming odds; if the battle is won, the victors triumph heroically, overcoming superior numbers. Wampler's understanding that his regiment had bested 4,000 of the enemy inflated the 1,720 bluecoats actually engaged at Ball's Bluff. It is consistent, however, with the inflation offered by the other side: General Orders No. 32, published by General McClellan on October 25, characterized the opposing southern force at Ball's Bluff as 5,000 strong, when in actuality it numbered 1,709 men.[80] In truth, the opposing forces were equal in strength. The losses were greater, in proportion to the numbers engaged, than at Bull Run.

The day following the clash, Wampler drew up Company H in a line of battle to cover the ford and turnpike, when he heard fighting resume, this time at Edwards Ferry, where he had noted enemy activity throughout the previous night. General Gorman had succeeded in ferrying 4,500 soldiers across the river. What Wampler heard was the 13th Mississippi Regiment attacking and being easily repulsed. Ann Mavin sent out food and coffee to her son and his men, before they lay down again to sleep in the cold and wet. That night, Gorman pulled his troops back across the Potomac, ending McClellan's attempt to dislodge the Confederates from northern Virginia by turning their left flank.

REORGANIZATION AND RECOGNITION

The Confederates did not yet realize that, for the time being, the danger of Federal invasion was over. Evans withdrew south of Leesburg to wooded bluffs overlooking Sycolin Creek, bivouacking at a site designated Camp Burt in honor of the commander of the 18th Mississippi, who had been mortally wounded at Ball's Bluff. Eppa Hunton later recalled feeling "cowardly" about yielding Leesburg to the Yankees after having won a victory northeast of town.[81] The retrograde left Company H alone and exposed on the Alexandria Pike. On October 23, Wampler was directed to move his unit to Fort Evans, but before he could close with the fort, he received a second hurried dispatch to rejoin his regiment at Sycolin Creek immediately, "or my command would be taken prisoners."[82] They remained at Camp Burt into November with but one interruption, another report of a Federal threat to Lovettsville. The 8th Virginia and 8th Louisiana moved nine miles north to Waterford, along with a squad of cavalry and two cannon. Companies B and H from the Virginia volunteers then joined two Louisiana companies in marching another ten miles to Lovettsville, where they spent the night on the cold, wet ground, tired and hungry, before returning the next day to Waterford. With nothing to show for their effort, Wampler's men trudged back through Leesburg to their camp on Sycolin Creek.[83]

Wampler now temporarily turned his company over to Lt. Festus Griffith and returned to his profession as a topographical engineer. Evans detached him to make a map of the battleground at Ball's Bluff. This occupied Wampler for a good week, from October 30 until November 7. The unaccustomed freedom also provided an opportunity to visit his family on Goose Creek and to hear Rev. Walter Williams, a VMI alumnus, preach in Leesburg.

Almost immediately upon returning to his regiment, Wampler attempted to discipline two soldiers who were fighting, when their comrades intervened, challenging his authority. He preferred charges against them all, and a court-martial was conducted over the following two days. The omission from his journal of any reference to the verdict suggests that Wampler's action was not vindicated. Blankets were distributed to soldiers who, by this time in late fall, must have suffered terribly from the nighttime chill. Colonel Hunton was welcomed on his return to duty, albeit temporarily, after convalescent leave for the fistula that limited his movement at Ball's Bluff. Kate came to visit her husband, and he accompanied her back to Leesburg. It was their last time together before the 8th Virginia left Loudoun County.

General Orders No. 15, published in Richmond the day after the engagement at Ball's Bluff, reorganized Confederate forces in northern Virginia. General Joseph E. Johnston was assigned command of the new Department of Northern Virginia, which consisted of three districts. The vital Potomac District, opposite Washington, was retained by General Beauregard. Its components were reconstituted, however, to organize units from the same state within a single brigade, to the extent possible. Consequently, the 21st Mississippi joined the other three Mississippi regiments in Evans's brigade at Leesburg, while Hunton's command was reunited with now Brigadier General Cocke, its commander at Bull Run, and his three Virginia regiments at Centreville. The transfer was not popular with the men of the 8th Virginia. Primarily Loudoun residents, the soldiers were accustomed to periodic, if sometimes unauthorized, visits to their homes, where they could obtain food, equipment, and clothing to supplement their sparse government issue. They reasoned that they knew the roads and pathways of Loudoun County far better than out-of-state troops and would fight hard to protect their homes. Exchanging the rich pastures, amenities, and relaxed camp life of Loudoun County for the discipline, military details, army fare, and enormity of the Confederate camp at Centreville was not at all an appealing prospect.[84]

The reorganization was accomplished in late November. The 8th Virginia could have covered the distance from Camp Burt to Centreville in a single day, but, for good reason, spent the night of November 21 at Zion Church, only seven miles from its destination. Maj. Norborne Berkeley organized a splendid dinner of turkey, pig, goose, duck, and biscuits to celebrate Thanksgiving. The following day, at the appointed noon hour, the 8th Virginia made its triumphal entrance onto the parade ground at Centreville. The other elements of Cocke's brigade were already formed up on line—the 18th, 19th, and 28th Virginia Regiments. As the band played "Lo the Conquering Hero Comes," these units, in turn, executed "Present Arms," and lowered their guidons in a ceremonial sign of respect. Cocke and Hunton both spoke, welcoming the 8th Infantry back into the 5th Brigade and complimenting its performance at Ball's Bluff, interspersed by "three cheers for the heroes of Leesburg!" from soldiers in the ranks.[85] To recognize the bravery of the 8th Virginia at Ball's Bluff, Mrs. Beauregard had made a flag from one of her silk dresses, which she presented to the regiment and which can be seen today at the Museum of the Confederacy in Richmond.[86]

The camp at Centreville was a magnificent sight, white tents spread over hills and fields in every direction. During the day, it may have reminded observers of a giant ant hill, figures scurrying in every direction, while soldiers practiced military drill at the squad, company, and regimental level. Brass bands competed for attention, filling the air with martial music. Regimental flags fluttered in the breeze. By day, sunlight glinted off metal barrels; at night, columns of smoke emanated from countless chimneys and open log fires.[87]

Despite their heraldic welcome, the men of the 8th Virginia were discontented. As the newest unit to the encampment, it is not surprising that they were assigned the least desirable bivouac site. Situated upon a rough slope, their rows of tents, with broad company streets in between, extended downward to the wet, marshy lowlands at the bottom, where, again not surprisingly, the lower-ranking enlisted personnel were billeted. The men were forced to sleep on the bare ground, devoid of the thick straw covering that had lined their tents in Loudoun County. Their displeasure was heightened by the absence of personal articles—bedding, camp furniture, extra provisions, cooking utensils—abandoned at Oatlands since the soldiers perceived a lack of transportation sufficient for their belongings.[88] Hunton disagreed, considering the movement to Centreville with twenty-eight wagons "the finest transportation that any regiment ever had in time of war."[89]

Soldiers in the 8th Virginia had many friends in regiments from neighboring locales, so an active social life soon evolved. Wampler visited with the Loudoun Guard, Company C of the 17th Virginia, renewing several acquaintances. He spent an evening with another old friend, Capt. James Towson, a VMI graduate commanding Company G, 17th Regiment, called on Capt. Welby Carter, Company H, 1st Virginia Cavalry, dined with Capt. Thornton Triplet, Company C, 19th Battalion, Virginia Heavy Artillery, and drank with Capt. S. W. Presstman, 17th Virginia, with whom his military career would become entwined. Capt. William Berkeley of Company D, 8th Virginia, joined Wampler in attending a large cavalry review. Col. James H. Williams of the 3rd South Carolina Volunteers stopped for a cup of coffee. The band of the 19th Virginia from Charlottesville came by to serenade Lieutenant Colonel Tebbs, once again the regiment's acting commander in Eppa Hunton's absence, providing enjoyment for Wampler and his men as well.

The nights had turned cold by the time the 8th Virginia reached Centreville, and the first snow fell on November 24. Wampler requisitioned overcoats for his men in Manassas. A week later, the troops were ordered to build cabins and settle into winter quarters, as General Johnston concluded that there would be no further major military operations that year. Timber had to be transported several miles, as closer stands of trees had already been used or destroyed. Wampler and his men first built fireplaces with stone chimneys for their tents, before engaging in the more time-consuming work of constructing log cabins. Spirits seemed to improve as the soldiers created a warm, personalized environment at Centreville, and it was not long before the encampment was affectionately referred to as "Cabinville."

Military regimen was not neglected. Roll was called at dawn; inspections and parades were conducted with regularity. During drill one day, Wampler was surprised to look up and see a balloon, by his estimation, some fifteen to twenty miles away in the direction of Washington. This was undoubtedly Prof. Thaddeus S. C. Lowe, who launched one of the first aerial surveillance balloons for the U.S. Army, creating quite a scare among the civilians of Leesburg. One beautiful Sunday, Wampler and Captain Towson rode over to Manassas to examine the battleground at Blackburn's Ford.

Soon after its arrival, General Cocke ordered the 8th Virginia to perform picket duty for the army gathered at Centreville, a responsibility shouldered by every regiment twice each month. The 8th Virginia was initially assigned to Picket Post No. 3 at Barnes Mill, a four-mile march over muddy roads from its campsite. The post was located in a desolate area of southern Fairfax County, where farmhouses were abandoned, fields barren, and fences burned. Solitary chimneys at irregular intervals marked the locations of residences ravaged by war. Every twenty-four hours, two companies were posted individually as advance pickets to the east of the mill, in the direction of Washington and Alexandria. The remainder of the regiment formed the reserve and gathered in shelters made of long saplings or poles, which rested against trees and were covered by boughs and branches to form lean-tos. Vermin, lice, and all manner of other insects populated the leaves and pine needles collected on the ground under the shelter by a succession of soldiers over several months.[90] As officer of the day, it was Wampler's duty to check the individual pickets periodically, during both day and night. Upon returning to camp, Wampler was proud to report any prisoners taken by his pickets.[91] Regiments were assigned to picket duty for seventy-two hours, from noon one day until the same time three days later, although the entire commitment consumed most of four days, with forming up and marching to and from the duty station.

Two full formations punctuated military life at Centreville. The first occurred on November 30, involving eleven thousand troops in a grand division review. Wampler's Loudoun County neighbors, Alfred Dulin and William McPherson, journeyed from Goose Creek to witness the spectacle, and Wampler took advantage of the opportunity to send letters back with them to Kate. The occasion was considered a complete success, with the troops in their best uniforms, cavalry mounted on their premier horses, and the weather perfect.[92] The review afforded the 8th Virginia its first opportunity to parade under the battle flag just adopted by General Beauregard. Two days earlier, Beauregard had published an order designating a special flag to be carried into combat to avoid the confusion in identifying colors at Bull Run. The red field with diagonal blue bars in the shape of St. Andrew's cross, holding white stars, soon became the standard military banner, although popularly mistakened later for the national flag of the Confederate states.

The second formation concerned the 1st Battalion, Louisiana Volunteers, Maj. Roberdeau Wheat's famed "Tigers." This colorful unit had its fair share of ruffians recruited from the docks, levees, and alleys of New Orleans.

Wheat seemed to be the only leader who could enforce any sort of discipline, and he had been severely wounded at Manassas. Disorderly conduct after tattoo one night caused several Tigers to be arrested and confined in the guardhouse. Their comrades tried to free them, knocking down the officer of the guard in the process.[93] The neighboring 7th Louisiana was called in to subdue the mutineers. Two ringleaders were sent before a court-martial the following day, found guilty, and sentenced to be shot at noon the next day. The brigade commander, Brig. Gen. Richard Taylor, son of the Mexican War general and former president whose death Wampler had lamented in 1850, directed that the firing squad consist of members of the convicted men's own company, against the advice of Wheat and others, who feared insurrection.[94] The first military execution in the Department of Northern Virginia must have had a profound effect on every soldier who witnessed it. Wampler described it this way:

> Monday, Dec. 9, 1861. Camp at Centreville (Execution). I have witnessed this day a sad & solemn sight, a military execution! Two of the N.O. Tigers were shot for attempt to kill an officer. Abt. 10,000 troops were drawn up in three sides of a hollow sqr to witness the execution as two stakes were prepared at the open side of the sqr. The prisoners were bro't & tied to these stakes standing when two squads (of 12 men each) of their own company were bro't to a front within abt. 20 yds. of them. The word was given at a moment when every breath was stilled, and as the rattle of the discharge of musketry thrilled on the ear, the eye saw two unfortunates fall in the agonies of death. 24 muskets were taken from the company and abt. one half were loaded with ball cartridge, the other half with blank cartridge. The company then draw lots as to who shall or who shall not be in the party of executioners until 24 shall have been drawn to do the work of death. They then are marched up & take each one a musket, not knowing whether he has a gun loaded with ball or blank. It so happened in this affair today that one of the guns of one of the executioners was not fired & upon investigation, it was found that the man in whose hands this gun was found was brother to one of the criminals, & the lot fell to him. Horrible, horrible, but necessary.[95]

Back in Leesburg, the new Confederate battle flag was introduced during a grand review on December 9. A deeply religious Christian, the garrison commander, Brig. Gen. D. H. Hill, interpreted this banner as a Confederate cross, distinguishing it from the Yankee flag. His predecessor, "Shanks" Evans, had been relieved on December 4, ostensibly for heavy drinking, which would blight the rest of his life, and because of his growing unpopularity among the local residents for imprisoning so many of them. Hill was highly impressed with the quality of his soldiers, "confident that they can whip the Yankees four to one."[96]

CHRISTMAS 1861

As Christmas grew near, Hill established a truce with General Stone, an old friend from his service in the U.S. Army. Three days before the holiday, the weather turned extremely cold and sleety. Hill worried about his troops suffering in tents—especially the Mississippi volunteers, who must have felt the cold far more than the local soldiers.[97] One Mississippian described his Christmas celebration as consisting of a sermon by Walter Williams, pastor of St. James Episcopal Church, a dinner with Mr. Hoffman, a member of the local gentry, and enjoying a letter from his wife. More spirited youths, like soldiers of the Richmond Howitzers, who spent the winter guarding the Burnt Bridge near Wampler's home, sought out "Fiddler's Green," a shanty belonging to a widow with three grown daughters, all of whom played the violin. Their Christmas ball was reported to have featured a sumptuous buffet, moonshine whiskey, hours of dancing to the women's music, and more.

The holiday celebration was not as jolly at Camp Cabinville. General Beauregard had instituted a policy allowing Christmas leave only to those soldiers whose families needed them at home. Wampler succeeded in obtaining passes for James Rose, whose mother was ill, and three other members of his company. Meanwhile, Wampler had been trying to obtain foodstuffs to send home. With the aid of James Simpson of Company I, he succeeded in conveying sugar and chestnuts, along with a bag of clothes, but efforts to ship a barrel of flour were thwarted when the intended carrier, his neighbor William Greenlease, failed to stop by and pick up the staple. In turn, Wampler received a pillow, turkey, jug of whiskey, and "a trunk full of good things" from Kate. Letters passed back and forth on a regular basis.

Christmas Eve began with a terrific windstorm that threatened to collapse Wampler's tent, so he was thankful to be able to move into his newly completed cabin before nightfall. It was two weeks later, however, before he installed a window. "A little party at Captain W[illiam] Berkeley's" constituted the sole recognition of the holiday for Wampler.[98] At 9:00 on Christmas morning, the commander of Company H started out to Picket Post No.

3 again, this time with five of the regiment's companies. After placing his men on outpost, he returned to the vicinity of Barnes Mill to take tea with some "ladies," along with Lt. Bob Gray of Company F, demonstrating that the forlorn area was not completely uncivilized.

AMERICUS HUTCHISON

At noon on the day following Christmas, Wampler's men were relieved by Company F and moved back to Barnes Mill to form the reserve. Wampler and Lt. Col. Tebbs dined with one of the ladies (referred to as "Miss Barnes," perhaps with tongue in cheek) with whom Wampler had enjoyed Christmas tea. The weather was clear but cold, when he returned to the old mill to take command of the reserve at 3:00 P.M.

Gathered around the fire with nothing to do but wait for an alarm, which they hoped would never be sounded, the men made crude attempts to relieve the tension and boredom by joking and chiding one another. A Baltimorean, John Marrett, made an obscene drawing on a piece of shingle and passed it to Americus Hutchison, asking, "How do you like your Mother?"[99] Hutchison flew into a rage, grabbed Wampler's sword from where it hung, and began chasing Marrett, hacking at his head, shoulders, and back. Marrett's screams stunned the other soldiers, who froze in place, but Wampler seized a musket and attempted to shoot Hutchison. The weapon would not fire. Marrett stumbled and fell, and Hutchison paused to deliver the coup de grace, when Wampler pressed his bayonet to Hutchison's chest, disarming him of the now broken sword. Hutchison's arms were bound, and sullenly he returned to Centreville under guard. Wampler accompanied Marrett for treatment of a severe cut on his head.[100]

Americus Hutchison was a farmer, twenty-two years of age and six feet tall, with dark hair, eyes, and a complexion. He had been enlisted by Wampler on July 13, when so many young Virginians came to the colors in the face of McDowell's threat from Arlington Heights. One of a dozen members of his family—mostly from an ancestral home called Peach Orchard in south Loudoun County—to serve with the 8th Virginia, the prisoner undoubtedly received many visitors during his long confinement in the guardhouse at Centreville, Wampler among them. Hutchison was returned to Company H on March 8, where he remained under guard until the twenty-fourth, awaiting court-martial. Instead, he appeared before a medical board convened to determine his fitness for military service. Two physicians for the

South Carolina Volunteers examined him and heard from witnesses who testified about his occasional attacks of mental derangement. Consequently, the board determined that Hutchison was not responsible for his actions and that he posed a danger to others. Considering him unfit for military service, the board recommended that Hutchison be released from confinement and returned to his family, where he could receive necessary treatment. General Johnston approved these findings, and so, by order of General Longstreet, Pvt. Americus Hutchison was issued a certificate of disability, dated March 31, 1862, thereby avoiding court-martial.[101] Wampler formally discharged him at morning formation on April 1. Ironically, the following day he was taken sick, and, two days later, Americus Hutchison died of typhoid pneumonia at Orange Court House.

The Americus Hutchison episode illuminates several characteristics of Morris Wampler's personality. His quick reaction when violence erupted bears the mark of leadership. While other soldiers were astonished and sat back to watch what developed, Wampler jumped into the fray, subduing the attacker. Wampler's considerate treatment of Hutchison in the three months before his death is also noteworthy. Rather than resort to what must have been a strong temptation to turn the entire matter over to a court-martial, Wampler had Hutchison medically evaluated. The captain even visited the private in the guardhouse, although there is no reason to believe that the two were close. These actions might be expected of a modern-day company-grade officer, but they were not so common in the mid-nineteenth century and suggest a compassionate approach to soldiering by the Company H commander.

Winter at Camp Cabinville

"Wednesday Jan. 1, 1862. Camp Cabinville near Centreville. Lovely day ushers in the Newborn Year. May God guide & direct me in the path of virtue & rectitude thro' this new year. May he release our beloved South from her present troubles, and confuse & scatter our enemies. God be merciful to me a sinner."[102]

So Wampler began the new year. It was a cold winter indeed, with snow falling regularly. When temperatures rose above freezing, the Centreville encampment became a sea of mud. Nonetheless, the 8th Virginia continued the training regimen established in the last month of 1861. Wampler naturally appreciated any variations in the routine. In addition to maintaining a regular correspondence with Kate, he was asked to write a petition to release the brother of a friend from prison. He also penned a letter to the children of a black couple, at their request. Wampler was ordered to sit on three courts-martial in January, serving as president of two. As a civil engineer, it is not surprising that he was placed in charge of improving roads extending from the camp, the streets within it, and wells that supplemented creeks as sources of water. He was further directed to improve the "policing" of debris. Lieutenant Colonel Tebbs decided to join his mess, a coterie of officers whose meals were prepared and served by the attendants or slaves who accompanied many Confederate officers into camp. Finally, Wampler narrowly averted disaster when Pvt. Bill Saunders accidentally discharged a musket inside his cabin, nearly wounding the company commander.

Wampler enjoyed the companionship of the regiment's clergy, Chaplains John Granberry and Charles Linthicum. He attended church every Sunday, often sitting through more than one service. Chaplain Linthicum had advertised in Loudoun County for books to help dispel boredom and ward off problems associated with idle soldiers: "Books, Books, Books is the continuing cry in camp. Good books will restrain evil, develop good, interest the mind, cultivate the affections, refine the nature, and profit the soul of man."[103] Wampler went a step further, organizing a debating society. The inaugural took place at Beauregard Lyceum on January 31, to consider the question, "Which is most gratifying to the senses, the contemplation of *Nature* or of *Art*."[104] The graduate of Miss Mercer's academy presented the opening arguments on behalf of nature and was succeeded by Linthicum on the side of art, after which each had an opportunity for rebuttal. Wampler contended that he had won. The next week posed the question, "Was Europe justified in Conquest of America?" There is no record of a victor on this matter.[105]

No doubt the Lyceum's name was an expression of the soldiers' lament over the departure of the popular commander of the Potomac District, who had been reassigned to the Western Theater after a series of public criticisms of the Davis government in Richmond.[106] Beauregard delivered a stirring farewell to his troops, vowing to return, and was then followed through Centreville by soldiers shouting, "Goodby, General, God bless you, General."[107] This early in his military experience, Wampler may not have fully appreciated the significance of losing a commanding general with whom he enjoyed a personal relationship. He had communicated with Beauregard shortly before his transfer, asking that Company H be converted to a light artillery battery. Negative responses soon returned from both the general and Judah P. Benjamin, Confederate secretary of war, who stated he could only accept a company reenlisted as infantry or heavy artillery.[108]

The 8th Virginia was assigned in the new year to a different picket post, No. 5 at the village of Germantown, west of Fairfax Court House on the north side of the Little River Turnpike. The distance was longer, the roads muddier after incessant snow, sleet, and rain. While in Germantown on February 7, at about 2:00 P.M., word came back to the reserve that the cavalry pickets, beyond their infantry counterparts, had been driven in by enemy activity. Wampler sent a company of infantry to strengthen the outposts, and then he and Sgt. Maj. John Hutchison ventured beyond the pickets in the direction of Fairfax on an independent scouting mission. They returned at 10:00 P.M. to a good scolding by Lieutenant Colonel Tebbs and the threat of being reported by Capt. Henry Carter of Company B. Fortunately for all concerned, no notice was taken by higher authority. However, two 8th Virginia soldiers were captured later that night.[109]

Throughout the winter, the soldiers at Centreville were cognizant of events taking place in other parts of the Confederacy. Wampler noted the bad news from Fort Donelson three days after its surrender on February 16. He also acknowledged the inauguration of President Davis in Richmond on Washington's Birthday. Closer to camp, cannon fire was frequently reported, initially from the direction of Evansport, south of Alexandria, and later from other points to the north and east. Nor was it uncommon for the regiment to be placed on alert—three-days' rations cooked, arms inspected, ready to march at a moment's notice.

Movement South

The long, cold winter, living in makeshift quarters, and being subject to military discipline for the first time after tasting the agony of battle all clearly weighed on the men of the 8th Virginia. By late February, the close proximity of their homes presented an irresistible temptation to take leave of army life, authorized or unauthorized. Wampler made note of his soldiers' coming and going. A notable example was C. J. Lowe, who returned from being absent without leave on February 9 and left again five days later, never to return. Indeed, General Hill, in Leesburg, was deeply distressed over the practice of furloughing experienced soldiers at a time when the opposing forces were gathering in strength, just across the river in Maryland.[110] It is not surprising, therefore, that on February 24, Wampler and Joe Carruthers, the acting first sergeant of Company H, were detailed on recruiting duty for thirty days. In addition to expanding the rolls, Lieutenant Colonel Tebbs instructed them to arrest as deserters and return to their companies any men found to be absent without authority.[111]

Wampler and Carruthers left camp early on the morning of February 24 and covered the twenty miles to Leesburg on foot, arriving at 3:30 P.M. The company commander continued on to Goose Creek and the sergeant headed home to Hamilton. Wampler found everyone apparently well and so immediately began his recruiting efforts by sending a notice to the Leesburg newspaper office to be printed as a handbill. He noted Confederate pickets stationed at the dam beside his mother's mill and heard cannon firing in the distance. When he ventured into town two days later, Wampler found great excitement, as the sick and baggage of Hill's troops were being evacuated. After catching up on the news from friends he had earlier made among the officer corps of the Mississippi regiments, Wampler again dined with John Orr, the town mayor and fellow engineer.

What Wampler learned was that on the same day he journeyed to Leesburg, Col. John W. Geary, a Mexican War veteran and property owner in Loudoun, was leading a Federal force into the county from Harper's Ferry. By week's end, Geary had set up headquarters at Lovettsville and was preparing to move farther south toward Leesburg. At the same time, McClellan, who had succeeded Lt. Gen. Winfield Scott as general-in-chief of the armies of the United States, was preparing to transport his forces down the Potomac to the Chesapeake in order to attack Richmond from the southeast.

Wampler could not fail to notice the increase in military activity around Leesburg. He walked to Fort Johnston, where he again conferred with his Mississippi friends. He observed the cannonading between Fort Evans and the Federal batteries across the river. Snow fell on March 2, the day the health of Wampler's stepfather began to fail. Wampler sent for Dr. Stovall, and the next day he walked into town for medicine for Mr. Mavin. While there, Wampler conferred about the deteriorating military situation with Maj. Henry Peyton, formerly in the 8th Virginia and now on Beauregard's staff. Returning home, he found Mavin in the throes of delirium, and for two days, Wampler and other family members sat up with the dying man. At 3:00 on the afternoon of March 5, William Mavin passed away. Wampler ordered a coffin. While he was in town the next day, arranging for a grave to be dug, his mother became ill and fainted at home. He feared that she would not last the night.

At midnight, Wampler heard the signal cannon notifying Confederate troops in the vicinity of Leesburg to fall back to Manassas Junction. The

Mississippians departed at once. Wampler stayed in bed until early on the morning of March 7. He discovered that the retreating southerners had burned wheat stacks and provisions that could not be transported with them. Any hesitation he may have felt about leaving his family amidst the uncertainty that lay ahead was outweighed by his sense of duty. Taking a hurried break-fast, Wampler said his goodbyes, climbed aboard Milton, and belatedly started for camp. He left behind his mother at the point of death and her husband's corpse in the adjoining room. Mavin was to have been buried at 11:00, but Wampler correctly surmised that the evacuation of Leesburg would interfere with the funeral. "This is the darkest day of my life when leaving all at the mercy of the ruthless & barbarian invaders." It would be nearly three months before he learned the fate of his family.[112]

The bluecoats left Lovettsville that same day, stopping briefly at Waterford, which had been spared the Confederates' torch by the sudden advance of the Federals. Continuing toward Leesburg, they halted again at Fort Johnston, where the U.S. flag was raised and the star-shaped earthwork renamed Fort Geary, by which it would be known by Union forces for the remainder of the war. Two Federal guns now looked down on the town below. Colonel Geary could see a valley with barns and fields in flames, but Leesburg itself was intact, and so he was able to take possession of its public buildings. At the same time, Federal troops were dispatched to Forts Evans and Beauregard, while another force pur-sued the retreating Confederates as far as Carter's Mill, where they found the bridge over Goose Creek had been burned.[113]

The entire Confederate army was now in motion, reacting to McClellan's amphibious flanking movement far to the southeast. The day after Wampler returned to Centreville, his company packed their wagons, formed them in line, and then stacked arms until orders were received to begin the march. While they waited, Wampler and Chaplain Linthicum were sent to nearby Brentsville to convey news of the withdrawal to Colonel Hunton, still at home, disabled by his fistula. Continuing on to Gainesville, where they ex-pected to rejoin their troops, they found instead only the advance element, and so Wampler and Linthicum proceeded to the outskirts of Warrenton, stopping at 10:00 P.M. at the Horner residence to await the regiment. The next day being Sunday, they attended church, while wagons and troops passed by all day. Wampler saw his neighbors, the Kepharts, in one wagon, as well as Lieutenant Colonel Tebbs's wife, but could learn nothing about his mother's health.

Their regiment eventually arrived, and Wampler and Linthicum rejoined them in moving westward, passing through Washington (Virginia), Sperryville, and Woodville, and enjoying the "beautiful mountanous [*sic*] country." Units in transit provided Wampler an opportunity to be reunited with old Maryland friends. He quickly found Capt. Patrick Henry Fitzhugh of the 26th Virginia from Baltimore, and the two in turn were warmly embraced by Brig. Gen. George H. "Maryland" Steuart Jr., recently appointed to command a brigade comprised of regiments from both sides of the Potomac. It is likely that Steuart and Wampler had been boyhood chums. Arriving at Culpeper Court House on March 14, Wampler became the house guest of a Captain Thomas and his family, with whom he attended church and played cards with the ladies. The march continued over the next several days, until the regiment went into bivouac two miles north of Orange Court House at a location dubbed Camp Taylor. Wampler was pleased when Eppa Hunton rejoined the regiment on March 21, hoping he had recovered sufficiently to remain for the duration of the conflict.

The 8th Virginia stayed at Camp Taylor until April 6, resuming the routine established at Centreville. Drill three times a day and dress parades helped restore military order and discipline. The Americus Hutchison matter was concluded. The company commander swore in five recruits, although three of them subsequently deserted. Brig. Gen. George E. Pickett was introduced to the brigade as its new commander, replacing Cocke, who had taken his own life. On the morning they broke camp, the foppish general conducted his first inspection of the troops.[114]

Two and a half weeks at Camp Taylor provided indelible memories for Wampler, some good, others not so good. He became involved in an unfortunate transaction with the Kees brothers, James and Robert. Wampler was offering his own gray horse for $250 cash and was persuaded by the Keeses to sell two mounts for them as well. Three days later, two men came to camp in search of the brothers for horse stealing. Wampler reimbursed the rightful owners and sent out the guard to arrest the thieves. Only James Kees was apprehended, and the next week he escaped from the brigade guardhouse, never to be seen again by the 8th Virginia. Fortunately, Wampler had enough money remaining to send one hundred dollars home to Kate via C. H. Nourse, who was passing through on the cars for Richmond. When the baggage finally caught up with the regiment, Wampler found that his map chest and two pairs of boots had been burned. Before departing Camp Taylor, someone also stole his revolver. All of these worries must have been more than offset in his own mind, however, by word that he had been commissioned a captain in the Confederate army's Corps of Engineers and ordered to report to General Beauregard for duty with the Army of the Mississippi.

Without the actual orders in hand, however, it was premature for Wampler to leave the 8th Virginia. The regiment was headed for Richmond, and Wampler continued along with it. Directed to strike tents and pack up, the soldiers were issued ammunition for the movement to Germanna ford across the Rapidan River. Moving out at midday, the soldiers tramped until 2:00 in the morning, covering sixteen miles and then, tired and hungry, lay down beside the road without blankets and shivered until dawn. The march continued for three more days until they reached Louisa Court House. Snow, hail, and cold rain contributed to the discomfort, making the roadway nearly impassable. Eppa Hunton remembered that "the roads were worse than I ever saw them."[115] Sleeping on the wet ground, Wampler's feet were frostbitten one night, causing him intense pain when he attempted to walk the next day. Once camped at Louisa, Wampler obtained a certificate of disability from General Longstreet, his division commander. Waiting at the home of Mrs. Bowen for the baggage to catch up, Wampler was reminded by the looks and manners of her little girl of his own daughter Annie.[116]

When the regiment finally started for Richmond, Wampler and Lieutenant Griffith rode the artillery train, which took over eight hours to travel a distance of 45 miles. They booked rooms at the Monument Hotel, and Wampler began preparing for his transfer to the West by purchasing new boots ($18), a trunk ($12), and a cap ($10.50). He also spent an afternoon with Eugenia Kephart from Belmont and entrusted a friend with another $100 to take to Kate. Finally, on behalf of the company officers, Griffith presented the departing commander with a non-regulation naval officer's sword, manufactured in Germany and smuggled through the blockade from England, presumably the only obtainable blade they could afford.

On April 15, Wampler finally left Company H, 8th Virginia Infantry, the unit he had recruited into service, organized as a fighting force, led in battle at Bull Run, commanded at the Burnt Bridge during the Ball's Bluff encounter, and trained and disciplined on the plains of Centreville over the long, cold winter. Despite his elation over receiving a commission as an engineer officer, he was undoubtedly saddened to leave the companionship of so many friends with whom he had formed strong bonds during nine months of service together. The regiment continued southeast to Lebanon Church to fight McClellan's Army of the Potomac in the Peninsula Campaign. The unit would later earn the sobriquet "Bloody Eighth" for its participation in the charge up Cemetery Ridge under the same George Pickett they had first met on the road to Richmond. Three years later, after another disastrous defeat at Sayler's Creek on April 6, 1865, there were but eleven surviving members of the regiment to be paroled at Appomattox. Of these, only three had fought at First Manassas.[117]

Wampler embarked on the long trip to Corinth, Mississippi, near a church across the state line in Tennessee, with the name suddenly on everyone's lips: Shiloh. Wampler got off the train in mid-afternoon at Lynchburg to buy an atlas so he would know exactly where he was headed. The rats kept him up most of the night at the Piedmont Hotel. The journey continued the next day, stopping at Wytheville for dinner and switching cars at Bristol. While enjoying breakfast the following morning in Knoxville, Tennessee, he was pleased to encounter Henry B. Latrobe, his friend serving as captain in the 3rd Maryland Artillery. By changing trains in Atlanta on Good Friday, Wampler had an opportunity to attend church, and have his coat and pants fixed, before continuing on to Montgomery, where he called on Mattie, another of the Kephart sisters. He escorted her to the Episcopal Church for Easter services and then spent the evening socializing with her.

Easter Monday found Wampler on his way to Mobile, first by the cars, then twenty miles by boat, gallantly escorting a lady from Virginia and her daughter. Before departing the next day, he had bought a saddle for $30 and hired a mulatto (or "Yellow Boy," as Wampler referred to him) for $10, along with calling on Miss Mary Lou Horton. The journey to Corinth took 43 hours in cars laden with troops of the 10th and 19th South Carolina, also being transferred to the West. The train rolled slowly northward through Mississippi fields planted with cotton and corn. Wampler kept Mrs. Tate in his protection and, upon arrival at Corinth on April 25, delivered her safely to her husband, Lt. J. B. Tate of the 51st Tennessee.[118]

After reporting to General Beauregard the following day, Wampler's first thought was to write to Colonel Hunton and Lieutenant Matthews back in the 8th Virginia. Wampler would serve with distinction as a Confederate engineer, but, like so many other officers before and since, the experience of command, of being responsible for the care and welfare of his men and leading them in times of danger, was one that he would never forget and would periodically miss. As a soldier, he would always be a member of the 8th Virginia Infantry.

Now new challenges lay before him, but they would not for long blot from his mind the friendships forged in his old regiment, or allow him to forget the wife and children left defenseless on the home front in Loudoun County. Indeed, while Captain Wampler was facing the trials and tribulations of being a soldier, his wife was encountering a different set of problems engendered by the war.

CHAPTER FIVE

➤➤➤

War on the Home Front

> May 12th/63. Married 11 years today. How time flies, & how many changes have taken place since then. War with all its horrors is upon us. We who were quietly at home had to be invaded by the band of Northern hirelings. Was ever such an unjust & cruel war, & oh how terribly the vandals have made us suffer. But we needed affliction, ere we forgot our Maker, and he wanted to lead us back to him. "For whom the Lord loves he chastens." Oh that as a People, & Nation we may bless, & praise him for our many, & great victories. And May We soon end this horrid strife, & permit our loved to return to anxious waiting hearts.

This passage from the "private journal" of Kate Wampler reflects her outlook on the world in which Morris left her, when he rode back to his duties as an infantry commander and, later, as a Confederate engineer.[1] Her thoughts repeatedly returned to her husband, as evidenced by extant writings from that time.

As bad as her situation often seemed, Kate realized that things would have been even worse for Morris, as a male southern sympathizer, had he remained in Loudoun County. At the same time, she prayed daily for his safety, wherever he might be, for it took weeks for her to learn of changes in his circumstances and location. To Kate, the dangers confronting Morris, thankfully mostly unknown to her, somehow seemed less threatening than the vulnerability of her family to the uncertainties of Loudoun County in the 1860s.

Despite his leaving her with their five children and his newly widowed mother with two more youngsters, Kate did not blame her husband for the separation. In her view the South had been violated, and Kate would have thought less of him had he not joined in the fight to protect the fledgling nation. Even if he had remained in Loudoun County, Wampler would not have escaped the war—it would only have affected him differently. He would likely either have been drawn into serving as a southern partisan or been arrested by the Federals as a suspected guerrilla and incarcerated in Old Capitol Prison in Washington, or possibly both. Indeed, Kate challenged the patriotism of men who called themselves southerners, yet stayed behind when the Confederate army pulled out. She had tended their home while Morris was away engineering for the Coast Survey and the railroads, and she could continue to hold the family together while he sacrificed for their new nation.

Kate's outpouring of emotion also reflects her abiding faith in God. She was painfully aware of the ability of people to inflict cruelty upon one another. A just Maker could not allow these sins to go unpunished. Once the God-fearing people of the South (among whom, as a daughter of Louisiana, Kate included herself) returned to the Lord, she believed, He would set aside their travails, enabling families to be reunited.

MAVIN'S MILL

The common Southern homestead during the Civil War was a plain, white-washed, two-story building constructed of timber and embraced by a long wraparound porch to shelter its walls and occupants from the sun. In the back stood servants' quarters, smoke- or meathouse, chicken hutches and animal pens, and an outhouse. Beyond were a vegetable garden and flower beds. The compound was presided over by a mistress, assisted by a trusted black "mammy," who oversaw the care and activities of the children.[2]

The Wamplers and their home on Goose Creek resembled this stereo-typical portrait of a yeoman family.[3] Kate managed the household, assisted by the faithful, one-eyed "Aunt" Annie. The house and its outbuildings resembled those in the standard caricature. Kate's immediate family (with their ages at the war's midpoint in 1863) consisted of Tommy (10), Kate (8), Annie (6), Julia (5), and Lena (2). Lena, or "Morrie" as she was known in later childhood, had arrived in 1861, during the hectic days preceding the war, the only Wampler born in Loudoun County. The extended family encompassed Ann B. Mavin, Morris's mother, who owned the homestead, and the two children by her second husband, Bobby and Anna. The large number of occupants lessened the likelihood of the residence being left unattended, an easy prey for marauders and scavengers.

The house rested in a grove of trees on seventy acres one mile west of the Belmont plantation home that had served as Margaret Mercer's academy, across Goose Creek at the bottom of a long, wooded ridge. The dwelling was sited on a slight elevation, a hundred yards back from Mavin's Mill. Surrounded by trees, the house's timbers had been sawed at the mill. Beside it was a small graveyard containing the mortal remains of the Cooke family, its earlier owners.[4]

Mavin's Mill was located about a mile south of the Alexandria–Leesburg Pike at a point on Goose Creek known as the lower ford. Old Ox Road extended eastward toward Alexandria. Transit across the creek was possible by means of boat, passing over the mill dam, or fording when the water was low. This was a well-known crossing, where George Washington had ferried over Goose Creek in March of 1771.[5]

William Mavin had immigrated from Northumberland County, England, in 1830, along with a brother and two sisters. They acquired the mill from the Cookes, who had purchased it from the family of John Hough, the original owner who petitioned the county court for its construction in 1759. Thus the structure was known successively by various names—Hough's Mill, Cooke's Mill, and, finally, Mavin's (often misspelled "Marvin's") Mill. In addition to the mill itself and the keeper's house, the waterside complex included a dam, guard gate, and mill race (to protect against a freshet), which had been adapted to serve as a passageway for boats on the Goose Creek Canal.

Just upstream from Mavin's Mill were the mouth of Sycolin Creek and the tall redstone piers for the bridge of the Alexandria, Loudoun & Hampshire Railroad, which was burned to deter the Federals from invading Loudoun County. Downstream, between the piers and the Burnt Bridge of the Leesburg–Alexandria Pike, the waters of the Tuscarora entered Goose Creek. Two miles farther north, Goose Creek emptied into the Potomac River at Edwards Ferry, soon to attain prominence as a crossing point for Federal forces.

Thus, when Wampler hurried back to Centreville with Confederate troops on March 7, 1862, he left his family in a rural setting, four miles southeast of Leesburg, the nearest locus for medical, mercantile, and mail services. The Wampler family resided at a prominent alternate crossing point to the turnpike and railroad bridges over Goose Creek, destroyed by southern sympathizers as tensions mounted in June 1861. While it was a prime vantage point to observe the passage of troops through eastern Loudoun County, Mavin's Mill was also a dangerous place for a woman to raise a family during a civil war. Moreover, the only males in the household were her son and her husband's half-brother, just 14 years old in 1863.

MOVEMENT OF ARMIES ACROSS LOUDOUN COUNTY

The 1860 census reported Loudoun County to have a population of almost 22,000 persons, including roughly 1,250 free blacks and 5,500 chattel owned by 670 slaveholders.[6] Fewer than 1,500 people resided in Leesburg, the county seat. The north county was pro-Union in sentiment, influenced by the Quaker contingent at Waterford and the sizable German population around Lovettsville, consisting mainly of small farmers who had emigrated from Pennsylvania. Neither faction held slaves. In contrast, the southern and eastern parts of the county contained large tracts of land worked by slaves.[7] The vote in favor of secession by approximately two to one reflected the division in sentiment throughout the area.

Loudoun residents opposed to secession crossed the Potomac to enlist in Federal units such as William Maulsby's Potomac Home Brigade and Henry Cole's Battalion of Maryland Cavalry. Some were driven to this decision by harassment and intimidation from Loudoun neighbors for being anti-secessionist.[8] At the same time, Marylanders disappointed by their state's retention in the Union moved in the opposite direction to join Eppa Hunton's 8th Virginia Infantry, Montgomery Corse's 17th Virginia Infantry, Turner Ashby's 7th Virginia Cavalry, or eventually Elijah White's 35th Cavalry and the 43rd Battalion, Virginia Partisan Rangers, of John Singleton Mosby.

Kate Wampler fretted over the treacherous position in which southern sympathizers were caught in Loudoun County. Located across the Potomac from Maryland, heavily guarded by Yankee pickets, and east of the foothills which Federal forces could never completely control, Loudoun residents were continually beset by bands of soldiers wearing both blue and gray, as organized units and irregulars, on horse and by foot.

The first successful invasion of Loudoun County began on February 24, 1862, when Col. John W. Geary crossed the Potomac at Harper's Ferry in command of the 28th Pennsylvania Infantry, reinforced by Michigan cavalry and two batteries. The citizenry in and around Leesburg was quickly informed of the rules of martial law imposed by the Federals. Shortage of paper had forced the local newspaper, the *Democratic Mirror,* to cease publication on January 15. In its place, on March 12, for a single edition only, appeared the *Advance Guard.* The Federal provost marshal declared a 9:00 P.M. curfew, forbade alcoholic beverages in town, and required residents to maintain clean streets. The Stars and Stripes were to be respected, and all U.S. property in private possession was to be turned in to the proper authorities. Permits were required to leave town; violators risked arrest and punishment. By June, two companies of cavalry, calling themselves the Loudoun Rangers, were being organized by Samuel Means, among the first Federal units recruited in Virginia.

Kate surely knew of these matters, which must have been perceived as threatening to the household of a secessionist officer. With her husband serving in the Confederate army in the West and the Yankees in nominal control of Leesburg and its environs, Kate was isolated behind Federal lines from March until September of 1862, when the Army of Northern Virginia returned to Loudoun County, fresh from victory at Second Manassas. Marching north from Bull Run, Rebel troops passed along the Alexandria Pike, close enough to Mavin's Mill for Kate to receive a smile from Maj. Gen. Thomas J. "Stonewall" Jackson that she would never forget. Her loyalty to the Southern cause could not have blinded Kate to the dirty and ragged look of many of the soldiers who trudged up the pike, an appearance commented upon by other observers of Gen. Robert E. Lee's army at this time.[9]

By late October, the Federal Army of the Potomac returned to Virginia from Antietam in belated pursuit of Lee's forces. They were followed across Loudoun County in November by Maj. Gen. Henry W. Slocum's Twelfth Corps, on its way to reinforce Maj. Gen. Ambrose Burnside at Fredericksburg.

Feeding all these troops depleted the region's agricultural stores. When assigned to Leesburg the previous December, Brig. Gen. D. H. Hill had observed, "This is a most lovely & wealthy county and the people are as kind as they can be."[10] Upon being ordered to withdraw the following March, he lamented, "We have abandoned the richest part of Virginia to the enemy."[11] One of Lee's prime reasons for entering the North through Loudoun in September had been its bountiful resources for his men and their horses. He wrote President Jefferson Davis, "I therefore determined . . . to draw the troops into Loudoun, where forage and some provisions can be obtained."[12] Within two months' time, from early September into November, two armies had restocked their larders from Loudoun's harvest.

Across the South the war was taking a heavy toll on women trying to provide for their families. By the following spring, there was precious little left for residents dependent for subsistence on Loudoun's farms. In late May, Kate encountered Dr. William B. Day, one of the few physicians remaining in the area. "[He] told me the Yankees made daily visits to Drainesville [sic] & are acting terribly. He thinks if the Southern Army does not come soon, some of the women & children must starve. Merciful Father avert such a fate. Surely our Army will come & not let such a fate happen to the border people, after their having shared all they had with them so nobly. . . . What times we live in. Dr. D[ay] did not know me. I am so thin & changed. This war changes me."[13] Kate's prayer was answered by the return of an army, but not the one for which she had petitioned.

March to Gettysburg

On June 3, 1863, a month after their invigorating victory at Chancellorsville, the men of Lee's Army of Northern Virginia began pulling out of the Fredericksburg area, initiating a flow northward by both the Federal and Confederate armies that would reach a climax one month later at Gettysburg. While Lee took a route west of the Blue Ridge, Maj. Gen. Joseph Hooker, commanding the Army of the Potomac, moved along a parallel axis east of the mountain range in order to shield the capital at Washington from the invaders. Maj. Gen. Oliver O. Howard's Eleventh Corps entered Loudoun County on June 17, the vanguard of over ninety thousand blueclad soldiers who would traverse the area over the following ten days, the largest body of troops to pass through Loudoun during the war.[14] Howard's corps pitched camp on Goose Creek opposite Mavin's Mill.

Kate got ready that afternoon, intending to go into Leesburg with her two oldest daughters, "But when I got as far as Mrs Moffetts, Mother [Ann Mavin] ran up to tell me there was a large force of Yankees camped in the neighborhood so I returned."[15] She soon learned they were Howard's men, and that they had pitched their round Sibley tents downstream at the Burnt Bridge and upstream near the log dam at Trappe Rock. "Oh what a sight the fields were near us, thousands & thousands of them camped, the dust several inches deep, not a sign of vegetation left, & dead mules to scent the once pure air."[16] Kate understood the Federals to be on their way to cut off Jubal Early's advance into Pennsylvania, not yet recognized by her as the lead element for the entire Army of Northern Virginia.[17] "Oh these are dreadful times. I am so glad dear M[orris] is not here. I pray he may be kept thro' all dangers safe from harm."[18]

The Eleventh Corps had marched from Centreville in a single day. The soldiers arrived on blistered feet, hot, tired, and dusty. Yet, Kate was pleasantly surprised at their demeanor. Some took supper from her, while others helped themselves to milk and butter, and she was pleased that they all paid for what they received. "They certainly were the best behaved Yankee troops

I've ever seen," she wrote, a commentary on soldiers under unit discipline versus the stragglers and marauders she encountered all too often.[19]

Compensating for handouts from a farmer or at a miller's house did not mean that the invaders paid for everything. Eleventh Corps soldiers bragged about "snatching" a sheep, chicken, or hog, and amused each other with accounts of mothers pleading not to take the food out of their children's mouths.[20] The northerners took thirteen head of cattle at Belmont, leaving behind only the tough meat on the bones of an old blind cow. Other farmers in the vicinity suffered similar losses. Picking cherries and blackberries and collecting honey further supplemented the basic rations on which the bluecoats had subsisted over the winter. With the arrival of the Federals came rain, the first in five or six weeks. It poured down on June 18 and 19, settling the dusty roads for the marchers and rekindling the hopes of local residents that a crop of potatoes and corn might yet be harvested. In late June, the best corn stood only knee high in the fields.[21]

As units arrived, Yankee officers commandeered quarters throughout the local area. Mattie Kephart informed Kate that Brig. Gen. Solomon Meredith, commander of 1st Brigade, 1st Division of Maj. Gen. John Reynolds's First Corps, and his staff were taking their meals at the Belmont plantation house. Kate's walk into Leesburg on June 23 was delayed at another general's headquarters (his identity unknown to her), where she was asked to take a sealed note to General Slocum at Williamson's hotel. Kate was surprised to find the Yankee "a perfect gentleman," and the town as quiet as if there were no soldiers present. She soon discovered a white soldier and a black man tied by their arms to the courthouse railing for racing through the streets, a sobering lesson for Slocum's troops. Mrs. Williamson insisted that Kate spend the night, and so when the general's adjutant offered her an overnight pass, she could not refuse.[22]

The war was never far from anyone's thoughts. Eleventh Corps soldiers slept wearing accouterments during their first couple nights in Loudoun County, unsure of whether the enemy might strike. The threat of bushwackers helped keep Union pickets alert. The sounds of artillery fire rolled down from the foothills of Aldie and Middleburg, Snickers Gap, and Thoroughfare Gap as opposing cavalries skirmished, heard clearly and noted by both the soldiers in blue and by Kate.

On June 24, Union engineers, directed by Brig. Gen. Henry W. Benham, laid a pontoon bridge 1,450 feet across the Potomac at Edwards Ferry, just north of where Goose Creek empties into the river. Another temporary bridge was installed across Goose Creek at Kephart's Mill, a half mile from the river, to facilitate passage of the Army of the Potomac. On June 25, a second pontoon bridge was set in place across the Potomac to the south of Goose Creek. In three days, 77,000 infantry and 15,000 cavalry, plus accompanying artillery and supply trains—a column estimated to be over 80 miles in length—flowed through eastern Loudoun County and over the temporary bridging.[23] Elements of the First, Second, Third, Fifth, Sixth, Eleventh, and Twelfth Corps, plus much of the cavalry and supply trains, passed within a mile of Mavin's Mill, either on the Alexandria Pike from Dranesville or moving northward from Gum Springs to Edwards Ferry. By June 28, Loudoun was clear of all units displaying the Stars and Stripes.

The Wampler family witnessed the drama of the Army of the Potomac on the march. Kate learned that Howard's men had departed Goose Creek on June 25, when her black servant, "Aunt" Annie, took Tommy to the campsite and returned disappointed that other scavengers had already taken everything of value that the Yankees had not burned. The following night, two Federal cavalrymen rode up and asked directions to the crossing, the lead element of troops of northern horsemen who would pass by on their way to Edwards Ferry. Kate marked her thirtieth birthday on June 27 by locking up the old reliable horse, Sally, to protect her from troopers who proceeded to take the geese and other possessions from the mill. Had a Federal officer not interceded one evening, Kate was convinced, they would have broken into the meathouse and taken the nag as well.[24]

Once they were gone, Kate walked down to see yet another temporary bridge the Yankees had built over Goose Creek, this one where the Alexandria–Leesburg pike was interrupted at the Burnt Bridge. The new structure had been constructed partly from timbers cut at Mavin's Mill. She could not help but admire it. That same day, the first after the Federals deserted Loudoun County, she observed soldiers of the 6th Virginia Cavalry, again patrolling the pike, apprehending enemy stragglers.[25]

BORDER WARFARE

All along the line dividing northern and southern states, fighting by irregulars posed a constant danger for civilian populations. The most famous Confederate in this type of warfare, the "Gray Ghost," John S. Mosby, operated in a wide swath across northern Virginia that included Loudoun County. "Breaking communications is the chief work for a partisan—it defeats plans and starts confusion by destroying supplies, thus diminishing the offensive strength of an army," he wrote.[26] To accomplish his objective, Mosby seldom operated as a unified force, preferring to divide his command into smaller detachments of fewer men, distributing uncertainty amidst the enemy and inflicting the greatest psychological impact on the Federal occupation force and the local citizenry.

While soldiers in Regular Army units customarily wore blue or gray, outfits operating independently were known to don the uniforms of their opposite number. One Federal unit created especially to gather intelligence about Confederate operations, the Jessie Scouts, was notorious for pretending to be southerners. At the same time, the famous Black Horse riders of Company H, 4th Virginia Cavalry, wore blue overcoats confiscated from Union soldiers.[27] So when Kate and the other residents of Loudoun County were approached by an individual or a small band of soldiers whom they did not recognize, their allegiance could not be identified with certainty based upon the uniforms on their backs.

Rich in agriculture, Loudoun County offered a plentiful breadbasket for both sides. The temptation of foraging on the bountiful Quaker and German farms in the Unionist north county was often irresistible for Confederate raiders. A notable example occurred in June 1864, when Mosby's men sought to gather wagonloads of grain there, only to be challenged by the Loudoun Rangers. Elijah V. "Lije" White's 35th Virginia Cavalry was sent into Loudoun in the fall of that year to rustle up beef for the Confederate army. The pro-slavery leanings of the remainder of Loudoun County justified to Northern brigands their appropriating anything of value from its residents. Kate and her neighbors were continually preyed upon by hungry stragglers, from both armies, looking for a chicken, a hog, or a bag of grain from the mill. Her ire was heightened when soldiers used her own wood to roast the family's chickens in the yard.

Sometimes it was not hunger but vindictiveness that motivated the intruders. At one point, a company of Yankee engineers opened the flood gate, setting the mill wheel racing. Had Tommy not seen it and informed his grandmother, who exhorted them to close the gate, the mill's mechanism would have caught fire. On another occasion, Kate's meathouse was broken into and its contents dumped into the mill race. She experienced an even more disturbing loss of irreplaceable family volumes from Louisiana, at a time when books were so scarce in some parts of the South that children had to bring their own in order to learn at school.[28] A ruffian named Charles Webster entered the Wampler house and helped himself to her library. Considered the "drillmaster" of Means's Loudoun Rangers, Webster was infamous among Southern sympathizers for ruthlessly killing an 8th Virginia officer engaged in recruiting earlier in 1862, for which Webster was subsequently tried and hanged in Richmond.[29] Webster completed his looting and departed with the threat that he would return to evict Kate and her children from their home. Determined not to betray her grief, Kate maintained her composure, silently reminding herself that brave Southern soldiers were facing far greater peril. But she was devastated by the experience and her losses.[30] Kate subsequently received word that some of the books had been given to a young lady, others were in the possession of a Northern riverboat pilot, and another portion had found its way into the hands of a Leesburg family. It is doubtful, however, that she ever recovered a single volume.

It was not uncommon to bring the family cow into the house to preserve the children's source of milk. Horses were also constantly in jeopardy. Kate's closest call with Sally occurred in the wake of Gettysburg, when Yankee cavalry suddenly entered Leesburg one Monday as she was visiting Mrs. Armistead Mott, the doctor's wife, in their home that now serves as the Laurel Brigade Inn. To Kate's astonishment, a soldier rode up and began taking Sally out of the Mott stable, exclaiming that he had orders to round up all the horses in town. Despite Kate's pleas and efforts to block his way, the trooper quickly disappeared with his prize. Throwing a shawl over her head for protection from the rain, Kate ran through the town's muddy streets, searching for help. A Federal colonel and then a major were either unable or unwilling to intercede. At last, she was directed to the commanding officer, who, upon being told by a trusted resident that the "pony" was unfit for military service, ordered it returned. "Miss Bettie Williamson told me she thought I was not afraid of the whole Yankee Army. I did not know I had so much spirit 'till this war. . . . What w'd dear M[orris] have thought c'd he have seen me facing the Yanks today."[31] While Kate's encounter was undoubtedly spirited, gender and class afforded Southern women significant protection in their confrontations with the hated Northern invaders.[32]

Traffic back and forth across the Potomac between Loudoun County and Montgomery County, Maryland, had been common before the war. Lije White had been born and raised in Poolesville, Maryland, and moved into Virginia only after purchasing farmland along the Potomac in 1856. White's Company B bore the nickname "Chiswell's Maryland Exiles," while his Company D was recruited from both Maryland and Virginia. A group of forty Southern sympathizers from around Poolesville had crossed the Potomac in August 1862, stopping next door to Mavin's Mill at Belmont, where they dried their clothes and enjoyed breakfast served by the Kepharts, before continuing into the mountains to join up with White's Comanches.[33] Being married to a Marylander, having lived in Baltimore before the war, and trying to maintain a household within walking distance of the Potomac, Kate was well aware of the jockeying across the river and efforts to rally Marylanders with Southern sympathies to their cause. Her personal feelings were sufficiently known by February 1865 that Lt. Edward Chiswell chose Mavin's Mill as the assembly point for twenty-two troopers from the Old Line State about 8:00 one night, before crossing the frozen Potomac by foot and surprising the 1st Delaware Cavalry camped near Edwards Ferry.[34] As was often the practice, upon returning, the Confederate raiders may well have shared their spoils with Loudoun residents confronting dire shortages in the war's closing months.

Mavin Mill's location just off the Alexandria–Leesburg Turnpike provided Kate an ideal vantage point to observe military units passing back and forth, heading toward Dranesville, ten miles to the east, or westward to Leesburg and the Blue Ridge Mountains beyond, which separated Loudoun County from the Shenandoah Valley. Lije White and his men, for example, swam their horses across Goose Creek beside the Burnt Bridge on their way down the pike to scout in Fairfax County in late February 1862. When Mosby led his first company of Rangers into Maryland in June 1863 for a raid of Seneca Mill, he returned to his base of operations via the Alexandria–Leesburg Turnpike right past Mavin's Mill.[35]

Anyone coming down the pike, military or civilian, might have information about the war to share with Kate. The news was not always accurate, however. Passed by word of mouth to individuals holding similar political views, desired outcomes sometimes took the place of fact in the telling. Furthermore, accurate or not, the news was not always initially accepted as true, especially when it ran counter to one's hopes or expectations. Kate's wartime experiences in Loudoun County provide several sharp illustrations of the distinction between reality and hope.

The Confederate cause received a double blow in early May 1863, when two of its best-known generals died at the hands of other southerners. The more devastating was the death of "Stonewall" Jackson as a consequence of being fired upon by fellow soldiers during the Battle of Chancellorsville. Surprisingly disturbing to the South, however, in light of his uneven military career, was the assassination of Maj. Gen. Earl Van Dorn by the husband of a woman whom the philandering cavalryman had allegedly seduced.

Lacking firsthand information, rumor, sometimes wildly inaccurate, frequently held sway in the minds of women isolated during the war.[36] Kate heard reports of both deaths within seven to ten days of their occurrence. On receiving two separate accounts of Jackson's death, she prayed they were false and that he was still alive, remembering his smile when she was introduced to him the preceding year. It was only a week later, when shown the Richmond newspaper accounts of his funeral procession, that she accepted the news as fact. Kate had known the Van Dorns in Baton Rouge, and, while she accepted the reports of the general's character flaws, she strongly felt that the new nation should come first and private grievances set aside until the crisis passed. Indeed, she wanted to believe the rumor, conceived shortly after Van Dorn's death, that the attacker had acted as an agent of the government in Washington. She wished that Morris (who had served with Van Dorn in the West) was with her to explain the tragedy.[37]

News from a firsthand participant could contain inaccuracies as well. George Washington Hummer was the enlisted aide to Col. Eppa Hunton at Gettysburg. Hunton was wounded in the leg in Pickett's charge up Cemetery Ridge and escorted to safety by Hummer, who led the colonel's horse back to Confederate lines. Five days later, Hummer swam the Tuscarora below Mavin's Mill and waited overnight at Kate's house for the swollen waters of Goose Creek to subside, before completing the trip to his home near present-day Sterling. He gave her an account of the battle as he knew it. Hummer recounted the decimation of the 8th Virginia by stating that only ten men had survived the battle unscathed. He also reported that two days later, Lee lured the Federals out of their defenses and took thirty thousand prisoners. A different source soon told Kate that the prisoner count was really forty thousand.[38]

The true story became known to Loudoun County as the dead and wounded not buried or captured in Pennsylvania were returned home. Gettysburg was, in Kate's words, "a terrible affair," as was the surrender at Vicksburg, which was made all the more devastating by earlier reports that it, too, was a Confederate victory. Kate had heard in late May, and again in early June, that Southern troops had "whipped the Yankees gloriously on the Mississippi," killing General Grant.[39] It was not coincidental, perhaps, that a few weeks later Kate first heard a public prayer for President Jefferson Davis, offered in Leesburg by pastor Walter Williams, causing "a thrill" to pass through her.[40]

The military operations most evident to Kate, of course, were those partisan activities closest to Mavin's Mill. Two prime examples were the encounter at Miskell's Farm and the clash near Belmont. Mosby led his men to Dranesville on March 31, 1863, in search of several scattered Yankee outposts in the vicinity, only to discover that the Federal forces had pulled back to more defensible positions. Turning west toward Leesburg, Mosby and his men stopped for the night at a farm five miles due east of Mavin's Mill. Early the next morning, the partisans were awakened by Dick Moran, a comrade who had stayed behind to spend the night with a friend, alerting them that a sizable force of enemy cavalry was on their trail not far away. The outnumbered Confederates nevertheless mounted and charged into the blueclad troopers as they entered the barnyard, accomplishing by surprise what could not have been done by sheer numbers alone. In a state of panic, the bluecoats broke and fled, chased down the Leesburg Pike by Mosby's horsemen.[41] Southern sympathizers in the area, Kate among them, took immense pleasure at the partisans turning the tables on the despised Yankees. When Moran was captured two months later and incarcerated in the Old Capitol Prison in Washington, Kate knew full well of his earlier role in sounding the alarm and reported that the northern press "boasted of having caught that Prince of bushwhackers Richard Moran."[42]

The second incident began the following February just across Goose Creek from Mavin's Mill on the fields of Belmont. Troopers from two Union regiments were camped there for the night, a portion of the 2nd Massachusetts Cavalry, commanded by Capt. J. Sewell Reed, and elements of the 16th New York Cavalry. The former patrol was guided by a deserter from Mosby's command named Charlie Binns, whom Mosby must surely have wanted to capture. The Rangers spent that same night at the Harrison farm, a couple miles up Goose Creek, and then laid an ambush the next day on the road network to the east of Belmont. The surprise of the attack was complete, routing the Federals and sending many fleeing back up the turnpike in the direction of Leesburg.[43] Kate knew the whole story, adding to her account the facets important to a mother trying to hold a household together in a land beset by raiders.

> Feb 22nd. Washingtons Birthday. The Yanks about 350 or 400 strong passed 2 nights in Leesburg, & this morning about 1 o'clock went to Belmont where they camped. Their first act was to take every piece of meat & the few herrings they had out of the meat house. They also broke the school childrens slates, took their books etc., fed away the hay, burnt the fencing, & did all the harm they c'd. Mrs K[ephart] was in M'd about 8 A.M. They left & after going a short distance divided, one set going the Farmwell road, & one set keeping the Pike. When near Palmers Major Moseby, who had been watching them while at Belmont & was ready for them fired into them & completely routed them, killing 22 among them Major Read who

had told Mr K[ephart] he intended to live at B[elmont] when the war was over, as he liked the place. They had a number wounded most of them supposed to be mortally. 82 were taken Prisoners, & over 100 horses were captured. We lost one a young man from near Upperville, Chappelier. We had only 3 wounded. 15 Yanks were seen in the River, which was coated with ice & drowned. I expect those that escaped will long remember Washington's Birthday 1864. For a wonder the creatures did not cross at our dam. Binns was with them, but the traitor escaped 'tho they suppose they captured his horse.[44]

As was often the case, the initial estimate of enemy casualties was inflated, for ten Federals were reported killed and seven wounded in the official report of the engagement, but the remainder of Kate's description held true.[45]

Leesburg was, of course, the nerve center of Loudoun County, as well as its collecting point for news, commerce, and travelers, military and civilian. When her family responsibilities permitted, Kate commuted the four miles to town and, at other times, learned what was going on there from neighbors and passersby on the pike. The threats posed by Mosby and White were magnified in the minds of many as tales of their exploits were retold and embellished. Kate later recalled with relish the nervousness of Federal soldiers deployed to hostile territory and in constant apprehension of surprise by the enemy.

In the spring of 1863, the Yankees being camped in L[eesburg] we had not heard for some weeks from our troops at the South so one morning the young ladies & myself started to a neighbors, a couple of miles off. We were finely mounted, one on an old bony horse, the other & myself on a little mule. I was riding behind, little cared we then for looks, a cart or an ox wagon being just as acceptable as any other mode of going. We did not know that Pickets had been placed on the road & much to our surprise we were halted & compelled to go several miles to the Town of L[eesburg] for a pass. It was drizzling & we certainly did not present a very enviable appearance as we rode up to the Provost Marshalls Office, & we were angry too at having to ride so far, on such a day. So we thought we'd give them some news. We rode to several of our friends but did not dismount, & told them to cheer up, their town w'd soon be rid of their unpleasant visitors, that White was near with a large force. All was said for the benefit of the soldiers who were patroling the streets. Little did we think how the idle words w'd bear fruit. That evening at dusk a Yankee officer rode up, & enquired of us the way to L. He had supplies for the troops there, was from Washington, but he did not get more than half way to Town before he met the troops, flying in great confusion, saying White was in pursuit. Their major, who was very fond of his toddy, had actually surrendered to his own men, & had left town without stopping to ascertain. Such demoralized troops you never saw. They left us 60 bushels of oats on the road, also several wagon loads of hard tack, which some of the poor cows in the neighborhood found indeed hard luck, as they died from an overdose of them.[46]

When Federal patrols and Confederate partisans were not fighting each other, they were often engaged in searching for Southern soldiers, and, in the case of the Federals, apprehending men of military age who appeared to be peaceful civilians by day but might be guerrillas at night. Once Mosby achieved success and became known, a series of enemy cavalry forays combed his area of operations, looking for Rangers.

Kate worried about men, mostly too young or too old for military service, taken by the Federals from neighboring homes, and she naturally empathized with their wives. Farmer William McPherson was fortunate to be released, along with his horse, the same day he was arrested. Neighbor Peter Adrain was not so lucky. George Kephart, the sixty-eight-year-old owner of Belmont, was mounted by northern troopers aboard a child's pony for the journey back to their camp in Maryland. His daughter Eugenia (known as "Genie") insisted that she be allowed to accompany him as far as the Potomac and persuaded Kate to come along to keep her company. The Yankees treated them politely, but it was, nonetheless, a sad parting on the riverbank. To everyone's surprise, Kephart was returned six days later. By 1864, dozens of Loudoun civilians were being detained as part of the Federal program to thwart Rebel conscription and deny succor to Mosby's raiders.

Nighttime searches by northern soldiers were by no means unknown to Kate. Perhaps surprisingly, distress over the invasion of her personal privacy is missing from her accounts of these incidents.[47] After the war, she recalled these intrusions and, with a touch of humor, one particular incident.

> Often & often have I gone over the house at night with them searching as they said "for Rebs." I early heard that the best way to get along with them was to put on a bold air, & tho often feeling as if exposure was certain, I never let them know. Oh how many of them used to sit in a large old fashioned cushioned chair, little thinking that underneath the cushion was grey cloth & other articles which w'd have caused them to turn us out, had they known it. They caused us to resort to many ingenious ways of eluding them & we were always ready with an answer, tho I assure you it was no easy matter to appear cool with 4 men with revolvers cocked & holding near your head, guarding you, & making you go with them & search the

house, but I must tell you an amusing incident . Ours was an old fashioned house. You went into the Cellar from a passage & the door of which looked like a closet, & one night to my great satisfaction one of the men who were searching the house for a Southern soldier who they insisted we had concealed went to the door & called out, "I've got him Cap," gave it a push, & went headlong down the cellar. I asked him if we w'd not have a light, as they had been ordering me to bring a light in so many places at once. I told them when searching in Dixie they ought to remember lights were scarce & they ought to bring their own.[48]

At the same time, the "peculiar institution" of slavery was readily shattered in areas like Loudoun County, where freedom in "Uncle Abe's" Union was within walking distance, and it was not difficult to find blue-uniformed soldiers offering protection. D. H. Hill had reported trouble with slaves running away from Leesburg in early 1862; at the same time, property owners in nearby Warrenton were forming night patrols to "keep the servants in order."[49] Could those blacks who remained behind be trusted not to reveal the location of hidden silver or the presence of a Southern partisan, who might be a family member? Despite the proximity of three Mosby Rangers in the yard one night in June 1863, Kate reported that a black family of six, including a four-week-old infant, departed their Loudoun home for the Federal lines.

Kate was caught up in a similar situation while spending a night at Belmont. The household was awakened by troopers from "Scott's 900," a New York cavalry unit camped nearby, trying to force their way into the meathouse. Mrs. Kephart, her daughter Genie, and Kate confronted them from a second-story hall window. As the officer in charge insisted on being admitted to the house, Genie hid her young brother, John, age fifteen. By the time the ladies had dressed and come downstairs, the house servant Jim had opened the kitchen door, allowing what seemed like forty soldiers to enter. The intruders searched the house "from garret to cellar," looking in every wardrobe and cupboard. They finally departed with a hired man, discovered in bed, and Jim, who had already packed his belongings and left in high spirits.[50]

OBTAINING THE ESSENTIALS OF LIFE

Regardless of their cost in food and feed, in spite of the threat posed by their presence, and oblivious to the extraordinary attention drawn to Loudoun County as a result of their activities, Southern partisans retained the allegiance of citizens sympathetic to the Confederacy. The resulting privation, devastation, and lawlessness that permeated the vacuum between Federal and Confederate authority has been characterized by one modern-day commentator as a "no-man's land."[51]

One of President Lincoln's first countermoves to the states seceding from the Union had been the announcement of a blockade to deny the import of manufactured goods, especially war munitions, and to prevent the South from acquiring wealth by exporting its cotton to Europe. The blockade was soon extended from Southern ports to its land borders. Families in northern Virginia initially looked for relief to friends and relatives in nearby population centers, such as Alexandria, Baltimore, Poolesville, and Point of Rocks, Maryland. It quickly became commonplace for women of all social strata to smuggle food, goods, and medicine into Virginia for their own families and others.[52]

Early in the war, on the occasions when Federal pickets were withdrawn from the Potomac, Kate and her friends crossed the river in search of items increasingly scarce at home. One easy means of concealing small articles, like medicines, was to sew them into clothing, although Kate employed other techniques as well. Her use of a hoop skirt to conceal larger items, such as hams, was by no means unique in the Southern blockade-running experience.[53]

> So one day a lady friend & several of the opposite sex & myself went in a leaky skiff across the Potomac. We went to a friends house but found that as the old Yankee Detective was left, the merchants did not dare to sell us anything. But what would woman's ingenuity do. We thought of the loved at home, & so determined to get what we c'd. Several kind friends called & they went into the stores & brought us things on their hoops, & we went home well loaded, our hoops doing all the carrying. I had 2 pairs of boys boots, a bolt of cotton, tea-writing paper, soda etc. & my friend was about as well supplied. But the worst part of the trip was crossing the canal as we had to walk over at the lock on a single plank but it was safely accomplished & tho I'm sure the Detective must have heard the squeak squeak of those boots. Got after a long walk to our boat. We again embarked & never was I more thankful to be on dear old Dixie shores but the smiles, happy looks which our supplies brought amply repaid all the trouble of getting them.[54]

Clothing, sugar, tea, flour, soap, and even writing paper were all in short supply in the South. Salt was sought by Kate, not merely as a condiment, but to preserve meat. Considered by many as a humanitarian necessity, the inclusion of medicine on the Federal contraband list was especially controversial, as it denied quinine, morphine, and other drugs vital to the Southern civilian populace, as well as to its military. Kate first looked to Doctors Day and Mott for medicine, and if that failed, like other southerners, she employed home remedies, often utilizing plants and herbs.

Obtaining shoes constituted the greatest challenge in the clothing department.[55] Those manufactured in the South were generally cut from a single pattern to fit either foot and delivered to the armed forces, not civilians.[56] Southern women were known to go to great lengths to make footwear from any hide, skin, or material available, to include wood, or by recycling leather initially used for another purpose, such as the tops of cavalry boots.[57] Again, Kate's experience paralleled that of her peers: "[S]hoes was the greatest trouble. I c'd make the tops out of cloth & then sometimes I c'd get them roughly soled. Once I had ridden a long distance to a tannery. I had gotten a few dollars in greenbacks (for by that time Confed money was useless) & made up. But alas the vile Yanks made a raid on the stores & my poor calf skin went & alas the little feet had to go cold & bare."[58]

Southern families readily turned to alternatives other than smuggling to meet their daily needs. Many folks had long before cut back to two meals a day. The clothing shortage, which became critical by the fall of 1863, led to increased borrowing and exchanging among friends.[59] Kate worked late many nights, mending and patching the children's clothes for wear again the next day. Merchants' shelves were almost bare, and the little that remained was offered at exorbitant prices, frequently quoted strictly in U.S. dollars, as Confederate issue became more worthless with each passing day. Kate was outraged. She prayed that the government in Richmond would take action against men who avoided military service to stay behind and protect their families and finances from suffering in the failing Confederate economy. "Alas for our cause if the Confederacy were made up of such Southerners," she lamented.[60] A demonstration of her devotion to the cause was Kate's investment of what must have been all of her modest savings in a two-thousand-dollar Confederate war bond in the spring of 1864.

As the conflict lengthened, the Federals drew the blockade tighter and tighter. At one point, reports were passed by word of mouth that Yankee soldiers were concentrating on Berlin (now Brunswick), Maryland, detaining river crossers and confiscating their parcels. Kate and several friends were prevented by a Federal "detective" from purchasing goods on one trip across the Potomac. Four Loudoun women, each in their twenties and all friends of Kate's—Bettie and Kate Ball, Ann Hempston, and Elizabeth White (Lije's wife)—were later arrested for smuggling across the Potomac and spent over a week in Old Capitol Prison before being released. The lifting of the blockade at Edwards Ferry in 1864 was one indication that Loudoun County was finally considered firmly under Federal control.

Kate continued to feel stymied, however, by the requirement to take "the horrid oath" of allegiance to the Union as a condition for being allowed to return to Virginia.[61] In their separate worlds, far apart, both Kate and Morris suffered terribly during the conflict. The justification, the common cause, the object of their mutual affection was the Confederacy. To take the oath would have been to repudiate the reason they had fought and endured.

EMOTIONAL REINFORCEMENT

These were dismal times for those left at home. The constant threat posed by soldiers and drifters, the deprivation of food, clothing, and household goods for young and old alike, the dread of casualties ignited by each fresh report of more fighting—all weighed heavily on the inhabitants of eastern Loudoun. Somehow the shared pain seemed to draw together those left at home, regardless of age or social position.

A fishing party came out from Leesburg and, before long, a half-dozen women had gathered with Kate at the creek. When one of the Divine girls from town fell in the water, she changed into a dress of Kate's at the house, while her clothes were being dried. Two neighbors came together to pick raspberries, or a group of women assembled, attired in their oldest threadbare costumes, to traipse through the fields in search of berries for supper. One such group stopped briefly to frolic with a black servant who was milking the McPherson's cow, their lightheartedness momentarily overcoming the gloom.

When not together at the water or in the fields or walking in pairs or threesomes to Leesburg in search of a letter or the latest news, the women along Goose Creek called upon one another, often spending the night, taking some children and leaving others behind with a relative or the help. Youngsters of similar ages welcomed the companionship, as did their mothers, an unstated reason being a mutual feeling of safety.

The stereotype of the Southern woman as plantation belle was belied by the grim realities of war. Survival required Southern women to be industrious, self-reliant, and resourceful. In the absence of their husbands and in place of their departed servants, those living in rural areas had little choice but to haul water, iron clothes, tend the garden, and mow hay for the few remaining animals. Confiscation of horses and wagons by both armies left the women cutting and carrying wood by hand. Kate was thankful to have a son to help her; others were not so fortunate.

Kate's only links to her husband were his letters, hurriedly scrawled in lead pencil. Outdated though they may have been by the time they arrived, their receipt put to rest, at least temporarily, Kate's unease over his well-being. The news conveyed was authoritative, and worth sharing with family and neighbors alike, just as one passed along a treasured newspaper. As the eldest child, the only son, and a lad approaching the acute sensitivity of puberty, Tommy seemed to need this connection with his father more than his sisters. On occasion, a separate note to the boy would be enclosed in one of Morris's letters to Kate.

When the conflict was young, prospects for success seemed bright, and their separation no more than a temporary one across the county line to the south. Kate and Morris could expect to hear from each other several times a month, thanks to the informal courier service provided by Loudoun residents visiting the troops camped at Centreville. Once he was transferred to the Western Theater and Loudoun County fell under Federal control, however, his letters were less regular, averaging no more than one a month, depending in part on movement by the western army.

Like so many other Confederate couples, maintaining an emotional bond with her husband depended upon the new national postal service.[62] Kate's access became even more limited when stranded behind Federal lines. She had to rely upon someone going to Richmond, or at least into an area controlled by the Confederates, to start a letter on its way to her husband. At the same time, Wampler addressed his correspondence to an intermediary known to both of them, who held it until arrival of a messenger from Kate. An individual at Culpeper Court House was used for this purpose in mid-1863. Loudoun's state senator, Charles B. Ball, was another go-between. As the armies moved north and south throughout Virginia, the contact person would change. Once Mosby's presence became established in northern Virginia, his troopers transported mail to and from Southern sympathizers residing in the border counties.[63] Kate may well have availed herself of this service.

It was not at all uncommon in nineteenth-century rural settings throughout the United States for a married woman to cherish one particular friendship of special intimacy and mutual trust with another female.[64] Kate's closest friend during the war years in Loudoun was Kate Ball, the daughter of Henry Ball, a prosperous landowner, who lived at Temple Hall on Limestone School road, north of Leesburg. Her siblings included a brother, Charles, who served as a captain in Company K, 6th Virginia Cavalry, until his death in the Wilderness in 1864, and two sisters, Sue and Bettie, also Kate Wampler's wartime confidantes.

Henry Ball's neighbor farther down the winding road, where it ends at the Potomac River, was Elijah White. Kate Wampler participated in the socializing between Mrs. Ball and Mrs. White, as they enjoyed each other's company during their husbands' absences, often calling upon one another while Kate was a guest at the Balls' residence.[65]

A third set of strong Southern supporters residing along the Limestone School road were the Balls' neighbors to the east, the family of Alfred Campbell Belt. These two families were drawn close together when Henry Ball and Campbell Belt were arrested by Federal authorities in March 1863. Neither man was in good health, yet despite numerous pleas for their release from family and friends, including Walter Williams, the sole clergyman remaining in Leesburg during the war, the Federals kept them incarcerated in Fort Delaware. The Balls attempted to stay in touch with their father via the telegraph office at Point of Rocks, Maryland, where Kate Wampler accompanied Kate Ball on one unsuccessful trip in late July 1863. In August, the two wives, along with other family members, visited the men in prison, after first being required to take the oath of allegiance to the United States. Kate Wampler was visiting at Temple Hall when the delegation returned and shared the news of their trip with those left at home. They had found Ball to be quite feeble, but Belt in better health, performing hospital duty for Rebel soldiers.[66] In September, the Confederate secretary of war signed an order confining two prominent Union sympathizers in Loudoun County until the two Southern hostages were released. Not long thereafter, Henry Ball and Campbell Belt were returned to their families.[67]

MOTHERING

The most poignant of Kate's experiences in her struggle to survive the chaos that encircled the family on Goose Creek involved her role as a mother of five. She could readily call the children to her to protect them physically

Col. Elijah White and party. Ann Hempston on the left, Bettie and Kate Ball
in the middle, and Mrs. Elizabeth White on Lije's left.
Northern Virginia Regional Park Authority.

from intrusions by troops, but guarding them against disease, a subtle scourge more deadly than bullets, was far more difficult. Sickness was regularly on her mind. Her own maladies were of little consequence. Scarlet fever and diphtheria attacked residents across the creek in 1863, and smallpox was prevalent in Leesburg the following winter. So when one of her youngsters was taken ill, Kate naturally feared the worst. Julia's fever, sore throat, and vomiting caused Kate to suspect scarlet fever, but when old Dr. Day answered her call for help by riding up the pike to examine the little girl, he made a less ominous diagnosis. Julia's upset stomach would not accept the castor oil at first, but Kate succeeded the next evening by mixing it with some toddy and peppermint. Another time, Kate was forced to treat Morrie's fever without a doctor's consultation and did so with oil and turpentine, holding the baby lovingly in her arms, when all else seemed to fail.

Physicians, like pastors, became scarce as the military's needs gradually stripped the civilian population of every able-bodied professional. Dr. Mott had followed after D. H. Hill when he left Leesburg, becoming chief surgeon on the general's staff by war's end, and Dr. Day eventually moved his practice to Richmond. Kate rode Sally through fields covered with deep March snow to carry Annie to Dr. Mott, when he was home in Leesburg on leave in 1864. The physician subscribed to the old school of medicine that promoted bleeding for certain ailments.[68] Fortunately for Annie, venesection was not a treatment recognized for her hearty cough, and, once again, Kate was reassured that her fears were excessive.

One of Kate's greatest scares took place one warm day in early June 1863. Kate and Sue Ball, along with Lucy McPherson, came to visit, and their hostess thought that the ladies would be free to chat if the party moved down to the creek bank, where the barefoot children could amuse themselves. Kate's three oldest girls—Katie, Annie, and Julia—all proceeded to wade in the water. When eight-year-old Katie came running out onto the shore, she stepped on a large water snake, obscured from view in the shade of a large sycamore tree. The snake bit Katie's leg, frightening her mother far more than the little girl. Kate immediately made a tourniquet above the bite with her garter, afterwards applying sour whiskey and salt to the incision. Upon hearing of the mishap, "Aunt" Annie encouraged Kate to kill a young chicken and bind it to the injured leg, which she also tried in desperation. While the therapeutic value of the sour mash applied externally is subject to speculation, Katie did benefit from the whiskey consumed for medicinal purposes and, lightheaded, enjoyed a sound night's sleep. Mr. McPherson killed the offending reptile, and the next day Bobby Mavin destroyed another large snake in a nearby field, along with two dozen eggs, and burned its nest. Other snakes had been found earlier in the spring, sunning in the garden and on the woodpile. Fortunately, the one that bit Katie proved to be nonpoisonous.[69]

Young Tommy attended Belmont school at the war's outbreak. In 1862, as enemy forays became more frequent, classes were dismissed prematurely at the cry, "The Yankees are coming," whereupon the children scattered. Consequently, Tommy never attended school beyond the third grade. Formal education behind him, one of his favorite pastimes was watering Federal horses. As a grandfather, long after the war, he looked back with pride on his deception in offering to lead a bluecoat cavalryman's steed down to Goose Creek for a drink and, once out of sight, riding off to deliver his charge to any southern partisan in need of a mount.[70]

Kate questioned her own patience with Tommy and the other children, but perhaps she had cause to be hasty and preoccupied in her thoughts. When at age four, Julia had grown too big for the crib, Kate dutifully turned to training the two-year-old to sleep there. "Mama fitchey me," Morrie cried when left alone in the crib, bringing tears to her mother's eyes. Over the many months since Morris had shared her bed, Kate had derived some measure of solace from sleeping alongside the baby. But now it was time to wean Morrie, despite the emotional need they shared for each other. Kate confided to her journal, "I missed the dear little creature, she is a great comfort."[71]

It was indeed a hostile environment in which to raise a family. Meeting the challenges of parenting without her husband was difficult for Kate, as it is for single mothers at any time. The multiple threats around her made Kate's responsibilities seem more daunting, however, and the unknown dangers confronting her husband so far away caused her to feel alone.

By war's end, Loudoun County had served as the battleground for forty-six skirmishes and military engagements of varying sizes.[72] Its citizens had suffered the hardships, deprivations, and despair attendant to extended residence amid opposing military forces. Once-prosperous farms had been depleted of livestock, outbuildings, wagons, and implements needed to restore agricultural production. Mills and manufacturing had been destroyed, railroad tracks and trestles torn up.[73] The county's social fabric was in tatters from the loss of 162 men who had died for the Southern cause (not counting those wounded in body and spirit), from the enmity generated among neighbors of differing political beliefs worth fighting over, and by the emancipation of one-quarter of its population who had been slaves in 1860. The turnpike past Mavin's Mill that conveyed Loudoun residents from Leesburg eastward, back toward the Union, had become deeply scarred with ruts and washes. Kate kept her family safe and together throughout this turmoil, surviving the war through her personal determination, ingenuity, indomitable spirit, and faith that some day, in some way, the fighting and destruction would end, and she, her husband and children could begin to rebuild the family life whose desolation paralleled that of Loudoun County.

CHAPTER SIX

>>>

The Route to Chief Engineer, Army of Tennessee

As the family of Kate and Morris Wampler grew with the addition of their fifth and final child in early 1861, their beloved South was also experiencing the pains of birth. The formation of new governmental entities south of the Potomac seemed to present sterling opportunities for Morris Wampler. He launched his personal campaign to serve in an engineering capacity in the new Confederacy on the day Jefferson Davis resigned from the United States Senate. In a letter dated February 21, 1861, addressed to Davis as "President Southern Confederacy," Wampler offered his services as *"Soldier* and *Engineer,"* specifically requesting a commission in the new army's engineer corps. He listed his usual references—Prof. Alexander Dallas Bache, Col. James D. Graham of the U.S. Topographical Engineers, Capt. Montgomery Meigs of the U.S. Corps of Engineers, and former Maj. Isaac I. Stevens. He also enclosed a letter of recommendation from Capt. Andrew A. Humphreys, serving with the U.S. Topographical Engineers.[1]

Wampler renewed his campaign in June, while working as a Virginia militia officer in support of the defenses being organized in northern Virginia. A follow-up letter to President Davis from Col. Eppa Hunton, endorsed by Maj. Norborne Berkeley, also of the 8th Virginia, recommended Wampler for a captaincy in the Confederate Corps of Engineers, characterizing him as a "valuable man." Hunton sent a similar recommendation to the newly appointed commander of Southern forces in northeastern Virginia, Brig. Gen. P. G. T. Beauregard. The adjutant general, Col. Thomas Jordan, replied on behalf of the commander, setting aside the request for a commission and conveying instead Beauregard's instructions that Wampler be employed as a topographical engineer to map Leesburg and the surrounding area threatened by Federal forces.[2]

While that initiative was underway, Wampler was at the same time pursuing an appointment to the Virginia Corps of Engineers. As president of the recently adjourned state secession convention in Richmond, John Janney was enlisted to appeal to Gov. John Letcher on Wampler's behalf. Janney highly commended Wampler for the (envisioned) Corps of Topographical Engineers, adding that it would please him personally to learn of the selection.[3] This effort was also fruitless.

It required Beauregard's personal intercession during the winter of 1861–62 for the applicant to achieve his objective. Wampler had reportedly impressed his senior officer with the maps he prepared of Loudoun County the previous summer.[4] Consequently, when Beauregard was dispatched to the West in late January 1862, Wampler's name was on the list of officers whom the general asked the secretary of war to send to his new headquarters. Citing the necessity of a strong defense at Columbus, Kentucky, as well as the importance of engineers in launching an offensive, Beauregard asked Richmond to assign him more engineer officers. In particular, he requested that four individuals already serving as captains with their state units be appointed engineers in the Provisional Army of the Confederate States (P.A.C.S.) and transferred to his western command.

THE CONFEDERATE CORPS OF ENGINEERS

The Confederate Congress had authorized an engineer corps, headed by an engineer bureau, in legislation enacted on March 6, 1861.[5] The nucleus of the Confederate Corps of Engineers had come, quite naturally, from the United States Army. Before the Civil War began, forty-eight engineer officers in the Regular Army were assigned to the Corps of Engineers and forty-five to the Corps of Topographical Engineers. With the support of a single company of engineer troops, generally numbering fewer than the officers, the Corps of Engineers concentrated on constructing fortifications, especially those guarding the coast, and were prepared in wartime to conduct sieges and supervise erection of field fortifications. Topographical engineers, on the other hand, were assigned the mission of developing information on terrain of military significance to field commanders. In peacetime, they complemented the Coast Survey by mapping in the West, primarily, and overseeing internal improvements to the nation's infrastructure, such as roads and lighthouses. These two organizations produced soldiers whose engineering skills and leadership were important to the nascent Confederate cause.

Eight officers resigned their commissions from the U.S. Corps of Engineers, with Bvt. Maj. P. G. T. Beauregard being the most prominent. Seven more left the topographical engineers to join the Confederate army. Each received a one- or two-rank promotion upon confirmation as an officer in the Regular Army of the Confederacy. Jeremy F. Gilmer, William H. C. Whiting, George Washington Custis Lee, and Martin L. Smith eventually ascended to major general, although not all in engineer billets. Other Confederate leaders, notably Robert E. Lee, Joseph E. Johnston, and Gustavus W. Smith, had been assigned earlier in their careers to the engineer or topographical corps.[6]

There the matter stood, as the Confederate Congress had in two separate acts authorized twenty officers and one hundred men in a company of sappers, miners. and pontoniers as its army's Corps of Engineers.[7] The congress failed to create a separate topographical corps, for which Wampler would have been ideally suited.[8] Maj. Josiah Gorgas served as acting chief engineer of the Confederate army, in addition to his primary duty as head of ordnance. State engineering departments, most importantly in South Carolina and Virginia, provided support as well, although their responsibilities were folded into the Confederate engineer corps late in 1861. Civilian engineers constituted another source of expertise. A celebrated example was "Stonewall" Jackson's favorite engineer, Jedediah Hotchkiss, who served as a civilian in the field for sixteen months before receiving a temporary appointment as captain of engineers.[9]

As it became evident that the war would not be decided by an initial defining battle or two, the paucity of engineers in uniform became critical. In his report of December 1861, Confederate Secretary of War Judah P. Benjamin recommended that five times as many engineers be authorized. The congress reacted by establishing a provisional engineer corps comprising fifty junior officers to serve until the war's conclusion.[10] Consequently, on February 12, 1862, Secretary Benjamin nominated sixteen individuals for appointment to the rank of captain in the Corps of Engineers of the Provisional Army of the Confederate States. Wampler was one of two candidates identified from Maryland, which, of course, had not joined the Confederacy. Later, after the total officer strength of the provisional corps had been doubled in April 1862, Gilmer complained privately that the hundred contained "not more than a *dozen* good men—men who can lay any claim to be called engineers," as almost half of the appointments came from "broken down" families in Virginia and South Carolina.[11]

CORINTH

Wampler's engineer credentials would not have been critically scrutinized upon his arrival in Mississippi, as the command there had far weightier matters confronting it. Corinth in late April 1862 was a depressing place for almost anyone but an ambitious officer reporting for his first assignment on the general staff. Earlier that month, the Confederate Army of the Mississippi, as it was then known, succeeded in surprising its adversary at Shiloh Church, Tennessee, inflicting casualties and confusion, only to have the larger Northern force batter the southerners the following day. Both sides were stunned by the extent of carnage and leery of renewing the contest. Wagons loaded with five thousand wounded soldiers, Federal as well as Confederate, streamed back into Corinth, the assembling area for the attack, overwhelming the local population of fewer than one thousand inhabitants and quickly turning the town into a vast convalescent center. Hotels, churches, stores, private residences, the local girls school (or seminary)— indeed, all the substantial buildings—were soon filled, not only with wounded, but with the sick and disabled. Measles and typhoid fever were rampant. More Confederates perished from illness in Corinth during the seven weeks following Shiloh than died in the battle itself.[12] Over thirty-two thousand cases of disease were treated during April and May 1862, diarrhea and dysentery being the most prevalent.[13] Stifling heat and a shortage of meat seemed to exacerbate these problems, further lowering morale. The extent of this deterioration in the ranks, however, may not have been immediately evident to a newly assigned officer.

Upon reaching Corinth, Wampler's first official act was to report to his new commander and benefactor. General Beauregard referred him, in turn, to Capt. Samuel H. Lockett of the Confederate Regular Engineers. The army's chief engineer, Maj. Jeremy Gilmer, had been wounded at Shiloh, and, ten days after Wampler's arrival, Col. John Pegram was appointed to succeed him. Several years younger than Wampler, Pegram and Lockett had each graduated from West Point, Pegram in 1854 and Lockett second in the class of 1859. At the engineer office, Wampler encountered French-born Capt. Leon J. Fremaux, who had been working as a state engineer for the Louisiana Board of Public Works, presided over by Braxton Bragg, at the time of that state's secession. Fremaux was serving with the Confederate army in northern

Col. John Pegram. The Museum of the Confederacy, Richmond, Virginia.

Virginia as commander of Company A, 8th Louisiana Volunteers, when appointed to the P.A.C.S. engineer corps in February 1862, at the same time as Wampler. Fremaux's personality was akin to Wampler's; he was a civil engineer more comfortable as a poet and artist than as a businessman.[14] Another officer on that list was Capt. David B. Harris, who, like Wampler, had drawn maps for Beauregard at Manassas. Harris had arrived in the Western Theater months earlier and been posted to Island Number 10 and Fort Pillow, before his current assignment as chief engineer at Vicksburg. The fourth engineer requested by Beauregard and commissioned on the initial P.A.C.S. roster,

Capt. Stephen Wilson Presstman of the 17th Virginia Infantry, would arrive at Corinth three weeks later. He was already an acquaintance of Wampler's and would become one of his best friends in the West.

Wampler was initially assigned to mapmaking—not surprising, as this was the facility that had so impressed Beauregard the preceding summer. It took several days to get started, however, since he first had to obtain a horse from the quartermaster and then found that the engineer department had no instruments with which to work. In desperation, he borrowed a compass from Fremaux and began reconnoitering and sketching in a pie-shaped sector formed by two railroads that crossed in the center of town: the Mobile & Ohio, running north and south, and the Memphis & Charleston, going east and west. Defensive positions in a semicircle to the north and east of town had been started by the Confederates before marching off to Shiloh. Troops assigned to Maj. Gens. Leonidas Polk and William J. Hardee returned to man the left and right, with the corps of the newly promoted Gen. Braxton Bragg responsible for the center. Maj. Gen. John C. Breckinridge's Kentuckians constituted the reserve. Fresh from disappointment and defeat at Pea Ridge, Arkansas, Maj. Gen. Earl Van Dorn's fourteen thousand ill-equipped soldiers arrived in Corinth in the weeks after Shiloh and were stationed on the right flank behind Hardee, out of concern for a possible envelopment by Maj. Gen. Henry Halleck, as his Federals pushed slowly southward. Wampler was assigned to lay out defensive positions on this flank astride high ground three miles outside town.

Traversing the marshes and bayous to the southeast of Corinth, Wampler prepared a map that Beauregard reviewed with him. In succession, he accompanied Generals Breckinridge, Hardee, Beauregard, and Bragg, along with their staffs and escorts, to point out proposed locations for batteries and rifle pits. Breckinridge was then ordered to furnish a detail of five hundred men to begin work, with Beauregard staying abreast of progress through evening briefings by Wampler and Lockett. After two days, work was interrupted late on May 3 by the first probe of Confederate pickets by Halleck's advance. Wampler expected a "grand fight" the next day, and so went out at 2:00 A.M. to supervise completion of the earthworks and assist in positioning Brig. Gen. Patrick Cleburne's troops along the front, with Breckinridge's reserve corps on the right.[15] Hours later, the weather turned cold, bringing rain. Returning to town at noon after accompanying Van Dorn on a reconnaissance, Wampler was not only tired and wet, but sick with fever and congestion. Confined by the staff surgeon to bed for three days, Wampler did not miss the expected encounter, as it failed to materialize. Exchanges of

Maj. Gen. Earl Van Dorn. Library of Congress.

cannonading between the two sides late on May 8 again held promise of a larger confrontation. General Beauregard ordered his staff to report at daylight the following day, and this time Wampler was not disappointed.[16]

At 8:00 A.M. on May 9, Wampler received orders to join Van Dorn's staff during a planned attack on Maj. Gen. John Pope, commanding the Federal lead elements. Pope's troops had extended beyond Halleck's support the previous day, when they were occupying Farmington, a village less than five miles directly east of Corinth.[17] Pope's intention was to execute a reconnaissance in

Samuel H. Lockett in the uniform of a West Point cadet.
U.S. Military Academy, 1859.

force to determine the strength and disposition of the Rebel defenses outside
Corinth. On the Confederate side, Bragg's corps was ordered to launch a
frontal attack, using Brig. Gen. Daniel Ruggles's division, along with portions of Van Dorn's command. Bragg joined Ruggles as he began to move
out, encountering only token resistance before taking Farmington by 10:00
A.M. Ruggles then opened fire with three batteries and advanced against the
main Federal force, consisting of a brigade, battery, and cavalry in support of

Capt. Leon J. Fremaux, ca. 1870.

pickets.[18] Beauregard had envisioned a coordinated offensive, with Van Dorn moving onto the Yankee flank and striking as the enemy pulled back. However, Van Dorn was an hour late getting into position, delayed by the swamps, thickets, and ravines outside the Confederate lines to the right. When at last Van Dorn's staff came into full view shortly before noon, Wampler saw stretched out before him double and triple lines of grayclad troops opposing a force drawn up in line of battle on the opposite ridge. For a brief period, the two sides traded artillery and musket fire. Van Dorn and his entourage were fully exposed to the projectiles, one staff member being shot through the lungs and another in the side. Wampler noted horses going down on either side of him, but he and his own white mount remained unscathed. Recognizing the threat posed by Van Dorn and their disadvantage in numbers, the Federals soon broke off the engagement and moved back across Seven Mile Creek to Pope's main body.

Van Dorn was astute enough not to follow into what might have become a trap and settled instead for burning the bridge and collecting the equipment, stores, and baggage left on the field by the retreating bluecoats. Wampler was pleased to acquire a bridle, halter, and saddle pockets.[19] Soldiers in gray were in good spirits that night after achieving a clear-cut victory, although the conflict at Farmington was best described as a "skirmish."[20] Losses were comparatively light, with Pope reporting 16 killed, 148 wounded, and 14 captured or missing. On the Southern side, Van Dorn and Ruggles suffered somewhere between 108 and 128 casualties.[21]

Beauregard was disappointed that Van Dorn had permitted the enemy to escape. If, as his biographer suggests, Beauregard himself contributed to the lack of complete success by his imperfect knowledge of the terrain to the right front, part of this responsibility may well have rested on Wampler's shoulders, for he drew the maps and briefed and escorted the commanding general.[22] However, Beauregard appeared "pleasant & agreeable" when Wampler called on him that evening.[23] Van Dorn undoubtedly shared in the fault by not insisting on a thorough reconnaissance before moving forward.[24] It is also possible that the two scouts sent to lead him into position may not have been as familiar with the terrain as expected. In any event, by nightfall Beauregard had directed that his soldiers fall back to their earlier positions to preclude exposure to an enemy counterattack on the flank.

The Federals subsequently reoccupied Farmington. As their presence outside the Confederate lines grew, so did Beauregard's apprehension. Wampler was sent once again to the right flank to lay off more earthworks. As forerunner to a retrograde movement, he accompanied Colonel Pegram and Captain Lockett on an examination of roads to the rear. The next day, Wampler returned with the 1st Louisiana Regiment as pioneers to improve the roadbed, but nearby skirmishing prevented them from making much progress. Again, he received orders to explore the countryside to the south, riding first to Danville and then to Rienzi. A mile past town, a squad of Southern cavalry overtook and arrested the engineer, mistaking him for a Yankee. He was released only after return to Rienzi and examination by the troop commander. His reconnaissance then continued to Kossuth, but before arriving back at Corinth, Wampler was detained again, this time by a "citizen" who drew a revolver and questioned him before being satisfied as to his identity.

Upon returning to the engineer office, Wampler was dispatched on May 20 to observe the enemy's breastworks from two outposts overlooking Farmington. He was accompanied by Captain Presstman, who had reported for duty only four days earlier. They were repeatedly fired upon, one round barely missing Presstman and striking a fence rail directly in front of Wampler. Late the next afternoon, Southern troops took positions to advance against the Yankees. The gray lines waited patiently the following morning for a signal cannon to announce that Van Dorn had succeeded in reaching the Federal left flank, only to be disappointed once again. The attack was consequently called off, and Wampler busied himself with riding along the defensive lines, making tracings of the enemy positions. On May 25, he accompanied Pegram to the far right to lay off an earthwork for a five-gun battery and magazine a mile beyond the Confederate lines. Wampler's "redan fort" protected the Memphis & Charleston rail line, but, more importantly, it provided cover for the road south to Danville. Assigned eight hundred soldiers for its construction, Wampler completed the project by 5:00 P.M. the following day, when General Van Dorn came out to inspect it. The enemy was firing heavy volleys with artillery and muskets, to which Van Dorn responded with three shots from the redan's rifled cannon.[25]

While Confederate troops were strengthening their positions and trading shots with the Federals, Beauregard and his corps commanders were meeting to decide what to do next. Halleck's increasing pressure upon a cantonment area rife with disease and short on food and water seemed to leave no realistic option but withdrawal. Once this decision was made on May 25, Beauregard encouraged activity, like Wampler's earthworks construction, to deceive an enemy that for weeks had expected the Confederates to abandon Corinth. The military depot came alive with activity and confusion, as sick and wounded, arms and ammunition, and equipment and stores of all sorts were sent to the rear. Wampler dispatched his own personal baggage before joining his friend, Maj. Henry Peyton, another Virginia veteran of Beauregard's army at Manassas, in the line of staff officers accompanying the commanding general. Where the Danville Road crossed the Mobile & Ohio Railroad, Wampler observed thousands of sick troops gathered beside the track, awaiting evacuation southward. Not long thereafter, Beauregard summoned him and Capt. John Otey, yet another Virginian serving as assistant adjutant on the general staff, to take a message to Van Dorn. If the sick were not transported that afternoon, Van Dorn's troops were to return to their positions in the line to provide cover overnight. Consequently, it was 3:00 A.M. before Wampler caught up with Beauregard's entourage, bivouacked outside Rienzi. After spreading his saddle blanket on the ground, the exhausted engineer was soon asleep.[26]

The retreat was effectively executed, despite suffocating temperatures and a shortage of water, which combined to produce heat strokes. A ruse froze Halleck's forces in place until the defenders had completely abandoned Corinth. Once the Federals realized in which direction Beauregard's troops had withdrawn, Pope's cavalry was soon in pursuit, harassing the retiring Confederates. Awakened after only a few hours of sleep, Wampler was sent by Beauregard to deliver orders to Bragg, camped eight miles away. On the return trip, he heard what appeared to be cannon fire a few miles to the south of Rienzi. It was in actuality ammunition exploding aboard a trainload of ordnance, baggage, and supplies stopped at Booneville. The Federal cavalry proceeded to capture hundreds of Confederates, mostly wounded, until interrupted and dispersed by Southern troopers. Wampler learned the next day from his servant Mac, who had been aboard the cars and had barely escaped being taken prisoner, that all of his personal items, including his bedding, had been destroyed. He was devastated. The clothing was replaceable. His portfolio and papers were not. Among them were drawings of a rotary engine and locomotive and his relics and accounts of the battles at Manassas, Leesburg, and Farmington. His flute, spyglass, compasses, and, most disturbing to him, the mementos of his family in faraway Virginia were all lost. "I would not have taken 5000$ for my trunk & its contents," he lamented.[27] The engineer's distress could have extended as well to his small telescope and drawing implements, in light of the severe shortage of surveying and drafting instruments throughout the South.

Beauregard and his staff continued moving south, generally following the railroad, but diverting at times along dark and winding roads through forest bottoms. Horses' hoofs and rattling sabers emitted the only sounds. At night, Wampler and Peyton slept on pallets under cover or in one of two tents pitched for them and their servants. On June 1, they reached Baldwyn. Foragers and commissary officers fanned out in all directions, hunting chickens, vegetables, and provisions of any kind. Engineers were also out surveying, asking local inhabitants for information about road networks.[28] Wampler participated in this endeavor. First, he examined roads southeast of Baldwyn for eight or ten miles, then went northward with two cavalrymen as escorts to check on the enemy and evaluate the roads toward Jacinto. He moved forward with caution, noting fresh tracks of Yankee horsemen, but encountered no troopers except his own cavalry, which halted and questioned him. Exchanging his weary white stallion for a brown horse, Wampler was next dispatched to Tupelo, twenty-five miles to the south. The town consisted of barely more than a railroad station and a few stores and saloons, erected as the Mobile & Ohio Railroad was being laid in 1860.[29] Reversing direction, he followed the rails north through Saltillo and Guntown, then back to Baldwyn. "Poor apologies for towns. . . . I have not yet been in a house in Miss. that bears any evidence whatsoever of refinement. This is a horrid State."[30] Upon each return, Wampler reported to the commander's headquarters at Dr. Lang's house. This time, after he gave Beauregard his hand-drawn map and explained the relative merits of the different stops along the railroad as campsites, the general offered him a toddy.

Several days later, the army began to move south again, causing disruption in the communities being abandoned. Slaves ran off, cavalry destroyed crops and confiscated mules, and residents packed up to leave amid rumors of almost everything imaginable.[31] Beauregard and most of his staff traveled by train to Tupelo on June 7. Wampler, however, was sent on horseback to reconnoiter the intermediate road network once again. No sooner had he finally arrived in Tupelo when Beauregard directed him farther south to Aberdeen by another circuitous route. Entering the rich black belt of Mississippi agriculture, Wampler was stunned by what seemed like "tens of thousands of acres of corn as high as my head."[32] His rewards upon returning from this assignment were a compass from the engineer department, a bridle from a friend, and letters from his beloved Kate, his mother, and two former comrades in the 8th Virginia. He wistfully noted the return to Virginia of young Tom Clagett, an enlisted soldier from Leesburg with whom he had formed a bond during these first days away from home in the Western Theater.

Wampler's preoccupation prevented him from foreseeing a change about to transform the Confederate Army in the West. Beauregard's health had been poor; a lingering throat ailment caused him serious discomfort. He consequently obtained a surgeon's certificate of disability and prepared for a respite of ten days to two weeks at Bladon Springs, a resort near Mobile. Wampler learned of these plans on June 15, but thought little of their significance, for he did not realize the extent to which his commander's stock had fallen in Richmond as a result of the perceived unilateral retreat from Corinth. Once Beauregard departed for Alabama, Davis quickly replaced

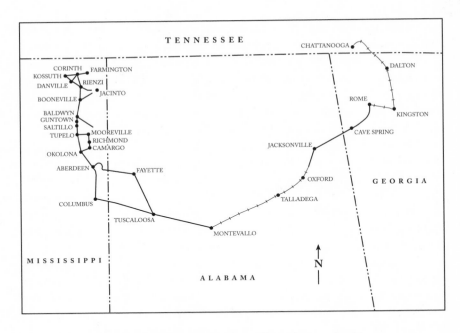

Wampler's War in the West: April 26–August 18, 1862.

him, assigning Bragg as permanent commander of the western department on June 20. Without even a farewell, Wampler was again separated from his benefactor.

ABERDEEN

The change of command from Beauregard to Bragg was made evident to most soldiers by an increase in discipline. If he knew nothing else, Bragg was a master at organizing and training troops. The new conscription act was strictly enforced, extending volunteers beyond their initial one-year enlistment. Deserters were shot. Alcohol consumption and other vices common to encampment were discouraged. Church attendance was emphasized. Quarters were improved, and wells were dug to a depth of ten to fifteen feet to provide the pure water lacking at Corinth. Despite customary complaining, it was not long before the constant drill and improved health of the army lifted the spirits of its soldiers.[33] During his first month in command, Bragg succeeded in molding a relatively effective army, capable of taking to the field.

As this transformation began, Wampler was ordered to relieve Lockett at Aberdeen and take charge of building two bridges across the Tombigbee River. He took along Lt. Walter J. Morris as his assistant. They left at once and, befriending a black man on horseback en route, arrived at noon on June 18. Wampler immediately rode down to the river and examined the bridge locations with Lockett, who was being posted to the defenses of Vicksburg, where he would distinguish himself. The incoming engineer was pleased to find excellent supervisors in the foreman, John Westbrook, and his assistant, William McCabber, carpenters and neighbors in town.

This was Wampler's first bridge construction project for the Confederate engineer corps, and his determination was evident in his decisive actions. Disapproving of Lockett's locations and plans for the bridges, Wampler altered them. A permanent bridge was placed at a bend in the river north of town, taking advantage of a rail roadbed and existing bridge piers on Matubba Creek. A floating bridge was sited farther downstream on a straight stretch to the east.[34] Wampler telegraphed Mobile, canceling the pile driver apparatus ordered by Lockett. Westbrook obtained lumber prices from one sawmill, but Wampler made a better bargain at another. He also wrote to Capt. George B. Pickett, encouraging him to bring his company of sappers and miners from the Tupelo area to assist in construction.[35] They arrived the next day and camped a mile outside town. Wampler had been authorized to impress slaves into service, compensating their owners for the labor, and he soon had forty-four slave hands at work as well. Initially, Wampler could not obtain food for his workers. When confronted, the commissary, Mr. Galloway, was drunk and ordered Wampler out of his office, cursing and even following to try and shoot him, before friends intervened. Wampler had Galloway arrested, and the matter was referred to Colonel Pegram. Within a week's time, a shipment of augers, adzes, and scrapers had arrived, the men were erecting trestles for the permanent structure, and a crew was improving roads leading to the bridges. Teams were impressed to facilitate the heavy hauling. Once the trestles were in place, the workers turned to the stringers and flooring. Preparing the landings and spanning nearby culverts were the final tasks. Eleven days after taking charge of construction, Wampler completed the permanent bridge. The floating span was finished a couple of days later.[36]

Wampler's posting at Aberdeen was made bearable because of the friendship he developed with the family of Martin L. "Doc" Strong. As a husband and father a thousand miles from home, Wampler found the warmth and civility of this wealthy plantation family the best remedy available for the

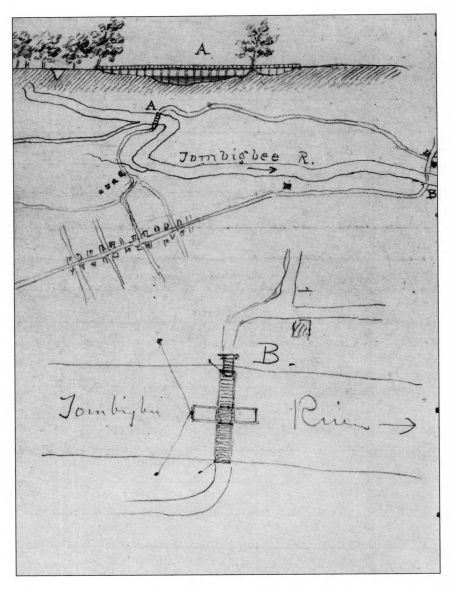

Field sketch of bridge locations at Aberdeen, Mississippi,
by J. M. Wampler, June 28, 1862.

homesickness that gnawed at him when alone. Doc was a few years younger than Wampler, and the son of Elisha Strong, a militia general who served in the War of 1812. His wife, the former Georgia Hill of Athens, was born in the same year as Kate Wampler and was the mother of a son and daughter of similar ages to the engineer's younger children. The Strong family wealth consisted of their slaves and plantation amidst the rich black soil of the Mississippi prairie near Strongs Station on the road to the railroad at West Point.[37] Indeed, Wampler put to use over twenty of General Strong's slaves, plus those of Doc Strong and Robert Paine, a Methodist Episcopal bishop who resided in town.

It is likely that Wampler was introduced to Georgia Strong by Captain Lockett's wife, who had accompanied her husband to Aberdeen. Soon Wampler and Morris were calling on the Strongs on a regular basis, taking dinner, playing music, and accompanying the family to church. Doc Strong introduced Wampler to his father, from whom he obtained use of a team of horses for his workers. Georgia Strong put Wampler in touch with Gabriella Brock and her daughter Sue, living at nearby Egypt Station, who made shirts for him and joined in his social circle. On more than one hot afternoon, Wampler and Doc rode to the bridges to inspect their progress and then took a cooling bath in the river. Dressed in their Sunday finery after church on June 29, the Strongs drove Wampler in their carriage to the permanent bridge, where he took the reins and was the first to cross.

With the completion of actual construction came the business of finishing the paperwork. Wampler made out an account of expenditures on the two bridges and sent Morris to Tupelo for payment. He returned undoubtedly buoyed over his brevet promotion to captain, but, unhappily, without the money. After two weeks of waiting, Wampler journeyed to Tupelo himself. He found great commotion among Beauregard's former staff officers, as some were being transferred and others requesting reassignment in the wake of their mentor's departure from command. Wampler and his friend Henry Peyton shared a desire to return to Virginia and decided to ask the Adjutant and Inspector General's Office in Richmond for a transfer. They were refused by Bragg. Wampler also wrote directly to Beauregard, expressing concern about the general's health and offering his services, once he returned to duty. Wampler learned that the Commissary Galloway had been dismissed as a result of his report. The matter apparently did not sit well with Pegram, however, and may have touched off his volley of correspondence with Wampler regarding appropriate expenses for the bridges. While waiting, Wampler and Peyton encountered Isham Harris, the governor of Tennessee in exile, who was continuously lobbying for return of Confederate forces to his home state, while serving as a civilian aide to the commanding general. Eventually, Pegram approved the bridge accounts, and Wampler returned to Aberdeen to pay off these debts.

Use of the floating bridge was soon discontinued, as it was apparently not as reliable as originally envisioned. The other structure also proved to be less durable than intended. As there is no local lore respecting the permanent bridge, it must have been swept away by a flood. The Tombigbee could grow five miles wide at flood level and rise thirty feet without climbing out of its banks. Wampler's stationary span had seemingly disappeared by February 1864, as it is not mentioned in reports of the northern prong of the U.S. Army's Meridian Expedition.

As the business of bridge building drew to a close, the engineer captain had time to address a personal need. Riding a succession of quartermaster mounts since arriving in Mississippi, Wampler had been in the market for a horse of his own. At Aberdeen, he finally settled on a little horse, six years old, for which he paid two hundred dollars. Searching for a short, distinctive name to match its appearance, Wampler decided on "Cupid." Captain Morris borrowed the animal three days later to ride with a lady, but, upon his return, Cupid got away and ran off into the woods, saddled and bridled with reins dragging. Wampler subsequently dispatched two servants, who failed to find the horse. Riding with Doc Strong the next day, Wampler found Cupid grazing, but again he broke away, leading them for miles, before another servant captured and returned the horse with only a cut on his left foreleg. Three days later, Cupid kicked Wampler as he was adjusting the saddle, dislocating his shoulder and severely bruising his thigh. The Strongs cared for him until he recovered, but when Wampler next rode Cupid to their plantation, the animal broke away once more, this time from a hustler, and ran until nearly dropping. In light of Cupid's unreliability, Wampler must have felt considerable apprehension as he climbed aboard the steed shortly thereafter to conduct an extended reconnaissance for the army commander.

SEIZING THE INITIATIVE

Confederate soldiers endured the regimen of Bragg and Hardee with the expectation of moving north back up the Mobile & Ohio track to confront the Federals now based at Corinth. The countryside had been depleted of forage, however, and an unusually hot, dry summer exacerbated the seriousness of an already poor water supply to the north of Tupelo. Upon learning that Halleck had sent Maj. Gen. Don Carlos Buell eastward along the Memphis & Charleston Railroad, Bragg was determined to deny the Federals access to the strategic rail center at Chattanooga. By uniting with Maj. Gen. Edmund Kirby Smith, commander of the District of East Tennessee, Bragg also envisioned regaining control of rich agricultural areas in central Tennessee. Consequently, Special Orders No. 4, dated July 21, 1862, directed that Bragg's infantry move by train to Chattanooga, via Mobile, retracing the eight-hundred-mile journey that Wampler had taken to arrive in Mississippi three months earlier. Artillery, cavalry, engineers, pioneers, and wagon trains would take an overland route, beginning at Wampler's bridging over the Tombigbee. The convoys would continue via Columbus, Mississippi, and Tuscaloosa, Alabama, and then through Will's Valley to Gadsden, Alabama, and Rome, Georgia, before arriving at Chattanooga.[38]

The following day, Wampler and Morris received orders, via courier, to conduct a reconnaissance to Columbus and Tuscaloosa. Crossing the Tombigbee and Buttahatchee Rivers and then the Looxapalila and Sipsey Creeks, Wampler made note of the condition of bridges and the availability of water. Proceeding slowly through poor farming areas, Cupid became overcome by the heat and suffered from thumps, a respiratory condition caused by exhaustion.[39] Four days and sixty-two miles, by Wampler's estimate, brought them to Tuscaloosa, the former capital of Alabama. Wampler's years of urban mapping enabled him to appreciate streets laid out precisely on a summit overlooking the Black Warrior River. He marveled at the beautiful effect created by rows of willow oaks down the middle and on both sides of broad boulevards. The travelers had their horses combed and rear hoofs shod before undertaking the return trip. Cupid was now more docile, due to loss of his right eye in a stable accident, which deeply distressed his owner.

The engineers followed a more northerly course back, through sparsely settled countryside, over rough, hilly roads, past dilapidated houses. When not singing or whistling, Wampler and Morris talked of home and family to lift their spirits. Arriving at the Tombigbee bridge, which he calculated to be ninety-five miles from Tuscaloosa by the upper route, Wampler was surprised to meet troops and wagon trains already moving toward Chattanooga. After a hearty welcome from the Strongs, he learned that Pegram had countermanded his original reconnaissance orders but not bothered to send after him. The new directive dispatched Wampler and his engineers all the way to Chattanooga, with instructions to report back periodically on road conditions to the 1st Louisiana Regiment, which would serve as pioneers for the convoy.[40]

Daytime rides with the ladies, music in the evenings, helping Mrs. Strong recover a runaway slave, and arranging for an ambulance to transport their baggage occupied Wampler's time until the horses were rested and ready for the trek to East Tennessee. With a sad goodbye to his surrogate family, Wampler started on his way on August 7, the party consisting of Morris on horseback and his servant, Oliver, driving the ambulance to which Wampler hitched his old black army mount. The load was too heavy for a single horse, and a quartermaster mule and harness were soon obtained to help with the hauling. Stopping at houses along the way for dinner at midday and supper and rest at night, they hurried to stay ahead of the longer trains of wagons that clogged the roads, adding clouds of dust to the sweltering ride. Reaching Montevallo, east of Tuscaloosa, after a week's ride, Wampler booked transportation on the Alabama & Tennessee Rivers Railroad. He calculated a saving of sixty miles overland, as the train rolled through Talladega and Oxford, depositing them at its terminus ten miles south of Jacksonville. On the road once more, this time through prettier mountain scenery, the little party stopped only for food and rest and to have their animals reshod. Reaching Rome, Georgia, Wampler attended services at the Episcopal church, while awaiting a passenger train east to Kingston, where a northbound artillery train pulled their car to Chattanooga. The entire journey of four hundred miles required twelve days to complete.

Wampler remained in Chattanooga only four days. His old Virginia colleague, David Harris, was now serving as Bragg's senior engineer, Pegram having transferred to be chief of staff for Kirby Smith. Bragg had divided his army into two wings, the divisions of Maj. Gens. Benjamin Franklin Cheatham and Jones M. Withers under Polk and those of Maj. Gen. Simon Bolivar Buckner and Brig. Gen. Patton Anderson under Hardee. Their effective strength was reported as 27,320 officers and men.[41] Harris assigned Wampler as engineer-in-chief of Polk's Right Wing. Wilson Presstman held the comparable position for Hardee and commanded that wing's pioneer company, which included forty-five excellent mechanics. Presstman was assisted by Capt. Edward B. Sayers, Lt. John W. Green, and Henry N. Pharr.[42] Wampler was delighted to see Brig. Gen. Thomas Jordan, although the Virginian and member of the Beauregard coterie was being replaced as the army's chief of staff. Wampler also enjoyed the company once more of Henry Peyton (and obtained whiskey from him at ten dollars a gallon) and was reunited with his servant Mac.

Bragg had reason to be pleased with the repositioning of his forces, for he had effectively used the railways to beat Buell to Chattanooga, consolidating two Confederate armies and exposing the enemy's flank and rear in the process. Now Bragg agreed that Kirby Smith should force the Federals out of Cumberland Gap and stand ready to help Bragg oust them from Middle Tennessee. The delegation headed by Governor Harris certainly subscribed to the latter objective, but another influential group favored reclaiming Kentucky for the Confederacy. Before Bragg could move out, whatever his destination, he had to wait for all his wagon trains to close with the main body at Chattanooga.

Finally, on August 17, Cheatham began crossing the Tennessee River, with Withers following right behind. Two days later, the engineers were authorized to requisition quartermaster supplies, rations, and medical items.[43] After reporting to Polk for orders, Wampler left Chattanooga on August 23. His party consisted of Captain Morris, Lts. George M. Helm and James D. Thomas, and Henry Pharr as engineers; a company of sappers and miners; the 1st Louisiana Regiment, commanded by Lt. Col. John A. Jacques, as pioneers; and at least a half-dozen wagons.

While Wampler accurately identified Jacques's troops as "pioneers," Confederates west of the Appalachians were not as precise in their use of engineer terminology. Technically speaking, sappers were soldiers employed in the construction of fortifications, trenches, or tunnels to undermine enemy positions. Miners laid mines, on land or at sea. These specialists would not normally have been expected to perform unskilled manual labor in the vanguard of an army on the move. On the other hand, pioneers were not mechanics or experienced in the building trades, but usually detailed from infantry units and employed in a far wider variety of activities. Sappers, miners, and pioneers were commanded by line officers but were provided technical direction by engineers.

Pioneers facilitated their own army's movement, while attempting to restrict the mobility of their opponent. They made and improved roads, cleared a line of battle, and constructed and repaired bridges. Pioneers cleared fields of fire by cutting underbrush in front of artillery positions; dug hasty field defenses, such as parapets and breastworks; built all manner of fortifications; threw pontoon bridges across waterways; and prepared shelters for field hospitals. They were even known, on occasion, to clear driftwood from a ford, corduroy a swamp, construct a bombproof, build a signal fire, fabricate a coffin, and bury the dead. Some of these tasks exposed pioneers to enemy fire, although most did not.[44] Conversely, to help thwart the enemy, they placed obstructions, such as fallen timber, in the middle of roadways, blockaded gaps to deny avenues of approach, and demolished bridging to hinder pursuit after the rear guard was safely across. Soldiers serving as pioneers carried their own firearms, although, while serving in this capacity, their primary weapons of war were spades, picks, and axes.[45]

Line units were assigned to periods of pioneer duty. Individual soldiers were also encouraged to transfer to the pioneers or were summarily detached from their parent outfits after being actively sought out for their mechanical skills, which were especially scarce in the Southern army. Recruits with experience as carpenters, carriage makers, and the like were assigned to the ranks of the pioneers as well. The attractions of this kind of service were that pioneers were rarely ordered to participate in direct assaults, infrequently performed picket or guard duty, and typically received cleaner quarters and better rations than other field soldiers. These advantages were further enhanced by the opportunity presented to the vanguard to forage for themselves ahead of the column trailing behind.[46]

Utilizing pioneers to help provide security, on August 24, Wampler's party slowly crossed the Tennessee River at Harrison, a deserted village northeast of Chattanooga, staying alert for Yankee bushwackers as they passed beyond the protection of Cheatham's pickets. When a pair of Union sympathizers was identified, Wampler and three other officers rode out and arrested them. The proximity of the 1st Louisiana, reinforced with daily scouting into the hills by the engineer officers themselves, helped steady their nerves as they waited for Polk to join his divisions and order the wing into motion. Harris had informed Wampler that he would not be provided with guides acquainted with the terrain to be traversed. This assistance would have to be obtained from loyal residents who knew the crossroads and bridle paths, as well as the main routes, particularly in the Cumberland Mountains. "Use your guides only so far as their knowledge extends, then sleep there and substitute other[s] in their places," Harris advised Wampler.[47]

On August 28, the entire army began to move. The Right Wing soon divided. Guiding Withers's brigades, Morris and Pharr took the road from Hickman's to Robinson's across the Sequatchie Valley with the sappers and miners and four companies of pioneers. Wampler remained with Helm, Jacques, and six companies of his regiment to lead Cheatham's division northward on the upper road to Pikeville. Mending bridges and repairing roadways as they went, Wampler's contingent began climbing Walden's Ridge outside Morgantown. For three miles, they trudged up the steep, rough road, finally encamping on the plateau at the top. A detachment of cavalry came forward before midnight to act as couriers. Three hours later, another courier arrived, bringing Wampler orders to lead the advance through Pikeville to Sparta.

The way down into the pastureland and grain fields of the Sequatchie Valley may have been even steeper than the ascent, and Wampler's party stopped often to mend the rough road. He dispatched couriers along the way to inform Harris and Morris of their progress. By mid-afternoon they were in Pikeville, and Wampler was able to report in person to Bragg and Harris. The two wings were reunited at this point, allowing Wampler to meet as well with Polk, Morris, and Pharr. The next day, the first of September, the column began ascending the more gradual grade onto the Cumberland Plateau. In addition to road repairs, Harris and Wampler were concerned about locating campsites near water. Coming out onto the main road, they found that elements of Cheatham's division had broken the march discipline by moving ahead along a road not improved by the engineer advance. Another problem arose in foraging for beef. Pickets would not allow Wampler's troops to pass, as they did not know the countersign, even after he wrote them permission "by order of General Bragg." Wampler finally rode out to give the officer in charge of the pickets "a severe tongue lashing," and then wrote a statement of the facts for Polk to pass along to Bragg. The engineer party arrived in Sparta the following day without rations.[48] Wampler's spirits were quickly lifted, however, upon hearing of Lee's smashing victory at Second Manassas.

At Sparta, Wampler first encountered the celebrated Brig. Gen. Nathan Bedford Forrest, who had been conducting raids in Middle Tennessee and was now assigned in support of the Right Wing. Forrest's riders quickly returned to the field, screening Bragg's army from the Federals at Nashville and reporting on Buell's movement out of that city. It was also at Sparta, on September 5, that Wampler learned of Bragg's decision to continue northward to Gainesboro, and Kentucky beyond, rather than turning west and advancing upon the Tennessee state capital.

Ordered once again into the van of Polk's wing, Wampler left at once for Gainesboro with a cavalry escort of eleven men, arriving at midnight.[49] As directed by Bragg, Wampler started early the next morning to examine two fords along the Cumberland River. Selecting the upper one, six miles from town, he sent his findings on the condition of the feeder roads and ford bottom to both Bragg and Polk.[50] A similar dispatch to Morris brought him forward with work parties to begin making repairs. Wampler also sent back intelligence to his wing commander. In a separate communiqué, he informed Polk of four or five local citizens who reportedly had been serving as Yankee couriers since the war began. These individuals allegedly owned two dozen horses and had three thousand pounds of bacon, corn, and fodder stored away. "Send me a Company of Cavalry," wrote Wampler, "& I will secure it all for the Army."[51] He concluded with a cautionary note about bushwackers on the north side of the river.

The next day a company of cavalry reported and, securing local guides, began looking for the Unionists. Over the next two days, Wampler and the cavalry escort arrested several men, administered the oath of allegiance to the Confederacy, and let them go. The search party also confiscated horses, corn, and other produce, but failed to discover the quantities of foodstuffs envisioned. Perhaps as a coincidence, Wampler also found that he could purchase a fine mare and a McClellan saddle from Yankee sympathizers at a fraction of their market prices. As this mission drew to a close, Wampler camped at the hamlet of Centreville, just below the Kentucky line.

Kentucky

Opportunity seemed to abound for the Confederacy in September 1862. Southern armies in the West were invading Kentucky and threatening Grant's command to the southwest. At the same time, Lee's Army of Northern Virginia was entering Maryland. Within the borders of the Old Line State, Confederates would entreat the populace to join their ranks, just as Bragg, Buckner, and Kirby Smith would do in Kentucky. Van Dorn and Maj. Gen. Sterling Price were expected to reclaim portions of western Tennessee and northern Mississippi. This was a time that would come to be viewed as the high tide of the Confederacy.

Wampler crossed the border into Kentucky at about 8:00 A.M. on September 9. Earlier in the morning, he had sent his cavalry escort ahead while he waited for the sappers and miners to come up. A report had arrived the previous evening that the Federals were evacuating Nashville en route to Cincinnati. There must have been talk as well of the need for Bragg's force to move quickly in order to stay between Buell and Kirby Smith's army already in Bluegrass Kentucky. Arriving at Tompkinsville about 1:00 P.M., Wampler was joined by Cheatham's troops shortly thereafter. Polk appeared that night.

Wampler took a day to reconnoiter in order to provide Polk with a map. He was in the saddle again at 4:00 A.M. on September 11, accompanied by Morris and an escort of forty troopers to sketch more maps, which were sent back by courier.[52] Behind them came the pioneer corps, directed by Helm and Pharr, and Withers's division, for whom Wampler had been directed to furnish a guide.[53] By 10:00, Wampler's party stopped to eat and feed their horses at Skaggs Creek, within nine miles of Glasgow.[54] Preparing to leave about noon, Col. William Allen and the 1st Alabama Cavalry dismounted for the same purpose. Allen had been instructed to consult with Wampler, who, as the wing's senior engineer, would provide information on the direction of march and sites for encampment.[55] A courier handed Wampler a dispatch from General Polk to move forward with his work party and reach Glasgow as soon as possible.[56] Leaving Allen behind, Wampler proceeded with caution, as he expected to encounter Federals, and reached Glasgow at about 4:00 P.M. Wampler posted pickets on all the accesses and "took possession" of the town.

> The Rebel ladies received us with waving handkerchiefs, & tears of joy at their deliverance from so cruel a despotism. I rode up to a house on the porch of which were several ladies, who manifested much real joy at the presence of Southern soldiers, and asked if they would direct me to some good reliable Southern Gentleman who could give me information & they wrung their hands & cried, & said, Oh! we are Southern! We are Southern! We are Rebels! Indeed we are! Oh! Do come in, etc. Oh! They wept so earnestly for joy, & fear but I soon assured them that a strong army of Southrons [sic] would follow me in abt 12 hours. They were very kind indeed. Abt. 2 hours later Col. Allens command got in & relieved my pickets.[57]

Amidst all this celebration, Wampler did not forget to write a quick report of his success to Polk, including the description of a good campsite for the division outside town, where the Louisville Road crossed Beaver Creek.[58]

Braxton Bragg arrived on September 13. At Glasgow, he issued a proclamation, as instructed by President Davis, describing his army as the liberator of Kentuckians from "the tyranny of a despotic ruler" and the protector of persons and property.[59] These were not-so-subtle references to the excesses of martial law imposed in the state by the Federal government. For the invasion to succeed, Bragg said, Kentuckians must embrace the Confederacy by enlisting in its army. Bragg was challenging Kentucky to live up to the promises of its representatives in the secessionist government and military or be abandoned once and for all by the South.

Wampler's Virginia friends began to filter into town, and he took time to meet with Harris, Presstman, and Otey, among others. While the army collected itself from its long march, Wampler accepted the hospitality of Glasgow's adoring female population, enjoying especially the supper and music provided by Miss Mollie Dodd. He tended to business by making a map of the environs, based on reconnaissance in all directions by his four subordinate engineers, protected, of course, by cavalry escorts.

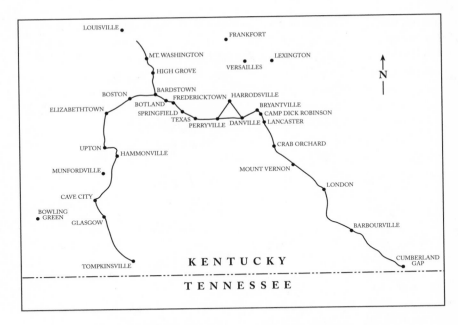

Wampler's War in the West: September 9–October 16, 1862.

Glasgow was located 30 miles due east of Bowling Green, where Buell's army had stopped on its way north from Nashville on a route parallel to Bragg's. To sever the railroad connection with Louisville, the nearest Federal supply depot, Bragg sent a Mississippi brigade to Cave City, ten miles north-west of Glasgow. Polk ordered Wampler to investigate the situation. He returned two days later, just in time to see his army's rear elements marching out of Glasgow on the road to Louisville. By hard riding over the next twenty-four hours, acquiring en route a splendid bay belonging to a Union man as a fresh mount, Wampler succeeded in passing Forrest's cavalry and reaching the extreme advance. Late on September 16, Wampler's party took posses-sion of the hamlet of Hammonville, seizing its post office and blacksmith shop—the latter needed to reshoe their horses. His situation report to Polk elicited a response describing a confrontation with the determined garrison of forty-five hundred Yankee soldiers at Munfordville, a town some ten miles to the south, between Wampler and Polk. The engineer party was directed to continue forward, reconnoitering and reporting on topography and other information of military consequence.[60] Amidst wild rumors of first Buell, then Breckinridge, heading his way, Wampler's contingent moved west to the railroad at Upton Station to tear down the telegraph wire linking it with Louisville.

The next morning, September 18, the party proceeded north on the road toward Elizabethtown. At Nolin's Creek, Wampler stopped to send a dispatch back to Polk, reporting on the food supply and enemy presence in the area. The local mills were not considered in working order, a conclusion he could reach authoritatively, given his experience at Mavin's Mill. Three miles back at Sonora on the rail line, he had discovered two hundred bushels of wheat intended for Louisville. The report also noted forage available near the roads, which was assessed to be of good quality. Understanding the Yankees to have abandoned Elizabethtown and hearing that John Hunt Morgan's troopers might have taken possession, Wampler announced his intention to continue forward.[61]

Moving farther north along the ridgeline with his escort, Wampler entered Elizabethtown that same day, to the hurrahs of men and women appearing to be Southern sympathizers.[62] Having perfected by now the technique for occupying a town, Wampler placed pickets and sentinels in key locations and once again seized both the post office and telegraph. To his delight, a cache of cavalry equipment was discovered, and the engineer officer helped himself to a good saddle. Couriers carried reports back to headquarters, squads reconnoitered the area, and the sappers and miners finally caught up with the advance. No sooner had they arrived, then word arrived from Forrest that the whole command was being ordered to Munfordville to confront Buell.[63] The engineer advance headed south, but, before reaching its destination, they encountered Forrest's troopers who this time informed them that the crisis was resolved, as the Federal garrison at Munfordville had surrendered. Wampler and his men turned north once again.

Forrest's cavalry passed through Elizabethtown the following day. The general told Wampler that Bragg's army was now on a forced march to Bardstown. The engineers quickly packed up, passed the commissary trains and then Forrest's own command, and kept riding to reach the head of the column as it entered Bardstown at 1:00 P.M. on September 21. The trains were late arriving, having been ambushed by Yankees concealed in the thick foliage between Boston and Bardstown. With the Rebels in town, everyone seemed to be a secessionist. Wampler set about making his usual topographical sketch to send back to Polk.[64]

Back at Munfordville, Bragg had lost valuable time in a show of force and subsequent negotiation to secure capitulation of the outmanned and strategically insignificant Federal garrison. Bragg chose not to pursue a greater confrontation with the Yankee army and headed instead to Bardstown, where he expected to replenish his supplies and join forces with Kirby Smith. "This campaign must be won by marching, not by fighting," Bragg explained.[65] His decision, however, opened the way for Buell to move uncontested into Louisville, where he, too, could gain reinforcements and logistical support preparatory to challenging his Southern opponents.

Arriving at Bardstown on September 22, Bragg was naturally interested in obtaining a situation report, as the proximity of the enemy invited constant rumors of their impending arrival. Forrest had his troopers drawn up in line around the courthouse, which was soon reinforced with a brigade of infantry and artillery.[66] Wampler briefed Harris on the situation and dispersed parties of engineers, accompanied by cavalry escorts, in all directions on general reconnaissance. The following day Wampler was able to make seven maps of the vicinity for Bragg and Polk. He also dispatched Morris and Pharr eastward to Danville to examine the terrain from a military perspective. Soon afterward, Hardee sent Presstman on a similar mission. Meanwhile, Southern troops continued to arrive and set up camps in the rolling hills surrounding the town, where they rested after their long march.

On September 25, Pharr reported back to Wampler that the roads to the east were of varying quality. Some sections were "piked" (or paved), but one ten-mile segment was rocky and uneven, requiring a good deal of work. Pharr also pointed out that Chaplin Creek was the only source of water between Mackville and Harrodsburg, an observation of profound military significance that soon would become evident.[67]

To herald the arrival of Confederate forces and emphasize the importance of garnering full support from the local residents, a grand flag raising took place in Bardstown on September 24. Troops formed up around the courthouse; military music stirred the populace gathered on the square. As the Confederate battle flag unfurled over the courthouse, the Washington Artillery of New Orleans fired a national salute. Generals Bragg, Polk, Buckner, Cheatham, Chalmers, and others all made short speeches.[68] Buckner had implored his fellow Kentuckians "to join the standard of freedom. If you are worthy of liberty you will win it. We have arms for all who will join us."[69]

Bragg went one step further, threatening to pull his army out of the state if its citizens did not rally to the Southern cause, now that they no longer suffered from the intimidation of Federal occupation.[70] He notified Richmond of this prospect in a letter the following day, pointing out that accessions to his ranks were negligible, leaving unclaimed most of the fifteen thousand weapons being transported for the legions of Kentuckians he had been led to expect. Bragg's interest in knowing more about retrograde routes to the east, in the opposite direction from the Federal force gathering strength at Louisville, and his creation of a logistical base at Camp Dick Robinson reflected his contingency planning in the event a withdrawal from the state proved necessary.[71] Before leaving Bardstown on September 28, Bragg and Polk, along with their staffs, including Wampler, attended church and heard a sermon based upon the passage "Strive to enter in at the straight gate" (a reference to Matthew 7:13).

While at Bardstown, Wampler sketched his design for a Confederate national flag and submitted it to President Davis. The Provisional Confederate Congress had established a committee to consider candidates for a national flag and seal. This undertaking generated considerable interest, as thousands of drawings were contributed by enthusiastic southerners like Wampler. He may well have been inspired by the patriotism displayed on September 24, or by a flag created earlier by Nicole Marchall of Louisville, which, according to local lore, was the first southern banner raised in Kentucky and was flown outside the home of Lt. Gov. William Johnson on the edge of Bardstown.

Mount Washington

The cobblestone turnpike outside the Johnson residence connected Bardstown and Louisville, forty miles to the north. Stone markers along the way indicated the distance in miles. Wampler and his escort started up the turnpike late on the morning of September 29. Despite the paving, the horses moved slowly on the uphill climb to High Grove, which looked down on a valley farther north. Col. John Wharton, whose 1st Cavalry Brigade supported the Right Wing, had selected this strategic location for his headquarters. Wharton coordinated cavalry elements of varying sizes used for videttes, guard, and police duty, special assignments, and, in the case of one company, as support of the engineer corps under General Polk. Wharton had 200 Texas Rangers (8th Texas Cavalry), 40 members of the 2nd Georgia Cavalry, and 4 partially armed companies with him at High Grove—fewer than 300 troopers in all.[72] Their pickets were positioned as far north as the outskirts of Louisville.[73] Continuing on, Wampler's party passed over the ridge at Riverview with a commanding view of the valley to the north and east, down and across the Salt River, and at sunset up the ridgeline into Mount Washington, a village of fewer than 500 inhabitants, 2 churches, and a secondary school.[74] They had ridden 20 miles from Bardstown.

Wampler entered the two-story frame hotel on the east side of the main street to book a room and obtain whatever intelligence was possible by listening to local gossip. He quickly learned that in Louisville earlier that day, Federal Brig. Gen. Jefferson C. Davis had shot and killed Maj. Gen. William "Bull" Nelson, a veteran of Shiloh and commander of the troops routed by Kirby Smith at Richmond, Kentucky.[75] At the Mount Washington hotel, Wampler also met a "Mrs. Church," whom he found to be "very intelligent & shrewd." Wampler determined to employ her as a "secret agent," and she readily agreed. Returning to Bardstown the next morning, he made the necessary arrangements and left again for Mount Washington three hours later. At 8:00 P.M., he was instructing his agent in how to produce and distribute incendiary handbills in Illinois and Indiana, where inhabitants in the lower portions of each state sympathized with the Southern cause. The following morning, he started Mrs. Church on her way.[76] That same evening, Wampler also enlisted one of his escorts, named Henton, to circulate outside Louisville and gather intelligence on the Yankee force assembling there. He would depart the next morning as well.[77]

Recruiting and employing intelligence operatives was not a customary role for a Confederate engineer officer.[78] Who was Mrs. Church whose potential as a southern operative was so obvious to Wampler? In all likelihood, she was the wife or consort of Nelson B. Church, a former captain in the Federal army. A native of Ohio, Church had been a locomotive engineer on the Louisville and Nashville Railroad when the war began. After enlisting a number of recruits into Company F of the 4th Regiment of Kentucky Cavalry, it was no surprise when he was elected their commander later in 1861. He took the unit to Bardstown in January 1862, and then his brief career as a soldier began to unravel. His regimental commander, Col. Jesse Bayles, reported that Church transported "a pretty woman" from Louisville to Bardstown and put her up in a nearby farmhouse. After Church was missing from his unit for an excessive period of time, Bayles went looking for him and surprised the two in bed together. Church explained that he was sick and the woman was his wife. Soon thereafter, the company commander was arrested for encouraging soldiers to desert, but he escaped custody and was shown as "Absent Without Leave" on the musters of March and April 1862. In June 1862, a Union surgeon diagnosed Church as syphilitic, and he was discharged from service. A newspaper reporter encountered him outside Mount Washington the day after "Mrs. Church" departed.[79] It is not unreasonable to speculate that, by this time, Church's paramour may well have been receptive to an assignment that would take her out of the area.[80]

At about the precise time on the morning of October 1 that Wampler was dispatching his agents, Federal soldiers were marching out of Louisville to confront the Confederate invaders of Kentucky. Buell was retaking the initiative from the Rebels. His army of 58,000 was organized into 3 corps, marching southeast on separate roads to Bardstown through Taylorsville, Mount Washington, and Shepherdsville.[81] The Second Corps, commanded by Maj. Gen. Thomas L. Crittenden and numbering about 22,000, moved toward Mount Washington. It was preceded by 5 companies of 350 troopers from the 4th Indiana Cavalry, under command of Col. Lawrence Shuler, in the far advance.[82] Several miles out of the city, they were surprised by Capt. Cyrus Ingles's 3 companies of the 1st Kentucky (Confederate) Cavalry. In the ensuing exchange of fire, Shuler's units lost 25 men killed and wounded. Vastly outnumbered, the Southern riders fell back to a succession of defensive positions from which they repeatedly delayed the Federals.[83]

After completing his business in Mount Washington that morning, Wampler proceeded with his cavalry escort up the turnpike toward Louisville. Passing Southern pickets, he came upon 20 or 30 Texas Rangers, by his estimate, who advised him not to go farther, as the enemy was advancing in large numbers. Responding that it was his duty to go ahead and see for himself, Wampler continued on for another mile and a half until he approached within 250 yards of Yankee horsemen. Behind the lead element appeared to be a regiment of cavalry. Wampler began to slowly withdraw. His foes came forward at the same pace. When he drew his small party into a line across the pike, the Yankees did the same. Not wishing to engage a superior force, Wampler's band began to retire once more. Shuler's troopers then veered off on a parallel road to the west. The two adversaries continued southward in tandem for four miles, when the Federals suddenly dashed onto the turnpike from the byway on Waterford Road, guns blazing. The forty Confederates were badly outnumbered and spurred their horses in flight. Wampler and ten companions arrived first at the burnt, two-span, wooden bridge over Floyd's Fork, a couple miles north of Mount Washington. They quickly formed a defense, opened fire, and successfully covered the retreat of their comrades. Wampler sent a messenger to Wharton for help, and what seemed like several hundred cavalrymen were soon at his side. As darkness ended the skirmish, Wharton punctuated the resistance with salvos from two brass six-pounders, positioned outside town on a ridge south of the Fork. The Confederates lost five men wounded, along with several horses, while they calculated three killed on the enemy side. Two Federal prisoners were taken, Capt. William A. Woodard of Company E, 4th Indiana Cavalry, and a private.[84]

Wharton and Wampler retired to Mount Washington, where each prepared a report of what had transpired. After dispatching his account, Wampler decided to go to Bardstown himself and, leaving at 10:00 P.M., arrived there at 4:00 in the morning. Three hours later, he was briefing the acting army commander and its chief engineer, David Harris, at their headquarters at Edgewood. Polk complimented Wampler on a satisfactory report. Before mapping his observations, Wampler dined with Harris and Brig. Gen. Daniel W. Adams, a Kentuckian who would bravely lead his brigade into battle one week later. Over the next thirty-six hours, the situation grew more grave, as Crittenden's corps pressed Wharton back, first to Mount Washington, then to Salt River, and finally to High Grove. As part of the headquarters evacuation on October 4, Wampler awoke his engineers before daylight and started them eastward on the road to Danville.[85] Wharton's troopers rode back through town later in the day, and by nightfall Bardstown was occupied by Federal soldiers.

PERRYVILLE

After leaving Bardstown, Bragg had conferred with Kirby Smith in Lexington and continued on to Frankfort to inaugurate a Confederate governor, Richard C. Hawes. Intended to be a lasting symbol of the South's claim to Kentucky, the ceremony on October 4 was brought to a hasty conclusion by enemy gunfire just outside the state capital. The shelling heralded the arrival of Brig. Gen. Joshua W. Sill's division, which had taken a fourth route out of Louisville, through Shelbyville, to divert attention from the main Federal offensive through Bardstown. Bragg, Kirby Smith, Hawes, and other Confederate dignitaries quickly departed for the Harrodsburg area, where Polk had been directed to bring the Army of the Mississippi. Bragg planned to unify the two Confederate armies in Kentucky, Polk's and Kirby Smith's, and then confront the main Federal force believed to be moving along the Shelbyville–Frankfort road.[86]

The Confederate order of battle leaving Bardstown on October 4 placed Polk's Right Wing in the lead, followed by Hardee's command. Wharton's cavalry was assigned to protect Hardee's column as a rear guard, for Buell's advance was not far behind. Polk's wing spent the night of October 4 in the vicinity of Springfield, but Wampler continued on to Texas or Cedar Grove, ten miles from Perryville. He made notes on the route as he rode through the beautiful countryside, along the ridge to Botland and then descending into a valley at Fredericktown that winds almost to Perryville. The next day Wampler arrived in Perryville, thirty-five miles east of Bardstown, as church bells were announcing the Sabbath. He stopped only long enough to have his horse's breast strap mended, before continuing another ten miles to Danville, a charming town about the size of Bardstown, but prettier, in Wampler's eyes. Cheatham's division moved north to Harrodsburg, while Withers's division was sent ahead to join with Kirby Smith.

The road between Perryville and Danville formed the base of an equilateral triangle, with Harrodsburg, ten miles north of each town, as the vertex. On October 6, Wampler was directed to confer with Harris at Bragg's headquarters at Harrodsburg.[87] About sunset the following day, Wampler became aware that Polk, along with Cheatham's division, had been ordered to move from Harrodsburg back to Perryville to counter the Federal forces gathering in that area. After finishing supper at the home of John Halsey, an old engineering colleague in Arkansas, Wampler gathered his escort and proceeded out of town. They slowly passed by the ribbon of gray and butternut soldiers trudging in the moonlight and reached Perryville shortly before midnight. The village of five hundred inhabitants was located in the state's geographic center at crossroads pointing in six directions. As Cheatham's four brigades began to arrive, they were directed to spend the night in a line of battle on Hardee's left.[88] Wampler's party, however, moved back about a mile or so to a grove, quite likely beside Crawford Springs, and slept for a couple of hours early on October 8.

Bragg remained convinced that Sill's diversionary movement represented the main Federal thrust. Kirby Smith was gathering his troops outside Lexington at Versailles and seemed to need reinforcement, while, in Bragg's conception, the force confronting Hardee at Perryville was a feint. Bragg had therefore directed Polk to "move with Cheatham's division to his [Hardee's] support and give the enemy battle immediately; rout him, and then move to our support at Versailles."[89] Even with the addition of Cheatham's division, Confederate troops at Perryville numbered only 16,000, of which over 1,000 were cavalry, as contrasted with the 50,000 soldiers available to Bragg in central Kentucky. Hardee had counseled Bragg on the evening of October 7, "Do not scatter your forces. There is one rule in our profession which should never be forgotten; it is to throw the masses of your troops on the fractions of the enemy."[90] Bragg was clearly violating that admonition.

Buell was equally confused. He believed that Bragg's forces were consolidated in the immediate vicinity of Perryville. He intended to concentrate there, too, but his three corps, consisting of fifty-eight thousand soldiers with varying battlefield experience, were widely separated in approaching the village. The corps under acting Maj. Gen. Charles Gilbert's advance was three or four miles west of Perryville on the Springfield Pike. Crittenden was close by but stalled on the Lebanon Pike to the south. Maj. Gen. Alexander McCook's corps was farther back at Mackville on a parallel road to the northwest. Buell himself was not about to check the disposition of his army, as he had been injured in a fall from his horse and appeared content to remain immobile at his headquarters at the Dorsey House, four miles west of town on the Springfield Pike.

Due to a summer drought, October of 1862 was unusually hot, and the availability of water exceptionally scarce. The march from Bardstown exhausted the thirsty blueclad soldiers, who had been without a good source of water for three days. Perryville held the promise of relief from the Chaplin River, as Pharr had reported almost two weeks earlier, and from its tributary, Doctor's Creek. Both were controlled by the Rebel army, along with the springs in and around Perryville. At 3:00 A.M. on October 8, a brigade in Brig. Gen. Philip Sheridan's division moved forward to fill their canteens from small pools in the bed of Doctor's Creek, two and a half miles west of town.[91] The Federals were soon challenged, however, by outposts of the 7th Arkansas on Peters Hill. Outnumbered, the Southern skirmishers drew back to the main line of Brig. Gen. St. John Liddell's Arkansas brigade.[92]

Wampler arose at 4:30 A.M. and was soon in the saddle with his escort. Riding through Perryville "amid the rattle of muskets," he arrived at the front about daybreak, as Liddell's 5th and 7th Arkansas regiments, accompanied by cannonading, were making an unsuccessful attempt to dislodge four Federal brigades from Peters Hill.[93] Wampler observed the enemy position and then returned to his line east of the Chaplin River to report what he had seen. While awaiting further orders, he found a position with good visibility on a ridge "where Hardee's left & Cheatham's right unite[d]" and dismounted to make an entry into his personal journal. His horse nibbled at some oats brought by its rider.[94] While Wampler reclined on the ground, Liddell's counterattack subsided, and a silence passed over the rugged terrain.

Bragg was not as content at this point as Wampler. The Confederate commander had awakened that morning expecting to hear the sounds of fighting. When he could stand the quiet no longer, the general headed for Perryville. Upon his arrival at about 9:30, he learned that Polk had convened a council of his commanding generals and concluded that the growing number of Yankees opposite them obviated Bragg's directive to take the offensive. Instead, Polk intended to employ a "defensive-offensive" strategy. Bragg remained determined to attack the Federals at once. Learning of the introduction of McCook's units on the Mackville Road, he must have also been concerned about becoming cut off from Kirby Smith to the north. Bragg therefore directed Cheatham to reposition his division to the right of Anderson and Buckner, in an attempt to overlap the Federal left and protect his access to the Confederate force at Versailles.

Wampler's tranquility was interrupted by orders that his wing, consisting of three of Cheatham's brigades, had been ordered to take an advance position on the Confederate right flank. Marching past the Crawford house, now serving as Bragg's headquarters, the Right Wing continued north along the Chaplin River road before halting to prepare for an attack, scheduled to begin at 12:30 P.M. Once again, Polk delayed. Wharton's cavalry brought news that the Federals were extending northward across the Mackville Road, and so Cheatham was ordered to move again in order to be in position to attack the enemy left. His soldiers waited impatiently a second time in the cornfield beside the Walker house.[95] Finally, they crossed Chaplin River, climbed the bluff along its west bank and, at about 2:00, assaulted what they believed to be the Federal left flank.

There, before Wampler's eyes, erupted a conflagration which Generals Bragg and Hardee considered "the severest struggle" they ever witnessed, according to Col. George W. Brent of Bragg's staff.[96] Wampler must have watched in amazement as Brig. Gen. Daniel Donelson's brigade, followed by Brig. Gen. A. P. Stewart's, moved forward into a crossfire from the blue line ahead and artillery farther out on the Yankee flank than the southerners had anticipated. Brig. Gen. George Maney was ordered to silence this Federal battery. Supported by effective salvos from their own artillery, the Confederates eventually captured the enemy guns, killing two Federal brigadier generals in the process—James S. Jackson and William R. Terrill. This "terrible contest," in Wampler's words, extended across Hardee's sector as well, as Cleburne, Adams, and Liddell's brigades joined with the rest of Anderson and Buckner's commands to battle McCook's First Corps and the few elements of Gilbert's Third Corps sent into the fray.

It is surprising that only twenty thousand of Buell's army engaged in this struggle for Kentucky. The Federal commander had become discouraged by the lateness of the deployment of his forces and was determined to attack the Confederates on the following day. An "acoustic shadow," caused by the severe topography where the fighting raged, combined with a strong wind out of the south to muffle the sounds of war from Buell's hearing at the Dorsey House, a mere two and a half miles from the battlefield. When firing was audible during his dinner with Gilbert at 2:00 P.M., Buell considered it to be ineffective "shelling the woods" and directed that the artillerymen stop

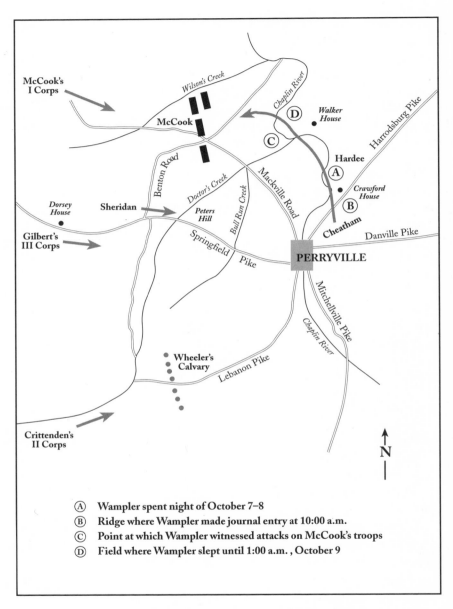

Wampler at the Battle of Perryville, Kentucky, October 8, 1862.

wasting their ammunition.[97] By the time Buell learned the full extent of the engagement, the battle was over and, soon thereafter, so was his career as an army commander.

As darkness descended about 5:30 P.M., Polk earned Wampler's respect by leading his men "with impetuosity." The bishop-general had mistaken the 22nd Indiana for a Southern regiment. Approaching the unit, Polk was challenged by its commander to identify himself. Realizing his error, Polk retorted, "I'll soon show you who I am, sir; cease firing, sir, at once."[98] He thereupon rode brazenly back to the Confederate lines and directed Liddell's brigade to open a devastating volley upon the Indianans, killing their commander. Wampler recorded that the fighting lasted for another ninety minutes after sunset. His eye for the aesthetic noted the full moon overhead and the grandeur of "bright flashes along the line as cannon & muskets did their deadly errands."[99]

When firing finally subsided, the Federal left had been pushed back a mile or so. The Southern forces occupied the battlefield, and went about the business of collecting guns, ordnance, and clothing. Threadbare Rebel survivors relieved the dead of hats, coats, pants, and shoes.[100] Twelve-pounder Napoleon guns were hauled away by teams that left behind the southerners' inferior smoothbore six-pounders. Bragg's army had sustained fewer casualties, 510 killed, 2,635 wounded, and 251 missing, compared with 845 Federals killed, 2,851 wounded, and 515 captured and missing. One-third of the Southern losses were sustained by Cheatham's units.[101] Nevertheless, "the victory ours," concluded Wampler, and a good many of his comrades agreed.

Perryville represented Wampler's most profound exposure to the intensity, confusion, and horror of a Civil War battlefield. Other than observing and reporting upon the disposition of enemy forces, however, the encounter had not imposed particular challenges on the engineer staff officer. There had been no paths to clear to enable units to maneuver, no fortified positions to build or reinforce, and no bridging to construct or destroy. On the other side of the battlefield, Federal topographical engineers were employed to reconnoiter terrain preparatory to emplacement of troops. At one point, engineers in blue were thrown into the fight, providing fire support to a Michigan battery.[102] At the contest's conclusion, the engineer staffs of both armies prepared maps depicting what had occurred from their varying command perspectives.

While Southern foot soldiers slept on the battlefield where the fighting had halted, surrounded by the dead, dying, and wounded from both sides, Wampler moved back to the field beside the Walker House, where Cheatham's troops had prepared for battle, and slept on a pile of corn and fodder. He was awakened about 1:00 A.M. to move out. Saddling his horse, he "rode by moonlight over the battlefield amid the dead bodies & groans of the wounded." Rebel surgeons were ministering to the casualties of North and South alike.[103] As Wampler passed through Perryville, grayclad pickets pointed out to him the line of Yankees visible by moonlight on the edge of town. When Buell finally launched an attack in the morning, his troops entered a village overflowing with the casualties of both armies, but the Rebel combatants had disappeared.

At sunrise, Wampler was reunited with Cheatham, who informed him that, rather than merely repositioning the lines, as Wampler had been led to believe, Polk's force at Perryville was being pulled back to Harrodsburg to meet a flanking movement by the enemy. His dinner that day at the Halsey house in Harrodsburg was the first meal Wampler had eaten since supper taken at the same table before leaving for Perryville.

THE LONG WAY BACK

Kentucky had not rallied to the Confederate banner as expected. Scarcely more than two thousand men enlisted, and Bragg believed that half of these subsequently deserted.[104] He understood the Federal army to be "largely superior" in numbers, making a decisive Confederate victory unlikely. Shocked to learn that his commissary held only enough flour and meal for four days' rations, the Confederate commander felt compelled to withdraw to an area that could sustain his troops. Reports of another Federal army descending upon his right flank from Cincinnati added to his unease. Autumn rains would soon make the crude roads through Cumberland Gap impassable. The discouraging news of Southern defeats at Iuka and Corinth in north Mississippi opened Middle Tennessee once again to Yankee control if Bragg did not redeploy his army.[105] Consequently, Bragg moved his headquarters to the Bryantsville area and then ordered his army to begin pulling out of Kentucky on October 13.

Wampler had already headed for Bryantsville with a fellow engineer, Lt. George M. Helm, and an officer on General Cheatham's staff, Col. Marcus J. Wright. Reaching Camp Dick Robinson on October 10, they conferred with Cheatham, who had also just arrived. The two engineers then reported to Harris, in his final days on the army's staff. He was probably unaware that orders had been issued by the war department on October 7, reassigning him to Beauregard's headquarters in the Department of South Carolina and Georgia.

As an engineer officer on Bragg's staff, Wampler was one of the first to receive an indication of the direction the army would be moving. On October 11–12, he was sent on repeated reconnaissance missions to the southeast, returning each time with sketches of what he observed. He also accompanied a contingent of sappers and miners to the battery bluff overlooking the Danville Road, where they set to work on defensive positions. Wampler had been asked to oversee their relocation from Bryantsville to Camp Dick Robinson so as to position the engineer troops to lead the army southward. Originally established as a base by Federal recruits, Camp Dick Robinson was reportedly an ideal site for a camp, with water available in nearby Dix River and shade provided by large oak trees.[106]

Shortly after midnight on October 13, Harris awoke Wampler to tell him that the artillery and other troops were being withdrawn from the bluff. He notified the sappers and miners to prepare to leave immediately. Once again, the engineer corps was at the head of the column. By the time a halt was called for midday dinner, they had ridden and walked nineteen miles through Lancaster to Crab Orchard and camped a mile outside town.

Lancaster was the junction where the column split. Kirby Smith's army had finally merged with Polk's at Camp Dick Robinson, but no single road south was adequate for the entire retrograde movement. While Polk's Army of the Mississippi continued on through Crab Orchard, Kirby Smith's Army of Kentucky headed in the direction of Big Hill. The latter element contained most of the supply trains. Wagons loaded with forage took two and a half days to pass a single point and were especially vulnerable to flank attacks by the pursuing Federals.[107] Wharton's cavalry brigade screened the right flank, while Wheeler's troopers protected the rear echelon. They were in almost continual contact with the enemy. Cavalrymen felled trees across the road, set up ambushes, harassed the enemy column, and did everything possible to delay the Yankee pursuit without being drawn into a pitched battle against what were invariably unfavorable odds.

At Crab Orchard the terrain changed from fertile Bluegrass to barren, rocky terrain, barely rich enough to feed the sparse population of eastern Kentucky. The macadamized surface ended, and the road became increasingly rough as it began the climb to higher elevations. Creeks and springs were still dry from the summer drought, and fodder for the animals was scarce. Soldiers exhausted from the rigors of the march and weakened by the lack of provisions were periodically detailed to do guard duty, serve as pickets, and perform as pioneers.

Polk's vanguard made especially good progress on October 14, passing through Mount Vernon to reach London, forty miles farther along the Wilderness Road. Wampler began to feel the effects of fatigue, exposure, hunger, and diarrhea. Soldiers without rations up and down the line endured the wearying days on the road and the cold, damp nights. Polk's column included wagons hauling muskets, ammunition, and merchandise of all sorts acquired in Kentucky, oxen dragging artillery, close to two thousand head of cattle driven by the 8th Texas Cavalry (Terry's Texas Rangers), and refugees with their household possessions and, in many cases, their slaves.[108] Wampler took special interest in the Hoskins family with seven children riding on horseback and in two carriages, along with several servants driving a pair of four-horse wagons. These fugitives accompanied Wampler beyond Barbourville to the home of Judge Pope, who was willing to accommodate them on the night of October 15. Cheatham's main body bivouacked farther back, alongside the road northwest of London at Pittman's Spring, the only adequate water source in the vicinity.[109]

The following morning the van started for Cumberland Gap. It crossed Cumberland Ford at mid-morning and continued on a long, gradual ascent along rough roads through the rugged foothills to reach its destination before sunset. The scenery was magnificent. Mountains were covered with forests to their summits, except in places where trees had been cut to permit unobstructed artillery fire. The opening itself was not easily visible from the line of march. Thinking like a military engineer now, if still somewhat aesthetic, Wampler noted "a remarkable feature in nature and naturally a very strong position in the Gap & at its highest point."[110] Moving through the gap, Wampler and his engineer party crossed the state line into Tennessee. At last, pure water was readily available from fine springs. Wampler enjoyed a good night's sleep in a little room used as a drugstore in the house where General Breckinridge's wife also stopped.

Continuing out of the mountains, once again in the company of the Hoskins family, Wampler's party passed by Tazewell, forded the wide Clinch River, kept on through a hamlet known as Priceville, and finally arrived at Knoxville three days later. Wampler had been forced to sleep in one of Hoskins's wagons, but otherwise, after leaving Kentucky, he had not fared badly, especially in comparison with the hardships endured by the army trailing behind.

Cold autumn nights and early snow in the foothills created a dismal environment for the bitter conclusion to the Confederates' invasion of Kentucky. Reports of soldiers nearly starving on the retreat were widespread, as were instances of men with inadequate clothing shivering in the cold. Invisible among a mountain population loyal to the Union, bushwackers preyed upon inviting targets in the caravan. The supply trains that were just reaching Cumberland Gap as Wampler rode into Knoxville experienced difficulty scaling the steep grades and had to be pushed by infantrymen. The going was slow, as a single stalled wagon invariably caused the entire procession of foot soldiers, wagons, and artillery to halt. Consequently, the rear guard of Bragg's army, Wheeler's cavalry corps, did not clear the gap until October 23.[111]

Booking a room at Bosworth's Boarding House in Knoxville on October 19, Wampler sat down to express his disappointment in the Kentucky campaign to an individual who had provided help in the past. "We whipped the Enemy" at Perryville, he wrote to General Beauregard, which made subsequent developments so puzzling. Wampler indicated the bewilderment of those around him at Bragg's withdrawal from Kentucky and recalled Beauregard's commitment to have him assigned to his staff in the future.[112] The supplicant was now aware that David Harris was returning to serve with Beauregard. Another Virginian on Polk's staff, Capt. John Otey, would soon receive orders to report to Charleston.[113] Wampler was discouraged and wanted an assignment there, as well. He was not alone in his discontent with General Bragg.

One of Braxton Bragg's biographers concluded that the Kentucky campaign caused nearly every Confederate to lose confidence in him.[114] Polk, Hardee, Kirby Smith, Breckinridge, and Cleburne were among the most outspoken critics of the western commander's leadership. Bragg never really challenged the Federals for control of Kentucky. He failed to join the Army of the Mississippi with the Army of Kentucky or fight all, or even part of, the enemy force, as Hardee had advised. Victory on the battlefield would have made the political statement needed to win the overt allegiance of Kentuckians with Southern leanings. The battle at Perryville was a tactical success for Bragg, as he crushed the Federal left, but of absolutely no strategic value. By leaving the battleground, the Confederates gave the impression that they were the losers, just as their subsequent retreat from Kentucky would confirm that the entire invasion had failed.

Many southerners, like Wampler, considered their side to be the victors at Perryville.[115] Certainly the performance of individual Rebel soldiers at Perryville was not questioned. Bragg conceded, "For the time engaged it was the severest and most desperately contested engagement within my knowledge."[116]

MIDDLE TENNESSEE

Knoxville was soon bustling with veterans of the march through Kentucky. Bragg and Polk arrived with their regiments and staffs, along with Harris, Otey, Capt. John F. Lay, and more of Wampler's Virginia coterie. The sappers and miners showed up on October 23. A captain newly arrived from Richmond informed Wampler that Beauregard had applied for him. His spirits sank when Bragg declared that he could not be spared, but Wampler retained a desperate hope that the war department would nevertheless accede to Beauregard's request. Bragg was ordered to explain the disappointing Kentucky campaign to the president in person and departed for Richmond. No orders arrived for Wampler. He bided his time by writing to his family and to Charles B. Tebbs in Virginia and Doc Strong in Mississippi. Dr. Thomas H. Clagett from Loudoun County stopped by to give a long account of what had happened since Wampler's departure and informed him of the death of Robert Mavin, his deceased stepfather's brother. Wampler was assured that his family was surviving, despite Yankee raids and deprivations. He asked Clagett to take $135 back to his wife, using Loudoun's state senator, Charles B. Ball, as an intermediary. Wampler submitted another design for a Confederate national flag, this time to the congressional committee. He was pleased by the arrival of his mare, ridden by his servant, Mac. Temperatures turned colder, and four inches of snow blanketed the ground. Capt. James Nocquet was selected to succeed Harris as the army's chief engineer, and Wampler reported to him. Yet there was still no word from Richmond.[117]

The boredom and anxiety were finally broken on October 28, when Polk sent for Wampler and issued orders for the sappers and miners to repair the roads westward through Middle Tennessee to Murfreesboro. While the troops were once again to be transported by rail, Wampler's engineer party was to prepare the way for overland movement of the artillery and the ordnance, commissary, and baggage trains. The engineers would be accompanied by one hundred pioneers from Lt. Col. Robert C. Tyler's 15th Tennessee Regiment.[118] Capt. George Pickett, remaining in command of the sappers and miners, led them on the road toward Kingston the next morning. Wampler passed the work party on his way to catch up with the engineer staff officers ahead. The following day, he stopped at Kingston to acquire a detail of cavalry to act as couriers and then continued on to examine a ford across the Tennessee River. Over the next several days, Wampler alternated between scouting and reporting what he saw, giving direction to his wing's engineer corps, and dining and spending evenings with his peers, Capts.

Edward B. Sayers and John W. Green, and with Lt. Helm from the Left
Wing engineer party. The van proceeded southwesterly along good roads
through the fertile Tennessee River valley to Smith's Cross Roads, where
Green and Helm veered off to report back to their headquarters. Starting
fresh the next morning, the engineers moved up and over Walden's Ridge
and, descending into the valley beyond, camped beside the Sequatchie River.
Exploring the road network in several directions, they continued by
Therman's, onto the Cumberland Plateau, and into Altamont. There
Wampler discovered the 15th Tennessee, a unit recruited largely from Southern sympathizers in downstate Illinois, drunk and causing trouble, a situation not satisfactorily resolved by a subsequent court-martial, which he considered to be a farce.[119]

The route through Middle Tennessee had been specified at the outset of
the movement.[120] At Altamont, Wampler received a special message from
Cheatham, indicating the roads that Polk wanted the batteries and trains to
take into Tullahoma. Polk and Cheatham were both Tennesseans and might
well have been expected to have firsthand experience and opinions as to which
routes their troops should use. Cheatham also indicated that an artillery officer,
well acquainted with the country, would be sent to assist the engineers.[121]
Cheatham had moved from Chattanooga, where Wampler last heard of him,
by rail to Bridgeport, Alabama, and consequently the engineers' courier had
not yet caught up to inform the general that the van was twenty-five miles
north of where the guide was told to meet it. The engineers thus found their
own way off the Cumberland Plateau via Pelham.

On the morning of November 6, Wampler reached his final destination,
entering Tullahoma ahead of his party. He must have been somewhat disappointed by the settlement, described in a contemporary newspaper account
as "[a] dismal, melancholy depot station. . . . A few scattered and squalid
tenements (crammed, jammed and damned . . . mud up to the eyes, not
having stone, nor curb."[122] Wampler ran into Lt. Col. John Jacques, his com-
patriot from the engineer advance into Kentucky, and they went together to
have a drink with General Cheatham, noted for his fondness of spirits. Unfortunately, on this occasion the libation ended in a heated argument between Wampler's two drinking companions.[123]

The Right Wing engineers arrived first and camped on a hillside at the
edge of town, leaving the bottom for their counterparts from the Left Wing,
when they appeared a day later. The weather turned bitter cold and windy
with snow, causing Wampler's head and jaw to ache. He continued to suffer
from diarrhea. After several days, as the temperature began to moderate, his

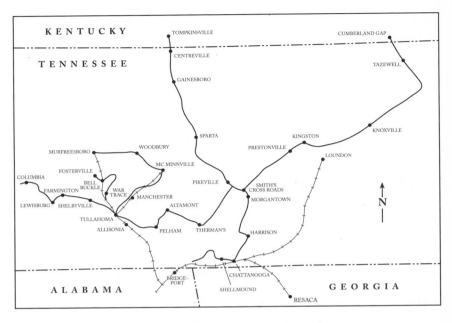

Wampler's War in the West: August 19–September 9, 1862,
October 16, 1862–July 24, 1863.

health improved, and he set about working again. Wampler directed Lt. Henry
C. Force to begin preparing a map of the town and its environs. Serving as
acting commander in Polk's absence, Cheatham sent Wampler to Bridgeport
to gather the mail. When he returned empty-handed, the general immediately sent him back over the same track, this time all the way to Chattanooga
to retrieve the wing's correspondence. Stockades and burnt dwellings provided grim reminders that, not long before, the area had been occupied by
the enemy. Passage through the long Cumberland Mountain tunnel outside
Cowan required pulling half of the train at a time. The bridges across the
Tennessee River at Bridgeport, which had been destroyed during the summer to slow the Federal advance on Chattanooga, were under repair. Wampler
had to remain at Bridgeport overnight before crossing the river by boat. He
was delayed again on the east side, awaiting a train to Chattanooga. While
there, he encountered Bragg and his staff on their way west to Tullahoma.

Once in Chattanooga, Wampler obtained supplies for Cheatham and used
the opportunity to mail personal letters home and socialize with friends. The
return trip required almost twenty-four hours to traverse one hundred miles,
causing the engineer captain at one point to buy bacon and flour for biscuits in

an attempt to satisfy his hunger and that of his traveling companions. He finally arrived in Tullahoma at midnight, only to find Presstman asleep in his bed, leaving the weary traveler to improvise for the remainder of the night.[124]

While the engineers remained busy, many soldiers, especially those from Tennessee, were rewarded for their arduous march through Kentucky by being granted leave to go home. Over the next ten days, Wampler's thoughts turned to his family, as well. He busied himself sending officers out on reconnaissance and attended to miscellaneous tasks, such as obtaining blankets for Lieutenant Force, even though he had none for himself. When Polk's command was directed to Murfreesboro on November 21, Wampler conveyed the orders to the sappers and miners and then started out on horseback with John Lay, now wearing the brevet rank of colonel. The two horsemen sang hymns, whistled, and talked to pass the time as they rode along at an easy gait. Proceeding by way of McMinnville, they stopped in a well-appointed hotel, where the smell of an oil lamp recalled happier days before the war, reminding the engineer once again of his separation from loved ones in Virginia. He was pleased to find Col. Marcus Wright of Polk's staff in town. The engineer and his traveling companion also bargained for new mounts, Wampler paying $275 for a little black stallion, which thoroughly delighted him. When they finally arrived at Murfreesboro, he expanded his socializing to include Lt. Cols. George W. Brent (a friend from Alexandria, Virginia) and George G. Garner, Bragg's acting chief of staff and adjutant general, respectively, Robert C. Tyler, and other acquaintances.[125]

Wampler found the army's engineer office in Murfreesboro in a state of flux. Now a major, James Nocquet had initially accompanied Bragg and other senior generals on reconnaissance throughout the locale. The French-born Nocquet's engineering expertise was seemingly well regarded, but his thick accent made him difficult to understand. Wampler appeared to get along with Nocquet better than most, quite possibly due to his facility with French. In the midst of shuffling commanders and staff, Bragg was not as comfortable with his senior engineer. He consequently dispatched Nocquet to oversee preparation of the defensive works guarding the bridge and ferry at Bridgeport.[126] When he departed Murfreesboro early on November 28, for what must have seemed a temporary assignment, Nocquet left Wampler in charge. Neither seemed aware of the opportunity being presented.

SUCCESS AT MURFREESBORO

Braxton Bragg had announced a major reorganization of his command on November 20, christening the new entity the "Army of Tennessee."[127] The former Right Wing of the Army of the Mississippi, commanded by Polk, became its First Corps; Hardee's Left Wing was converted into the Second Corps; and once Kirby Smith's troops closed with the main body, they would constitute the Third Corps. Wheeler and Wharton, by now brigadier generals, were assigned to lead cavalry brigades in support of the First and Second Corps, respectively. Brig. Gen. Nathan Bedford Forrest and Col. John Hunt Morgan headed independent mounted brigades. The aggregate strength reported in field returns for the First and Second Corps exceeded 60,000 soldiers, of which only 30,649 were considered effective and present for duty (excluding 9,000 troopers in the cavalry brigades).[128] The plan for a third corps was abandoned in mid-December, when Bragg was ordered to send 10,000 troops to Mississippi.

The commanding general was anxious to concentrate his army around Murfreesboro to counter Federal forces gathering thirty miles north in Nashville. A number of the soldiers returning from Kentucky were barefooted and ragged, although Bragg seemed satisfied that clothing, shoes, and blankets were being supplied as rapidly as possible. Outbreaks of typhoid, scurvy, dysentery, and pneumonia were widespread. Nevertheless, on November 24, Bragg reported, "The health and general tone of my old Army of the Mississippi (now Polk's and Hardee's corps) were never better."[129]

Bragg was still embroiled in a contest with some of his subordinate commanders to assign blame for failure of the Kentucky campaign. At the same time, some key staff were critical of his leadership. Others were thought to have loyalties elsewhere—to Beauregard, in particular—as the former commander had originally assembled the staff now supporting Bragg. In the midst of sorting out friend and foe, Bragg worked incredibly long hours, often attending to administrative minutiae and delegating work inconsistently. One new member to his staff remarked that "Bragg is said to be difficult to please. He told me that he was exacting 'but tried to be just.'"[130] In the swirl of these pressures and suspicions, Bragg directed Wampler to report to him later on the same day that Nocquet was assigned to manage construction projects from the logistics center at Chattanooga, as chief engineer of Department No. 2. The opening was thereby created for the commanding general to designate Wampler "as chief of the engineer corps until further orders."[131]

The appointment was completely unexpected by Wampler. It certainly was not a promotion he had lobbied to obtain. He bore no ill feeling toward Nocquet, and, indeed, the two frequently socialized together. At the Frenchman's insistence, Wampler had even joined his mess. Nor had Wampler asked Bragg for special recognition. Quite the contrary, sharing the collective frustration over his commander's handling of the Kentucky campaign,

Wampler had attempted to rejoin Beauregard. Bragg was certainly aware of Wampler's personal attachment to Beauregard, having vetoed the proposal that Wampler and Presstman be transferred to Charleston.[132] Never one to turn his back on an opportunity, however, Wampler immediately immersed himself in the duties of the Army of Tennessee's chief engineer.

The captain reported to the commanding general each morning for orders. He deployed his staff of engineer officers on reconnaissance, twice riding to the front lines with Force to pass him through the pickets. He met repeatedly with Jacques and Tyler, commanders of troops serving as pioneers. Helm was employed in making a map of the Perryville battlefield. A light snow fell, activating the rheumatism in Wampler's left shoulder, but this was not a time to be distracted.

When Nocquet returned from Bridgeport, he and Wampler reported together to Bragg. The army commander must have liked what Wampler was doing, for the French officer was sent back to the Tennessee River to oversee construction of the bridges and batteries there. Nocquet packed his personal possessions, taking along a draftsman, clerk, cook, and orderly. Pickett's sappers and miners were ordered to accompany him. Meanwhile, Wampler furnished Bragg with six tracings of the surrounding terrain. Within hours of the general's inquiry about the bridge over Duck River at Shelbyville, Wampler provided a spot report on its condition and estimated repair time, along with identifying a good ford in the immediate vicinity as an alternative.[133] Wampler's value as a topographical engineer to a commander confronting a large adversary on unfamiliar ground clearly outweighed that of a more senior engineer who was less skillful in gathering intelligence and awkward at working with commanders and staff.

Wampler continued to push his officers. As assignments were completed, others were made. One subordinate departed to repair a road crossing; another was sent to find existing maps of the region and whatever drawing materials were available. Correspondence flowed back and forth between the engineer office and corps headquarters. Wampler continually updated Bragg's map as new information was received. On at least one occasion, true to form, the commanding general took time to delve into a list of officer assignments being made by his chief engineer. In the midst of this activity, Wampler was surprised one evening by the sudden appearance of Henry Pharr, who was believed to have been killed at Perryville. He had been captured instead.

Morris returned from the field with news that the enemy was at Franklin, twenty-eight miles to the west of Murfreesboro, in position to threaten the Confederate left flank. Soon thereafter, Wampler delighted in watching Yan-

kee prisoners being marched from an engagement at Hartsville past his office down the town's windy, icy street. Reportedly, a large quantity of stores
was also captured by the southerners. The engineer office also received information regarding entrenchments around Nashville, which was duly recorded
and disseminated.[134] Engineers directed construction of three railroad bridges
to facilitate the army's mobility to respond to a Federal attack anywhere along
its line. Completion of one bridge required payment of costs totaling almost
$850. A succession of couriers arrived and departed, orders were received,
delivered, and executed. As the hectic pace continued, Wampler's headaches
and rheumatism seemed to intensify. However, he would not permit himself
to take time off.[135]

Captain Wampler had demonstrated competence in the engineering skills
required to develop defensive positions at Corinth, construct bridges at Aberdeen, prepare a route of march for an army on the move, gather intelligence on the enemy's whereabouts
and disposition, and, of course, conduct reconnaissance and make topographical drawings to facilitate tactical decisions. Now he was supervising
other engineers performing these tasks.[136] At the same time, Wampler was
maturing as a leader as he directed his peers in the field. The hardships of
war, including prolonged separation from home, were muted by the satisfac-
tions attendant to expanded authority and visibility. While the execution of
day-to-day responsibilities was important, his success would be measured by
the commander's perception of this performance. There was no apparent
cause for concern in this regard, however, as he appeared to be satisfying a
general with the reputation of being very difficult to please.

Eight months on the trail with the Confederate Army in the West had
brought Wampler to his present position. No more seasoned or able engineer officer was serving in that command. Other than his cohort, Capt. David
Harris, his predecessors had held the rank of colonel or major. Wampler was
doing the job as a captain, and, at age thirty-two, he was older than many
general officers wearing blue or gray. Morris Wampler had every reason to be
proud of his appointment and performance of duty as chief engineer, Army
of Tennessee.

CHAPTER SEVEN

> > >

The Engineer Corps in Tennessee

December 1862 was an eventful month for the Army of Tennessee. Gen. Joseph E. Johnston came to inspect the command on the fifth, the day after assuming leadership of the Western Department, which encompassed the forces under Gen. Braxton Bragg, Lt. Gen. Edmund Kirby Smith in East Tennessee, and Lt. Gen. John C. Pemberton in Mississippi. Johnston concluded that "Bragg's troops are in fine condition. Healthy looking & well clothed. In fine spirits too."[1]

Later that same week, President Jefferson Davis arrived to evaluate the Army of Tennessee. Davis sought a firsthand assessment of the Army in the West, after summoning Bragg and Lt. Gen. Leonidas Polk to Richmond to confer on the withdrawal from Kentucky and receiving a disturbing request from Kirby Smith for transfer anywhere outside Bragg's command. A grand review of the troops of Polk and Lt. Gen. William J. Hardee attracted a large crowd of civilian spectators. The president also "found troops there in good condition and fine spirits," making note, as well, of the enemy's close proximity at Nashville.[2]

The frigid Tennessee weather turned balmy as Christmas approached. Murfreesboro glowed from its own lights and those of soldier campfires ringing the community. Parties, receptions, races, drinking, and frolicking enlivened the encampment. Colder temperatures soon returned, however, accompanied by a hard rain that dampened holiday spirits at the gala balls before and after Christmas.

EVACUATION

The chief engineer of the Army of Tennessee was one of the few staff officers not enjoying the frivolity. Fatigue, extended periods outside in the cold and damp, exposure to infectious disease common in the close confines of bivouac, and inconsistent sanitary measures had finally caught up with Morris Wampler in early December, just as these conditions disabled hundreds of thousands of other soldiers throughout the war. In December 1862 and January 1863, the Army of Tennessee recorded over sixty thousand patients in its medical system. Less than one-fifth were suffering from battle wounds; many were ill with diarrhea and dysentery.[3] In addition to sickness, the increased work schedule and pressure of being the army's senior engineer weakened a soldier who had endured the rigors of almost four months of campaigning. During that period, Wampler traveled overland from Aberdeen, Mississippi, through Alabama and Tennessee, into Kentucky, and then back to Tullahoma, before settling in Murfreesboro.

The faintness Wampler experienced may have been attributable to dehydration, brought on in part by a shortage of clean drinking water in an area suddenly occupied by tens of thousands of soldiers, along with their horses, mules, and oxen. Harmful bacteria in the commissary combined with contaminated water to ravage Wampler's digestive system. His recurring stomach problems degenerated into a chronic bowel infection, most likely a strain of true dysentery. Concentration on staff work became impossible due to severe headaches, in all likelihood the result of dehydration and low blood sugar, reducing the absorption of nutrients. The accompanying muscle aches in the arms and legs could have been a symptom of the infection attacking Wampler's body or a sign of another bout with rheumatism, from which he had suffered since serving in the Coast Survey. Common use of the term "rheumatism" may have been what is known today as "reactive arthritis," or Reiter's syndrome.[4]

Despite the absence of a precise medical diagnosis, Wampler knew he was far sicker than at any other time in his adult life. He tried to leave his bed to work, but could not do so. A high fever continued for nearly three weeks. By December 28, it became obvious that the chief engineer could not remain at his post, especially in light of the developing military confrontation. Confederate cavalry reported the Federal army moving toward Murfreesboro. Bragg organized his line of battle and ordered troops to draw ammunition and two days' rations.[5]

Wampler's orderly, William, found help to move the stricken engineer to the depot, where he was placed aboard a train going south and east, away from the Yankee threat. After traveling from early morning, the evacuee finally arrived at Resaca, Georgia, shortly before midnight. Thoroughly exhausted and barely cognizant of his whereabouts, Wampler was lifted from the car, carried to the home of his engineer comrade, Capt. John W. Green, and confined to bed. The Greens' plantation house was situated on a hilltop overlooking the Western and Atlantic Railroad, passing one hundred yards to the east. Benefiting from the family's nursing and personal care, a sharp contrast to living conditions in the field, Wampler gathered strength and gradually recovered. By mid-January, the patient was pleased that he could walk about his room without assistance. He was still very weak, however, and it was January 23 before he could finally join the family at the dinner table.[6]

Regaining his strength, Wampler became concerned about expiration of the thirty-day furlough granted him on December 28. The pass was based upon a surgeon's certificate of disability, the standard policy in the Army of Tennessee for soldiers suffering from illness. The army was now taking disciplinary action against invalids who failed to report to their duty stations upon expiration of leave.[7] Wampler despaired over his absence during the Battle of Murfreesboro (or Stones River, as it was known to the Federals). The three-day clash had left both sides with casualties exceeding 30 percent of their effective troop strength. Wampler believed that the Army of Tennessee could have benefited from his direction of its engineer corps. At the conflict's conclusion, once again, Bragg had withdrawn from the battlefield, leaving the Federals to declare victory and renewing talk that he had lost his nerve.

Wampler also dreamed of home, wondering about his life after the war. How he wished to return to Virginia to see his family. He asked one of the Green girls to have a dress made for Kate and corresponded with her, using Charles Ball as intermediary. The patient clipped a newspaper advertisement for ninety-five acres of timbered land seven miles outside Atlanta. His inquiry elicited the description of a prime location near both a railroad and the Chattahoochee River, streams and springs providing pure stone water, and an old locomotive engine to run machinery that conveyed with the property. Clearly, he envisioned the Wampler family resettling near peaceful Atlanta after the war, far from the fighting which had swept back and forth across Loudoun County by early 1863. Until the conflict ended, however, a loyal southerner must be prepared to defend his homeland, and so he inquired, as well, about cartridges for a Yankee pistol obtained after Kirby Smith's victory at Richmond, Kentucky.[8]

At last, on February 6, Wampler had sufficiently recovered to return to Tennessee. The comfort received from the Green family reminded him of the warmth he had known with the Strongs in Mississippi. He would stay in touch with the Greens, as he had done faithfully with Doc and Georgia Strong. Carrying a box lunch, packed by Mrs. Green and her daughters, Wampler boarded the train and traveled until sunset, when he arrived in Chattanooga. He reported at once to the provost marshal to resolve any questions concerning his expired furlough and then set about to reestablish himself in the engineer corps.

GENERAL BRAGG'S ENGINEERS

The following day, Wampler dined with two engineer colleagues, Capt. George B. Pickett and Maj. James Nocquet, at the latter's office in Chattanooga. They were joined by French-born Capt. Francois L. J. Thysseus, another engineer officer assigned as aide-de-camp to Maj. Gen. Earl Van Dorn. As commander of a company of sappers and miners, Pickett had provided support for Wampler in Mississippi and on the march through Kentucky, and the two would work together again in the months ahead. Pickett's company was currently employed by Nocquet in building a pontoon bridge at Battle Creek. Components were also being assembled for a second bridge. At the same time, Pickett supervised slaves furnished by the State of Alabama in construction of stockades to defend the crossing point on Battle Creek.[9]

As chief engineer of Department No. 2, Nocquet was assisted by Lt. James D. Thomas, a fair-haired, twenty-six-year-old graduate of Western Military Institute at Georgetown, Kentucky. Before the war, Thomas had been engaged for five years as a civilian engineer, constructing railroad bridges and laying track. He enlisted as a private at Bowling Green, Kentucky, and was immediately assigned as a draftsman for Nocquet. An eye problem hindered Thomas's opportunity for promotion. By early 1863, however, he had received a commission in the P.A.C.S. Corps of Engineers. Advancement was slow for Thomas, like other engineer officers, despite the fact that his father was a member of the Confederate Congress and lobbied the secretary of war repeatedly on his son's behalf.

The next day, Wampler continued westward via the railroad. When the train reached Bridgeport, Alabama, Capt. Wilson Presstman climbed aboard. He had been charged with preparing fortifications to protect the railroad bridge recently rebuilt over the Tennessee River, reconnecting the trunk line between South Carolina and Tennessee. Presstman was now on his way to the headquarters of the Army of Tennessee to assume the duties of chief engineer. This was a somber revelation for Wampler, who had lost the position due not to poor performance or lack of ability, but to illness beyond his control. His disposition brightened somewhat at the warm greeting extended by his comrades in Tullahoma.[10]

Presstman and Wampler reported together to General Bragg on February 9. Presstman was relieving Capt. Salvanus W. Steele, who had held the post of chief engineer since Wampler's evacuation. Appointed to the Provisional Corps of Engineers from Maury County, Tennessee, in October 1862, after commanding a pioneer unit in the Army of the Mississippi, Steele was being reassigned to Maj. Gen. Joseph Wheeler's newly formed cavalry corps.[11] Wampler would remain on the headquarters staff, working on special assignments as second in line behind the chief engineer.

General Bragg's engineer corps at this time was impressive in the skills and experience, both military and civilian, which its officers brought to their assignments. Capts. Edward B. Sayers and John W. Green were serving as chief engineers of Polk's and Hardee's corps, respectively. A six-foot, blue-eyed, thirty-four-year-old Irishman, Sayers had learned engineering in his homeland and in England over a five-year period, before emigrating to America. For six years prior to the war, he was assistant engineer for the city of St. Louis as a member of the state engineer corps. Sayers claimed to have been offered a captaincy in the U.S. Corps of Engineers before choosing an acting appointment on Gen. Albert Sidney Johnston's staff at Bowling Green in October 1861. Sayers was involved in the construction of fortifications at Clarksville, Tennessee, and served as well at Fort Donelson and Fort Pillow, where he impressed Maj. Jeremy F. Gilmer, then chief engineer of the Western Department. Later, as chief of the engineer bureau in Richmond, Gilmer would be a steady supporter of the immigrant.[12]

Assisting Sayers was now acting Lt. Henry N. Pharr. A professional engineer before the war, Pharr had enlisted in the 1st Arkansas Mounted Rifles in June 1861 and was soon wounded in the right leg by a musketball at the Battle of Wilson's Creek. By the following February, he had succeeded in obtaining a transfer to the engineer staff of Brig. Gen. Lloyd Tilghman in Kentucky and subsequently joined Polk's staff.[13]

As chief engineer of Hardee's corps, Captain Green was older than many of his military peers. He was a civil engineer by profession, having spent twenty years in the lumber industry. Swept up in the euphoria at the war's outbreak, he had enlisted in the 4th Louisiana Battalion, rapidly rising to sergeant and then acting adjutant. Green had left the army and was serving as senior engineer for the Vicksburg, Shreveport, and Texas Railroad, when, in July 1862, he was appointed a first lieutenant in the engineer corps.[14]

Reporting to Captain Green were four lieutenants—George M. Helm, John F. Steele, Henry C. Force, and Robert P. Rowley. Like Sayers, Helm also began his career as a Confederate engineer at Bowling Green and served with Capt. Samuel H. Lockett the following spring at Corinth, Mississippi, conducting reconnaissance of the area's road network. The Mississippian was a veteran of the march through Kentucky and later collected information about the Nashville and Chattanooga Railroad when Wampler served as the army's chief engineer. General Hardee considered Helm to be intelligent, energetic, and efficient.[15]

Of the four lieutenants, Steele had the most in common with Wampler, as a civil and topographical engineer of ten years' experience. Like Green, Steele had served a term in the ranks, enlisting in the 4th Alabama from his home state. He earned Brig. Gen. William H. C. Whiting's recommendation for a commission after working on his staff during construction of Southern fortifications along the Potomac River early in the war. Steele also received the commendation of Presstman, who described him as "zealous and efficient" and "highly accomplished," along with "practical experience as a Civil Engineer." In lobbying for a captaincy in the engineer corps, Steele wrote of "my standing as to scientific acquirement, military efficiency as an Officer, [and] high social standing," the latter referring, in part, to his attendance at the prestigious University of Virginia, a distinction that Wampler surely would have liked to share.[16]

Henry Clay Force was mustered into service at Tuscaloosa, Alabama, in April 1861 by Capt. Robert E. Rodes. Force was soon thereafter appointed regimental color sergeant of the 5th Alabama. He was discharged one year later, but returned to uniform in the summer of 1862, upon receiving an appointment as first lieutenant in the engineer corps. Force had apparently impressed his first commander, for the new officer was assigned to the Army of Northern Virginia to serve on the staff of now Brigadier General Rodes, who had practiced civil engineering before the war and was now commanding an infantry brigade. Force returned to the West in November 1862, being added to Wampler's engineer complement at Tullahoma.[17]

Lt. Robert P. Rowley's extensive professional experience, civilian and military, must have made less-qualified senior officers uncomfortable. Rowley had completed three years as chief engineer of Arkansas, when his state seceded and its troops, less the engineer corps, transferred to the Confederate army. Caught up in Southern patriotism, Rowley crossed the Mississippi

River and enlisted in the 4th Tennessee Infantry at Fort Pillow in August 1861. Brig. Gen. Gideon Pillow quickly recognized Rowley's capability with a field appointment as first lieutenant, assigning him to duty at Island Number 10. Rowley proceeded to prove his competence as a military engineer to a succession of prominent or soon-to-be influential superiors—Major Generals Breckinridge and Samuel Jones; Col. John Pegram; Major Gilmer; and Capts. Samuel H. Lockett and David B. Harris. Rowley performed a wide range of military engineer functions, from constructing earthworks on the Mississippi River to supervising slaves building a bridge outside Tupelo, Mississippi. By the winter of 1863, he became discouraged about his prospects for advancement in the engineer corps and applied for a captaincy to the chief of ordnance, Col. Josiah Gorgas. Bragg finally agreed to transfer Rowley back to Arkansas, once he could be spared. In the meantime, this very experienced lieutenant was engaged in building bridges on the Elk River near Tullahoma.[18]

Several junior officers and civilians were also assigned to the headquarters engineer office. Andrew H. Buchanan brought sterling credentials to the Corps of Engineers. For seven years before the war, he had held the position of professor of mathematics at Cumberland University in Lebanon, Tennessee, in addition to working as a civil engineer. Buchanan joined the corps as a topographical engineer early in 1861, serving at Nashville with Gilmer late that year. By early 1863, he had obtained a commission as a lieutenant and was assigned as a mapmaker on the headquarters staff of the Army of Tennessee.[19]

James K. P. McFall was appointed a lieutenant in the engineer corps on May 1, 1862, after prior service as a sergeant in Company H, 1st Tennessee Infantry, based upon his experience in railroad construction before the war. He had reported to Wampler during the engineer advance into Middle Tennessee in late October of that year. About the time of Wampler's return, McFall was being employed to survey the Tennessee River to determine how and where to obstruct it, if necessary.[20]

Conrad Meister served as draftsman, one of the relatively few Germans in Confederate service, unlike the Union army, which had a sizable number of Teutonic soldiers. He had initially joined Captain Pickett's company of sappers and miners in New Madrid, Missouri, rising to the grade of sergeant. His skill in topographical drawing soon earned Meister a place on the headquarters staff.[21] Two civilians also worked in the engineer headquarters, Assistant Engineer J. C. Wrenshall and Clerk George B. Blakemore, about whom little is known.

Robert C. Tyler in a brigadier general's uniform. Library of Congress.

Robert P. Rowley in a lieutenant colonel's uniform.
From *Confederate Veteran*, April 1899.

Two other engineers, Amos S. Darrow and Walter J. Morris, were assigned at that time to the Army of Tennessee. Darrow was S. W. Steele's
counterpart as the engineer with Morgan's Cavalry at McMinnville. While
serving as an acting commissary sergeant in the 25th Louisiana Infantry,
Darrow had demonstrated qualities that led to his selection as assistant engineer with the field rank of second lieutenant.[22]

Walter J. Morris of Polk's engineer staff was on thirty days' leave of

Lt. James K. P. McFall, ca. 1870, in the uniform of Knights Templar.
Tennessee State Library and Archives.

Lt. Andrew H. Buchanan after the war. From *Confederate Veteran,* May 1895.

absence, quite possibly to care for his business in East Tennessee. Morris had been appointed a first lieutenant in the engineer corps in October 1862, after serving with a field commission as an engineer lieutenant on the staff of General Tilghman, commanding Forts Henry and Donelson. It was at the latter post that Morris had been taken prisoner in 1862. His skill as a draftsman distinguished Morris from his peers, and so he was charged with preparing numerous maps for the Army of Tennessee in 1863–64. At the time Wampler returned to duty, Morris was engaged in topographical work to accompany Lt. Gen. Leonidas Polk's official report on his command at the Battle of Murfreesboro.[23]

In sum, Wampler returned to an engineer corps of nineteen officers, including the three-man contingent at Chattanooga, most of whom had considerable professional experience. These were, by no means, the only engineers supporting the Confederate war effort west of the Appalachian Mountains. Outside the Army of Tennessee, engineer officers were serving on the Mississippi River, in the Trans-Mississippi, and in other western departments, such as Kirby Smith's Department of East Tennessee. Some engineers filled authorized billets but were not recognized as officers in the Confederate Corps of Engineers. The latter category included engineers holding state commissions, wearing rank presented in the field but not acknowledged by Richmond, or working for the various engineer departments as civilians.

With one apparent exception, the Frenchman Nocquet, these officers shared a camaraderie and the seeming respect of their superior officers.[24] By February 1863, all had seen action on the battlefield. Their rank was well below the commanders they served, as "the old Army" had found captain and lieutenant to be appropriate seniority for leaders of small field parties, the role of many engineer officers in peacetime. Neither the blue nor gray army had yet recognized the increased responsibility and multiple functions performed by engineers in support of armies and corps consisting of numerous units with tens of thousands of soldiers. For Wampler and these other Confederate engineers, the adventure of establishing a new nation and fighting to ensure its survival, along with the opportunities for leadership and recognition thereby afforded, must have dimmed in attraction. By 1863, they were well aware of the reality of hard field duty, danger from combat and disease, separation from loved ones, and minimal pay as low-ranking officers in an economy overheated by inflation, with no reasonable hope for cessation of hostilities in sight.

In Garrison at Tullahoma

Wampler rejoined an army in defensive array along the Duck River, positioned between the Federal force around Murfreesboro and its own base in the strategic transportation network feeding into Chattanooga. The Confederate presence in Middle Tennessee also afforded access to the region's rich agricultural production. Bragg's headquarters at Tullahoma was astride the Nashville and Chattanooga Railroad. To his left and right front, aligned along the Duck River, were corps under Polk and Hardee. Polk's left wing was centered at Shelbyville; Hardee's right wing was headquartered in Tullahoma. Guarding their left and right flanks at Columbia and McMinnville, respectively, were cavalry under Van Dorn and Wheeler.

The Army of Tennessee was in the midst of a six-month hiatus in operations, the longest such interlude enjoyed by any Confederate army during the war. Bragg was at his best when afforded an opportunity to recruit, discipline, train, and equip soldiers. When Wampler returned, individuals present for duty numbered over 49,000, of whom almost 37,000 were considered effectives. This latter number approached 53,000 by mid-May, before 11,000 of Bragg's troops were transferred to Mississippi.[25] Wampler reported in to Bragg just as Gen. Joseph E. Johnston was completing yet another inquiry into what action should be taken, if any, regarding command of the Army of Tennessee. Johnston found the army "well clothed, healthy, and in good spirits," and consequently counseled President Davis against removing its commanding general.[26]

Wampler was returning to a commander in his mid-forties who, since the war's outset, had aged considerably, both physically and mentally, by contemporary accounts. Bragg's infrequent social contacts with subordinates added to his stern, rigid, officious persona. An inability to inspire those around him may have been caused, in part, by poor health. In addition to chronic nervousness, Bragg suffered from headaches, dyspepsia, and an outbreak of boils during the winter and spring of 1863.[27] Reserving judgment on Bragg's failings and apparently satisfied that his own brief performance as chief engineer had met with the approval of the commanding general, Wampler undertook his new engineering assignments with confidence and commitment, within the limits of his own precarious health.

He began by surveying the town's line of defense from horseback with Presstman, Green, and Pharr. By its completion later in the spring, more than a dozen gun emplacements reinforced almost five miles of breastworks, arranged in a semicircle to protect Tullahoma to the north, east, and west. Special attention was given to places where the perimeter was broken by a road or railroad track. Defensive positions looked out over a half mile of cleared stumps, abatis, and swamp, with woods and thicket beyond. Well inside the perimeter, just north of town was a star-shaped fort, called Fort Rains for Brig. Gen. James E. Rains of Nashville, killed in the fight at Murfreesboro.[28]

The weather was warm for February, and the engineers rode around the defensive line a second time before Wampler laid out new breastworks on the right, or east flank. He and Buchanan directed the men as they began work, but several days of rain left the construction sites wet and muddy. During this period, Wampler's cartographic skills were employed to help Wrenshall complete work on a map. When Presstman was away from headquarters, Wampler reported to Bragg as acting chief engineer.[29]

The return of wet, cold days and nights brought a recurrence of Wampler's rheumatism. By month's end, he also suffered from an attack of erysipelas in his arm, leading to an examination by the staff surgeon, Dr. D. W. Yandell, and his assistant Dr. A. A. Powell. Poultices and iodine washes seemed to help.[30]

The town of Tullahoma provided little in the way of social life for Bragg's staff officers. An out-of-town journalist described the community as, "A shocking place. (I mean for a gentleman!) A dismal, melancholy depot station. . . . A few scattered and squalid tenements (crammed, jammed, and damned . . .) mud up to the eyes; not having stone, nor curb."[31] Wampler relied upon music to lift his spirits. Sometimes he took up the flute, accompanied by his orderly, William, on the violin. Locating a melodian, another companion played, while Wampler and Meister sang, or the Marylander returned to his wind instrument. He once again engaged in correspondence with family and friends at home, including Kate, his mother, Eugenia Kephart, Chaplain Linthicum, and Capt. Albert Matthews, now commanding Wampler's former company in the 8th Virginia. Matthews reported the regimental news, but the absent husband and father was undoubtedly more interested in the account of Yankee "depredations" in Loudoun County.[32]

While the army headquarters improved its field fortifications, cavalry skirmishing flared up periodically at the front. On March 5, a confrontation at Thompson's Station, near Spring Hill, produced over a thousand Yankee prisoners. Wampler noted them being herded past his office in Tullahoma several days later. Another skirmish occurred on March 10 near Murfreesboro, resulting in the capture of an artillery piece of interest to the southerners. Wampler watched his colleagues try unsuccessfully to fire it. The engagement most threatening to the Confederates, however, erupted at Van Dorn's headquarters in Spring Hill. Recognizing the enemy's numerical superiority, the Rebel cavalrymen attempted to withdraw to the south, across Duck River into Columbia. When the swollen river prevented Van Dorn from erecting a pontoon bridge, however, he was forced to fight his way out. Feinting toward the Union right, his troopers escaped to the east, eventually ferrying across the river at Chapel Hill.

Wampler was consequently ordered to Columbia to oversee the installation of a bridge. He received authorization to call upon the nearest troop commander for labor, in addition to hiring, buying, or, as a last resort, impressing slaves and materials.[33] The engineer left Tullahoma on March 13, covering the twenty-four miles to Shelbyville before dark, when he stopped to visit with General Polk, telegraph Presstman, and billet with his comrades, Sayers and Pharr. The town had a reputation for being pro-Union and was reportedly bristling with civilians listening for information to relay to Maj. Gen. William S. Rosecrans, twenty-five miles to the north.[34] The next morning, Wampler continued on his way via Farmington and Lewisburg, "riding over the worst roads I ever saw, my poor horse suffering with scratches." For one so well-traveled, that was quite an indictment. The ground east of Columbia was rocky and uneven, the road no wider than a path, winding through glades, perpetually wet in spots, and hemmed in by nettled cedar trees, brambles, and briars. Consequently, the weary traveler decided to spend the night at Columbia, when he learned that Van Dorn was staying even farther ahead, outside of town.

The compacted gravel turnpike southwest from Columbia, in the direction of Mount Pleasant, was a refreshing change from the rough ride the preceding day. The terrain opened into a broad fertile area with prosperous, well-kept farms. Wampler enjoyed the warm sunshine and birds singing as he rode seven miles to Hamilton Place, Brig. Gen. Lucius Polk's home and occasional headquarters, where Van Dorn was visiting.[35] The colorful cavalryman was enjoying breakfast when the caller arrived shortly after 9:00 A.M. Van Dorn stated that his bridge was so near completion that Wampler's services were not needed, but that any observations he might make as a professional engineer would be most appreciated. The general informed his guest of the enemy disposition to his front and requested that this information be relayed to Bragg, along with a description of the poor network of lateral roads. The task was indeed daunting. "The liveliest effort of the mind could not conceive of roads in as bad condition as I found them," Wampler wrote. Van Dorn's objective was to convince Bragg to construct a bridge farther west toward Centreville, offering access to the rich valleys branching off Duck River and, more importantly, opening flanking routes to Franklin and Spring Hill. Van Dorn succeeded in persuading the army commander, for the engineer office was subsequently directed to construct a bridge twelve miles west of Columbia.[36]

On his way back to Tullahoma, Wampler stopped at the construction site, an old pioneer ford where Brig. Gen. Don Carlos Buell had crossed on pontoon bridges with the Army of Ohio on its way to Shiloh. Maj. Hampton L. Boon, Van Dorn's chief quartermaster, who had no engineering experience, had been assigned the task of erecting a bridge. After conferring with him, Wampler returned by the same route he used earlier, staying once again with Sayers and Pharr and calling this time on General Cheatham. Wampler was not so preoccupied with his travels that he failed to enjoy the wild flowers coming to life, and he stopped to gather poppies and anemones to send home to Kate in a letter. His six-day trip to Columbia had covered 136 miles.

Wampler arrived at headquarters in time for a series of military reviews. By March 1863, discord between Bragg and his generals appeared so contentious that the war department ordered Gen. Joseph E. Johnston to assume command of the Army of Tennessee. Arriving in Tullahoma, Johnston reviewed Hardee's corps, ten thousand strong, drilling on the parade ground for an hour or more before a host of onlookers. The 20th Tennessee proudly displayed a Confederate battle flag made by Mrs. Breckinridge from her wedding dress and presented to the regiment for its bravery at Murfreesboro. After reviews, Hardee was accustomed to hosting tournaments, horse races, serenades, and dances.[37]

Learning that Mrs. Bragg was battling typhoid fever, giving her husband more than enough to worry him, Johnston postponed announcing his control of the army. Johnston himself had taken ill by the time that Bragg returned to duty. It is doubtful that Wampler had heard the speculation that Johnston would take command or appreciated the imminent threat to Bragg's leadership, as he made no mention of it in his journal.[38]

The following week, Hardee's troops were on display again, this time in a grand review for Col. William Preston Johnston, the son of deceased Gen. Albert Sidney Johnston. Colonel Johnston was serving as aide-de-camp to President Davis. He, too, had been dispatched to Tullahoma to assess the state of the army. Johnston observed drills performed by the Kentucky Brigade at Manchester and by Polk's corps at Shelbyville. Afterward, on a bright, cool day, Wampler escorted the inspector on a ride along Tullahoma's line of defense, which Johnston subsequently described to Davis:

> I examined these fortifications, which are a line of slight redoubts extending in a semicircle from the Fayetteville to the Manchester road. Our advantage of ground is not very obvious, although the engineer in charge assured me it does exist, and the earthworks are low redoubts, not flanked by rifle-pits, except for some 20 yards or so. To my eye they seemed too far in advance of the crest of the hills. On the slope an abatis of heavy felled timber extends 1,500 feet to the front of each redoubt, making a zone of

that width about 3 or 4 miles in length. The works are either too strong or
too weak. They are too weak to rely upon, and too strong to abandon to
the enemy. Much labor has been wasted on them, unless they shall be put
in condition to be held by a small force against a larger one. General Bragg
says heavy intrenchments demoralize our troops, and that he would go
forward to meet the enemy, in which case that abatis would be an obstruc-
tion, to say the least.[39]

Another remarkable individual, Col. William Orton Williams, called
upon Wampler and Presstman during this period. The engineers must have
become acquainted with him before the war, as all three had resided in the
area around Washington, D.C. Two months after their chat at Tullahoma,
Williams and an accomplice were hanged as Confederate spies by Union
forces at Franklin, Tennessee.[40]

PROMOTION IN THE CORPS OF ENGINEERS

During the winter of 1863, Wampler entered into another kind of campaign,
this one with the Confederate War Department. Having served as a captain
for almost two years, while watching other officers, junior in years and experience, advance to higher rank, Wampler believed that he, too, was entitled
to promotion. He thereby joined forces with Presstman to obtain joint recognition as majors.

As captain was the highest rank initially permitted to P.A.C.S. officers in
the Corps of Engineers, the war department had engaged in the practice of
selectively promoting deserving candidates as artillery majors, while retaining them in engineering capacities.[41] In September 1862, the Confederate
Congress finally permitted P.A.C.S. engineers to serve as field-grade officers,
authorizing one colonel, three lieutenant colonels, and six majors.[42] As a
matter of personal policy, however, the chief of the engineer bureau, Col.
Jeremy F. Gilmer, chose not to nominate the full number approved for field
grade, in order "to excite the ambition to greater devotion and activity to
merit advancement" among the many company-grade aspirants. This approach had the added virtue, to Gilmer's mind, of allowing time for worthy
candidates to make themselves known to the war department.[43]

By February 1863, the pressure for upward mobility seemingly caused
Gilmer to request nominations from senior field commanders.[44] Gen. P. G. T.
Beauregard recommended his chief engineer in Charleston, Maj. David B.
Harris, for promotion to lieutenant colonel, while at the same time naming five
other officers as candidates for major, including Wampler and Presstman.[45]

These two, in turn, undertook to solicit endorsements from their patrons in the Army of Tennessee, Bragg and Hardee, respectively.[46] Presstman quickly obtained a letter of merit from Hardee, but Wampler found Bragg to be cautious, as usual, apparently uncertain of the propriety of Wampler's request. Once he sensed this reluctance, Wampler addressed the matter of his personal integrity in a letter to Bragg, explaining his collaboration with Presstman and pledging to make the ultimate sacrifice, "lose my Commission & go in the ranks," rather than advance at the expense of a friend and comrade in arms.[47] Bragg ultimately consented, but his recommendation, along with those of Hardee and Beauregard, produced nothing for the two engineers in Tennessee. Consequently, Wampler wrote to Beauregard, urging his benefactor to pursue the matter with Richmond.[48]

Disappointed once again, Wampler took his case directly to the chief of the engineer bureau. The supplicant traced his dedication to the Southern cause back to the response to John Brown's raid on Harpers Ferry and reviewed his contributions before and after formation of the Confederacy. He reminded Gilmer that a pair of full generals had written on his behalf and pointed out his seniority as a captain in the engineer corps.[49] In his mind, Wampler might have blamed the lack of appropriate recognition, as others did, on staff assignments rather than being in a line unit, or on his service in the West, as opposed to Gen. Robert E. Lee's Army of Northern Virginia, the perceived favorite of the war department.[50] Indeed, Lt. Col. Alfred L. Rives, Gilmer's assistant bureau chief, acknowledged, "Merit at a distance is sometimes unrewarded for want of proper representations."[51]

Presstman was equally discouraged. If officers of Nocquet's ilk were valued by the engineer corps, Presstman wrote, he preferred to serve in another capacity. He expressed to Wampler a desire to return home to an assignment in Virginia. It is interesting to note that weeks before Gilmer's call for candidates for promotion, Nocquet had gratuitously gone on record in support of Wampler and Presstman's advancement.[52]

While Wampler and Presstman struggled with their individual careers, an opportunity was opening for engineer officers across the Confederate army. In March 1863, the Confederate Congress in Richmond approved the proposal of the chief of engineers to organize specific engineer units. The legislation authorized a company to be raised in each infantry division and one troop of mounted engineers in every cavalry division.[53] Provision was made for transferring line officers to lead these units. Engineers were to be collected into four regiments. The 1st Engineer Regiment was designated for the Army of Northern Virginia, although General Lee successfully resisted

Maj. Gen. Jeremy F. Gilmer. The Museum of the Confederacy, Richmond, Virginia.

interference in what was already the largest engineer contingent assembled under a single Confederate commander. The 2nd Regiment was earmarked for the Southeast, from Virginia to Alabama, but only scattered units were ever formed. The 3rd Regiment was organized in the Army of Tennessee in 1864, after Brig. Gen. Danville Leadbetter was appointed its chief engineer. A fourth unit, a battalion of mounted engineer troops, was created in the Trans-Mississippi.[54]

The formation of specific engineer units naturally opened a stream of nominations and applications for commissions. For example, General Polk recommended nine "western men," who, with two exceptions, had proven themselves in his own engineer department. Those individuals serving with the army as assistant engineers, but without formal commissions, saw this as an opportunity to enter the officer ranks and applied directly to the bureau in Richmond. On the other hand, Maj. Gen. Dabney Maury's approach was not unique in a time when engineers were scarce. He unilaterally transferred his cousin into the engineer department.[55]

As chief engineer of the Army of Tennessee, Wampler had recommended a number of his assistants for commissions. Upon returning from convalescent leave, he renewed his efforts to obtain a commission for Henry Pharr. Wampler pointed out that when taken prisoner at Perryville, Pharr nearly suffered the fate of a spy, because he was not a commissioned officer in the Confederate army. Once Pharr's case was favorably resolved, Wampler turned his attention to obtaining a captaincy for another comrade, 1st Lt. George Helm.[56] Whether pursuing his own promotion or advocating the advancement of his colleagues, Wampler had learned the necessity of perseverance in dealing with Richmond.

The Bridge at McMinnville

Spring was now in full bloom in Middle Tennessee. Wampler enjoyed a bright, beautiful Easter Sunday, writing to Kate, Nocquet, and other friends. Captain Green's wife and father arrived from Georgia, producing a joyous reunion with their former patient. The reverie was interrupted, however, by news that the railroad bridge outside McMinnville had been burned by the Yankees, or their sympathizers, on the night of April 7. A spur jutted off the Nashville and Chattanooga Railroad at Tullahoma, connecting it with McMinnville, thirty-five miles to the northeast. Morgan's cavalry was stationed there, guarding the Confederate right flank and protecting Bragg's access to the agricultural area east of Murfreesboro. The rail line was an important supply route, and so the Army of Tennessee dispatched a senior engineer to rebuild the bridge.

Wampler immediately began to make preparations. He telegraphed for a gravel train to be sent from Chattanooga and organized an engineer detail to be ready to depart the next morning. He was disappointed when the train started late and then, after loading heavy timbers near Manchester, broke down sixteen miles south of the McMinnville bridge. The engineers finally reached the work site at 10:00 P.M. on April 9.

Preparations resumed early the next morning. The train returned to Manchester for a detail of fifty men led by 1st Lt. Pleasant J. Cummings, Company D, 33rd Tennessee Infantry. He had been assigned to conscript duty in the area, making him available for any contingency.[57] While Wampler acquired rations, Cummings's men began framing and pitching tents and clearing debris, to include the wreck of a locomotive. Meanwhile, the work train shuttled back and forth to Manchester, transporting lumber, picks and spades, rope, and even a barrel of whiskey.

Wampler surely found the burnt bridge spanning Hickory Creek to be an imposing structure. Connecting banks 225 feet apart, the superstructure was designed to provide a rail surface 50 feet above the water at normal depth. The crew first began to reconstruct the sills, the horizontal foundation resting on the footings. When Wampler attempted to erect the first trestle, tying the piers together, a timber slipped, injuring a workman and prompting a telegram for more rope and a tackle. The party also requisitioned a second handcar. The bents, or crosswise sections supporting lateral as well as vertical loads, went in slowly. Progress was delayed by heavy rain. When precipitation continued for four consecutive days, the creek rose too high to continue construction. Workmen killed a hog, causing Wampler to intervene in the ensuing controversy to reassure its owner that he would be fairly compensated. Federal prisoners passing by created another distraction. Eventually, the idle crew returned to work, building a footbridge across the creek. The return of clear weather coincided with resumption of progress on the railroad structure itself. By expertly employing the locomotive to raise trestles into place, Wampler succeeded in erecting all four by April 19.

Conrad Meister's visit in the midst of the project helped divert Wampler's attention from engineering to socializing, as the two comrades spent an evening sharing eggnog with three young ladies, chaperoned by Mrs. Lock, Wampler's landlord in McMinnville. Sunday provided the opportunity to accompany one of the girls, Julia Spurlock, to church. The eggnog and conversation did not cease with Meister's departure, as Cummings took his place as Wampler's companion.

When work resumed on Monday morning, the crew was ready to complete the bridge surface. The rails lay on crossties resting, in turn, on the board lengths called stringers, running the length of the bridge. Installing these timbers required only a single day. On the morning of April 21, the engineer work party completed laying track across the bridge. At 11:00 A.M., Wampler drove an engine and tender over and back, signifying completion of the project.[58]

Any celebration was shortlived. General Rosecrans, the Union commander of the Department of the Cumberland, had determined to push the Confederates out of the area bounded by Stones River on the west, Cumberland River to the north, and Caney Fork to the east of McMinnville. To accomplish this objective, he formed a task force commanded by Maj. Gen. Joseph J. Reynolds, consisting of a division, two attached brigades, and a cavalry detachment, totaling well over six thousand men. Elements of the three Federal corps advanced slowly southward in a display of force intended to hold the enemy's attention, while the Reynolds expedition moved in the direction of McMinnville.[59]

A Federal raiding party led by Col. Eli Long started out at 2:00 A.M. on April 21 to interdict the McMinnville railroad. It consisted of Long's 4th Ohio Cavalry, along with elements of the 2nd Kentucky Cavalry and 1st Middle Tennessee Cavalry. Simultaneously, Reynolds's main body approached McMinnville and, avoiding detection, captured John Hunt Morgan's new wife and came close to taking the Rebel chieftain himself. Arriving at his destination about 10:00 A.M., Long first struck the rail line southwest of Morrison Station, midway between McMinnville and Manchester. Moving farther in the direction of Manchester with the intention of destroying a lengthy trestle, Long's party paused to ambush a train heard approaching from the south. Its crew apparently learned of the Yankee interruption, however, and backtracked to Manchester. Disappointed, Long turned and proceeded back up the track to Morrison Station, destroying bridging as he went.[60]

Wampler first received a report of a Yankee raid to the south, while waiting for the northbound train to cross the Hickory Creek bridge. When it failed to appear, he concluded that the account was true. Two couriers arrived, announcing, first, that the enemy was approaching McMinnville in force and, then, that they were only three miles away. Wampler's train headed toward town, but reversed direction and chugged back to the bridge, when he discovered Federal cavalry already there. The engineer mustered his men, ordered them aboard the three cars, and then crossed over the footbridge to recover his baggage and pistol. The train started off prematurely, causing Wampler to scramble after it to climb aboard. When enemy horsemen approached, firing a volley at the fleeing southerners, Cummings and his cohorts jumped off and ran into the woods, but Wampler stayed aboard with his engineering detail. The engine gradually picked up speed, leaving its pursuers behind. More danger lay ten miles ahead at Morrison Station, where two hundred of Long's cavalrymen awaited. Wampler spotted the stockade filled with bluecoats. The raiders had torn up the track, thrown logs across the rails, and burned the bridging and trestle. As the train slowed, the Federals rushed forward. At this point, Wampler and his men abandoned the cars and headed into the brush. He briefly tried to organize the twenty southerners into a defensive line, but they panicked and ran, with their leader close behind. The engineer party quickly scattered.

As night fell, Wampler stopped at a small house seven miles from Manchester. He was still close enough to the Yankees to observe their campfires and the railroad bridges burning in the distance. His feet were sore and his overcoat left behind, but he retained the valise with his personal papers. Arriving in Manchester the next morning, the fugitive boarded a train for Tullahoma to render a report. Undoubtedly, the headquarters of the Army of Tennessee was too preoccupied with the fighting erupting across its front to take much interest in the narrow escape of its engineer party.[61]

Colonel Long's troopers burned Wampler's locomotive and cars, along with the depot at Morrison Station. Over the next week, Reynolds's soldiers moved through the area defined by Rosecrans, foraging, picking up straggling Rebels, and destroying everything of military value. In addition to tearing up the railroad, Reynolds reported capturing 180 prisoners, taking hundreds of head of livestock, and burning food stores, supplies, and equipment.

Wampler remained in Tullahoma only one day before being dispatched on another mission. He received orders to go to Bridgeport and inspect its fortifications. Departing on April 23, the engineer was pleased to share his car with the Green family, returning to Resaca. Disembarking at his destination, Wampler encountered Brig. Gen. John K. Jackson, commander of the District of Tennessee River, who was boarding for Chattanooga, after completing his own examination of the earthworks. He expressed displeasure that Wampler had not arrived sooner to consult with him, criticism the engineer attempted to deflect by showing orders dated just that morning. Then, he set about to explore the defensive positions, resulting in the following critique.

> I found the works here generally superior to any temporary earth works I have yet seen in the south. I would call particular attention to the 3 magazines in Nos. 1, 3, & 5. (see sketch) They are well constructed as to durability, ventilation & drainage, but I think at the angles too lightly covered with earth. Were the depth at these places equal to the depth of the apex of the cover over the center of the roof then the objection I think would be removed. The Magazines are Subterranean Chambers.
>
> Abt. 6 ft deep & 8 x 12 feet large. They are formed of framing of 6" stuff lined with inch $1/4$ oak boards inside & outside, leaving an air chamber of 6" depth entirely around, above & below, and outside this entire air

chamber is 2 feet thickness of Sawdust, and outside the Sawdust is earth. *Work No. 1* is a *square redoubt* arranged for guns in barbette, commanding a circlelar [*sic*] area whose radius averages abt. 1 mile.

Work No. 2 is a simple *redan* with a good command, arranged for Guns in Barbetts. *Work No. 3* is an indented line, of formidable proportions, with faces well directed to best advantage, with three traverses thro' each of which is a covered way, to facilitate communication. This is also arranged for Guns in Barbette, & has an excellent command. Near this and on the opposite side of R. R. cut is a small work No. 4, a redan for one Gun in barbette merely to command a deep cut in small Branch of Memphis & Ch[arleston] R. R. to Jasper, which would, if not protected, afford cover to an advancing foe.

Work no. 5 is a double Redan with two distinct Templates, the *main surface* being about eight feet higher than the *secondary.* The *main* has a fine command, guns in barbette, and, while *it* is easily commanded by an opposite hill of much greater altitude & abt. $^1/_4$ mile distant, still, on acct. of its height above the *secondary,* it entirely covers the secondary. This is an ingeniously constructed work, & all possible advantage is taken of the ground. The secondary part of this work does not face the hill above alluded to, but faces the valley in front & cross fires with the other batteries.

The works are connected by indented lines of *rifle pits,* located advantageously but at one place (marked B) is subject in some degree, to enfilading fire from the hill above alluded to. I would suggest that the earth work forming the *Rifle pits* on either side of No. 5, marked C & D, be strengthened to withstand artillery fire, as in event of the men being driven from the main work to the secondary, a cross fire of rifles could be kept up to the front on No. 5 to prevent storming.

All the works above referred to, can bear upon hill A—tho' the hill has greater elevation than any or all of the works. It would be inexpedient for our forces to occupy Hill A, except by skirmishers or sharpshooters as it is commanded by another hill, & that, by still another & so on in succession, leading from our forces. It is also easily accessible to the enemy by a road, pretty well covered from our fire.

Since every thing has been done on this side of the River that could be done—except the trifling additions, above suggested—and all possible advantage taken of the ground, it would be well to take advantage of a high & accessible bluff (marked E) on the other side of the River which well commands the Hill A, our only bugbear, and has a much greater elevation than Hill A, with plunging fire, at distance of abt 1 mile or $1^1/_4$ mile.

I consider this last mentioned position one of importance, and learn from inquiry, that it is of easy access to us from the table land which communicates with it.[62]

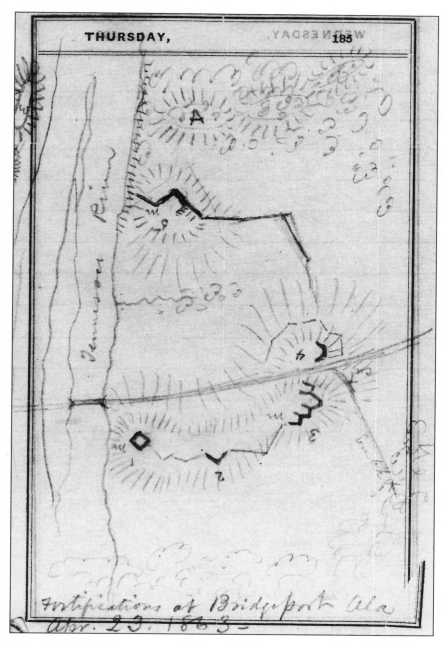

Field sketch of fortifications at Bridgeport, Alabama, by J. M. Wampler, April 23, 1863.

Wampler's report of the fortifications at Bridgeport is the most complete of his extant military engineering studies. It is based on a day spent examining the defensive positions with Lt. Thomas S. Newcomb, the engineer officer on site. A native New Yorker, Newcomb's credentials as a civil engineer had qualified him to serve with the Confederate engineers since October 1861. While in Corinth, Mississippi, the following spring, he received a field commission from General Beauregard as acting first lieutenant in Capt. George Pickett's company of sappers and miners. Newcomb and Wampler had messed together on the march from Knoxville into Middle Tennessee.[63]

Returning to Tullahoma by train the following morning, Wampler learned of the redeployment of Hardee's corps to Wartrace. Confederate response to the Federal incursions around McMinnville had been to relocate Hardee's troops farther up the Nashville and Chattanooga tracks. Bragg intended for the enhanced Confederate presence in that vicinity to influence the Federals north of Hoover Gap, thereby protecting the rail line connecting Manchester with McMinnville. While waiting for the Yankee raiding party to pull back, Wampler and Presstman evaluated bridge sites across Duck River to facilitate their army's rapid movement. Once the Federals withdrew, Wampler was ordered to repair the bridges and put the McMinnville & Manchester Railroad in operational condition once again. He was authorized to hire, buy, or impress any necessary labor or materials.[64]

Starting out from Manchester on April 27, Wampler's engine could go no farther than the first burnt trestle, eight miles to the northeast. After assessing the situation, he hurried back to Tullahoma for tools and, returning to Manchester, enlisted a detail of one hundred men. They camped for the night at the trestle and began work at 6:00 the next morning. By early afternoon two new bents were installed, along with other repairs. The work party then proceeded up the track, restoring three successive trestles, before finally reaching the bridge over Hickory Creek. The engineer found it "badly damaged," and so he settled once again at Mrs. Lock's home.

Assembling the materials for these repairs was challenging. Lumber and rope came from Tullahoma. Bolts and crossties were more scarce. While awaiting supplies, Wampler enjoyed bathing in the cool creek water and meeting the "very pretty" Miss Victoria Wade, quite possibly a pseudonym. By midday on May 2, an engine and cars were able to cross the bridge, enabling the engineer party to move two and a half miles into town to regrade and rebuild its railroad switch.

Wampler observed his birthday in McMinnville by attending church, while permitting his men a day off to observe the Sabbath. The loved ones at home in Virginia were very much in his thoughts. Later in the week, he would send more money to Kate, employing Lt. Col. C. B. Tebbs, formerly of the 8th Virginia, as intermediary. Wampler had made the acquaintance of Maj. O. P. Chaffie, a quartermaster officer assigned to Wheeler's cavalry corps, which was providing horses and wagons to the engineers. Together they called on the chief of cavalry and his senior engineer, Wampler's former colleague, Capt. S. W. Steele. The thirty-three-year-old ended the day by sleeping on the table in the engineer office.

Completing work on the switch the following day, Wampler dismissed half of his crew at a time, sending them back to Manchester by train. Suffering from another attack of dysentery, he remained behind at Mrs. Lock's for a couple of days before finally leaving McMinnville for the last time. The bridge over Hickory Creek had provided Wampler an opportunity to apply his expertise at civil engineering to a formidable structure important to the Confederates. By doing so a second time within four weeks, he demonstrated determination and tenacity, when another type of personality might have become discouraged. With this challenge behind him, Wampler reported once again for duty at engineer headquarters in Tullahoma.[65]

PREPARING FOR RESUMPTION OF BATTLE

The raids on McMinnville marked the beginning of the Federal spring offensive in Tennessee. The Northern army was gathering strength, increasing pressure on its counterpart to the south. The threat posed by Yankee cavalry and infantry moving down the turnpike from Franklin toward the Confederate left flank at Spring Hill focused Van Dorn's attention on strengthening his defenses. He consequently asked General Polk for an engineer officer and some intrenching tools.[66] The request was relayed to Presstman, who telegraphed the engineer bureau in Richmond for five hundred shovels.[67] The chief engineer selected Wampler to go back to Columbia and build fortifications for Van Dorn. Wampler began to put his personal affairs in order before leaving, when suddenly word reached Tullahoma that the cavalry leader had been killed.

Earl Van Dorn had been shot in the head by Dr. George Peters, a prominent physician in Spring Hill, the cavalry outpost north of Columbia. The doctor entered Van Dorn's headquarters at the Cheairs House, ostensibly seeking a pass. Fleeing from the building after the attack, the assassin mounted his horse and fled through the Federal lines, never fully answering for the murder in court. A dapper, diminutive man, soft-spoken and cultured, Van Dorn was attractive to the ladies, earning the reputation as a womanizer.[68]

His affair with the vivacious twenty-five-year-old wife of the doctor, who was twice her age, led to the shooting on May 7, five days after Thomas J. "Stonewall" Jackson fell at Chancellorsville from bullets fired by his own soldiers. Like Jackson, Van Dorn enjoyed prominence throughout the South, although, in Van Dorn's case, it was hardly merited by performance on the battlefield. Despite the tawdry circumstances surrounding his murder, Van Dorn's death stunned Wampler and his colleagues, not unlike the shock felt in Virginia at Jackson's passing. Van Dorn was a member of the Army of Tennessee and personally familiar to its officer corps, while Jackson was known in the West through reputation alone. It is likely that Wampler was particularly distressed at the death of the general he had worked closely with at Corinth, when first assigned to the Confederate Army in the West, and then conferred with outside Columbia shortly before his demise.

At the same time, the western army received news of a great victory in Virginia over Maj. Gen. Joseph Hooker at Chancellorsville. Wampler's elation was tempered by learning that the bluecoats under Maj. Gen. Ulysses S. Grant had occupied Jackson, Mississippi. He was further discouraged to hear that two regiments of Southern cavalry were captured in front of Shelbyville.

The engineer department nevertheless methodically went about the business of assisting units in the field. Presstman consulted with the staffs at Shelbyville and Wartrace. Blakemore and Meister were dispatched to help Polk's corps with their defenses. Wampler made repeated visits to check preparations at nearby Fort Rains.[69]

On May 20, Wampler was once again on the road to assess Confederate earthworks. He rode Toby to Allisonia, where the Nashville and Chattanooga Railroad crossed Elk River. The breastworks were dug into the west bank, guarding the rail trestle over the water. They were far simpler and less extensive than the defensive positions at Bridgeport, and so he was able to complete his inspection, dine with a local family, and return to Tullahoma before nightfall. His report was completed the following day.[70]

Wampler's next assignment took him fifteen miles northwest along the rail line to map the topography in front of Hardee at Wartrace. Maj. Gen. Patrick Cleburne had deployed brigades at Tullahoma, Wartrace, and Bellbuckle, a village five miles farther up the track. Railroad Gap and Liberty Gap beyond Bellbuckle provided two prime avenues of access into the area occupied by Southern forces. Cleburne assigned Brig. Gen. St. John Liddell's brigade to picket these passes. Two other depressions, Dismal Hollow and Hoover's Gap, provided ingress to the right of Liddell and were patrolled by Wheeler's cavalry.[71] Months earlier, Hardee had gone on record in opposition to this deployment, basing his view in part on the report of his engineers, Captain Green and Lieutenant Helm. Hardee would continue to argue with Bragg that his line was overextended and that Hoover's Gap was too far away to be defended without a large force.[72] Wampler was asked to assess this topography for his own headquarters. Lieutenant Steele would perform the same function in front of Polk's corps.

Wampler and Steele rode north together for a while, before heading in different directions. Along the way they learned that the Federals were once again in McMinnville. Spending the night at Green's camp, outside Hardee's headquarters in Wartrace, Wampler began to reconnoiter the next morning, riding first past Fairfield and then through Hoover's Gap as far as the Southern cavalry pickets. He turned west past Dismal Hollow and, then, suffering from a headache, spent the night at Mr. Hoover's, on an elevation overlooking Liberty Gap. His discomfort persisted the next morning as he continued five miles to Bellbuckle. Riding along a high knoll, the engineer was able to view Murfreesboro, fifteen miles or so in the distance, through his telescope. He stopped at Bellbuckle only long enough for his horse to graze and then turned north again through Railroad Gap to Fosterville. A thunderstorm and bad directions along the way caused the traveler to spend an extra night on the road before concluding his reconnaissance.[73]

On the clear, warm morning of May 28, Wampler rode once again toward Wartrace. He headed for Hardee's headquarters at Mrs. Mary Irwin's house, where he had socialized while stopping there two days earlier. Her home was located two miles outside of town, next to Beech Grove plantation amid rolling hills, some of which were cultivated, while others were covered with magnificent trees. Wampler was entertained by Mrs. Irwin, two other ladies, and one of General Hardee's daughters. Hardee's two engineer officers were also present, along with Mrs. Green, back from Resaca. During the afternoon, a tall, handsome man was introduced to Wampler, who "was much pleased with his face & manners." The newcomer was Clement L. Vallandigham, former Democratic congressman from Ohio and candidate for its governorship, before he was arrested for expressing seditious sentiments by the commander of the Department of the Ohio, Maj. Gen. Ambrose Burnside. Vallandigham was subsequently banished by Rosecrans into the Confederacy. A later arrival was an "Englishman on Tour of Observation," Lt. Col. Arthur James Fremantle of the Coldstream Guards, who remarked upon the distinguished, soldierlike appearance of both corps commanders present, Hardee and Polk.

After Polk and Vallandigham returned by ambulance to their quarters in Shelbyville, the remaining guests settled into a pleasant evening of music and conversation with the ladies. The fellowship concluded with prayers offered by the elderly Stephen Elliott, bishop of Georgia. The ladies presumably stayed with Mrs. Irwin, and Fremantle spent the night in Hardee's room at Beech Grove, while other officers were billeted at Chockley Hall, General Cleburne's hotel headquarters opposite the depot at Wartrace. Wampler, however, simply crawled into Helm's tent in the engineer camp.[74]

Wampler remained at Wartrace for two days, working with Green on a map of the front and engaging in more socializing with the ladies. He plotted his reconnaissance upon returning to Tullahoma, along with drawing seven dollars for expenses incurred on the trip. Other routine matters consumed his days until June 6, when orders arrived to pack up the engineer department at once and rejoin Bragg, who had moved his headquarters to Shelbyville. By nightfall Wampler was reunited with Sayers and Pharr, and the next morning they established their office in a vacant house.

The Marylander stayed in Shelbyville only one additional night, for he received orders to relieve Nocquet as chief engineer, District of Tennessee River, and departed the next morning. Wampler arrived at Chattanooga by train in late afternoon of June 9, settled into the engineer office, and ended the long day by dining with Captain Thysseus, who, with Van Dorn's death, was between assignments.

ENGINEERING AT CHATTANOOGA

The senior engineer position in Chattanooga would be critical to the Army of Tennessee in the weeks ahead. Wampler's forty-five days in the billet illustrate the diverse roles of a Confederate engineer. The challenges he faced were similar to those confronted by military engineers across the South, as surveyed by James L. Nichols in his definitive treatment of Confederate engineering.[75]

Wampler's reassignment had occurred because the commander of the Department of East Tennessee, Maj. Gen. Simon B. Buckner, was pressing the engineer bureau in Richmond for Nocquet and two topographical engineers to be sent to Knoxville. Distressed at the prospect of Yankee raids interrupting service, presidents of East Tennessee railroads were petitioning the Confederate government for better protection.[76] Topographical engineers were scarce, but Nocquet could be spared, as Wampler was available, since he no longer occupied an authorized billet on the headquarters staff of the Army of Tennessee. As Wampler would still be working for Bragg in his capacity as commander of Department No. 2, the crusty general had less cause to complain. Hence, the engineer bureau ordered Nocquet to report to Buckner, and Wampler to succeed Nocquet.

It took over a week to complete the handoff of responsibilities. The two engineer officers rode around the area, examining where fortifications could best be erected, considering the winding Tennessee River and multiple rail lines that made control of Chattanooga critical to Confederate retention of the Deep South. Nocquet had earlier identified twelve specific locations as part of a strategic survey for the defense of Chattanooga. The positioning of the earthworks and magazines had been precisely indicated on a sketch accompanying Nocquet's report to Gen. Joseph E. Johnston. A formidable construction challenge lay ahead, one that would be nowhere near completion when the Federals eventually occupied Chattanooga in September 1863.[77]

Wampler's first undertaking was to clean up the engineer office. He engaged a Mrs. Myers to reside there and take charge of their dining. Next, he employed a clerk to handle the correspondence and assist with the voluminous recordkeeping and map production. As Nocquet apparently carried off all the office furnishings to his new assignment, it was necessary to order a full complement from Pickett's company of one hundred sappers and miners at Battle Creek, over twenty miles due west of town, and longer by road. The items arrived by wagon the following week. They included three pine drawing tables and stools, a desk, strongbox, and triangles made of poplar. Pickett apologized to Wampler for his inability to fashion the T squares requested. Hinges and locks were unavailable to Pickett, so he suggested procuring them in Chattanooga.[78]

The new incumbent encountered a critical shortage of maps at Chattanooga, a problem common to Confederates throughout the war. Areas traversed by Southern armies were, with few exceptions, uncharted at the war's outset. The precise measurements made by the Coast Survey were restricted primarily to the shorelines, and the U.S. Army Corps of Topographical Engineers had focused on the Trans-Mississippi. These surveys were generally unavailable to Confederate commanders, anyway. The very few trained topographical engineers in the South, like Wampler, were readily assigned to other engineering tasks, for lack of skilled personnel to undertake them. Although Wampler was a trained cartographer, he had ascended to positions encompassing far broader responsibilities. The Army of Tennessee was fortunate to have Captain Morris with Polk's corps and Capt. Wilbur F. Foster in Knoxville, two other capable mapmakers in its engineer ranks.[79] Once tactical maps were drawn, however, the southerners did not have the capability of reproducing them in mid-1863. Coincidentally, on the other side of the picket lines, the Union Army of the Cumberland was far advanced in the use of photography and lithographic presses to make and publish maps.[80]

The engineer bureau in Richmond could be of little assistance. Indeed, in July 1863, Gilmer wrote to Presstman asking for copies of whatever general maps or drawings were available of important localities. Battlefield maps were expected to accompany commanders' field reports, but Gilmer specifically inquired about these as well. He also requested that maps be drawn specifically to reflect information gathered on reconnaissance, so that national leaders in Richmond could familiarize themselves with terrain and follow the movement of armies far away. Gilmer offered Presstman the standard military shibboleth for a headquarters shortage in any particular expertise—find a soldier in the ranks with the required drafting skills and have him detailed for temporary duty to the engineering office to draw maps.[81]

Wampler was reliant on whatever maps he could find or have sketched. One of his initial acts as chief engineer was to advertise for a map of Tennessee. He wrote to Presstman for Rae's Map of Tennessee but was told that only a single copy was available in Shelbyville. Wampler dispatched Lieutenant McFall on surveys north, west, and east of Chattanooga for information needed to prepare maps. When Lieutenant Thomas reported to the engineer office, he was assigned to assist McFall. The chief engineer repeatedly rode out himself to acquire a firsthand understanding of the surrounding terrain. Nor was Wampler reluctant to borrow a map from anyone, as the prominent Tennessee politician, Brig. Gen. John C. Brown, found when he met Wampler, shortly after the new chief engineer began work.[82]

Staff engineers, like Wampler, were subjected to enormous quantities of paperwork. Construction projects under their supervision obviously entailed large sums of money for materials, as well as for hired labor, including the cost of slaves pressed into service with or without their owners' consent. Two weeks after assuming his new duties, for example, Wampler sent a special requisition to Richmond for twenty thousand dollars to underwrite engineering activities in his district. An allocation in that amount was entered onto a ledger, subject to withdrawal in accordance with treasury department procedures. Strict accounting required retention of vouchers indicating where funds were expended. Regulations also prescribed a file of official letters, a book on materials, and a roll of personnel employed. Wampler was also expected to send to the engineer bureau on the proper form the names of soldiers entitled to receive increased pay for being detailed to construction projects.[83]

As chief engineer in Chattanooga, Wampler faced the same kind of meticulous accountability he had experienced under Alexander Dallas Bache in the Coast Survey. The Confederate engineer assumed formal custody for an array of construction implements, including 287 shovels, 150 picks, and a hammer and file. Careful accounting for a spirit level and a prismatic compass, scarce instruments in the blockaded South, appeared to be reasonable. He also signed receipts for a myriad of office and drawing supplies—259 envelopes, 23 pieces of India rubber, 16 sheets of large drawing paper and 50 sheets of tracing paper, 6 paint saucers, 4 drawing pens, 2 bottles of red ink, a protractor, 1 box of water colors, and even 1,145 blank forms, to mention only a partial list.

Military engineers, North and South, recognized Dennis Hart Mahan at the U.S. Military Academy as the undisputed authority on fortifications. Thus, it is not surprising that Wampler receipted for three copies of the professor's *Complete Treatise on Field Fortification,* the bible of the operational engineer. In turn, he was expected to issue a volume to each of his officers.[84]

No sooner had Wampler become chief engineer of the Tennessee River District, then he received written guidance from the engineer bureau. Gilmer instructed him to continue Nocquet's work in superintending construction of fortifications at Chattanooga. In addition, the new chief engineer was expected to obtain and report topographical information of military significance, especially concerning the construction and maintenance of bridges over the many rivers in his area of responsibility. Gilmer was seeking once again to compensate for the shortage at the war department of reliable maps depicting the Western Theater.[85]

Shortly after assuming his new duties, Wampler was directed by Brig. Gen. John K. Jackson, the senior officer at Chattanooga, to accompany him on a reconnaissance to Loudon. The chief engineer joined other staff officers and troops aboard a train which required seven hours to cover eighty miles up the main line in the direction of Knoxville. Wampler found Loudon to be ugly. His forays into the surrounding countryside, however, revealed landscapes replete with beauty, but full of bushwhackers.[86]

While in Loudon, Wampler was delighted to be introduced to Ella Newsom, referred to later as the Florence Nightingale of the Southern army. Mrs. Newsom was the attractive and wealthy widow of a physician. She dedicated her time and money to caring for Confederate battle casualties. Wampler may have first become familiar with her work at Tishomingo Hotel Hospital in Corinth, where she faced a particularly difficult challenge of finding hospital garb to replace her patients' bloody, muddy clothes.

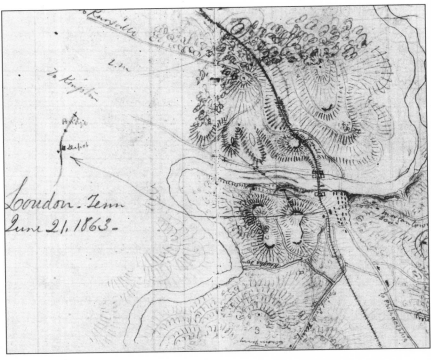

Field sketch of Loudon, Tennessee, by J. M. Wampler, June 21, 1863.

When Wampler met her at Loudon, Mrs. Newsom was in charge of a hospital at Chattanooga.[87]

Upon returning to Chattanooga, Wampler was delighted to receive a package from Charleston, South Carolina, containing the buttons and gold lace needed for his dress attire. An engineer's uniform was similar to that of other Confederate officers, consisting of cadet gray coat, dark blue trousers with a broad gold stripe down the outer seam, and red silk net sash. An engineer's tunic was edged in buff facing, which was reportedly unavailable in Charleston. As a staff officer, Wampler may have worn a cocked hat, adopted from the French army, or, more likely, a kepi or forage cap of dark blue with braid in two gold strands indicating the rank of captain. The same thickness of lace braid at the sleeve and three horizontal bars on the collar also designated his rank. An officer's collar and cuffs were plain gray. What distinguished an engineer were coat buttons bearing a raised Old English "E." The seven buttons lining the tunic were one-eighth inch larger than those of other officers. Black cravat, ankle boots, and leather sword belt with tassels completed the attire.

Wampler's friend in Charleston, Capt. G. Thomas Cox, could not find engineer buttons and purchased instead a set of general staff buttons displaying an eagle surrounded by stars. Cox was able to send eleven yards of lace for the sleeves, in accordance with Wampler's earlier request. Looking ahead to a possible promotion, Wampler also obtained a set of major's stars for his collar. Cox's three purchases cost thirty-five dollars, yet Wampler's uniform remained incomplete. The Confederacy's limited resources and the small size of its engineer corps, as compared with the infantry, artillery, and cavalry, made distinctive engineer accouterment especially scarce.[88]

The demand for insignia and accessories was growing in the early summer of 1863, as the act authorizing the organization of engineer regiments was being implemented. A commission with the engineer troops did not carry the same prestige as an officer in the Corps of Engineers. Yet an opportunity was provided for those seeking promotion, at a time when advancement in the basic engineer branch was severely limited. Presstman and Green reluctantly applied to be regimental commander or deputy commander of engineer troops in the West, positions in the grade of colonel and lieutenant colonel, respectively.[89] At the same time, the bureau in Richmond directed senior engineers in the West to begin organizing companies of engineer troops. Nocquet received such instructions for Buckner's Department of East Tennessee, as did Presstman for the Army of Tennessee. Gilmer intended that men should be selected from throughout the ranks for their skills as carpenters, masons, blacksmiths, wheelwrights, boat builders, caulkers, saddlers, shoemakers, and what were considered other mechanical branches of labor.[90] As a practical matter, many of the soldiers most qualified and interested in serving in the engineer troops were already members of companies functioning as sappers and miners. The bureau went so far as to identify acting engineer company commanders for Bragg's divisions, to include two of Wampler's associates, Pharr and Force. Permanent officers would not be appointed until a company or regiment was completely formed.[91]

Gilmer must have been surprised when officers considered to be highly qualified declined to surrender their commissions in the engineer corps for higher rank in the engineer troops. Lieutenant Force refused such an appointment, as did Capt. John G. Mann and 1st Lt. Felix R. R. Smith. Mann had originally been commissioned by Gov. Isham Harris as a first lieutenant of engineers in the Provisional Army of Tennessee and subsequently served as Cheatham's acting signal officer. There is no record that he was ever formally recognized as an officer by the Confederate Engineer Bureau. At the time he declined to join the engineer troops, Mann wore the assimilated rank of captain, while functioning as chief of engineers with Forrest's cavalry.[92] Smith had also served as a lieutenant in the Tennessee army in 1861, assigned to the staff of Brig. Gen. Felix K. Zollicoffer. He did not receive an engineer commission in the Confederate army until a year after declining Gilmer's offer.[93] At the same time that Mann and Smith were turning their backs, Gilmer claimed that a great number of able civil engineers were eagerly waiting to join the officer corps as lieutenants with the engineer troops.[94]

By the end of June 1863, the roles and missions of Confederate engineers had coalesced into a single policy statement, General Orders No. 90, which Wampler would rely upon in the days ahead. The senior engineer officer with an army in the field was responsible for the proper execution of all engineer functions. The duties of an officer of engineers encompassed reconnaissances and surveys to ascertain information concerning roads, bridges, fords, water courses, and other prominent topographical features. He was expected to select the sites and prepare plans for offensive and defensive positions, to include field forts, batteries, rifle pits, trenches, and river and harbor obstructions. He was also accountable for all public funds and property under control of the engineer department. The senior engineer would receive orders from both his commanding general and from the engineer bureau and, in turn, provide sketches, drawings, and maps to both. The scarcity of trained engineers caused the army to limit their role to staking out locations for proposed field fortifications. The war department was clear that soldiers and hired laborers would construct earthworks under the direction of line officers. Troop commanders were also expected to provide escorts for engineers who were directing an expedition or conducting reconnaissance. With this directive, the adjutant and inspector general, as well as the engineer bureau chief, intended to clarify the mission of the Corps of Engineers, preventing intraservice misunderstandings. While plausible for garrison soldiering, once a contingency arose, adherence to formal regulations assumed secondary importance.[95]

ARRIVAL OF THE ARMY OF TENNESSEE

As the engineers struggled with their doctrine, roles and missions, a serious contingency, although not unexpected, was brewing for the Confederates in Middle Tennessee. Bragg had built up the size and equipment of his army, only to see its strength reduced to fewer than forty-three thousand effectives by the order to send reinforcements to Mississippi.[96] His diminished force was spread across a seventy-mile front from Shelbyville to McMinnville. He seemed to have no strategic plan other than protecting the breadbasket in Middle Tennessee and positioning his troops between Rosecrans and Chattanooga. Bragg spent six months after the engagement at Murfreesboro perfecting his static defenses, especially at Shelbyville and Tullahoma. Somehow he did not appreciate the implied significance of the Yankee raids on McMinnville in April and May. His line could be easily skirted or penetrated through defiles in the rugged hills north of Duck River.

By June, the Federal Army of the Cumberland was also enjoying its sixth month of relative inactivity, which troubled the war department in Washington, fearful that the Confederates would take advantage of the seemingly endless lull to enlarge their forces at Vicksburg. Hence, Rosecrans was under increasing pressure to engage his counterpart. On the morning of June 23, which was followed by seventeen consecutive days of rain, the Northern army finally stirred, the main thrust directed at Hardee on the Confederate right, while diversionary activity kept Polk pinned at Shelbyville. When Bragg eventually understood the nature of the Federal advance, he consolidated his army in the elaborate defenses at Tullahoma. A Yankee foray sent behind him to cut the rail line at Decherd, however, convinced Bragg to abandon the earthworks at Tullahoma in order to deny Rosecrans unimpeded access to Chattanooga, which, at the same time, would block the Confederates' route to its transportation hub in the southeast corner of Tennessee. After first considering defensive positions along the Elk River near Decherd and farther back at the mountain at Cowan, the Army of Tennessee instead continued its retrograde movement across Sewanee Mountain toward Chattanooga. If the fall of 1862 had been the high tide of the Confederacy, July 4, 1863, was arguably the beginning of the end. On that date, Lee started his withdrawal from Gettysburg, Vicksburg surrendered to Grant, and the Army of Tennessee retreated out of the Tennessee heartland.

What had Bragg's engineer corps done to facilitate its army's relocation? As far back as September 1862, the engineer bureau had directed Sayers to reconnoiter the countryside in Middle Tennessee and send to Richmond the kinds of detailed information subsequently specified in General Orders 90. Sayers was also expected to report on topography to the departmental engineer, James Nocquet. In the spring of 1863, Captain Green on General Hardee's staff had prepared a map of the road network in his corps sector, which assisted division commanders in assessing the fords through Duck River to the rear and the roads leading to Tullahoma. In mid-June, Pharr had laid out fortifications protecting the Fairfield Turnpike for a construction detail of one thousand men in Polk's corps. Upon arriving at Tullahoma, Sayers and Morris had been instructed to oversee the preparation of breastworks by Polk's corps to strengthen the Confederate line. Engineers, such as Helm, were also assigned to guide brigades and divisions over unfamiliar terrain. At Allisona, Polk's corps destroyed the rail and vehicular bridges over the Elk River, swollen by daily rains during the last week of June, a mission which may well have involved the engineers. Finally, Polk's engineers were requested to repair the road leading over Sewanee Mountain as far as University Place, a tract of land where, ironically, before the war the bishop-general had laid a cornerstone for the University of the South.[97]

What the engineers had not done was to destroy the long tunnel through the mountain at Cowan. It has been said that Bragg had a blind man's eye for terrain.[98] In their haste to reach Chattanooga, neither Bragg nor his headquarters engineer department had paused to clog the rail artery at its most vulnerable point.

Wampler took note of the army's concentration at Tullahoma on June 29. The next day, he learned of "Reports & dispatches that 2000 Yankees are coming to destroy Bridges at Bridgeport, & on the River elsewhere."[99] Clearly, the heightened Federal activity was generating intelligence with varying degrees of reliability. The trick was to separate truth from rumor. Wampler twice accompanied Maj. William D. C. Lloyd, inspector general on Jackson's staff, across the Tennessee River to check picket stations and examine key terrain, such as the gap in Missionary Ridge. Wampler was also sent to inspect pontoon bridging positioned at Kelly's Ferry, seven miles west of Chattanooga, where the Tennessee River widened, becoming more shallow and placid. He reported back to Jackson that the guard was being depleted by officers recalling their men, using the excuse that they were absent from their commands without leave.

In a separate report, Wampler called Jackson's attention to the poor condition of the road connecting the ferry with Chattanooga. It was barely more than a wagon path and, in his opinion, "in very bad condition. Indeed I hardly think it possible to take a Gun & Caisson to the Ferry or from the Ferry to this place without breaking the carriage." While recognizing the present shortage of labor in the Chattanooga area, he urged that improvements be made in order to maximize the utility of the crossing.[100] Soon thereafter, on July 3, Wampler recorded that "General Jackson sent for me this A.M. to go to Kelly's Ferry & have the Pontoon bridge put over at once, & remain there & superintend the work."[101]

In December 1862, Nocquet had sent Gilmer a concept plan for a pontoon train, complete with specifications, drawings, and cost estimate. As a former French officer, it is not surprising that Nocquet eschewed the lighter, Russian-style pontoon with tarred canvas stretched over a wooden frame, the kind preferred by the Federal Army in the West, for a heavier wooden version similar to that used by Napoleon's army. Nocquet's plans prescribed reinforced sections 18 feet long and 4 feet across with a 2-foot depth. They would be transported on wagons with 11-foot flatbeds and positioned in the water side-by-side, approximately 16 feet apart, from center beam to center beam. Planking 12 feet wide would provide the treadway that connected the bateaux.[102]

Nocquet had, however, initiated a somewhat grandiose application of the "ponton" (as it was referred to by the Confederates) to the bridging requirements of the Army of Tennessee. His ambitious approach envisioned 100 pontoon boats in a company of pontoniers, as compared with the 16 boats and 100 men in the equivalent unit of the French army, which Gilmer considered the standard.[103] Nocquet also sought a special rations allowance for mechanics in its ranks, at a time when Gilmer was just putting forth his proposal for the formation of basic and distinct engineer units. Gilmer challenged Nocquet's insistence on incorporating unique features into his pontoon design, such as vertical sides, longer and narrower dimensions than the French or U.S. models, and a sharp prow. The chief of the engineer bureau much preferred simpler, more conventional lines, far easier to fabricate in the field. "The present time does not seem to be propitious for a young nation with limited resources and in time of war to make a grand experiment apparently at variance with past experience," Gilmer concluded.[104] Not long after this critique, Wampler was engaged to make "drawings & calculations for plan of Pontoon Train & boats."[105]

At Nocquet's direction, but apparently in accordance with Gilmer's guidance, Pickett's company of sappers and miners subsequently built and installed pontoons across the Tennessee River just above the mouth of Battle Creek, approximately twenty miles due west of Chattanooga and six to seven miles above Bridgeport. During the morning before Polk's corps arrived at the river bank on July 3, a freshet caused by the heavy rains broke this bridging apart at its center. Half of the bateaux were pushed by the current up against either shore, and the engineer officers seemed incapable of reconnecting them. The alternate route across Battle Creek to Jasper was unavailable, because the swollen creek could not be forded. The problem was addressed by a twenty-one-year-old artillery officer in Cheatham's division, Capt. William W. Carnes, who had resigned from the U.S. Naval Academy in the spring of 1861, his senior year. Carnes succeeded in navigating the sections back into place through the heavy waters, which must have chagrined Pickett, Morris, and Sayers, the engineer officers on hand.[106]

Pickett's workmen had constructed a second set of pontoons for use elsewhere on the river, which, in early July, was positioned at Kelly's Ferry. Nocquet had earlier identified the river crossings at Battle Creek and Kelly's Ferry to General Johnston as the obvious approaches to Chattanooga from the west.[107] As Polk's corps was using the bridge at Battle Creek to cross the Tennessee, Hardee's corps stayed north of the winding river, passed through Jasper, and arrived at Kelly's Ferry on July 5 and 6.

Wampler had immediately begun to employ his crew on the afternoon of July 3 to throw the bridge across the river. Hard rain elevated the water level, introducing driftwood, which complicated the task. Starting early again the next morning, individual boats were positioned, one by one, and chess (or planking) was laid across them to form the roadway. The job was finally completed by 3:30 P.M. on the day before Hardee arrived. Wampler was surprised that evening when Presstman appeared in Chattanooga with Bragg's advance. The army continued arriving over the next several days.[108]

Once the army had finished using the bridging, the question arose of what to do with it. Polk's corps was completely across the Battle Creek pontoons by late on the afternoon of July 4, and, as he had no further use for the bridge, the bishop-general offered the structure to Hardee's corps and Wheeler's cavalry. He informed Bragg as well, and asked that the engineer officer in charge be directed how to dispose of the structure. Bragg's chief of staff responded that one of Cheatham's brigades should remain on the west side of the river to defend the crossing. Heading for Kelly's Ferry farther to the north near Jasper, Hardee responded that he would have no need for the bridge but recommended that Polk protect rather than destroy it. On his way to the crossing at Bridgeport, Wheeler also wanted the pontoons preserved. Polk continued fussing about having to guard them. Caught in the middle, Pickett remained in place until the bateaux were eventually towed back to Chattanooga.

Wampler received a (false) report on July 6 that the Battle Creek bridge had been destroyed by Confederate troops, causing him to ask Jackson for instructions regarding his companion structure. On July 12, Pharr was dispatched from Chattanooga with a steamer to retrieve the second pontoon bridge at Kelly's Ferry.[109]

Wampler's engineer office grew more active as the Army of Tennessee assembled at Chattanooga. When Force reported for duty with Wampler, the lieutenant was sent on topographical reconnaissance along the critical road over Signal Mountain toward Anderson to the northwest. Then he and Wampler spent three days reconnoitering the area around Shellmound, astride both the river and railroad near Bridgeport. At the same time, Wampler contested the replacement of his orderly (a musician by trade) with another, deemed less suitable, arguing unsuccessfully with Maj. Richard Whiteley of the Georgia Sharp Shooters.[110]

On July 9, the engineer office received orders to expand the fortifications defending Chattanooga. Wampler began the next day to lay off two works on the sharp rock cliff facing north with command over the Tennessee River. Stretching to the right was MacLellan Island, and Wampler quickly sent men to clear its timber, both to obtain building material and to improve the line of sight. Wampler divided the detail of 600 to 750 workers who reported each day between the two projects, with Helm and Force assigned to oversee their progress.

The senior engineer issued a directive to reinforce the proviso of General Orders No. 90, regarding supervision of soldiers employed as laborers. Wampler instructed the officer in command of each fatigue party to divide his detail into two reliefs, to facilitate greater use of the limited tools on hand. The officers in charge were to remain at the project, directing the labor, until the end of the duty day at 5:00 P.M. The engineers' concern for property accountability was reflected in assigning these line officers responsibility for the tools, which were to be drawn from the guard each morning and carefully laid out in piles at nightfall. Any lost or stolen implements would be charged to the supervising officer.[111]

July was very hot that year, and an occasional afternoon shower provided little relief from the heat. After ten days dedicated to developing defensive positions, Wampler took a Sunday break to accompany a party of officers on a ride to the top of Lookout Mountain, where the cooler air was inviting. He was disappointed, however, that haze prevented observation across the Tennessee River Valley, sixteen hundred feet below. Returning to town, Wampler continued work the following week on what would become a single fortification known as Battery Smart (now the location of the Hunter Art Museum). When confronted by the Federals, the Confederates would mount eighteen to twenty guns at Battery Smart. Guarding its eastern flank were two smaller forts.[112]

The Confederate army seemed to be settling into the area in and around Chattanooga. Once again, a weary Braxton Bragg appeared to be without strategic vision, content to provide for his command and defend its encampment

in a small corner of Tennessee, while conceding most of the state to his oppressors.[113] Wampler had by this time served fifteen months with the Army
of Tennessee and its predecessor, the Army of the Mississippi. The opportunity that had once appeared so bright was now faded with Beauregard's departure, the disappointing adventure in Kentucky, and the stagnation in his
own career as a military engineer, commencing with health problems at the
year's outset. Transfer to the West had not lived up to its initial promise. It
was time for a change.

CHAPTER EIGHT

>>>

Ten Days at Charleston

The train crept along the Western and Atlantic tracks from Chattanooga, one in an almost continuous succession returning from the front, where troops and war materiel had been exchanged for soldiers in invalid status and private citizens, fleeing the impending conflict or involved with the war effort in some support capacity. Joseph Howell, a mechanical engineer from Augusta, Georgia, seated next to Captain Wampler, was in the latter category. When Wampler's mind drifted away from their conversation, he must have thought of the rapid series of activities over the preceding twenty-four hours. Just the day before, on July 23, 1863, he had received orders from the engineer department of the Army of Tennessee to proceed at once to Atlanta and take charge of the fortifications under construction. Clearly, his friend and comrade-in-arms, Capt. Wilson Presstman, now serving as the army's chief engineer, anticipated that Wampler would remain in the city for an extended period, as the orders specified that reports detailing his work and that of the parties under him be submitted on a weekly basis.

This reassignment disappointed Wampler, as he had applied for transfer to northern Virginia to be near Kate and his family. Engineer officers were scarce commodities in the Confederate army, however, and experienced ones like Wampler were in increasing demand as commanders became more cognizant of the importance of preparing defensive positions to hold their own against numerically superior opponents. Consequently, his request for transfer had not been supported by Gen. Braxton Bragg's headquarters, and unless an adequate replacement could be identified, which seemed unlikely, Wampler could expect to remain in the West indefinitely. In all likelihood, however, the precarious position of Lee's army in the wake of Gettysburg would not have permitted a visit home by a newly assigned officer for some time to come.[1]

Atlanta

The train finally pulled into the station at four o'clock, having required almost twelve hours to traverse a distance of scarcely more than one hundred miles. Wampler suffered extraordinary delays in obtaining his two horses and baggage from the boxcar, but finally checked into the Atlanta Hotel, the new city's first hostelry, if no longer its finest.

While by no means the largest community in Georgia at the war's outset (that distinction belonged to Savannah, with the capital seated at Milledgeville), Atlanta was nonetheless critical as a rail center, the linchpin for transportation between the Confederacy's seaboard and its western states. Ordnance and supplies imported on blockade runners waited at the Atlanta Depot for shipment to armies in the West. The city's industrial capacity was vital to the war effort. Atlanta factories produced all manner of personal gear, ranging from spurs and canteens to revolvers and cartridges. Cannon, rifles, and swords were manufactured here, as were clothing, buttons, and shoes. Rolling mills turned out railroad iron, gunboat plates, and other heavy armament. Consequently, by the time of Wampler's arrival, the city had become headquarters for the quartermaster department of the Army of Tennessee.[2]

As the war moved nearer its logistics hub in 1863, the Confederate army began to heed the calls from Atlanta for assistance in constructing defensive works. Maj. Marcus H. Wright, commander of the Confederate States Arsenal in Atlanta, was promoted to the rank of colonel and placed in charge of the city's defense forces.[3] Capt. Lemuel P. Grant, chief engineer of the Department of Georgia, began building defensive positions at fords and bridges along the Chattahoochee River to the north of the city and eventually continuing with a perimeter along the higher terrain. Wampler surveyed the situation the day after his arrival, riding out to look at the lines selected for fortification in the company of Wright and Grant.

Before beginning work, Wampler addressed some personal matters. He attended the Presbyterian Church, hearing a sermon, or what he considered to be a "lecture," on the matter of slavery. Settling his hotel bill of twenty-four dollars for three days' room and board, he relocated to a room at the Masonic Hall, which he considered charming, as its windows overlooked the square, depot, and hotels on Marietta Street. Meals were arranged with Mrs. Leonard at a reasonable rate of $4.50 per day. Daily forage, consisting of 12 pounds of corn and 14 pounds of fodder, was drawn from the quartermaster for each horse. Wampler also discovered the Atlanta Pistol Works, where he purchased two navy revolvers for $110 (Confederate) and exchanged his derringer, valued at $125 in the same currency.[4]

Wampler began work by obtaining an office and draftsman and requisitioning paper, drawing tables, a 50-foot tape line, spirit level, and maps—the stock in trade of a topographical engineer. Having set up his base of operations, he returned to the Chattahoochee River with Grant to determine the exact location of proposed fortifications. The next day, the new engineer started construction, supervising a party of thirty-eight blacks. Completing one section, he staked out another to begin the following week. But it would not be his project to continue.

A dispatch from General Bragg directed Wampler to report to Col. Jeremy Gilmer, chief of the engineer bureau in Richmond. Wampler asked to remain two or three weeks to complete the project on which he was working. A second dispatch, this one from Gilmer, ordered him to report to Lt. Col. David B. Harris, General P. G. T. Beauregard's chief engineer in Charleston. This time it was Captain Grant who appealed for a delay, but the telegram in reply extended Wampler for only a few more days. General Beauregard was pressing for "efficient" engineer officers to be sent to Charleston to help counter Federal forces busily constructing batteries outside that city.[5]

On the eve of his departure, Wampler dined with Grant, a routine the two had fallen into quite readily. An indication of the friendship that had developed during his short time in Atlanta was the popular McClellan saddle that Wampler presented to his comrade, worth at that time in the South, by his own estimate, as much as one hundred dollars. Early on August 5, Wampler reluctantly loaded his horses on a freight train headed for South Carolina, and an hour later started out himself. After stopping a day in Augusta, he repeated the ritual by first shipping his animals and then boarding a crowded overnight train to his final destination.

CHARLESTON IN AUGUST 1863

Wampler arrived in Charleston at 8:00 on August 7. What he found may not have matched his expectations. The city was missing part of its center portion, which was destroyed by fire in December 1861, and much of its population, since women and children were instructed in July to leave and had not yet returned, if they ever would. Free blacks, who had helped extinguish blazes before the war, were increasingly relied upon as volunteer firemen, as the regular firefighters were now working for the military. It was a community committed to evading the blockaders waiting outside the sandbar beyond Charleston harbor and resolute to withstand the siege of Federal warships and Union legions poised to strike.

In September 1862, General Beauregard had been summoned to Charleston out of the military exile to which he had been relegated upon leaving command of the Army of the Mississippi. The balls and parties in celebration of his appointment had ceased by the time of Wampler's arrival, although social gatherings were not completely extinct. A "musical soiree" or sumptuous dinner could still be arranged, especially if the purpose was to entertain the representative of a European state, such as Lt. Col. Arthur James Fremantle of Britain's Coldstream Guards or Charles Girard of France, both of whom visited Charleston just weeks before Wampler's appearance.

Fremantle commented on the seeming luxuriousness of the city, despite the deterioration of its paving and lighting and the large number of boarded-up shops. Most of the horses and carriages had been sent away, and the wharves were largely deserted, adding to the city's lifeless appearance. Girard was struck by the great similarity in appearance of the population, clothed alike in wool, cotton, or linen, all locally manufactured and generally of drab colors, gray being predominant. The dress of masters and servants was largely indistinguishable, except that slave women were not permitted to wear the veil. Black mourning dress was increasingly common. The growing scarcity of servants had caused ladies of the genteel class to undertake the unfamiliar chores of housekeeper, chambermaid, and laundress.[6]

When fighting first erupted on the barrier islands that separated the harbor from the ocean, folks lined the Battery wall overlooking the port to observe the naval and artillery fire. Rooftops and cupolas also provided optimum vantage points. By the time Wampler arrived in Charleston, however, the sounds of cannonading had become commonplace, drawing attention only when especially heavy or prolonged.[7]

Maj. Gen. Quincy A. Gillmore, arguably the North's premier engineering and ordnance officer, commanded Federal forces outside the city. Gillmore was committed to a four-part campaign plan. He would first take possession of the lightly defended lower end of Morris Island to the south of the harbor, which would be used as a base of operations. Secondly, he would take Battery Wagner. Battery Gregg at the north end of the island would then, in all likelihood, be abandoned by the Confederates. Once Northern forces controlled all of Morris Island, Fort Sumter could be destroyed by heavy artillery fire, the third step. The Union fleet would finally be free to remove the channel obstacles, steam past the other shore fortifications, and reach Charleston itself.[8]

Step one was accomplished on July 10, with support from masked batteries quietly constructed on Folly Island, immediately south of Morris Island. Federal troops pushed forward as far as rifle pits two hundred yards in front of Battery Wagner, and by nightfall they were in possession of three-quarters of Morris Island. An attack the following day was turned back, so over the next week Gillmore proceeded to construct four batteries to support a larger offensive against Wagner. This assault by five thousand soldiers in blue on July 18 has been memorialized for being spearheaded by black troops of the 54th Massachusetts regiment, which lost two-thirds of its officers and 40 percent of its men by the time it reached the battery's ramparts and was repulsed.[9] Having surrendered the elements of surprise and momentum, Gillmore was now convinced that the Confederate obstacle could not be taken by charging across the sand to its walls, and so turned to the longer, but time-tested approach of laying down trenches and engaging in siege warfare.

Arrayed against the Federal forces was a formidable combination of fortifications and defensive innovations. The entrance to Charleston Harbor was protected by Fort Moultrie on Sullivan's Island at its north and Battery Gregg on Cummings Point, the northernmost tip of Morris Island, to the south. Farther down the island was Battery Wagner. To the west of these bastions stood Fort Johnson on the north shore of James Island, where laborers were busily constructing a series of additional batteries. In the harbor itself were two small islands containing the invincible Fort Sumter near the harbor entrance and the antiquated Castle Pinckney, just offshore from Charleston. Complementing these fixed defenses were two ironclad rams, which had already made one foray against the Yankee blockaders on January 30, 1863. Shortly after Wampler's arrival, on August 14, a small "torpedo boat," named the *Hunley*, joined the city's naval defenses.[10] Navigational obstructions included a log, rope, and chain barrier stretched across the main ship channel. Explosive devices or "torpedoes," floating, electrical cannisters, were mounted on spars or moored throughout the harbor.[11] The innovative ves-

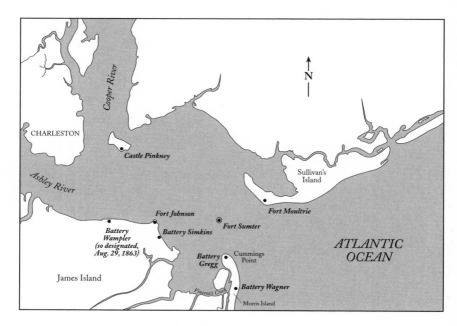

Defenses of Charleston, August 1863.

sels and obstacles placed in the water were as valuable for their psychological deterrence as for the actual damage they inflicted. Balloons performed aerial reconnaissance overhead, manned, if possible, with an engineer officer cognizant of the topography.[12]

CHALLENGES CONFRONTING CONFEDERATE ENGINEERS

CHARLESTON, S. C. July 17, 1863–11:30 A.M.
General S. COOPER, Adjutant and Inspector General:
Contest here is now one of engineering. With sufficient time, labor, and long-range guns, our success is very probable, owing to plan of defense adopted. Otherwise it is doubtful in proportion to the lack of those three elements of success.

G. T. BEAUREGARD[13]

A career engineer officer in the Regular Army before the war, including service in the Mexican campaign, General Beauregard considered himself first and foremost a military engineer. It is not surprising, therefore, that in selecting sites, building and manning defenses, and restoring fortifications after attack, he relied upon engineers who reported directly to him through his senior engineer, David B. Harris, Wampler's mapmaking colleague before First Manassas and supervisor in the West.[14]

Maj. William H. Echols served as chief military engineer for South Carolina, Harris's counterpart at the district level. A West Point graduate and member of the Confederate Regular Army, Echols's broad perspective is reflected in the wide variety of roles he saw for engineers—"carpenters, boat builders, ship-carpenters, masons, blacksmiths, teams, stevedores, overseers, pilots, boatmen, sailors, fishermen, gardeners, railroad overseers, timber hewers, wagon drivers, firemen, & laborers."[15]

As a newly assigned engineer, what problems could Wampler expect to encounter while working under the direction of these senior officers? To begin with, reliable transportation was needed between Charleston, Forts Johnson and Moultrie, and the outposts most under fire, Fort Sumter, Battery Wagner, and Battery Gregg. Along with acquiring two rafts of hewn timber for cargo transport, Echols had collected and repaired thirty rowboats capable of carrying one thousand men as reinforcements. He also arranged for sufficient pairs of oars to be made. Once supplies reached the barrier islands, mules were needed to carry the materials to their destination. To help defend Battery Wagner against ground attack, spiked planks were fabricated in Charleston and carried to Morris Island aboard the steamer that served as a daily ferry, once Federal firing stopped after dark. A bib of spikes and "frous de loups," each containing pointed stakes, in front of the battery, required repeated restoration. Incoming naval and artillery fire necessitated regular replacement of the platforms and carriages supporting siege and field pieces defending these fortifications. The demand for more sandbags grew proportionately with the intensity of the artillery exchange, and women across the state responded to the call.[16] The engineer on Sullivan's Island was given the task of preparing bags sent to Fort Sumter. They were packed two-thirds to three-quarters full and then tied, using unraveled sacks for strings, if no alternative was available. The literal "life or death" cries for more sandbags caused the engineers to post a guard at the receiving end to insure that these defensive building blocks were employed to meet engineering requirements and not diverted for purposes identified by the infantry or other claimants.

Provision of and care for labor was a continuing challenge. Engineer personnel on duty at fortifications under fire had to be rotated regularly, requiring replacements to be continually selected, notified, and transported in a timely manner. Responsible men were needed to plant the torpedoes that served as land mines in front of defensive positions on Morris Island. Carpenters were in constant demand for erecting and rebuilding protective structures.

The supply of slave labor was never equal to the requirement. General Beauregard repeatedly implored plantation owners to make blacks available to construct and repair field works. Estimates of the need for slaves ranged from 2,500 to 5,000 laborers, but the engineer department reported receiving an average of only 591 slaves per month for 30-day tours during the period from October 1862 through June 1863, with 74 of that number typically sidelined due to sickness. Harris asked Gov. Milledge L. Bonham to request that laborers report with spades or entrenching tools.[17] When they did not, the engineer department was called upon to supply these implements, in addition to furnishing overseers. At installations on Sullivan's and James Islands, easily accessible to the mainland, the engineers attempted to thwart escapes by posting guards. At Fort Sumter and Battery Wagner, engineers were concerned that injury or sickness would result in slaves being returned to their masters in poor condition, discouraging plantation owners from providing replacements. Consequently, Major Echols urged his subordinates to ensure that good water and adequate rations were set aside for black laborers. He soon resorted to ferrying slaves back and forth to Morris Island after dark, so they could work each night before intensive Yankee shelling resumed the following morning.[18]

BATTERY WAGNER

Wampler quickly settled into the city, making arrangements for his horses and belongings. He reported to the departmental engineer office and found Harris laid up from heat prostration suffered during a regular visit to Morris Island.[19] It was not long afterwards, on August 12, that Wampler and another engineer, H. W. Stewart, received orders from Echols to proceed to Morris Island and relieve William Hume and William Tennent, two South Carolina engineers assigned to Batteries Wagner and Gregg, respectively.[20] At 6:00 that evening, Wampler and Stewart started out by small boat, stopping first to report at Fort Sumter. Arrival on the beach alongside Battery Gregg was timed at dusk, when fading light made the landing a less obvious target for Yankee artillerists. It was 8:15 before Wampler reached Battery

Wagner itself, where he was greeted by Capt. Charles S. Hill, a Marylander serving as the garrison's ordnance officer.

Hill's wartime career had paralleled Wampler's, beginning with service in the 1st Virginia Infantry Regiment, continuing with the Army of Tennessee as an artillery and ordnance officer, and then being reassigned to Charleston in the spring of 1863. Captain Hill had impressed one Charlestonian as "good looking, dandified, [and] conceited."[21] Whether Wampler shared this assessment is unknown, but he must have been gratified to find a familiar face on this dangerous, desolate island far from home.

Morris Island measured almost four miles in length. It was a low, flat, thin sand barrier running north and south alongside the channel that turned slightly westward into Charleston Harbor at Cummings Point. Battery Wagner was situated at the narrowest point on the island, three-quarters of a mile south of Battery Gregg on Cummings Point. Referred to by General Beauregard as the "Neck Battery" after being sited in 1862, the fortification was subsequently named for Lt. Col. Thomas M. Wagner, a South Carolina state senator and militiaman who lost his life in an artillery accident at Fort Moultrie later that same year. The battery's two main salients faced southward and together traversed the island, 275 feet wide at that point. In front of its rampart curved a moat that filled with water at high tide. The ditch beneath the front parapet was lined with fraise work, lances and boards holding pointed stakes, while the terrain beyond was thickly planted with land "torpedoes," explosive cannisters buried with Rains fuses upward to be detonated by weight.[22] A slight ridge 250 yards away contained dug-in positions, manned by 75–80 pickets and sharpshooters during the day, with double that number at night.[23]

Extending back from the land front were two wings. On the left side, a heavy traverse, over 200 feet in length (including the sally port), provided protection toward the sea. The right or westward parapet paralleled Vincent's Creek and the marshland separating Morris Island from James Island. Only a breastwork formed the rear perimeter, toward Battery Gregg. Lacking a true rear wall, the fortification was technically an enclosed "battery" rather than a "fort," as it has mistakenly been called.[24] It was entirely an earthwork, reinforced only with palmetto logs. The battery's ability to absorb enemy explosives was enhanced by the extra fine quality of the island's quartz sand, causing holes gouged out by incoming rounds to be quickly and naturally filled in by falling particles. Inside these ramparts were several magazines and a large bombproof, 30 by 130 feet, subdivided to provide for a hospital and capable of holding as many as 900 soldiers. In the words of General Gillmore, "Battery Wagner was beyond question a work of the most formidable kind."[25]

Wampler found a wide variety of artillery here, manned mainly by South Carolinians. The left flank was armed with two field howitzers, which were smoothbore cannon with low muzzle velocity, used as an anti-personnel weapon by throwing shell, grape, or canister at a high trajectory. Next to them was an 8-inch seacoast howitzer, among the largest of that category, weighing almost 3 tons and capable of propelling a shell 1,800 yards. On the sea face were mounted two 10-inch Columbiads and a 32-pounder rifled gun.[26] The Columbiads were smoothbore cannon with long range and high elevation, the battery's most effective weapon against Yankee monitors, capable of hurling projectiles weighing 128 pounds.[27] On the left salient was another 8-inch howitzer and a 42-pounder carronade, an antiquated, short, light form of naval ordnance, dating back to 1774, which the Federals had largely discarded but the Confederates employed as an anti-personnel weapon, using shell, grape, and canister. On the curtain of the land face were positioned pairs of 8-inch navy shell guns and 32-pounder navy guns, vintage 1845, of limited value against their more modern rifled counterparts. Finally, two 32-pounder carronades, an 8-inch siege howitzer, and a 10-inch light seacoast mortar protected the right flank along Vincent's Creek. Requiring only small charges of powder to launch a variety of projectiles at high elevations, the mortar was the battery's most effective weapon against the Federal entrenchments. Another 32-pounder carronade was positioned to overlook the waterway.[28]

The Confederates selected their most dependable troops for duty at Battery Wagner.[29] Beauregard attempted to restrict the garrison strength to about a thousand men, in order to limit casualties from artillery fire.[30] Troops were regularly rotated back and forth, primarily to James Island, in recognition of the limits which the human body and spirit could endure during a siege.[31] The Confederate Signal Corps was intercepting and decoding messages between Federal land forces and their naval counterparts, providing some expectation that a warning would be received in sufficient time to send reinforcements before another ground assault was launched.[32] The size of the garrison's population during Wampler's tour remained upwards of 1,135 soldiers, of which approximately three-fourths were infantry and the remainder artillery troops. Included in the former number were twenty sharpshooters, some armed with Whitworth rifles bearing a telescopic attachment that enabled a marksman to hit a head peering above the Yankee trench line as far as five hundred yards away.[33] Also stationed on Morris Island were a dozen or so

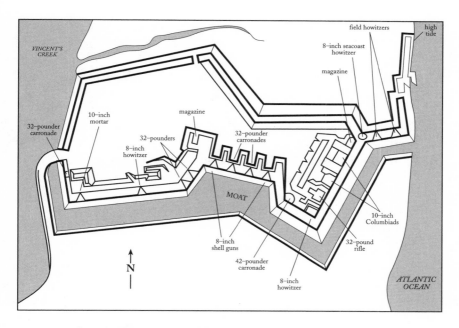

Battery Wagner, August 8, 1863. Graphic from *A Treatise on
Coast Defence,* published 1868.

cavalrymen who served as couriers, dodging exploding shells as they rode
back and forth across the one-thousand-yard stretch of unprotected sand
between Battery Wagner and the signal station on Cummings Point.

What was the morale of the troops Wampler was joining? The answer
depends on the source. During a visit in early August, General Beauregard
had found the garrison to be in "fine spirits."[34] One report received in Charleston, however, claimed that discipline was bad, "Commissioned officers too
drunk to know what they are about."[35] Certainly, living conditions at Battery
Wagner were harsh. With clear skies and August temperatures hovering around
100 degrees, soldiers were susceptible to heat prostration. Water was scarce.
Nearby wells had acquired a strange taste, which was attributed to the mass
graves outside the ramparts, lightly covered with sand, containing the remains of hundreds of blueclad soldiers who had perished in the assault of
July 18. It was not uncommon for a bursting shell or high wind to uncover
entire corpses or miscellaneous body parts. Horse carcasses rotted on the hot
sand. The locations of wells farther away in the sand hills were known to
enemy artillerists, who fired without hesitation when observing them in use.

Limited quantities of water imported from the mainland were barely sufficient for the sick and wounded.[36] The fare was hardly better than the water,
consisting frequently of mush and tough beef, which at one point, when
diagnosed as being "putrid," was discarded on the beach, where it naturally
attracted a swarm of bright-colored insects.[37] Swarms of mosquitoes, house-
flies, sand fleas, lice, and gnats abounded. The bombproof offered little relief. Stifling heat, suffocating smoke from coal oil lamps, and sights, sounds,
and smells of countless amputations in the adjacent hospital area made an
extended stay within its confines unbearable. Some soldiers consequently
preferred to seek cover from incoming rounds behind the traverses outside,
where at least there was a chance of catching a breeze.[38] Sleep was never assured, as the battery fired, and was fired upon, regularly throughout the day
and night, and large details of soldiers were called upon after dark to man the
forward rifle pits and repair breeches in the ramparts.

THE YANKEE AGGRESSOR

Just 540 yards in front of the battery was General Gillmore's third parallel,
with Northern engineers poised to dig closer.[39] Work parties of as many as
500 men, black and white, veterans and recruits, worked at night under
enemy fire, sapping trenches in a zig-zag pattern closer and closer to Battery
Wagner. A giant sap roller, a cylindrical basket filled with sand, inched forward to provide protection for workers. Once completed, a parallel was immediately manned by sharpshooters, howitzers, and Requa batteries—a 25-
barrel predecessor to the machine gun capable of firing volleys of as many as
175 shots per minute.[40] Federal soldiers endured the same miserable climate
and topography as their Southern counterparts. Contagious disease was a
constant fear in the lowlands surrounding Charleston. Alligators were in-
digenous in fresh water. Storms filled trenches with as much as 18 inches of
brine, making work unpleasant, if not impossible. Backed by a far richer
and more extensive support system, including nurses such as Clara Barton,
the hardships may have seemed more bearable to the bluecoats. Not to be
overlooked was the reality that Northern troops were delivering far more
ordnance onto their enemy than they were receiving.

The Confederates also preferred digging after dark. A day or two before
Wampler's arrival, the Federals began illuminating the Southern defensive
positions. State-of-the-art calcium lights shot a jet of hydrogen-oxygen into
enriched alcohol, which, when ignited, heated a small ball of lime. Its inventor,
Thomas Drummond, claimed the glow reflected in a parabolic mirror was eighty-

three times brighter than conventional lamps.[41] Southern workers repairing damage inflicted by artillery shells could be blinded by this brilliance, thereby posing as distinctive targets for Federal artillerists. Fatigue parties consequently learned to move and work in whatever shadows were available. Drummond lights also made steamers approaching Cummings Point more vulnerable to fire, causing transit of reinforcements, laborers, munitions, materiel, and supplies to be shifted to small boats less visible to Union spotters and harder to hit.[42]

An impressive array of artillery supported the approximately 7,000 Federal troops on Morris Island. When Wampler arrived, the Yankees were maintaining a steady barrage upon Fort Sumter, Battery Wagner, and Battery Gregg. The guns included 10-, 8-, 6.4-, and 4.2-inch Parrotts, 5-inch Whitworths, and Coehorn and 10-inch mortars firing an array of shot and shells from a dozen battery locations. The decided Union advantage in any artillery duel was due to its extensive fielding of rifled artillery pieces, most notably Parrotts, with distinctive iron bands reinforcing the breeches. The vastly improved accuracy produced by rifling, along with far greater projectile weight, resulted in penetration two to three times deeper into targets than smoothbore ordnance.

Off Morris Island stood the South Atlantic Blockading Squadron, consisting of ironsides, monitors, wooden gunboats, and a flotilla of tugs, tenders, and other support vessels. Small boats, dispatched from the combatants, were assigned picket duty each night to detect attempts to pierce the blockade. The squadron's most formidable vessel was the *New Ironsides,* 230 feet long and covered with a belt of iron extending four feet below and three feet above the water line, which made it seemingly impervious to cannon fire. The ship's complement had been increased from its peacetime crew of 165 seamen to 400 men in order to service its fourteen 11-inch Dahlgren smoothbores and two 150-pounder Parrott rifles, evenly divided between the port and starboard sides.[43] One broadside could unleash 1,000 pounds of explosive and metal flying toward the enemy. The monitors *Catskill, Montauk, Passaic, Patapsco,* and *Weehawken* were poised for action as well.[44] These were of the new Passaic class, flat-decked with revolving turret and armed with one 15-inch Dahlgren smoothbore and either an 11-inch Dahlgren smoothbore or an 8-inch Parrott rifle. A monitor's two guns could deliver 600 pounds of ordnance in a single firing.[45] Ten wooden gunboats mounted an assortment of weaponry, and an additional five mortar schooners were particularly active in the August bombardment.

General Gillmore was nevertheless disheartened by what he misperceived as the defenders' strategic advantage in artillery and manpower. His report to Maj. Gen. Henry Halleck, general in chief in Washington, cited twice as many men and more than five times as much artillery at General Beauregard's disposal than were available to the attackers. Gillmore also acknowledged unexpected losses from his effective fighting force due to sickness, which would soon disable him as well.[46]

AUGUST 12–16: THE FIRE BEFORE THE STORM

Captain Wampler was quickly given a taste of soldiering on Morris Island. The evening he arrived, the battery commander, Col. George Harrison, opened fire on the Yankee trenches, employing seven guns and the mortar, with five-minute intervals between each, in coordination with Fort Sumter and Battery Simkins on James Island. The barrage was successful, as little was accomplished by the Federal work detail that night. It was not long, however, before the enemy's artillery responded, using their calcium lights for target illumination. After a brisk exchange, the cannonading settled down to occasional firing. Toward daylight, work resumed on repairing the damage done to the battery. Four defenders were killed, plus Capt. John Gary of the Lucas Battalion, South Carolina Heavy Artillery, who, Wampler noted, received a severe head wound that proved to be fatal. It had been a long time since Wampler had seen a fellow officer mortally wounded, and its impact on him at an outpost where he was new and naturally apprehensive must have been particularly sobering. Nevertheless, the next day, Wampler turned his full attention to the engineering tasks at hand.[47]

As the incoming chief engineer at Battery Wagner, Wampler inherited certain problems and expectations. General Beauregard continued to insist upon building a covered way, presumably as a trench, between Batteries Gregg and Wagner.[48] He had also approved the suggestion that guns and carriages on Morris Island be painted a sand or neutral color as camouflage, but the absence of any follow-up may have been an indication that he was only lukewarm to an idea not his own, or, perhaps, that this color paint was not readily available.[49] Brig. Gen. Johnson Hagood of the 1st South Carolina Volunteers had directed Wampler's predecessor to erect and repair infantry banquettes (the treads upon which firers stood behind a parapet) to the front and back.[50] The prospect of the enemy landing between the two Confederate batteries and attacking Wagner from its rear was of some concern, and indeed the subsequent Federal plan of attack requested that a marine battalion with boats and howitzers be ready to land on Morris Island.[51]

In addition, the traverse circle of the recently received Columbiad on the sea wall and the bed for the 10-inch mortar did not provide proper seating for these weapons, adversely affecting their accuracy.[52] Col. Lawrence Keitt, battery commander the prior week, had also raised the possibility of laying pipe beneath the ground to carry water into Battery Wagner from wells in the sand hills, which would have been the perfect undertaking for an engineer with Wampler's background.[53] Requisition, receipt, preparation, and installation of adequate numbers of sandbags was an ongoing challenge, for as many as one thousand were required each night to strengthen defensive positions and repair the damage done by incoming rounds.[54] Finally, Major Echols was pushing for the installation of additional pikes and "frous de loups" in the battery's front ditch.[55]

To undertake these tasks, Wampler had available as many infantry personnel as could be spared from picket duty and other details. Two work parties were the norm, one before and one after midnight, each comprising about 75 men. Two hundred or so slave laborers were also imported each night from Fort Johnson and Sullivan's Island. Productivity was reduced by incoming mortar fire, a typical rate being at least one round every three to four minutes.[56]

Wampler took advantage of the brief cessation of firing at sunrise on Thursday, August 13, to bathe in the ocean, a somewhat dangerous practice sporadically engaged in by soldiers on both sides of the trench lines.[57] Afterwards, he assembled a detail of 150 men to work in two reliefs on revetments of the 10-inch Columbiad chamber on the sea face. Repairs were also accomplished on the platform for the 32-pounder and carronade on the flank, to include making ladders. The carronade was shifted repeatedly during the bombardment, as needed.

At 9:30 A.M., the U.S. schooner *Racer* began firing at intervals of ten minutes, and after stopping for the dinner hour, mortars from the Federal land batteries opened fire, continuing to disrupt the engineering.[58] At the same time, wooden gunboats moved to within 5,000 yards of Fort Sumter and commenced firing with rifled guns.[59] Yankee crews also attempted to repair their earthworks, damaged by rounds from Battery Wagner, but were halted by Confederate sharpshooters and artillery.[60] Naval and land firing with shells and mortar rounds intensified in the mid-afternoon against Wagner, Sumter, and Gregg. Wampler continued working his men, however, putting up a banquette on the left salient and, after dark, filling a hole blown in the traverse and reinforcing the sandbags protecting the lookout. By 10:00 P.M., the two sides had settled into a "warm cannonade and shelling."[61]

Occasional firing resumed from mortar schooners alongside the *New Ironsides* the next morning and from Parrott guns on shore in the afternoon. Sharpshooters kept up a steady exchange of fire. Wagner's artillery opened up at intervals, tempting the attacker's work parties to resume operations and then surprising them with sudden and vigorous shelling.[62] Anguished screams from Northern workers wounded in the trenches told Confederate pickets that their artillery fire was having effect. Four shots at the gunboats from the battery's rifled 32-pounder at midday, however, all fell short. Wampler continued to direct engineering details building banquette steps, shifting the 32-pounder's platform and traverse and rebuilding the revetment for its embrasure, working on the seacoast gun platform, and moving a carronade to the flank. One cannonier was shot by a Federal sharpshooter through the wrist, but otherwise the defenders were not interrupted by enemy fire until the tempo picked up late in the evening.[63]

Saturday, August 15, was also remarkably quiet with only occasional firing by Yankee mortars and rifled cannon, on land and at sea. At 10:30, two mortar schooners began firing, one at Wagner and the other at Gregg. The *Racer* delivered thirteen shells at Battery Wagner, and the schooner *Dan Smith* expended ten shells before halting for midday dinner.[64] The pattern of the preceding day was repeated when the land batteries opened up late in the afternoon.

Only the fire of Federal sharpshooters caused Wampler's laborers to seek cover. The lull in incoming artillery fire permitted him to resume work on the embrasure for the 32-pounder shortly after sunrise. An additional fifty men were employed making banquette treads for the rear breastwork, which was being strengthened in response to the concern about an attack from the rear. By afternoon, Wampler's attention had turned to constructing steps for banquettes on the rear face, repairing the traverse for a gun there, and fixing a lookout for observation. At the same time, it was noted that the mere sound of Confederate mortars discharging from Batteries Wagner, Gregg, and Simkins caused the Northern work parties, consisting primarily of blacks, to drop their tools and run for cover before the rounds landed.[65]

The good day's work and the heavy shelling after dark brought a cessation in engineering projects that night. Federal batteries exchanged brisk fire with the four Confederate fortifications, including Sumter, delivering both mortar rounds and shrapnel on Wagner. The mortar shells were consistently long, falling to the rear of the battery, until redirected by signals from the Union fleet. Wampler also noted signal lights flashing from Federal picket boats as they jockeyed into position offshore, looking for blockade runners.

Rockets were used to alert the land batteries of boats approaching Cummings Point, which then became instant targets. At 9:30 P.M., the defenders fired the rifled 32-pounder at a monitor that strayed too close to the sea face. As she immediately moved away, the Confederates concluded that they had struck her.[66] Later, a small boat with a shallow draft passed silently down Vincent's Creek, presumably sent to notify the monitors of Confederate craft approaching Cummings Point.[67] At midnight, Wampler retired.[68] Everyone on the island must have been startled by a general discharge from artillery pieces across the entire land face of Battery Wagner at 2:00 A.M., interrupting once again the work of enemy sappers.[69]

Col. Lawrence Keitt of the 20th South Carolina Volunteers had returned to Battery Wagner at 7:00 P.M., on August 15, relieving Colonel Harrison as commander. He quickly discerned the severe shortage of sandbags. From the battery's artillery commander, Capt. Charles Chichester, Keitt learned that all guns were in working order, but the mortar was inaccurate due to a cracked bed, requiring replacement. Receipt of a chassis would permit a 32-pounder to be mounted on the left salient, where it would be most effective. Keitt noted with alarm that his engineer-in-charge had no timbers, nor had he received instructions from the engineer office concerning construction of a new bombproof. In light of the bifurcated chains of command, the incoming battery commander could only beg that Captain Wampler be directed to undertake such a project and that necessary materials be sent at once to Cummings Point and then transported by raft up Vincent's Creek to Battery Wagner.[70]

Wampler was already on record as in favor of a bombproof chamber on the west side of the battery. He had also endorsed the artillery commander's suggestions that the 32-pounder smoothbore be repositioned where it could be most effective, mounted on the land face in the salient angle, in place of an 8-inch shell gun, and that the 42-pounder carronade firing grape and shell be relocated for maximum advantage against enemy working parties.[71]

Firing ceased about 5:00 A.M. Sunday. It remained strangely quiet all morning. Wampler took advantage of the opportunity to employ a detail of fifty men on the infantry banquettes on the west face, toward Vincent's Creek and the harbor, and on the revetment and wind sail in the middle gallery. He reported minimal damage from firing overnight. Walking up the beach to the signal station at Cummings Point, Wampler sent a dispatch to Charleston for sandbags and other supplies. At noon, firing resumed between the enemy's land batteries and Fort Sumter. Troops of the 20th South Carolina policed the battery for balls, shells, other expended ordnance, and scrap metal, which could be melted down to produce ammunition.[72] Wampler's men continued working until dark, repairing the gun chamber revetment for the old 10-inch Columbiads on the left and making additional sharpshooter stands on the parapet above the bombproof. The engineer had intended to implant additional spikes in the battery's front ditch, but uncertainty as to the exact location of the underground torpedoes changed his mind. A bale of two thousand sandbags arrived in time for the men to spend the hours until midnight filling them. It was almost twelve o'clock when the battery's guns resumed operation after a long cessation to receive and post replacement troops. The defenders fired sixty-one shells by morning. The enemy appeared to Wampler to be reluctant to answer, although they did so intermittently, employing only mortars.[73] The relative calm should have signaled that something extraordinary was about to happen.

AUGUST 17: THE STORM BREAKS

Naval gunfire during the preceding days originated exclusively from Federal gunboats and mortar schooners. The monitors offshore prepared for an extended engagement by taking on coal, and the *New Ironsides* distributed barrels of rum to other vessels that would take part in a new attack. The original starting date of August 14 was postponed when General Gillmore fell ill. At last, on August 17, the Union navy steamed into action.

As agreed, Gillmore opened the offensive before daylight using all his land batteries. Admiral John Dahlgren, commanding the blockading squadron, boarded the monitor *Weehawken,* which fired the first naval shot at Wagner from 1,000 yards away at 6:45 A.M. Five other monitors soon joined in the action—the *Catskill, Montauk, Nahant, Passaic,* and *Patapsco.* As the tide rose, Dahlgren led the monitors closer, to within 500 yards of Wagner. The *New Ironsides* was forced to stay farther back, as her draft would not permit maneuvering close to shore. Being more vulnerable to Rebel fire, the eight wooden gunboats also remained at longer range, where their guns could nonetheless be effective. The warships were answered, first, from Batteries Wagner and Gregg, and then by a rifled gun at Fort Moultrie. The fort's commander quickly received orders to cease fire, however, as a large work party of slaves employed in front of his fort was presumed to be in danger by the attention drawn to Moultrie by being involved in the fight. The *New Ironsides* received thirty shots, primarily from Battery Wagner, while at the same time delivering a succession of punishing broadsides. The defenders tried every kind of projectile in their inventory, but none was particularly effective against the armored combatants. The most devastating shot fired by Battery Wagner struck the *Catskill*'s pilot house, spraying three-by-five-inch fragments of iron, killing Capt. George W. Rodgers, the fleet commander, and Paymaster J. G. Woodbury, and injuring two other seamen. Upon silencing Battery Wagner in mid-morning, Dahlgren transferred to the *Passaic* and led the *Patapsco* to within two thousand yards of Fort Sumter, the real strategic objective, where they opened an uneven exchange of fire, heavily in their favor. Union artillery ashore reinforced the two monitors, laying a heavy bombardment on Sumter.[74]

On shore, August 17 started badly for the soldiers at Battery Wagner and became worse as the morning progressed. The rounds that awakened the garrison at 5:00 A.M. came from Parrott guns near Thomas Island, at a slightly oblique angle to Wagner's land face, placing the rear of its gun chambers on the sea face within the potential impact area. An extraordinary amount of cover was knocked from the top of the bombproof and blown from the traverses shielding the guns, increasing their vulnerability. It was not uncommon for as much as seven feet of sand to be removed in a heavy bombardment.[75] Trunnions were broken off two guns, rendering them unserviceable.[76]

At 8:40 A.M., the garrison was forced to take cover and wait for abatement, as the incoming fire intensified. For the first time, it came simultaneously, rather than consecutively, from Union land guns and mortars in conjunction with the fleet offshore. A cloud of dust and smoke enveloped the battery. Shells exploded on the bombproof and magazines and in the battery's interior at a rate unknown in earlier barrages. The defenders listened grimly to rounds screaming overhead, which produced terrible tremors when exploding in the compound.

Broadsides from the *New Ironsides* sent shells bouncing into the battery, where they buried themselves before detonating. Spherical shells, weighing over 300 pounds, from the monitors' 15-inch guns literally skipped across the water and into the fortification's interior to shower its occupants with sand and metal. Conical shells from the rifled Parrotts burrowed into Wagner's ramparts. Projectiles fired by mortars rained down vertically, indiscriminately striking shelters and traverses, weapons and gunners, anyone caught in the open. Long fuses increased the likelihood of shells exploding inside the earthwork.[77]

Veterans, as well as soldiers newly posted to the earthwork, tried to focus on other thoughts to block out the mortality all around them. Like some others stationed on Morris Island that summer, Wampler's aesthetic awareness could not have been blinded to the contrast between what lay on either side of him. To the east, warships produced roars far louder than thunder, shaking the ground with chilling reverberations. To the west rested Charleston, the queen city, its roofs and steeples gleaming in sunlight.[78] Caught in the middle were Wampler and the defenders of Battery Wagner.

Crowded into the bombproof that served as battery headquarters, Wampler sat down and began to compose a letter, "My dear wife and child . . ," when a 15-inch shell exploded, sending fragments in every direction. One severed his spine. Wampler died without making a sound. The chair cut in two, his body crumpled beneath the table.[79] The fatal shot was delivered by one of the monitors remaining abreast of Battery Wagner—the *Catskill, Montauk, Nahant,* or *Weehawken*—the only 15-inch artillery trained on Battery Wagner late that morning. The origin was most likely the *Catskill,* according to the report made by Admiral Dahlgren.[80] The firer was no more aware of the effect of his round than Capt. Robert Pringle had been of the death of Captain Rodgers aboard the *Catskill* by a shot from his 32-pounder earlier that morning.

Only the remains of officers and selected soldiers from the immediate Charleston area were carried back to the city, the rest being buried behind the battery. Wampler's body, along with the day's wounded, was transported to Charleston by steamer on Monday evening.[81] The deteriorating effect of the August heat caused the burial to take place the following day, even though a metallic coffin could not be found. As one of the first Confederate officers killed in the defense of Charleston who was not a South Carolinian, the disposition of Wampler's remains presented something of a problem for local authorities. The dilemma was resolved by the family of Lewis M. Hatch, who agreed to allow Wampler to be interred in their plot at Magnolia Cemetery, just outside the city limits. The four-dollar fee for a private burial, as compared with three dollars charged for a soldier's grave, was presumably paid by that family as well. Colonel Hatch was a prominent Charlestonian, a commission merchant and insurance agent before the war, serving in 1863 with the 23rd South Carolina Infantry.

A few of Wampler's friends and comrades, Marylanders and Virginians from General Beauregard's staff who could leave their duty posts for this solemn occasion, gathered at the graveside. Most likely, the small group included Lt. Col. David Harris, who was older and more senior in rank and prestige than Wampler, but a friend nonetheless. They had begun the war together, mapping northern Virginia for Beauregard, and later worked in tandem on the march through Kentucky and the battlefield at Perryville. When Harris had first been reassigned to the Army in the West and then to Charleston ahead of Wampler, the two remained in touch through mutual

David Bullock Harris in a major's uniform.
Valentine Museum, Richmond Virginia.

friends. Harris now saw Wampler to his grave, only a year before he, too, would expire on South Carolina soil, a victim of yellow fever.

The fallen engineer's companion on the ride to Murfreesboro, Bvt. Col. John Lay, was present and subsequently described the service to Kate Wampler in a letter. An officer in the 4th Virginia Cavalry at the war's outbreak, he was now Beauregard's inspector general. Another Virginian, Bvt. Col. John M. Otey, had been posted to General Beauregard's adjutant general office at Centreville

Capt. Lemuel P. Grant. Georgia Department of Archives and History.

and in the Army of Tennessee and was now assigned in a similar capacity with the Department of South Carolina, Georgia, and Florida. Marylander Charles Hill, who had welcomed Wampler to Battery Wagner just a few days earlier, was now part of the departmental headquarters staff and would have paid his last respects as well. A second Maryland friend, Capt. G. Thomas Cox, had followed a parallel path to Wampler's through the war, joining the 1st Virginia Infantry in early 1861, obtaining orders to report to General Beauregard at Corinth as an engineer officer in April 1862, and being reassigned to Charleston as an assistant

Capts. G. Thomas Cox and Charles S. Hill. From T. C. De Leon, *Belles, Beaux and Brains of the 60's* (New York: G. W. Dillingham Company, 1909).

Col. Lawrence Keitt. South Caroliniana Library, Columbia, South Carolina.

to Harris the following October. Their friendship was evident thereafter through regular correspondence back and forth and by Cox's recent acquisition of engineer accouterments for his chum. It would have been fitting for Tom Cox to attend Wampler's last rites.[82]

These officers had all formed an allegiance to Beauregard in northern Virginia during the Confederacy's halcyon months at the war's outset. Upon his summons or on their own initiative, they had followed him, first, to the campaign west of the Appalachians, and then to Charleston. It was not difficult for southerners to warm to Beauregard, the hero of Fort Sumter and victor at Manassas, a man of vision for a cause dearly in need of visionaries, and a personality with just enough eccentricities to be thought a genius by many. Wampler's ambition had also led him to aspire to join Beauregard's inner circle. He made a favorable impression at Manassas, but even with the general's sponsorship, months passed before he could rejoin his mentor as an engineer officer with the Army in the West. He arrived just in time for Beauregard's less-than-heroic departure as its commander. As a newly assigned staff officer, Wampler renewed the relationship sufficiently during their brief time together at Corinth to feel comfortable soliciting a recommendation for promotion to the chief of engineers, which the general readily gave. Summoned once more, at a time when the "Napoleon in Gray" desperately needed engineers, Wampler was just beginning to reestablish that rapport when the war ended for him after only ten days at Charleston. Morris Wampler was not destined to become a member of Beauregard's coterie, and his dream of being promoted to field-grade rank and serving with the general until the war's end and, perhaps, even afterwards would not be realized. Nonetheless, it was Beauregard's intercession with the war department in Richmond that earned for Wampler the distinction that most ennobled him and by which he would be remembered, that of Confederate engineer.

Epilogue

The premature death of Capt. John Morris Wampler, C.S.A., does not diminish his importance as a Confederate engineer. His experience, before and during the Civil War, may serve as a case study in mid-nineteenth-century engineering, while helping to illuminate the attraction of engineer professionals to and their performance in the Confederate States Army. Wampler's personal accounts sharpen contemporary understanding of the disposition, military contributions, and ground-level perspective of Southern staff officers. His story takes place primarily in the two major theaters of the war. He served with what Richard McMurry has called "Two Great Rebel Armies." Wampler's experience as a tactical unit commander in northern Virginia undoubtedly made him a better field engineer, when assigned to the Confederate Army in the West. His final days were spent in one of the conflict's extended sieges, adding another hue to this portrait of a nineteenth-century engineer at war. In addition to expanding appreciation of Confederate engineering, Wampler's life may also offer insights on talent and ambition, success and failure, that remain valid to readers entering the twenty-first century.

AFTERMATH IN CHARLESTON

Within two weeks of his death, a battery was named in Wampler's honor by Gen. P. G. T. Beauregard. The battery was one in a series along the north shore of James Island that bore the appellations of Confederate officers killed in the early months of the siege of Charleston. Cheves, Gary, Pringle, and others lent their surnames to defensive positions that completed the "circle of fire" around the perimeter of Charleston Harbor, protecting the city against naval attack at close range. Battery Wampler was armed with a double-banded Brooke gun, the Confederates' heavier, rifled counterpart to the Federals' Parrott, and a 10-inch Columbiad transferred from Fort Sumter.[1]

Battery Wagner held out until September 7, when sappers completed a fifth trench only forty to fifty yards from the Confederate salient, providing General Gillmore's troops an ideal point of departure for a sudden attack.

The defenders succeeded in evacuating by stealth at night from what Beauregard realized was an untenable position. Their efforts to spike the guns failed, however, when the explosives left behind failed to detonate. Battery Gregg was abandoned at the same time.

Occupation of the north end of Morris Island probably generated greater joy in the northern camp than despair among the defenders of Charleston. By holding Battery Wagner as long as possible, Beauregard and his troops bought sufficient time to establish another line of defense behind Morris Island. Consequently, the Confederate leadership considered the campaign a success. By maintaining the viability of Charleston as a fortified coastal city, they caused the Federal fleet and its blockaders to continue to commit resources that otherwise could have been utilized to hasten the closure of Mobile and Wilmington, the other Southern ports remaining open for commerce. Blockade running at Charleston came to an end with Gillmore's capture of Cummings Point at the harbor's mouth. Almost another year and a half passed before military pressure on Charleston reached the point where the Confederates were finally forced to abandon the city in February 1865.

While the struggle outside Battery Wagner had not been decisive in the fall of a center of Southern political power, it was significant for the employment of black troops by the Union army, the extensive use and coordination of naval gunfire and rifled artillery from shore batteries, and experimentation with innovations such as calcium lights to illuminate the enemy and Requa guns to lay down a withering anti-personnel fire.[2] The contest for Battery Wagner in the summer of 1863 also represented a milestone in the development of military engineering in the nineteenth century for the successful application of age-old siege warfare on a grand scale in a low tidal area and for the continuous efforts of Southern engineers to strengthen and repair an earthen fortification sufficiently to prevent its surrender in the face of a bombardment with an intensity and duration extraordinary for that time. Considering all these factors, the heroic contributions of Wampler and his fellow engineers enabled the South to achieve a strategic victory on Morris Island.

RECONSTRUCTING A FAMILY AT HOME

Kate was visiting her dear friends, the Balls, at Temple Hall, when she received news of her husband's death, most likely on August 22, 1863. A letter arrived much later, describing the funeral and disposition of his property. Its author was Col. John F. Lay, one of Wampler's companions in the western army, as well as at Charleston. Lay related that Wampler had left written instructions upon departing for Battery Wagner. The personal effects of the deceased—his trunk, valise, papers of value, watch, and rings—had been deposited for safekeeping in a bank in Columbia, South Carolina, a hundred miles from the siege. They would subsequently be transferred to Richmond. Lay's communiqué was sent via Charles B. Tebbs in Richmond, who had served as one intermediary for Wampler's communications with his family, when Loudoun County was isolated behind Union lines. Tebbs added his own letter of condolences. He was a close friend of Wampler's from their days together in the 8th Virginia, when Tebbs had served as deputy commander to Eppa Hunton. It was not until the following January before Kate finally received the official notification from Richmond of her husband's death.

> Extract from the Report of Brig. Genl. R. S. Ripley of the defense of Charleston from the 1st to the 20th August 1863: "17th. Battery Wagner, which had received its full share of the enemy's fire was but little damaged, but sustained a serious loss in the death of Capt. Morris Wampler of the Engineers, a gallant and accomplished officer, who was killed by a shell from the enemy's fleet, while faithfully performing his arduous duties."[3]

Kate did not wait before embarking on her own quest to learn what she could of Morris's demise and to collect his belongings. In November, she started for Richmond with a friend. They journeyed by horse and buggy as far as the railroad, where they sold their rig and took the cars to Richmond. Kate was warmly embraced by acquaintances in the Confederate capital and consequently did not begin the return trip to Loudoun until late December.

Once they left the train on their way home, the wayfarers were forced to rely upon any farmer passing by to offer a wagon ride. Christmas found the twosome in a little cabin in the foothills, watching stars shining through the roof at night, their holiday celebration consisting of a portion of turkey and cakes. On New Year's Day, the sojourners were in Upperville, where they took great delight in a skirmish between Yankee and Southern soldiers, which appeared to the women to be a victory for their side. At long last, in early January, Kate reached her home on Goose Creek, "& the little ones I longed to see."[4]

The family stayed on Goose Creek until the war ended. Loudoun County was then in shambles. The members of Kate's immediate family in Louisiana were deceased, so she headed where prospects appeared brightest for providing for her family. She took her children to the one place associated in her own mind with happy memories of starting a life with Morris. The Wamplers returned to Baltimore.

To support her family, Kate turned to two traditional sources of income for a widow.[5] First, she advertised herself as a seamstress, and, when that failed to produce sufficient earnings, hung out the shingle for boarders. At the same time, she engaged in her own personal campaign to find out more about Morris's wartime service far from home, to promote his career posthumously, and to perpetuate his memory. Kate corresponded with Mrs. Mary A. Snowden, who provided assurances that the grave was being cared for by the Charleston's Ladies Memorial Association, which she had founded. Correspondence with Generals Beauregard and Thomas Jordan, the Creole's former adjutant general and chief of staff, was intended to gain her husband belated recognition as a major in the Corps of Engineers. Jordan wrote, "I hasten to answer that your husband, to the best of my recollection, had been promoted to be a major of Engineers before he fell; and there can be no hesitation in giving him that rank." Jordan went on to recall, rather condescendingly, "I knew him early at Manassas & Centreville and saw a good deal of him and of his modest worth."[6] There had, in fact, been no actual promotion, a technicality that did not preclude the family from inscribing "Major" on Wampler's gravestone in Charleston. To memorialize the nexus with Beauregard, Kate presented to the City of Charleston the sword given her husband by his officers in the 8th Virginia to be displayed near that of his mentor. Kate even corresponded with Georgia Strong in Aberdeen, Mississippi, by then a widow herself, who warmly remembered Morris's stay during the summer of 1862. Mrs. Strong wrote of her family's grief upon learning of his demise, shortly after receiving "a beautiful letter" from him at Charleston.[7]

Kate remained in Baltimore through the decade of the 1870s. By then, her family had begun to scatter. Tommy married a Maryland woman and returned to Virginia to pursue a career as a photographer and later as a small-town newspaper publisher. Kate followed him to Front Royal, Charlottesville, and Culpeper, but also returned to her wartime friends in Loudoun County. In 1894, she applied to the State of Virginia for a pension as a war widow, receiving an annual sum of forty dollars. Kate never remarried. Sixty-one years after her husband's death, at age ninety-one, she died at the Home for the Incurables in Washington, D.C., from complications arising from being dropped out of a wheelchair.

Tombstones often obscure more than they reveal. Hers, at Leesburg, reflects the focus of her life: "Kate N. Wampler. Born in Louisiana, June 27, 1833. Died November 27, 1924. Wife of Capt. J. M. Wampler, C.S.A. Engineer, Fort Wagner, Charleston Harbor. Killed August 17, 1863." Where is

mention of the beautiful Baton Rouge lass? Of the mother who derived comfort during the war by keeping her baby close to her in bed, with the cow
protected in the kitchen? Of the brave woman who crossed the Potomac in
search of food from Yankee soldiers? Of the great-grandmother known affectionately to her family as "Bunner"?

WHY GO SOUTH?

Looking back over fourteen decades to observe the Civil War, it is natural to
wonder what motivated the vast majority of southerners, who were neither
plantation owners nor slaveholders, to risk their lives fighting for secession.
There is no single explanation for Wampler's commitment to the Confederate States of America. Patriotism is one thread running through his life. It
was evident in 1850, as Wampler's riverboat paddled up the Mississippi to St.
Louis, where, he recorded, "triumphantly waved, the flag of flags, the glorious Star 'Spangled Banner'."[8] Love of country occupied his thoughts again
later that summer, when Wampler mourned the death of President Zachary
Taylor. Patriotism reappeared intermittently throughout his writings; for
example, he makes an ironic reference in 1851 to one "indisolvable Union."[9]
He certainly took pride in being a part of his government's premier scientific
department, the U.S. Coast Survey. Influenced in part, perhaps, by those
around him, by late 1860, Wampler had transferred his allegiance from the
Federal government to his native South. He characteristically devoted himself to this new cause with the same passion that stirred his blood for the
Stars and Stripes in earlier times.

Certainly, opportunism was also a motivator for casting his lot with the
Confederacy. Wampler's civil engineering practice in Baltimore was far from
a huge success, falling short of expectations when he burned his bridges with
the Coast Survey and embarked upon what seemed like promising alternatives in the private sector. The establishment of a fledgling national government in Montgomery, Alabama, appeared to Wampler to be a chance to
associate himself with something great, just as he thought he was doing in
Texas and Arkansas with the railroads upon severing his ties with Alexander
Dallas Bache and company. When the peacetime government made the transition to war, Wampler was just as eager to sign up and serve as a military
engineer. If that was where the opportunities lay, then that was where he
would make his mark, and perhaps his fortune as well. No one knew for
certain in 1861 where this new Confederacy would lead for those willing to
cast their lots with it.

Wampler seemed to have very little to lose of a material nature. He owned no real property and possessed no slaves, so his motivation would not have been the preservation of a social system tied to his own personal wealth. Mavin's Mill utilized the services of a male slave, and "Aunt" Annie kept Kate company during the war. Wampler certainly employed slave labor as a Confederate engineer when constructing defensive positions, and he retained the personal services of a manservant when traveling with the Coast Survey and engineering with the Confederate army in the West. Wampler's references to blacks reflect his caring nature, as he engaged in writing or reading on their behalf, acted as a guide for a lost traveler, and, in at least once instance, tended to minor medical needs. A life spent, by choice, almost entirely within the South's racial construct would seem to indicate acceptance of its class system. Like so many southerners, Wampler felt a strong loyalty to the state, which encompassed its laws and mores as well.

As the fighting wore on, Wampler's commitment to the Confederacy was surely reinforced by those around him. Strong personal bonds are formed among soldiers with shared experiences, especially during times when mortality is at risk whenever fighting resumes and in the close daily contact of soldiering apart from one's family and loved ones. Using his uncommon facility with the written word, Wampler sustained this emotional bond during separations from his comrades-in-arms. This closeness is reflected in the correspondence he continued with Albert E. Mathews, Henry Peyton, and Samuel E. Fox, to cite but a few names from Wampler's service with the 8th Virginia. Short absences from Wilson Presstman, James Nocquet, and others in the West also generated letters. Had he performed his entire service with the 8th Virginia, amid close friends from the same locale, Wampler's psychological reinforcement would have come from within his unit. Parenthetically, his reputation at home would have related directly to his performance as a soldier. Hundreds of miles from Loudoun County, the solitary soldier fastened himself instead to other emotional anchors.

Wampler stayed in regular contact, not just with loved ones back in Loudoun County, but with the Strongs in Mississippi and the Greens in Georgia, surrogate families who had willingly opened their homes and shared their lives when he needed them. How could Wampler have retained his respect with these close friends and colleagues had he given up the Confederate cause that had brought them together? Long after any dreams of position or fortune had faded and in spite of a growing homesickness for his wife and children, Captain Wampler continued to do his duty as an officer in the Confederate States Army.

The Fate Awaiting the Tennessee Engineers

How would the war have ended for Wampler had he survived the ordeal at Battery Wagner? Would he have received greater recognition through promotion as a Confederate engineer? For an answer, one may look at the career of Wilson Presstman, a personal friend, peer, and ideal surrogate. They were the same age, and both from Baltimore. Wampler already knew Presstman when they soldiered at Manassas, where each served as an officer of the line. They received their commissions as captains in the Provisional Army of the Confederate States on the same list and were ordered to report to Beauregard in the West, at his request. Until Wampler's death, their assignments were remarkably similar. While Wampler served as senior engineer for Polk's Right Wing on the march through Kentucky, Presstman filled the corresponding billet in Hardee's Left Wing. When illness forced Wampler out of the position as chief engineer of the Army of Tennessee, his permanent replacement, six weeks later, was Captain Presstman. No sense of jealousy or resentment is evident in Wampler's demeanor toward Presstman, as he continued to follow his companion's comings and goings, lent him money on occasion, and communicated regularly, even when they were no longer in a superior-subordinate relationship. Indeed, it was after Presstman had ascended to chief engineer that Wampler entered with him into the joint endeavor to obtain promotions to the rank of major.

Presstman had worked as a railroad engineer before the war, marrying into a prominent family in Alexandria, Virginia. His social qualities and principles of honor and duty, remembered by those who knew him, are reminiscent of Wampler, as well. On the day his state voted for secession, Presstman joined the regiment forming up in Alexandria, the 17th Virginia Infantry, serving as commander of Company I. Leading his unit to the plains of Manassas, he was badly wounded in the skirmish at Blackburn's Ford that preceded the Battle of Bull Run. While recovering, he supervised work parties improving roads and railways, as the army wintered at Centreville. For thirty months, Presstman served in the rank of captain. The promotion campaign undertaken with Wampler finally reached fruition in November 1863, when Richmond informed Presstman of his appointment to major in the Confederate Provisional Corps of Engineers. During mid-1863, Presstman assumed responsibility for the 3rd Regiment of Engineer Troops being organized in the West. He was subsequently succeeded by Brig. Gen. Danville Leadbetter as chief engineer of the Army of Tennessee. It was as an engineer regimental commander that Presstman was promoted to major, and then to lieutenant colonel in 1864. He received the latter advancement after direct intercession by Beauregard.[10]

A fatal irony befell the former railroad engineer on January 30, 1865, when Presstman was crushed by the ash box of a tender, after he stumbled while attempting to run across the track in front of an engine on the Piedmont line in North Carolina. Presstman's tragic end does not imply that a similar fate would have awaited Wampler, as few engineer officers were killed in the war. With the exception of David B. Harris, who died of illness, none of Wampler's other colleagues perished during the conflict. Wampler could, however, have been expected to rise to field-grade rank, as did his cohort. He may also have made a successful transition back into civil engineering, with the sponsorship of benefactors like Beauregard and Marcus J. Wright, who prospered in the decades following the war.[11]

Many of Wampler's colleagues in the West completed honorable service as Confederate engineers and were released back into civilian life at the war's conclusion. Maj. George B. Pickett and Capt. Salvanus W. Steele surrendered in late April as part of Hardee's corps in North Carolina. Capts. Henry C. Force, Leon J. Fremaux, and Walter J. Morris were all paroled at Meridian, Mississippi, in May 1865, as members of Lt. Gen. Richard Taylor's Department of Alabama, Mississippi and East Louisiana. Capt. George M. Helm and 1st Lt. Thomas S. Newcomb capitulated at Athens, Georgia, and Catawba Bridge, South Carolina, respectively. Capt. Henry N. Pharr and Lts. James K. P. McFall and Andrew H. Buchanan also applied for parole. The last of Wampler's engineer comrades to surrender was Lt. Col. Robert P. Rowley, serving as an officer in Gen. Edmund Kirby Smith's Army of the Trans-Mississippi.

By war's end, other western engineers were already out of action. Capt. Felix R. R. Smith and 2nd Lt. James D. Thomas were both captured in the Atlanta campaign in 1864 and paroled in mid-June 1865 from a camp in Sandusky, Ohio.

At least two Confederate engineers were captured, exchanged, and returned to service until the war's end. Maj. Samuel H. Lockett surrendered at Vicksburg on July 4, 1863, and, upon being paroled, resumed his duties with the Confederate army, rising to the rank of colonel in the engineer corps. Similarly, Capt. John G. Mann was captured on December 28, 1863, behind the lines at Collierville, Tennessee, but exchanged the following week. He continued on the staff of Nathan Bedford Forrest throughout the remainder of the conflict.

The circumstances surrounding the capture of a select few engineer officers

arouse suspicion. In August 1863, Lt. Amos S. Darrow was detained in Rochester, New York, where he had allegedly gone to visit his brother. One of Jeremy
Gilmer's favorites, the Irish-born Capt. Edward B. Sayers, surrendered at Chickamauga, Georgia, on September 19, 1863. He was exchanged the following month,
but upon returning to the Rebel lines, he was relieved from duty in the Department of Tennessee and transferred elsewhere. Sayers continued serving the Southern cause until the war's end.[12] The termination of Conrad Meister's service as a
draftsman for the engineer corps is not in doubt. The week after Wampler left
Chattanooga, Meister crossed over to the enemy at Stevenson, Alabama. Identified
in Union records as a "Lieut. of Topographical Engineers," the German-born
deserter was permitted to return to his adopted home in New York City.[13]

The story of James Nocquet is more fascinating. A small Frenchman with a
black beard, Nocquet was reputed to have served as an engineer under Marshal
Bazaine in Algeria and may have also presented himself to Americans as holding
a doctorate degree. His service with the Confederate army began in September
1861, under Brig. Gen. Simon Bolivar Buckner in Kentucky. Nocquet was acting
chief engineer at Bowling Green until the arrival of Maj. Jeremy Gilmer, who
was apparently impressed by the Gaul, considering his support over the next two
years. Nocquet's name, along with Wampler's, was on that first list of captains
appointed to the Confederate Provisional Engineer Corps on February 15, 1862.
From Fort Donelson, Nocquet was assigned as chief engineer of Maj. Gen. John
C. Breckinridge's division at Baton Rouge and Port Hudson, Louisiana. Gilmer
transferred him to the Western Department in October 1862, so that his specialized knowledge of the Louisville area could be put to use during Bragg's occupation of Kentucky. Arriving too late to make a contribution, with Gilmer's bless-
ing, Nocquet was promoted to major and assigned as chief engineer of Bragg's
army in the West.[14]

It was at this point that Nocquet and Wampler became acquainted, leading
one month later to the Marylander replacing the Frenchman, who was sent to
Chattanooga to construct fortifications with the title of chief engineer, Department No. 2. In June 1863, Wampler replaced Nocquet again, as Gilmer reunited
Buckner with the major as his chief engineer for the Department of East Tennessee. In the fall, now Major General Buckner was reassigned to command a corps
under Bragg, and Nocquet was next seen representing Maj. Gen. Thomas C.
Hindman, a division commander in the Army of Tennessee, in discussions of
strategy at McLemore's Cove on September 10, 1863. Nocquet's broken English,
lack of understanding of the topography, and unfamiliarity with the enemy's
order of battle or the Southern forces irritated the army commander—a repeti-

tion of characteristics exhibited the previous November that caused Bragg to replace him.[15]

Shortly thereafter, Nocquet disappeared. By the end of October, the engineer bureau was inquiring as to his whereabouts. Leadbetter and Buckner reported the facts as they knew them. Nocquet had left the army to purchase engineer supplies in Tennessee. Depending upon the account, he was dressed either in civilian clothes or in a uniform stolen from a general officer. He apparently took with him $150,000 intended for the construction of bridges and defensive works in East Tennessee, Confederate money which he subsequently exchanged for more-negotiable Tennessee bank bills. It must have been difficult for then Maj. Gen. Jeremy Gilmer, the Confederate army's chief engineer and his former patron, to submit this report to the secretary of war and recommend that Nocquet be stricken from the rolls as a deserter.[16]

Nocquet may well have been accompanied through the Union lines by the elusive Capt. Francois Thysseus. The two Frenchmen would have been obvious companions. Thysseus had studied at St. Cyr, served as lieutenant in the French cavalry, and was an accomplished draftsman and painter, a fine drill master, and an adept swordsman. Since arriving in the United States, fifteen years before the war, he had been engaged as a professor of military tactics and engineering at the University of Nashville. There is, however, indication that he was less than fully successful as an officer in the Confederate army. Other than performing reconnaissance for Maj. Gen. Earl Van Dorn in Arkansas, while serving as his aide, there is no record of accomplishment by this engineer with the impressive credentials. At a time when commanders were desperate for engineering expertise, Thysseus was allowed to remain in a billet that could be filled by any officer of the line. In August 1863, Thysseus was apparently charged with being "intemperate." As a consequence, he could well have been discontent with his lot in the Southern cause. From having lived and soldiered in Tennessee, his knowledge of the area would have made Nocquet's Gallic friend the ideal partner with whom to desert. At his own request, on August 24, 1863, Thysseus was granted a thirty-day leave of absence "for the benefit of his health." Nothing was heard of him again.[17]

USE OF ENCRYPTION

Then there is the matter of several enciphered annotations in Wampler's personal wartime journals. What is the origin of these characters and what do they mean? The Confederate army did not employ a single code or ciphering device. The Vigenere square, the use of identical texts (such as dictionaries) as codebooks, and single and polyalphabetic substitution were all employed by commanding officers free to select their own codes and ciphers to shield messages from inquisitive Yankee eyes.[18] Wampler's cryptography does not appear to have been drawn from a unit cipher. It appears instead to have been fabricated for his own private recordkeeping by borrowing from the encryption design used by the Masonic fraternity.[19]

Wampler's affiliation with freemasonry had been terminated by his suspension from National Lodge 12 in 1856. Subsequently, during the long, cold winter spent in the Confederate Army of the Potomac, encamped at Centreville in 1861–62, Wampler added his name to a petition to establish a military lodge of the Masonic Order, in order to hold meetings wherever the regiment was stationed. The request was granted by warrant of the Grand Lodge of Virginia on January 25, 1862.

Two of the six specimens of Wampler's ciphers originated during this encampment. Two others are dated in March of 1862, during the retrograde movement toward the Peninsula. Another entry is over a year later, when Wampler was in Chattanooga. The sixth example, a series of paired words, is found in an account book, presumably entered sometime from late 1862 to mid-1863.

The last exhibit may be considered first, as it might have served as a sampler, providing the writer, unaccustomed to cryptology, an opportunity to practice transferring letters into symbols. What it reveals about Wampler's thoughts is of interest as well. The absence of a date to complete the final entry in no way obscures what was on his mind.

[encoded]

right	might	war
hope	doubt	joy
activity		success
exertion		valor
duty		struggle
battle		victory
peace	by	

The other five encrypted entries, interspersed in their open contexts, were:

Clear Text	Encoded
December 1, 1861, Centreville	
"wrote"	*to Ida Mitchell*

February 10, 1862, Centreville
    "Bob Clowe called yesterday"   *took letter to Ida*

March 9, 1862, near Warrenton
    "Chaplain & I went to Warrenton
    to Church"   *communion*

March 23, 1862, Camp Taylor
    "Chaplain preached"   *wrote to Ida by Chaplain*

July 14, 1863, Chattanooga
    "Working on Fortifications. Got"   *letter from Ida. Answered it.*
    "very warm"

Who is Ida Mitchell? The obvious reason for a military officer to en-
code diary entries in time of war is to protect information that could be of
value to the enemy. Ida Mitchell could have been a Confederate spy. Yet no
such woman is known to have been a Southern operative. Furthermore,
Wampler makes other notations of clandestine activity in his journals in
plain English. In Kentucky, on September 29, 1862, Wampler writes of meeting "Mrs. Church, & finding her very intelligent & shrewd, I engaged her
to go into Illinois & Indiana to distribute & publish documents." Two days
later, he sees her off on a mission to foment dissent among Southern sympathizers in two Union states. This activity is recorded in clear text. Wampler
was fond of using aliases to protect the identity of female associates, like
"Idy Saltmarsh," "Miss Barnes," and "Victoria Wade," designations connected with their whereabouts. It is also possible that the name "Ida Mitchell"
could also be a fabrication, both to permit Wampler to shroud her identity
and to allow her to pick up mail at a post office with anonymity.

After Wampler made an encrypted record of writing to Ida at Camp
Taylor, near Orange, Virginia, he included in a series of thoughts on March
27, 1862, "[Chaplain] Linthicum gone on secret duty to Maryland." Was this
an intelligence-gathering mission for Gen. Joseph E. Johnston's army, not
unlike other occasions when the unchallenged mobility of respected professional men, physicians and clergy, was utilized by the South for undercover
work? Or did Chaplain Linthicum's "secret duty" relate instead to Wampler's
secret letter to Ida Mitchell?

The clergyman certainly knew what was going on, which might suggest
that it was indeed completely moral or for military purposes. It does not explain,
however, the encryption of the word "communion" on March 9, 1862. Was "com-

munion" another code word? Wampler was, of course, Episcopalian, and Linthicum a Methodist, albeit a Northern Methodist, which indiscretion Eppa Hunton did not soon forgive him, but there is nothing obvious in the sacrament itself that would explain its being encoded. Little is known of Robert Clowe, the carrier of the February 10 letter to Ida, other than his being a private in Captain Wampler's Company H, 8th Virginia Infantry. A captain, a chaplain, and a private do not obviously add up to an undercover military operation.

Another possibility is that Ida Mitchell belonged to the Eastern Star, formed in 1855 as the female counterpart to the Masonic Order. This would have accounted for the use of signs resembling the standard Masonic Cipher and provided justification for complicity by a member of the cloth. Wampler's lukewarm membership in the fraternal order and the earliest encryption prior to renewing his Masonic ties through establishment of the military lodge at Centreville combine to discount this prospect.

A more plausible explanation is that Wampler had engaged in a liaison with Ida Mitchell. His journals are replete with references to ladies with whom he came into contact. With the possible exception of those designated by code words, like Idy Saltmarsh, these relationships may be understood to be as innocent as they appear. Why refer openly to a number of women encountered in his travels as an engineer and later as a Confederate officer and then encrypt Ida Mitchell's name? Would Kate or one of his military comrades have recognized Ida's name if they came across it in his writings and wondered about the exchange of correspondence? There is no mention of a Mitchell family in Kate's journal or in the 1860 census of Loudoun County. Nor does Wampler enter these notations when returning to the Leesburg environs from the camp at Centreville. Wampler's relocation to Virginia shortly before the war had not left much time for flirtation. Five years in Baltimore might have provided greater opportunities. Chaplain Linthicum hailed from outside Baltimore (in the community now known by his family name). He was returning to Maryland after being given the communiqué addressed to Ida Mitchell. Mrs. Clara Mitchell, offering millinery and children's clothing, lived next door to the Wamplers in Baltimore in 1859 and 1860, although there is no indication that she was known as Ida and no record that she had a daughter by that name.

Ida Mitchell's residence in the Maryland–Virginia area, which is her most likely location since this is where Wampler spent the five years prior to the war, could also explain the single encoded journal entry after he was transferred to the West. There is also a suggestion soon after Wampler arrived in the West, on May 27, 1862, that he wrote to Mitchell, as he notes in his journal, "Wrote letters to . ,————, wife, mother & Berkeley." Correspondence with the Confederate Army of the Mississippi would have been more difficult than with the Army of the Potomac, where messages could be hand-carried, especially if Ida Mitchell lived outside the Confederacy in Maryland. Are the two words, "very warm," in July 1863 that follow the encrypted reference to receiving a letter from her in Chattanooga intended as a double entendre?

The identity of Ida Mitchell will, in all likelihood, remain a mystery. If nothing else, Wampler's clandestine correspondence, recorded in code, reinforces his lifelong penchant for the companionship of women. Morris Wampler grew up in a women's world, absent a father or brother in his immediate family and schooled in a female academy presided over by a dominant, albeit enlightened, female educator. In such an environment, the young man learned refinement, not the pastimes and vices of men. These cultivated interests drew Wampler naturally to the company of women and, in turn, made him especially attractive to them. As a stranger in St. Louis and New Orleans in the early 1850s, as a resident in Baltimore before the war, and while stationed as a Confederate engineer officer in Aberdeen, Mississippi, in 1862, Wampler was accepted by the cultured families in these societies. Similarly, when posted in the West, his background and prewar exposure to the North allowed him to easily make friends with officers reared outside the Confederate states or abroad. Presumably Wampler's attractiveness arose from a facility in music, languages, literature, and religion, and, no doubt, because he was unusually well-traveled in the United States of his day.

Engineering for the Confederacy

In contrast to Wampler's liberal education, many military officers serving in the Corps of Engineers before the Civil War were trained at the U.S. Military Academy, where its venerable professor, Dennis Hart Mahan, wrote the treatise on field fortifications that was the discipline's scripture. Early Mahan disciples had honed their engineering prowess in the Mexican War. Civil engineers, like Wampler, brought with them into military service a different combination of skills, developed through surveying, bridge and railroad construction, city planning, and supervising the work of unskilled laborers. Mastering the military applications of their discipline was the challenge for these citizen-soldiers, while West Point graduates confronted the nontactical engineering tasks required to support Civil War armies on the move. Exploration and land development beyond the Appalachian Mountains infused into the staffs of the engineer departments in the western armies an inventiveness and aptitude for field expedients, when textbook solutions authored by urban eastern engineers were impractical or materials unavailable. Engineering, military or civilian, entailed strict accountability of funds, equipment, and supplies, plus efficient utilization of personnel resources. Wampler learned early in his career with the Coast Survey of the inevitability of ledgers and paperwork for any engineer working within the confines of a bureaucracy.

Due both to the shortage of trained engineers and to his own movement through the Southern states during sixteen months as a Confederate engineer, Wampler engaged in all the major functions of a military engineer in the field. His experience, of course, was apart from more specialized assignments in river and harbor obstructions or the experimental use of balloons for observation or submersibles to blow passageways through the Yankee blockade. A question persists as to whether the Confederate army overlooked a valuable resource by not utilizing Wampler's unique knowledge of Galveston Bay to thwart Federal encroachment on the Texas Gulf coast.

As a veteran of the acclaimed Coast Survey, Wampler's reputation was made as a topographical engineer. His ability to draw maps first brought him to General Beauregard's attention and then continued as his hallmark with field commanders wherever he served. Wampler's first military engineering project entailed construction of field fortifications outside Leesburg, Virginia. Upon reporting to the Confederate Army of the Mississippi, he quickly undertook reconnaissance and preparation of hasty defensive positions outside Corinth. Opportunities for bridge construction materialized at Aberdeen and, later, at McMinnville. On the march through Kentucky, Wampler served in the vanguard, ahead of the pioneers, identifying the route and insuring its clearance and preparation for the wagons and men that followed. He was also used to gather intelligence on the enemy's strength and whereabouts. When required, like all combat support soldiers, Wampler was expected to fight as an infantryman. Returning to garrison engineering in Middle Tennessee, Wampler engaged in road and bridge reconnaissance and repaired rail lines sabotaged by Union troops and sympathizers. In the position of chief engineer for the Army of Tennessee and for the District of Tennessee River, he shouldered an administrative burden, while supervising other professionals engaged in engineering. His most notable experience erecting pontoon bridges took place outside Chattanooga (after an earlier, less-successful installation at Aberdeen) late in his tenure with the Army of Tennessee. At Atlanta, Wampler returned to laying out defensive positions for a campaign that would not be fought for another year.

Wampler took his final exam in military engineering on Morris Island, repeatedly repairing the defenses of Battery Wagner (including laying land mines), while under siege and subject to naval and artillery bombardment. It is ironic that he should perish due in considerable measure to pressure exerted outside Battery Wagner by the engineering of enemy sappers. A life devoted to engineering ended as a consequence of the engineer expertise of his adversaries.

In undertaking his duties, Wampler's experiences were typical of military engineers in the Civil War. Long days on a work site and extended exposure to the elements required him to be active, energetic, and physically fit. As much of the considerable travel necessary to perform these missions was accomplished on his own steeds, Wampler also had to be a good horseman. He could not afford to be overly deliberate, as the tactical situation could change quickly. Field commanders wanted information from reconnaissance in a timely fashion, and expected it to be concisely described and accurately mapped. Therefore, Wampler had to be cognizant of tactics and attuned to the military advantages and disadvantages of terrain, an army's ability to traverse a particular area, road conditions necessary for use by units and their trains, and the camping, water, and forage requirements for a field army. In designing and building fortifications, Wampler, like other military engineers, needed an appreciation of ordnance and the characteristics of projectiles, as well as the problems inherent in permanent fortifications regarding ventilation and drainage for inevitable water seepage. Clear thinking and inventiveness were expected, but a civil engineer who put on the uniform of his military counterpart could not rely on common sense alone. Wampler also had to acquire a basic understanding of the profession of arms and be proficient at those military engineering specialties for which there were no civilian counterparts.[20]

Wampler's accounts of his war experiences, especially in his personal journals, are especially credible due to his untimely death. Entries in his own hand on the morning of August 17, 1863, suggest a practice of making notations as events unfolded, enhancing the accuracy of his observations. Veterans who survived the War of Northern Aggression or the Great Rebellion, depending upon their orientation, were free in later years to engage in revisionism, either consciously or as a result of failing memories. The bombardment begun by U.S. gunboats outside Charleston Harbor on August 17, 1863, froze Wampler's commentary for all time. It is unfortunate that somewhere along the way since then, his personal correspondence, especially that intended for Kate's eyes, has been lost, as, in all likelihood, it would have furnished personal impressions to help fill out his story.

As an officer in the Confederate States Army, Wampler made a personal commitment. Like his peers in the 8th Virginia, the Army of Tennessee, and those who sacrificed in the defense of Charleston, he took a stand against a government that he had once served with pride, but viewed in a different light in the 1860s. As fighting wore on, Wampler's foremost hope was not for victory on the battlefield, but for peace. Like many others around him, he grew tired of campaigning, of being separated from loved ones and friends in Maryland and northern Virginia, of the sickness exacerbated by the hard life of a soldier in gray.

Morris Wampler, Confederate engineer, did not live to see national peace and the reunification in its wake. His life has a lasting meaning, nonetheless, for what it says about a man with intelligence and education who valiantly struggled to find his way at a time of unprecedented change and crisis in the nation. Wampler did not achieve lasting fame as an engineer or as a soldier. His practice faltered. His inventions were unsuccessful. His fidelity as a husband is even in question. But Wampler's life tells us something valuable about both the strength and frailty of human nature when confronting crisis. Wampler faced the daunting challenge of being a father with no role model from his own formative years and little opportunity to be at home and participate in raising his children. He continued striving for a niche in the geographic and industrial expansion taking place about him. Others prospered; he did not. Wampler performed commendably as a military engineer, even though he was not promoted. Through it all, however, he persevered. Unbeknownst to him, he ultimately achieved success in that he left a legacy as a Confederate engineer, even if he did not gain the material achievement and recognition he sought.

Before the war drew to a close, Magnolia Cemetery outside Charleston suffered vandalism at the hands of Federal soldiers who occupied the city. The cemetery's wooden lodge was dismantled, the chapel emptied of pews, and the forest of oaks chopped down by troops permitted to camp on the grounds.[21] In 1871, the bodies of South Carolinians killed at Gettysburg were moved from Pennsylvania into a special section reserved for Confederate soldiers. Wampler's remains were transferred to this plot as well in January 1900, into a grave vacated by a body disinterred for burial elsewhere. By that time, his once-impoverished family had recovered sufficiently to afford a three-foot tombstone displaying the Masonic compass and level. Its size caused Wampler's memorial to stand out amidst the smaller, more modest headstones of standard issue on the surrounding graves.

His tombstone now stands in my den. For almost a full century, John Morris Wampler's grave was neglected. When I came upon it in 1985, after literally decades of searching, I discovered the stone broken, running the risk that his burial site would soon be unmarked. I engaged a mason to carve and erect an exact replica and carried the original, broken into three pieces, home to be mended and preserved. As his grave had been neglected, so Wampler's life has been overlooked for far too long. Reconstructing his life through multiple sources, Wampler can now be appreciated as not only a Confederate engineer, but as a variety of everyman, confronting a rapidly changing world and coping as best he could, before perishing in his most profound fight with adversity.

Notes

Primary sources cited without location, to include journals and letters, remain in possession of descendants of Kate and Morris Wampler. References to the *War of the Rebellion: A Compilation of the Official Records of the Union and Confederate Armies (OR)* are to series 1, unless otherwise indicated. References to Combined Military Service Records, War Department Collection of Confederate Records, Record Group 109, National Archives, Washington, D.C., are indicated as CMSR, NA. NA, of course, is an abbreviation of National Archives. All correspondence cited between John Morris Wampler and Alexander Dallas Bache that is retained by the National Archives is found in Correspondence of A. D. Bache, Superintendent, 1843–1865, Coast and Geodetic Survey, M642, RG 23, and is simply annotated with the roll number and NA after the date.

Prologue

1. *OR,* vol. 28, pt. 1: 470.
2. Wampler, Journal, Aug. 17, 1863.
3. *OR,* vol. 28, pt. 1: 470–71.
4. Madeleine Vinton Dahlgren, *Memoir of John A. Dahlgren* (New York: Charles L. Webster and Co., 1891), 408.
5. *OR,* vol. 28, pt. 2: 287.
6. John Johnson, *The Defense of Charleston Harbor, Including Fort Sumter and the Adjacent Islands, 1863–1865* (Charleston, S.C.: Walker, Evans & Cogswell Co., 1890), 123; and *War of the Rebellion: Official Records of the Union and Confederate Navies in the War of the Rebellion* (Washington, D.C.: U.S. Government Printing Office, 1902), series 1, vol. 14: 474 (hereafter referred to as *ORN,* followed by series, volume, and page numbers).
7. *OR,* vol. 28, pt. 1: 84.
8. Johnson, *Defense of Charleston Harbor,* 471–72.
9. Stephen R. Wise, *Gate of Hell: Campaign for Charleston Harbor, 1863* (Columbia: Univ. of South Carolina Press, 1994), 95.
10. Wampler, Journal, Aug. 17, 1863.

11. Col. John F. Lay to Kate Wampler, Aug. 19, 1863; and Samuel Jones, *The Siege of Charleston* (New York: Neale Publishing Company, 1911), 258.

12. Robert C. Gilchrist, "The Confederate Defence of Morris Island," *Yearbook of the City of Charleston, 1884*, 380–81; and S. A. Ashe, "Life at Fort Wagner," *Confederate Veteran* 35 (July 1927): 254.

Chapter One:
"The Only Boy Educated at Belmont"

1. The dates and circumstances regarding the deaths of Morris's brother and sister remain a mystery. What is certain, however, is that neither reached majority, and, by the middle of the next decade, Morris was his father's sole surviving offspring.

2. Ezra J. Warner, *Generals in Gray: Lives of the Confederate Commanders* (Baton Rouge: Louisiana State Univ. Press, 1959), 290–91.

3. Frances King Kelly, "The Gifted One: A Brief Biography of Margaret Mercer, 1791–1846, Educator, Emancipator and Heaven's Advocate," unpublished MS, Saint David's Episcopal Church, Ashburn, Virginia.

4. Ibid.

5. Ibid.

6. Caspar Morris, *Memoir of Miss Margaret Mercer,* 2nd ed., rev. (Philadelphia: Lindsay & Blakiston, 1848), 135–36.

7. Yardley Taylor, *Memoir of Loudon [sic] County, Virginia* (Leesburg: Thomas Reynolds, 1853), 23–24.

8. Charles P. Poland, Jr., *From Frontier to Suburbia* (Marceline, Mo.: Walsworth Publishing Company, 1976), 131–33.

9. Taylor, *Memoir,* 6–7.

10. Joseph Martin, *A New and Comprehensive Gazetteer of Virginia, and the District of Columbia* (Charlottesville, Va.: Moseley & Tompkins, Printers, 1835), 77.

11. Brenda E. Stevenson, *Life in Black and White: Family and Community in the Slave South* (New York; Oxford Univ. Press, 1996), 126. An additional charge would be levied for extracurricular instruction in subjects such as music and drawing. Catherine Clinton, *The Plantation Mistress: Woman's World in the Old South* (New York: Pantheon Books, 1982), 135.

12. "A Brief History of the Parish Church of Saint David, Belmont (Within the Bounds of Old Cameron Parish), Ashburn, Virginia," Saint David's Episcopal Church, Ashburn, Virginia.

13. Kelly, "The Gifted One."

14. J. Harry Shannon, "The Rambler Writes of Miss Margaret Mercer," *(Washington, D.C.) Sunday Star,* Dec. 15, 1918, 2.

15. Philip di Zerega, "History of Secondary Education in Loudoun County, Virginia" (M.A. thesis, Univ. of Virginia, 1948), 40; and George C. Rable, Civil

Wars: Women and the Crisis of Southern Nationalism (Urbana: Univ. of Illinois Press, 1989), 21.

16. Margaret Mercer, *Popular Lectures on Ethics, or Moral Obligation: For the Use of Schools* (Petersburg, Va.: Edmund & Julian C. Ruffin, 1841).

17. Ibid., appendix.

18. Lucy Lee Pleasants, *Old Virginia Days and Ways* (Menasha, Wisc.: George Banta Publishing Company, 1916), 84–86.

19. Boarders paid $125 for a half-session tuition and $10 a month board, plus $10 for French and $33 for music instruction, presumably offered to Morris Wampler without charge. Statement issued by Belmont Academy to Miss Sarah E. Linton, Oct. 1, 1838, in the papers of Louisa Hutchison.

20. Morris, *Memoir of Miss Margaret Mercer,* 138.

21. Ibid., 146.

22. "A Brief History of the Parish Church of Saint David, Belmont."

23. Morris, *Memoir of Miss Margaret Mercer,* 147. John H. B. Latrobe's contributions to America far exceeded his considerable artistic accomplishments, however. He spent over a half century as the railroad lawyer for the Baltimore and Ohio, arguing important cases in federal and state supreme courts, negotiating rights with the Czarist regime in Russia, and promoting the union of the Morse telegraph with the B&O. Inventor, poet, philanthropist—Latrobe's friendship with Mercer may have evolved from their mutual interest in the American Colonization Society.

24. Shannon, "The Rambler Writes of Miss Margaret Mercer," 3.

25. "A Brief History of the Parish Church of Saint David, Belmont."

26. Morris, *Memoir of Miss Margaret Mercer,* 174–76. See also J. Harry Shannon, "The Rambler Writes of the Old Belmont House," *(Washington, D.C.) Sunday Star,* Dec. 8, 1918.

27. "A Brief History of the Parish Church of Saint David, Belmont."

28. Miss Mercer was also very proud of the modernization within her own house: "The dressing-room is the most complete establishment; I have the most perfect pump, which draws the water from the bottom of the well into the dressing-room; then a large boiler with a flue, which passes entirely round the room, and will keep it perfectly warm at all hours; a large reservoir for warm water, and a spacious bath; the compartments are furnished each with a cup and basin, and there can hardly be anything sweeter or more convenient" (Kelly, "The Gifted One").

29. Morris, *Memoir of Miss Margaret Mercer,* 168.

30. Poland, *From Frontier to Suburbia,* 103.

31. Penelope M. Osburn, "Historic Leesburg Often Took Part in Great Events," *Virginia and the Virginia County* 7 (Jan. 1953): 16.

32. Samuel M. Janney, *Memoirs* (Philadelphia: Friends' Book Association, 1881), 93–95.

33. For a good overview of the Belmont school, see J. Harry Shannon, "Margaret Mercer's Academy for Young Girls," *(Washington, D.C.) Sunday Star,* Dec. 22, 1918.

Chapter Two:
Alexander Dallas Bache and the Coast Survey

1. *(Washington, D.C.) Daily National Intelligencer,* Sept. 22, 1846; and Allen Johnson and Dumas Malone, eds., *Dictionary of American Biography* (New York: Charles Scribner's Sons, 1958), 6: 545.
2. Richard Hugh Slotten, *Patronage, Practice, and the Culture of American Science: Alexander Dallas Bache and the U.S. Coast Survey* (New York: Cambridge Univ. Press, 1994), 1.
3. *The Public Statutes at Large of the United States of America* (Boston: Charles C. Little and James Brown, 1845), 2: 413.
4. Benjamin Apthorp Gould, "Address in Commemoration of Alexander Dallas Bache," *Proceedings of the American Association for the Advancement of Science* 17 (1868): 36.
5. Jeannie Tree Rives, "Old Families and Houses—Greenleaf's Point," *Records of the Columbia Historical Society, Washington, D.C.* 5 (1902): 59.
6. Slotten, *Patronage, Practice,* 50–51.
7. Ibid., 169.
8. Mitchell King to Bache, July 10, 1855, Correspondence of A. D. Bache, Superintendent, 1843–1865, Coast and Geodetic Survey, Roll 124, M642, RG 23, NA.
9. Joseph Henry, "Memoir of Alexander Dallas Bache, 1806–1867," *National Academy of Sciences, Biographical Memoirs* (1869), 1: 185.
10. Charles Dickens, *American Notes* (London: Oxford Univ. Press, 1957), 116.
11. "United States Coast Survey," *American Journal of Education* 1 (Aug. 1855): 104.
12. Alexander Dallas Bache, *Reports of the Superintendent of the Coast Survey,* Ex. Doc. No. 6, 30th Cong., 1st Sess., 1847, p. 50; Ex. Doc. No. 1, 30th Cong., 2nd Sess., 1848, p. 61; and Ex. Doc. No. 5, 31st Cong., 1st Sess., 1849, p. 59.
13. Cutts to Bache, May 31, 1849. Correspondence of A. D. Bache, Superintendent, 1843–1865, Coast and Geodetic Survey, Roll 31, M642, RG 23, NA.
14. Bache Report, 1849, 22.
15. Gould, "Address in Commemoration," 27.
16. Joseph Wraight and Elliott B. Roberts, *The Coast and Geodetic Survey, 1807–1957: 150 Years of History* (Washington, D.C.: U.S. Government Printing Office, 1957), 16.
17. Henry, "Memoir of Alexander Dallas Bache," 195.
18. Slotten, *Patronage, Practice,* 165.

19. Wampler, Journal, Dec. 26, 1849.
20. C. M. Gruener, "Rutherford B. Hayes' Horseback Ride Through Texas," *Southwestern Historical Quarterly* 68 (Jan. 1965): 354.
21. William W. Pratt, ed., *Galveston Island Or, A Few Months Off the Coast of Texas: The Journal of Francis C. Sheridan, 1839–1840* (Austin: Univ. of Texas Press, 1954), 30.
22. Wampler to Bache, Jan. 24, 1850, Roll 38, NA.
23. Ibid., Mar. 4, 1850.
24. Wampler, Journal, June 13, 1850.
25. Ibid., June 15, 1850. Wampler repeatedly used underlining to emphasize what he considered to be key words. In accordance with typesetting practice, any underlining in the original quotations appears in italics.
26. Ibid., June 17, 1850.
27. Ibid., June 23, 1850.
28. Ibid., June 24, 1850.
29. Ibid., June 25–28, 1850; and John F. Stover, *Iron Road to the West: American Railroads in the 1850s* (New York: Columbia Univ. Press, 1978), 1–2.
30. Wampler, Journal, July 9, 1850.
31. Brainerd Dyer, *Zachary Taylor* (New York: Barnes & Noble, 1967), 405.
32. Wampler, Journal, Sept. 24, 1850.
33. Ibid., Oct. 20, 1850.
34. A. H. Saxon, *P. T. Barnum: The Legend and the Man* (New York: Columbia Univ. Press, 1989), 164–65.
35. Wampler, Journal, Oct. 8, 1850.
36. Justin Winsor, ed., *The Memorial History of Boston* (Boston: James R. Osgood and Company, 1881), 4: 54.
37. George C. D. Odell, *Annals of the New York Stage* (New York: Columbia Univ. Press, 1931), 5: 408.
38. Gould, "Address in Commemoration," 38.
39. Bache to Wampler, Nov. 11, 1850, Roll 38, NA.
40. Slotten, *Patronage, Practice,* 72.
41. Wampler to Bache, Nov. 11, 1850, Roll 38, NA.
42. Ibid., Nov. 13, 1850.
43. Ibid., Nov. 18, 1850.
44. Wampler to Bache, Oct. 13, 1851, Roll 51, NA.
45. Wampler to Bache, Dec. 19, 1850, Roll 38, NA.
46. Bache to Wampler, Jan. 21, 1851, Roll 51, NA.
47. Wampler, Journal, Feb. 12, 1851.
48. Wampler to Bache, Jan. 15, 1851, Roll 51, NA.
49. Ibid., Apr. 2, 1851.
50. Ibid.
51. Wampler, Journal, Mar. 13, 1851.

52. Alexander Dallas Bache, Report of the Superintendent of the Coast Survey, Sen. Doc. No. 3, 32nd Cong., 1st Sess., 1851, 80.

53. Wampler, Journal, Feb. 14, 1851.

54. Ibid., Feb. 6, 1851.

55. Ibid., Feb. 28, 1851.

56. Ibid., Jan. 10, 1851.

57. Ibid., Jan. 14, 1851.

58. Ibid., Jan. 8, 1851.

59. Ibid., Jan. 4, 1851.

60. Ibid., Apr. 2, 1851.

61. Wampler to Bache, Mar. 15, 1851, Roll 51, NA.

62. William Chambers, *Sketch of the Life of Gen. T. J. Chambers of Texas* (Galveston: Galveston News Office, 1853), 50–53; and Llerena Beaufort Friend, "The Life of Thomas Jefferson Chambers" (M.A. thesis, Univ. of Texas, Austin, 1928), 134–36.

63. Bache to Wampler, Apr. 12, 1851, Roll 51, NA.

64. Ibid., June 16, 1851.

65. Wampler, Journal, Apr. 2, 1851.

66. The account of progress made by the topographical party under his charge was received and accepted by the superintendent on July 26. Bache to Wampler, July 26, 1851, Roll 51, NA.

67. Ibid., July 14, 1851.

68. Wampler to Bache, Aug. 21, 1851, Roll 51, NA.

69. Ibid., Aug. 28, 1851, and Bache to Wampler, Aug. 30, 1851, Roll 51, NA.

70. Wampler to Bache, Sept. 9, 1851, Roll 51, NA.

71. Bache to Wampler, Oct. 8, 1851, Roll 51, NA.

72. Wampler to Bache, Oct. 14, 1851, Roll 51, NA.

73. Ibid., Oct. 28, 1851.

74. Bache to Wampler, Nov. 22, 1851, Roll 51, NA.

75. Zinc was used to protect the iron fastenings from the chemical reaction with saltwater, and copper kept worms and other growth off the boat's bottom. Wampler to Bache, Jan. 29, 1852, Roll 67, NA.

76. Stevens to Wampler, Mar. 13, 1852, Correspondence of A. D. Bache, Superintendent, 1843–1865, Coast and Geodetic Survey, Roll 67, M642, RG 23, NA.

77. Bache to Wampler, Nov. 3, 1851, Roll 67, NA.

78. Wampler to Bache, Feb. 14, 1852, Roll 67, NA.

79. Bache to Wampler, May 3, 1852, Roll 67, NA.

80. Wampler to Bache, October 13, 1852, Brock Collection, Huntington Library, San Marino, Calif.

81. Montgomery C. Meigs, "The surveys, plans, and estimates for supplying the cities of Washington and Georgetown with water," Ex. Doc. No. 48, 32nd Cong., 2nd Sess., 1853, p. 8.

82. Washington District Corps of Engineers, *History of the Washington Aqueduct* (Washington, D.C., 1953), 5.
83. Bache to Wampler, Feb. 11, 1853, RG 23, NA.
84. Meigs, "Surveys, plans, and estimates," 9.
85. Washington District Corps of Engineers, *History of the Washington Aqueduct*, 6.
86. Russell F. Weigley, *Quartermaster General of the Union Army: A Biography of M. C. Meigs* (New York: Columbia Univ. Press, 1959), 59–62.
87. Wampler to Bache, Mar. 8, 1853, Roll 86, NA.
88. Williams to Bache, Feb. 16, 1853, Correspondence of A. D. Bache, Superintendent, 1843–1865, Coast and Geodetic Survey, Roll 97, and Bache to Wampler, Roll 86, NA.
89. Wampler to Bache, Jan. 31, 1853, Roll 93, NA.
90. Ibid., Apr. 1, 1853.
91. Bache to Wampler, Apr. 4, 1853, Alexander Dallas Bache Collection, American Philosophical Society, Philadelphia, Pa.
92. Capt. H. W. Benham, Assistant in Charge, U.S. Coast Survey, to Wampler, Apr. 15, 1853, Correspondence of A. D. Bache, Superintendent, 1843–1865, Coast and Geodetic Survey, Roll 86, M642, RG 23, NA.
93. Another veteran of fifteen years' service with the Coast Survey, John N. Maffitt, went on to fame as "the prince of privateers." Maffitt was the agency's leading hydrographer on the Carolina coast. Since he was married to a North Carolina woman, it is not surprising that Maffitt was one of seven Coast Survey professionals to defect to the Confederacy. Maffitt initially served on the staff of Gen. Robert E. Lee on the South Atlantic seaboard. He subsequently became the best of the blockade runners, while serving as captain of the *C.S.S Florida*, and was never captured. Although their tours of service on the Coast Survey overlapped, there is no reason to believe that Maffitt and Wampler ever met.

CHAPTER THREE: THE ANTEBELLUM YEARS

1. William Edwards Clement, *Plantation Life of the Mississippi* (New Orleans: Pelican Publishing Company, 1952), 30–42; *Craighead v. Wilson*, 59 U.S. (18 How.) 199 (1855); and U.S. Supreme Court, *Transcripts of Records and File Copies of Briefs*, 1855, vol. 2, case nos. 40 to 67, Office of the Clerk, Washington, D.C.
2. Kate Nugent Wampler, Nugent Family Tree, with commentary (holographic).
3. John Francis Hamtramck Claiborne, *Mississippi, as Province, Territory, and State, with Biographies and Notices of Eminent Citizens* (Jackson, Miss.: Power and Barksdale, 1880), 1: 415.
4. Allen Johnson and Dumas Malone, eds., *Dictionary of American Biography* (New York: Charles Scribner's Sons, 1958), 10: 355–58; and James P. Shenton, *Robert John Walker: A Politician from Jackson to Lincoln* (New York: Columbia Univ. Press, 1961), 127–31.

5. The insignificance of Atlanta at this time is reflected in Wampler's omission of its name in his account, noting, instead, the nearby Stone Mountain.

6. Wampler, Journal, Apr. 28–July 31, 1853.

7. Shenton, *Robert John Walker*, 133.

8. For a complete treatment of railroad expansion during the decade of the 1850s, see John F. Stover, *Iron Road to the West: American Railroads in the 1850's* (New York: Columbia Univ. Press, 1978).

9. Ibid., 62 and 102.

10. The two railroad lines solely in Arkansas were the Mississippi, Ouachita and Red River Railroad and the Little Rock and Napoleon Railroad.

11. D. L. Phillips, *The Early History of the Cairo and Fulton Railroad in Arkansas* (Missouri Pacific Railroad Company, 1924), 35–37; "Report of the Cairo and Fulton Railroad Company, *Rail Road Reports*, 1856, 6; and Cairo and Fulton Railroad Company, *Proceedings of the Board of Directors of the Cairo and Fulton Railroad, and the Report of the Chief Engineer Upon the Preliminary Surveys* (Little Rock: True Democrat Office, 1854), 5–6.

12. Wampler, Journal, Dec. 1, 1853.

13. Ibid., Nov. 11–Dec. 25, 1853.

14. Ibid., Jan. 30–Feb. 19, 1854.

15. Ibid., June 2–12, 1854.

16. Robert C. Black III *The Railroads of the Confederacy* (Chapel Hill: Univ. of North Carolina Press, 1952), map: "The Railroads of the Confederate States as of June 1, 1861."

17. Stover, *Iron Road to the West*, 61.

18. For complete treatments of the economic and political development of Baltimore during the middle and late 1850s, along with the social turbulence and criminal unrest, see Sherry H. Olson, *Baltimore: The Building of an American City* (Baltimore: Johns Hopkins Univ. Press, 1980), 108–10; and Clayton Colman Hall, ed., *Baltimore: Its History and Its People*, vol. 1: *History* (New York: Lewis Historical Publishing Company, 1912), 154–57.

19. Wampler to Swann, Nov. 11, 1856, Baltimore City Archives.

20. In this case, "falls" indicated a creek or stream.

21. *Wampler v. The Mayor & City Council of Baltimore*, Baltimore City Superior Court, 1860, Maryland State Archives; and Olson, *Baltimore*, 136–37.

22. Maryland Institute for the Promotion of the Mechanic Arts, *Annual Report of the Board of Managers and Treasurer* (Baltimore: Samuel Sands Mills), 1857–58, p. 34, and 1859, p. 75.

23. *Woods' Baltimore City Directory*, 1858, 1858–59, 1860.

24. Coroner's Inquisition, Sept. 30, 1858, Baltimore City Archives.

25. *Laws and Acts of Incorporation Relating to the Covington and Ohio Railroad* (Richmond: James E. Goode Printer, 1867), 44. Taking cognizance of the available labor pools, the chief engineer advocated use of white labor on the western end of the line and a black workforce on the eastern side. Not only was

black labor cheaper to employ, he stated, but "It is more steady and reliable than any other; and when work is carried on entirely with it, the riots and turn outs, so common on public works, where large numbers of white laborers are employed, never occur." Ibid., 64. See also 12–14, 43, and 101.

26. Wampler to Charles B. Fisk, July 22, 1858, William Jones Rhees Papers, Huntington Library, San Marino, Calif.

27. Henry Mankin file, Maryland Historical Society.

28. Wampler's chief assistant was the son of a prominent Baltimore mapmaker, Jonas Martinet, who had immigrated from Switzerland.

29. Award in Case of *J. M. Wampler vs. The Hampden Improvement Association,* Mar. 7, 1861, Scharf Collection, Maryland State Archives.

30. Wampler to Bache, Apr. 4, 1860, Roll 226, M642, RG 23, NA.

31. Wampler would have probably subscribed to the definition of "graphodometer" reported in his city newspaper, as he was, in all likelihood, the source for the article. "A graphodometer is a machine which can be constructed in the form of a buggy wagon and ridden in, like one anywhere around the country, up hill or down, east or west, north or south, over any kind of road, and which will automatically record, with perfect accuracy, a correct profile of any route passed over, the angles of deflection right or left, and the distance travelled, forming, in fact, a complete automatic surveyor" (*Baltimore Weekly Dispatch,* Apr. 2, 1859).

32. Lts. G. K. Warren and H. L. Abbot, Top. Engrs., to Capt. A. A. Humphreys, June 17, 1859, Correspondence on Invention of J. M. Wampler and J. Barrows Hyde, 1859, Unregistered Letters, Reports, Histories, Regulations, and Other Records, 1817–1894, RG 77, NA. Warren went on to become a general officer and corps commander in the Union Army during the Civil War.

33. Orders, Office Explorations and Surveys, War Department, January 20, 1859, Correspondence on Invention of Wampler and Hyde, Unregistered Letters, etc., RG 77, NA.

34. The author is indebted to Capt. Albert Theberge, NOAA Corps (Ret.) for this technical analysis of Wampler's graphodometer.

35. Warren and Abbot to and from Wampler, Jan. 27–May 27, 1859, and with Humphreys, May 22, 1859, Correspondence on Invention of Wampler and Hyde, Unregistered Letters, etc., RG 77, NA.

36. Allan Nevins, *Ordeal of the Union,* vol. 1: *Fruits of Manifest Destiny, 1847–1852* (New York: Charles Scribner's Sons, 1947), 155, 379.

37. Allan Nevins, *Ordeal of the Union,* vol. 2: *A House Dividing, 1852–1857* (New York: Charles Scribner's Sons, 1947), 36–37, 323–24, 397–98, 466, 470.

38. Poland, *From Frontier to Suburbia,* 168–70.

CHAPTER FOUR: THE 8TH VIRGINIA

1. Wampler, Journal, Dec. 20, 1860.

2. Ibid., Mar. 19, 1861.

3. Poland, *From Frontier to Suburbia,* 185.

4. *OR,* vol. 2: 911; and James M. McPherson, *Battle Cry of Freedom* (New York: Ballantine Books, 1989), 280.

5. Col. Eppa Hunton to Wampler, May 16, 1861.

6. Requisition No. 451 of Quartermaster's Office to Superintendent of the Loudon [*sic*] & Hampshire Rail Road, May 22, 1861.

7. Hunton, Certification (undated), J. M. Wampler, Engineers, C.S.A., CMSR, NA.

8. M. W. Strother, Madison Cavalry, to Wampler, June 3, 1861.

9. Wampler to Col. J. F. Gilmer, June 25, 1863.

10. *OR,* vol. 2: 917.

11. Wampler to Davis, June 14, 1861, Letters Received by Confederate Secretary of War, 1861–65, M437, RG 109, NA; and Provost Marshal pass, Head Department of Alexandria, Camp Pickens, Virginia, June 10, 1861.

12. Alfred Roman, *The Military Operations of General Beauregard* (1884; reprint, New York: Da Capo Press, 1994), 1: 80; and Head Quarters, Virginia Forces, to Harris, May 3, 1861, David Bullock Harris Papers, Special Collections Library, Duke Univ.

13. Thomas Jordan to Hunton, June 23, 1861.

14. Again, others, including Edmund Berkeley, later laid claim to the same distinction. See Edmund Berkeley, "War Reminiscences and Others of a Son of the Old Dominion, 1824–1917," unpublished MS, p. 25, in the estate of John Divine.

15. Eppa Hunton, *Autobiography of Eppa Hunton* (Richmond, Va.: William Byrd Press, 1933), 26–27.

16. Lee to Hunton, June 1, 1861, Records of the Virginia Defense Forces, M998, RG 109, NA; and *OR,* vol. 2: 915, 917.

17. Hunton, Certification (undated), J. M. Wampler, Engineers, C.S.A., CMSR, NA.

18. Wampler to Hunton, June 21, 1861.

19. At about the same time at Martinsburg, Virginia (now West Virginia), Col. Thomas J. Jackson preserved railroad rolling stock by having it dismantled, moved overland, and then reassembled. Whether Hunton or Jackson learned and copied from the other is unknown. James I. Robertson Jr. contends that the idea originated with Jackson in his definitive biography, *Stonewall Jackson: The Man, the Soldier, the Legend* (New York: Macmillan, 1997), 245–46.

20. Hunton, *Autobiography,* 27.

21. Ida Dulaney, "The Diary of Mrs. Ida Dulaney, Oakley Plantation, Upperville, Va.," in the estate of John Divine.

22. No engineers were practicing in Loudoun County at the war's outset. The design and execution of fortifications were clearly beyond the ken of the farmers and merchants who inhabited the area. Wampler's unusual reference to Fort Evans as Fort "Wampler" in his personal journal leads to the conclusion

that he was instrumental in its construction, and so it would have not been unlikely for him to be involved in the other earthworks as well.

23. Dennis Hart Mahan, *A Complete Treatise on Field Fortification, with the General Outlines of the Principles* (New York: Wiley and Long, 1836), 33.

24. Beauregard, June 6, 1861, David Bullock Harris Papers, Special Collections Library, Duke Univ.

25. D. H. Hill to his wife, Feb. 13, 1862, Daniel Harvey Hill Papers, U.S. Army Military History Institute.

26. *(Leesburg, Va.) Democratic Mirror,* June 5, 1861.

27. Hunton, *Autobiography,* 28–29, 32.

28. John Divine, *8th Virginia Infantry* (Lynchburg, Va.: H. E. Howard, 1983), iv.

29. Ibid., 1; and Randolph Abbott Shotwell, *The Papers of Randolph Abbott Shotwell* (Raleigh: North Carolina Historical Commission, 1929), 1: 89.

30. Divine, *8th Virginia Infantry,* 53–87.

31. Almost one-third of those initial Leesburg enlistees left the ranks, through desertion (10), absence without leave (although possibly returning) (12), or resignation (2). Another 11 soldiers would be wounded, captured, or both, during or immediately following the battle at Gettysburg. Five more were captured in other engagements. Of the 75 soldiers identified by Divine as serving in Company H with Captain Wampler during the war's first year, only 15 would apply for parole in the spring of 1865. Two would die of wounds suffered in battle; another 3 would succumb to disease. Ten were captured, and the largest number, 17 by actual count, deserted. Desertion rates were highest when the 8th Virginia was closest to home and family—during the first invasion of the North in the fall of 1862 and, again, nine months later when the Army of Northern Virginia trudged back from Gettysburg. It is likely that some of these foot soldiers later returned to active duty by volunteering for more glamorous cavalry service under the leadership of John Singleton Mosby or Elijah V. White, notably Charles L. Myers, John L. Cornwell, John W. Muse, and Samuel Ryan. Divine, *8th Virginia Infantry,* roster.

32. Colonel Evans and his South Carolinians had already been recalled to Manassas a couple of days earlier. Hunton, *Autobiography,* 29.

33. Maj. Norborne Berkeley brought along a daguerrean saloon from Leesburg, and the old-time photographic gallery served briefly as Colonel Hunton's headquarters in the field. Hunton related how hundreds of soldiers were drawn to the conveyance under the mistaken impression that they could have pictures taken for the loved ones far away. For this and other reasons, the regimental commander was not reluctant to abandon the headquarters on wheels. Ibid., 32, 43; *OR,* vol. 2: 545; and Wampler, Journal, July 18, 1861.

34. *OR,* vol. 51, pt. 1: 31–32.

35. Roman, *Military Operations of General Beauregard,* 99.

36. *OR,* vol. 2: 545.

37. Edward Porter Alexander, "The Battle of Bull Run," *Scribner's Magazine* 41

(Jan. 1907): 87–88; and Joseph E. Johnston, *Narrative of Military Operations, Directed, During the Late War Between the States* (New York: D. Appleton and Company, 1874), 42. A different version surfaced early in the twentieth century, contending that Eppa Hunton first learned of the Yankee flanking movement and alerted his Confederate superiors. See Hunton, *Autobiography*, 33; and *Richmond Times-Dispatch*, Aug. 3, 1904. Alexander's account would allow for credit to be shared, as he acknowledged that Evans had reported being notified by two couriers almost simultaneously, one from his pickets and the other conveying the signal message.

38. William Smith, "Reminiscences of the First Battle of Manassas," *Southern Historical Society Papers* 10 (Oct.–Nov. 1882): 436–37; Hunton, *Autobiography*, 36; and William C. Davis, *Battle at Bull Run: A History of the First Major Campaign of the Civil War* (Baton Rouge: Louisiana State Univ. Press, 1981), 200–201.

39. Roman, *Military Operations of General Beauregard*, 11.

40. Edwin C. Bearss, *First Manassas Battlefield Map Study* (Lynchburg, Va.: H. E. Howard, 1991), 11.

41. Divine, *8th Virginia Infantry*, 3.

42. The 2nd Wisconsin and portions of the 69th New York were clad in gray. The 33rd Virginia and 6th North Carolina wore blue. Both the New York Fire Zouaves and Wheat's Louisiana Tigers donned uniforms trimmed in scarlet. Everyone seemed covered with the dust of a hot summer day, muting differences in color. See Edward Porter Alexander, *Military Memoirs of a Confederate* (New York: Charles Scribner's Sons, 1907), 39.

43. Roman, *Military Operations of General Beauregard*, 106.

44. John Hennessy, *The First Battle of Manassas: An End to Innocence, July 18–21, 1861* (Lynchburg, Va.: H. E. Howard, 1989), 107.

45. *The Democratic Mirror*, July 31, 1861.

46. *OR*, vol. 2: 545.

47. Davis, *Battle at Bull Run*, 232.

48. *OR*, vol. 2: 546.

49. Hunton, *Autobiography*, 44; and *The Democratic Mirror*, July 23/24, 1861.

50. Roman, *Military Operations of General Beauregard*, 471–72.

51. Shotwell, *Papers*, 96.

52. Roman, *Military Operations of General Beauregard*, 132.

53. Divine, *8th Virginia Infantry*, 4.

54. Wampler, Journal, Oct. 4, 1861.

55. E. T. Crowson, "Aftermath of Battle," *Virginia Cavalcade* 18 (Spring 1969): 34.

56. Wampler, Journal, July 25 and Sept. 3, 1861.

57. Hunton, *Autobiography*, 45–46, 62–64.

58. *The Democratic Mirror*, July 24, 1861.

59. Ibid., Aug. 8, 1861.

60. Wampler, Journal, Oct. 4, 1861.
61. Shotwell, *Papers*, 93.
62. *The Democratic Mirror*, Aug. 8, 1861.
63. David Hunter Strother, "Personal Recollections of the War," *Harper's New Monthly Magazine* 33 (Sept. 1866): 412.
64. *The Democratic Mirror*, Sept. 11, 1861.
65. Wampler, Journal, Sept. 21, 1861.
66. I have added the parenthetical "or Leesburg" in this subhead for a specific reason. While no longer known by any name other than the Battle of Ball's Bluff, immediately following the engagement, Confederates, including Morris Wampler, referred to the fight as having occurred at Leesburg, in keeping with the Southern practice of naming battles for the nearest town, as opposed to a prominent topographic feature, ergo Manassas instead of Bull Run and Sharpsburg instead of Antietam. The North won the war and, consequently, their characterizations are the ones in general use today.
67. *OR*, vol. 5: 347.
68. Wampler, Journal, Oct. 15, 1861.
69. Beauregard to Evans, Oct. 20, 1861, Gen. P. G. T. Beauregard Papers, Manuscript Division, Library of Congress.
70. Shotwell, *Papers*, 111.
71. Kim Bernard Holien, *Battle At Ball's Bluff* (Orange, Va.: Moss Publications, 1985), 30–37.
72. R. W. Hunter, "Men of Virginia at Ball's Bluff," *Southern Historical Society Papers* 34 (1906): 259–60.
73. Hunton, *Autobiography*, 52.
74. *OR*, vol. 5: 366–67. One account assigns a heroic role to Captain Wampler and his company. Mason Graham Ellzey, a VMI graduate and surgeon in the Confederate army, wrote: "Capt. Morris Wampler, of the 8th Va., one of the ablest Civil and Military Engineers this country has ever produced,—who, with his company, had been detailed to guard the Goose Creek Bridge against the advance of 8000 union troops, under Burnside, who, it was known, had advanced as far as Dransville [*sic*]; hearing the firing, and (because he knew the country) . . . without waiting for orders burned the bridge and double quicked his men across to the Jackson house, rejoining his command just in time to met the attack of the enemy at that place." Mason Graham Ellzey, "The Cause We Lost and the Land We Love," unpublished MS, 35, in the estate of John Divine. It is conceivable that Wampler's pickets could have observed that McCall had in fact withdrawn from Dranesville before the battle at Ball's Bluff reached a crescendo, and hearing this, Morris repositioned his troops to meet the enemy, as Evans did at Bull Run. The fact that the two known firsthand accounts from Company H, Wampler's and that of Private Randolph Abbott Shotwell, both omit any reference to this redeployment,

when they are so careful to include other noteworthy happenings, argues against crediting Ellzey's telling of combat by Company H that day.

75. Divine, *8th Virginia Infantry,* 4–6.
76. Elijah V. White, *History of the Battle of Ball's Bluff* (Leesburg, Va.: Washingtonian Print, 1904), 17–20.
77. Wampler, Journal, Oct. 21, 1861.
78. John Divine, Wilbur C. Hall, Marshall Andrews, and Penelope M. Osburn, *Loudoun County and the Civil War: A History and Guide* (Loudoun County, Va.: Civil War Centennial Commission, 1961), 31.
79. Kim Bernard Holien, "The Battle of Ball's Bluff," *Blue and Gray Magazine* 7 (Feb. 1990): 53.
80. *OR,* vol. 5: 291.
81. Hunton, *Autobiography,* 57.
82. Wampler, Journal, Oct. 23, 1861.
83. Ibid., Oct. 26–27, 1861.
84. Shotwell, *Papers,* 128.
85. *The Democratic Mirror,* Dec. 4, 1861, and Shotwell, *Papers,* 131.
86. Berkeley, "War Reminiscences," 36.
87. Shotwell, *Papers,* 131.
88. Ibid., 130–32.
89. Hunton, *Autobiography,* 61.
90. Shotwell, *Papers,* 137–38.
91. Wampler, Journal, Dec. 16, 1861.
92. G. Moxley Sorrel, *Recollections of a Confederate Staff Officer* (New York: Bantam Books, 1992), 16.
93. Crowson, "Aftermath of Battle," 36.
94. Richard Taylor, *Destruction and Reconstruction, Personal Experiences of the Late War* (New York: Appleton, 1879), 21–22.
95. Wampler, Journal, Dec. 9, 1861.
96. Hill to his wife, Dec. 9, 1861, Daniel Harvey Hill Papers, U.S. Army Military History Institute.
97. Hill to his wife, Dec. 22, 1861. Daniel Harvey Hill Papers, U.S. Army Military History Institute.
98. Wampler, Journal, Dec. 24, 1861.
99. Shotwell, *Papers,* 143.
100. Wampler, Journal, Dec. 26, 1861.
101. Americus Hutchison, CMSR, RG 109, NA.
102. Wampler, Journal, Jan. 1, 1862.
103. Divine, *8th Virginia Infantry,* 8.
104. Wampler, Journal, Jan. 31, 1862.
105. Ibid. and Feb. 4, 1862. Literary societies, debating clubs, and theatrical productions were common to many encampments. See James I. Robertson Jr., *Soldiers: Blue and Gray* (New York: Warner Books, 1991), 89.

106. Naturally, Beauregard was not popular with everyone. In the opinion of one subordinate officer, "Beauregard left his army in the most deplorable condition" characterized by "demoralization, negligence, and the lax discipline which permitted the soldiers to assume a bearing which verged on actual insubordination." B. Estvan, *War Pictures from the South* (New York: D. Appleton and Company, 1863), 109.

107. T. Harry Williams, *P. G. T. Beauregard: Napoleon in Gray* (Baton Rouge: Louisiana State Univ. Press, 1955), 115.

108. Benjamin to Wampler, Feb. 3, 1862, Letters Sent by the Confederate Secretary of War, 1861–1865, Roll 3, M522, RG 109, NA. The members of heavy artillery units were drilled both as gunners and as infantrymen.

109. Wampler, Journal, Feb. 7–8, 1862.

110. Hal Bridges, *Lee's Maverick General: Daniel Harvey Hill* (New York: McGraw-Hill, 1961), 31.

111. Tebbs to Maj. Gen. James Longstreet, Feb. 22, 1862.

112. Wampler, Journal, Feb. 24–Mar. 7, 1862.

113. Divine, et al., *Loudoun County and the Civil War*, 37–38.

114. Wampler, Journal, Mar. 19–Apr. 6, 1862.

115. Hunton, *Autobiography*, 64.

116. Wampler, Journal, Apr. 9–10, 1862.

117. Divine, *8th Virginia Infantry*, 38.

118. Wampler, Journal, Apr. 12–25, 1862.

Chapter Five: War on the Home Front

1. Kate Wampler, Journal, May 12, 1863.

2. Jean Witherspoon, "Woman's Part in the Confederate War," *The Lost Cause* 8 (Feb. 1903): 105–6.

3. Rable, *Civil Wars*, 6.

4. J. Harry Shannon, "The Rambler Writes of the Old Mavin Mill," *(Washington, D.C.) Sunday Star*, Oct. 27, 1918, 3.

5. Eugene M. Scheel, "John Hough's Mill at Goose Creek's Lower Ford," *Loudoun Times-Mirror*, Sept. 29, 1977.

6. *(Leesburg, Va.) Democratic Mirror*, Dec. 12, 1860.

7. Divine, et al., *Loudoun County and the Civil War*, 11.

8. Poland, *From Frontier to Suburbia*, 187.

9. Douglas Southall Freeman, *R. E. Lee* (New York: Charles Scribner's Sons, 1934), 2: 354–55.

10. D. H. Hill to his wife, Dec. 4, 1861, Daniel Harvey Hill Papers, U.S. Army Military History Institute.

11. Bridges, *Lee's Maverick General*, 34.

12. *OR*, ser. 2, vol. 19, pt. 2: 590.

13. Kate Wampler, Journal, May 28, 1863. Kate's lament on how the war had aged

her was repeated by other women across the South. See, for example, Catherine Clinton, *Tara Revisited: Women, War, and the Plantation Legend* (New York: Abbeville Press, 1995), 112–13; and Rable, *Civil Wars,* 157.

14. John Divine, "The Passage of the Armies Through Loudoun: 1861–65," *Bulletin of the Loudoun County Historical Society* 2 (1960): 47.

15. Kate Wampler, Journal, June 17, 1863.

16. Kate Wampler, untitled reminiscences, undated.

17. Charles S. Wainwright, *Personal Journals, 1861–1865* (New York: Harcourt, Brace, and World, 1962), 222.

18. Kate Wampler, Journal, June 18, 1863.

19. Ibid., June 19, 1863.

20. Avery Harris, "Personal Reminiscences of the Author from August 1862 to June 1865, War of the Rebellion," unpublished MS, p. 77, Avery Harris Papers, U.S. Army Military History Institute.

21. Emory Sweetland, personal papers, Michael Winey Collection, U.S. Army Military History Institute.

22. Kate Wampler, Journal, June 23, 1863.

23. A. B. Johnson, "Union Army on Way to Gettysburg," unpublished MS, 1963, in the estate of John Divine.

24. Kate Wampler, Journal, June 27, 1863.

25. Ibid., June 28, 1863. For an overall account of the migration, see also John W. Schildt, *Roads to Gettysburg* (Parsons, W.Va.: McClain Printing Company, 1978).

26. John S. Mosby, *The Memoirs of Colonel John S. Mosby,* ed. Charles Wells Russell (Boston: Little, Brown, 1917), 126.

27. Alexander Hunter, *The Women of the Debatable Land* (Washington, D.C.: Corden Publishing Company, 1912), 29.

28. Kate Wampler, Journal, May 17 and June 21, 1863.

29. Briscoe Goodhart, *History of the Independent Loudoun Virginia Rangers, 1862–65* (Washington, D.C.: Press of McGill & Wallace, 1896), 30–31, 33–35, and 205–8.

30. Kate Wampler, untitled reminiscences, undated.

31. Kate Wampler, Journal, July 13, 1863.

32. Drew Gilpin Faust, *Mothers of Invention: Women of the Slaveholding South in the American Civil War* (Chapel Hill: Univ. of North Carolina Press, 1996), 201.

33. John Divine, *35th Battalion Virginia Cavalry,* 2nd ed. (Lynchburg, Va.: H. E. Howard, 1985), 8.

34. Frank M. Myers, *The Comanches: A History of White's Battalion, Virginia Cavalry* (Baltimore: Kelly, Piet & Co., 1871), 357.

35. Kate Wampler, Journal, June 11, 1863.

36. Rable, *Civil Wars,* 65, 156–57.

37. Kate Wampler, Journal, May 17, 1863.

38. Ibid., July 8 and 10, 1863. The magnitude and importance of the confrontation at Gettysburg led to all manner of accounts reverberating throughout the South for weeks thereafter. See Rable, *Civil Wars,* 211.

39. Kate Wampler, Journal, May 27 and June 8, 1863.

40. Ibid., Aug. 21, 1863.

41. Mosby, *Memoirs,* 190–95, and Hugh C. Keen and Horace Mewborn, *43rd Battalion Virginia Cavalry, Mosby's Command,* 2nd ed. (Lynchburg, Va.: H. E. Howard, 1993), 44–48.

42. Kate Wampler, Journal, May 17, 1863.

43. Keen and Mewborn, *43rd Battalion,* 112–14; and John Scott, *Partisan Life with Col. John S. Mosby* (New York: Harper & Brothers, 1867), 200–203.

44. Kate Wampler, Journal, Feb. 22, 1864.

45. *OR,* vol. 33: 159.

46. Kate Wampler, untitled reminiscences, undated.

47. Women west of the Mississippi were not so fortunate at the hands of guerrilla bands with Southern or Northern sympathies. Michael Fellman, "Women and Guerrilla Warfare," in *Divided Houses: Gender and the Civil War,* ed. Catherine Clinton and Nina Siber (New York: Oxford Univ. Press, 1992), 148–52; and Rable, *Civil Wars,* 158–59.

48. Kate Wampler, untitled reminiscences, undated.

49. J. Michael Welton, ed., *"My Heart Is So Rebellious": The Caldwell Letters, 1861–1865* (Warrenton, Va.: Fauquier National Bank, 1991), 99.

50. Kate Wampler, Journal, June 10, 1863.

51. Stephen V. Ash, *When the Yankees Came* (Chapel Hill: Univ. of North Carolina Press, 1995).

52. See, for example, Mrs. Burton Harrison [née Constance Cary], *Recollections Grave and Gay* (New York: Charles Scribner's Sons, 1911), 58.

53. See, for example, Mrs. John P. Sellman, "Experiences of a War-Time Girl," *Confederate Veteran* 35 (Jan. 1927): 19–20.

54. Kate Wampler, untitled reminiscences, undated.

55. Welton, *My Heart Is So Rebellious,* 126. See also Celine Fremaux Garcia, *Celine: Remembering Louisiana, 1850–1871,* ed. Patrick J. Geary (Athens: Univ. of Georgia Press, 1987), 130.

56. Mary Elizabeth Massey, *Ersatz in the Confederacy: Shortages and Substitutes on the Southern Homefront* (Columbia: Univ. of South Carolina Press, 1952), 38.

57. Ibid., 80–85.

58. Kate Wampler, untitled reminiscence, undated.

59. Massey, *Ersatz in the Confederacy,* 98.

60. Kate Wampler, Journal, May 14, 1863.

61. Ibid., February 17, 1864.

62. Faust, *Mothers of Invention,* 115–18.

63. Keen and Mewborn, *43rd Battalion,* 13.

64. Clinton, *The Plantation Mistress,* 175.
65. Myers, *The Comanches,* 9–10, 91, 96–97, and 102.
66. Kate Wampler, Journal, Aug. 18, 1863.
67. Myers, *The Comanches,* 220.
68. Poland, *From Frontier to Suburbia,* 233.
69. Kate Wampler, Journal, June 5, 1863.
70. Adelaide Wampler Kundahl to author, Nov. 18, 1995.
71. Kate Wampler, Journal, May 15, 1863. "Fitchey" was, in all likelihood, the baby's mispronunciation of "fetch."
72. Poland, *From Frontier to Suburbia,* 184.
73. James W. Head, *History and Comprehensive Description of Loudoun County Virginia* ([Leesburg:] Park View Press, 1908), 182.

Chapter Six:
The Route to Chief Engineer, Army of Tennessee

1. Wampler to Davis, Feb. 21, 1861, J. M. Wampler, Engineers, C.S.A., CMSR, NA.
2. Jordan to Hunton, June 23, 1861.
3. Janney to Letcher, May 2, 1861.
4. Shannon, "The Rambler Writes of Miss Margaret Mercer," 3.
5. *Acts and Resolutions of the First Session of the Provisional Congress of the Confederate States* (Montgomery, Ala.: Shorter & Reid, 1861), 40–41.
6. William M. Robinson Jr., "The Confederate Engineers," *The Military Engineer* 22 (July–Aug. 1930): 299–301.
7. *Acts and Resolutions of the First Session of the Provisional Congress of the Confederate States,* 40–41; and *Provisional and Permanent Constitutions of the Confederate States* (Richmond: Tyler, Wise, Allegre and Smith, 1861), 29.
8. In 1863, the Union army took specific action to combine its engineering functions into a single corps.
9. William J. Miller, *Mapping for Stonewall: The Civil War Service of Jed Hotchkiss* (Washington, D.C.: Elliott & Clark Publishing, 1993), 93.
10. James M. Matthews, ed., *The Statutes at Large of the Provisional Government of the Confederate States of America* (Richmond: R. M. Smith, 1864), 237–38.
11. Jeremy F. Gilmer to his wife, Oct. 12, 1862, Jeremy F. Gilmer Papers, Southern Historical Collection, Chapel Hill, N.C.
12. Robertson, *Soldiers,* 145.
13. Larry J. Daniel, *Soldiering in the Army of Tennessee: A Portrait of Life in a Confederate Army* (Chapel Hill: Univ. of North Carolina Press, 1992), 70.
14. Garcia, *Celine: Remembering Louisiana,* xx.
15. Wampler to Breckinridge, May 3, 1862.
16. Wampler, Journal, April 30–May 8, 1862.

17. *OR,* vol. 10, pt. 2: 168–69.

18. Ibid., pt. 1: 809, and pt. 2: 171; Daniel Ruggles, "The Battle of Farmington, Tennessee [*sic*]," *Southern Historical Society Papers* 7 (July 1879): 330–31.

19. Wampler, Journal, May 9, 1862.

20. Joseph R. Mothershead, Journal, Confederate Collection, Tennessee State Library and Archives.

21. *OR,* vol. 10, pt. 1: 805, 808, and 810–11. The imprecision in accounting for Confederate losses is caused by Ruggles's statistics totaling 99 aggregate casualties, as compared with 119 cited in his written report.

22. Williams, *P. G. T. Beauregard,* 151.

23. Wampler, Journal, May 9, 1862.

24. Robert G. Hartje, *Van Dorn: The Life and Times of a Confederate General* (Nashville: Vanderbilt Univ. Press, 1967), 178.

25. Wampler, Journal, May 12–26, 1862.

26. Ibid., May 28–29, 1862.

27. Ibid., May 30–31, 1862.

28. Samuel A. Agnew, Diary, vol. 4 (Apr. 1862–Sept. 1863), June 2–3, 1862, Southern Historical Collection, Chapel Hill, N.C.

29. Ruth Loden Johnson, "A History of Tupelo" (M.A. thesis, Mississippi State College [Univ.], State College [Starkville], Mississippi, 1951), 6.

30. Wampler, Journal, June 4, 1862.

31. Agnew, Diary, vol. 4, June 4–6, 1962.

32. Wampler, Journal, June 10, 1862.

33. See, for example, George Thompson Blakemore, Diary, 9, Confederate Collection, Tennessee State Library and Archives.

34. Emory A. Morgan, vice president, Monroe County (Miss.) Historical Association, letter to author, Oct. 1, 1996.

35. Wampler used the term "sappers and miners," by which Pickett's company was known at that time, whereas these troops were probably what are now, in retrospect, considered "pioneers."

36. Wampler, Journal, June 17–29, 1862.

37. U.S. Bureau of the Census, *Eighth Census of the United States: 1860,* Monroe County, Miss., 514; and W. A. Evans, *Who's Who in Monroe County Cemeteries* (Aberdeen, Miss.: Mother Monroe Publishing Company, 1979), 117.

38. *OR,* vol. 17, pt. 2: 656–57. The trains traveled from Tuscaloosa to Rome, Georgia, through Wills Valley and Gadsden. Wampler's route, however, more closely followed the path prescribed for the batteries through Talladega.

39. Thumps is caused by an animal working so hard that the respiratory rate exceeds that of the heart. Oxygen is depleted by working beyond endurance, which could certainly happen during an extended ride through Alabama in the middle of summer. The horse cannot take in enough air and breaths faster and faster. The name originates from actually hearing the heart thumping.

40. Wampler, Journal, July 22–29, 1862; and John Pegram, [Orders], July 22, 2862, Engineers Office, Tupelo, David Bullock Harris Papers, Special Collections Library, Duke Univ.
41. *OR,* vol. 16, pt. 2: 784.
42. Sayers to Gilmer, Aug. 20, 1862, Jeremy F. Gilmer Papers, Southern Historical Collection, Chapel Hill, N.C.
43. Record Book of the Army of Tennessee, Aug. 19, 1862, Huntington Library, San Marino, Calif.
44. For a firsthand account of life as a pioneer, see Lewis N. Wynne and Robert A. Taylor, eds., *This War So Horrible: The Civil War Diary of Hiram Smith Williams* (Tuscaloosa: Univ. of Alabama Press, 1993).
45. One problem of a hybrid unit of soldiers from different regiments was the variety of firearms they brought with them, creating a nightmare in supplying ammunition. Bragg attempted to solve this problem in late May 1861, by standardizing their arms, directing that a short rifle be issued to every pioneer. Message from W. W. Mackall to Bragg with annotation by the commanding general, May 31, 1863, Braxton Bragg Papers, William P. Palmer Collection, Western Reserve Historical Society, Cleveland, Ohio.
46. Wynne and Taylor, eds., *This War So Horrible,* 13, 34, 145.
47. Harris to Wampler, Aug. 20, 1862.
48. A year later, Maj. Gen. William S. Rosecrans found the country traversed by Bragg's army to be "destitute of forage, poorly supplied with water, [tied together] by narrow and difficult wagon roads." *OR,* vol. 30, pt. 1: 49.
49. Hardee's wing proceeded by way of Carthage, rather than Gainesboro. While Wampler examined the fords up ahead, Harris was providing Bragg with information on water courses and springs along this alternate route. Harris to Bragg, Sept. 7, 1862, Braxton Bragg Papers, William P. Palmer Collection, Western Reserve Historical Society, Cleveland, Ohio.
50. Wampler to Polk and Bragg, Sept. 6, 1862, David Bullock Harris Papers, Special Collections Library, Duke Univ.
51. Wampler to Polk, Sept. 6, 1862, Wampler, Engineers, C.S.A., CMSR, NA.
52. Special Orders No. 14, Headquarters, Right Wing, Sept. 10, 1862.
53. *OR,* vol. 16, pt. 2: 808; and Maj. George Williamson, Assistant Adjutant General, Right Wing, to Wampler, Sept. 10, 1862.
54. Cheatham's division took a more westerly route to Glasgow via Peters Creek.
55. *OR,* vol. 16, pt. 2: 808.
56. Polk to Wampler, Sept. 11, 1862.
57. Wampler, Journal, Sept. 11, 1862.
58. Wampler to Polk, Sept. 11, 1862, J. M. Wampler, Engineers, C.S.A., CMSR, NA. For a discussion of Allen's role, see Kenneth A. Hafendorfer, *They Died by Twos and Tens: The Confederate Cavalry in the Kentucky Campaign of 1862* (Louisville, Ky.: KH Press, 1995), 370–71.

59. *OR,* vol. 16, pt. 2: 822; and *Louisville Daily Journal,* Sept. 27, 1862.
60. William B. Richmond, Aide de Camp to Polk, to Wampler, Sept. 17, 1862.
61. *OR,* vol. 16, pt. 2: 843.
62. Bragg had declared September 18 to be a day of rest and thanksgiving, commemorating the bloodless victory at Munfordville, but Wampler was apparently unaware of the commanding general's intention that his soldiers pause and give thanks. Ibid., 842.
63. Ibid., 848–49.
64. Wampler, Journal, Sept. 16–21, 1862.
65. David Urquhart, "Bragg's Advance and Retreat," *Battles and Leaders of the Civil War* (New York: Century Company, 1884), 3: 601; and *OR,* vol. 16, pt. 1: 1090.
66. Three days later, on September 25, 1862, Forrest was relieved from duty from the Army of the Mississippi and reassigned to recruit and operate against the enemy in Middle Tennessee. *OR,* vol. 16, pt. 2: 876–77.
67. Pharr to Wampler, Sept. 25, 1862, Braxton Bragg Papers, William P. Palmer Collection, Western Reserve Historical Society, Cleveland, Ohio.
68. Will Frank Steely and Orville W. Taylor, eds., "Bragg's Kentucky Campaign: A Confederate Soldier's Account," *Register of the Kentucky Historical Society* 57 (Jan. 1959): 51; and Wampler, Journal, Sept. 24–25, 1862.
69. *Louisville Daily Journal,* Oct. 2, 1862.
70. Bruce Catton, *Terrible Swift Sword* (Garden City, N.Y.: Doubleday, 1963), 414.
71. *OR,* vol. 16, pt. 2: 876, 883.
72. Ibid., 881.
73. *(Louisville) Daily Democrat,* Sept. 28, 1862.
74. *New York Times,* Oct. 10, 1862.
75. For comprehensive accounts of the shooting, see the *Chicago Times,* Oct. 3, 1862, providing a diagram of the crime scene, and "The Murder of General Nelson," *Harper's Weekly* 6 (Oct. 18, 1862): 671, recounting the dialogue of the principal characters.
76. Wampler, Journal, Sept. 29–Oct. 1, 1862.
77. The horseman was, in all likelihood, William Henton, assigned to Company K of the 6th Kentucky Mounted Infantry. See William Henton, 6th Mounted Infantry (Kentucky), C.S.A., CMSR, NA. This was not an extraordinary assignment for a rider on point. Colonel Wharton had earlier requested United States or Kentucky currency for use "in secret service." *OR,* vol. 16, pt. 2: 882.
78. The Confederate Signal Corps was the service responsible for its army's intelligence-gathering activities. Before the signal corps was established as a distinctive branch in 1862, however, intelligence operatives like Edmund H. Cummins, Thomas H. Clagett Jr., and William H. Norris were assigned to the engineer corps.
79. *New York Times,* Oct. 9, 1862, 1.

80. Nelson B. Church, 4th Regiment Kentucky Cavalry, SC 425,548, Pension Application File, RG 15, NA.
81. *OR,* vol. 16, pt. 1: 1028.
82. Hafendorfer, *They Died by Twos and Tens,* 524, 565.
83. Ibid., 568.
84. Wampler, Journal, Oct. 1, 1862; and William A. Woodard, 4 Regiment Indiana Cavalry, CMSR, NA. Not surprising, in light of recurring exaggerations in estimates of enemy strength on both sides during the war, the Louisville press initially reported sixty Indiana cavalrymen attacked by five hundred Rebels. *Louisville Daily Journal,* Oct. 2, 1862. A less sensationalized account appeared two days after the skirmish. *Louisville Daily Journal,* Oct. 3, 1862. See also the *Chicago Times,* Oct. 3, 1862.
85. Wampler, Journal, Oct. 2–4, 1862.
86. Thomas Lawrence Connelly, *Army of the Heartland: The Army of Tennessee, 1861–1862* (Baton Rouge: Louisiana State Univ. Press, 1967), 254.
87. Harris had just returned that afternoon from Danville, where he had been sent by Polk to confer on proposed defenses around Bryantsville, protecting the supply depot at Camp Dick Robinson. Harris to Bragg, Oct. 6, 1862, Braxton Bragg Papers, William P. Palmer Collection, Western Reserve Historical Society, Cleveland, Ohio.
88. Cheatham's division consisted of Brig. Gen. Daniel Donelson's 1st Brigade, Brig. Gen. A. P. Stewart's 2nd Brigade, and Brig. Gen. George Maney's 3rd Brigade. A fourth brigade under Col. Preston Smith would arrive later and not become engaged. Marcus B. Toney, *The Privations of a Private* (Nashville, Tenn.: Privately printed, 1905), 42; J. J. Womack, *The Civil War Diary of Capt. J. J. Womack* (McMinnville, Tenn.: Womack Printing Company, 1961), 62; and Marcus Joseph Wright, Diary, Oct. 7, 1862, Confederate Collection, Tennessee State Library and Archives.
89. *OR,* vol. 16, pt. 1: 1096.
90. Hardee to Bragg, Oct. 7, 1862, Military Papers, Filson Club, Louisville, Ky.
91. *OR,* vol. 16, pt. 1: 1024.
92. Ibid., 1158.
93. Barnett's Illinois battery traded fire with a Confederate battery for an hour or so, as regiments from Illinois and Arkansas contested control of Peters Hill. *OR,* vol. 16, pt. 1: 239, 1083.
94. Wampler, Journal, Oct. 8, 1862.
95. It was in this field that a yellow cur snapped at the legs of Cheatham's soldiers marching to battle. They kicked at the dog to keep him away, and the following morning he was found lying dead. Sam R. Watkins, *"Co. Aytch": A Side Show of the Big Show* (New York: Collier Books, 1962), 63.
96. George W. Brent, "Memoranda of Events Connected with the Kentucky Campaign," Oct. 8, 1862, Braxton Bragg Papers, William P. Palmer Collection, Western Reserve Historical Society, Cleveland, Ohio.

97. Kenneth A. Hafendorfer, *Perryville: Battle for Kentucky* (Utica, Ky.: McDowell Publications, 1981), 242.

98. Arthur James Lyon Fremantle, *Three Months in the Southern States* (New York: Bradburn, 1864), 166–67.

99. Wampler, Journal, Oct. 8, 1862.

100. *Cincinnati Daily Enquirer,* Oct. 17, 1862.

101. Ibid.; *OR,* vol. 16, pt. 1: 1036; and Luke W. Finley, "The Battle of Perryville," *Southern Historical Society Papers* 30 (1902): 247.

102. *OR,* vol. 16, pt. 1: 1030, 1041.

103. *Cincinnati Daily Enquirer,* Oct. 17, 1862.

104. Grady McWhiney, *Braxton Bragg and Confederate Defeat* (Tuscaloosa: Univ. of Alabama Press, 1969), 1: 322.

105. *OR,* vol. 16, pt. 1: 1093.

106. *(Cincinnati) Daily Commercial,* Nov. 8, 1862.

107. Ibid.

108. Edwin C. Bearss, "General Bragg Abandons Kentucky," *Register of the Kentucky State Historical Society* 49 (July 1961): 219–20.

109. Ibid., 225.

110. Wampler, Journal, Oct. 16, 1862.

111. Henry W. Graber, The Life of H. W. Graber: *A Terry Texas Ranger, 1861–1865; Sixty-two Years in Texas* (N.p.: H. W. Graber, 1916, 181–84; Benjamin Franklin Burke, *Letters of Pvt. Benjamin F. Burke: Written While in the Terry's Texas Rangers, 1861–1864,* comp. Jessie Burke Heard (Texas: n.p., 1965), 20; R. Lockwood Tower, ed., *A Carolinian Goes to War: The Civil War Narrative of Arthur Middleton Manigault, Brigadier General, C.S.A.* (Columbia: Univ. of South Carolina Press, 1983), 51; Watkins, *Co. Aytch,* 66–67; and *OR,* vol. 16, pt. 2: 976–77.

112. Wampler to Beauregard, Oct. 19, 1862, J. M. Wampler, Engineers, C.S.A., CMSR, NA.

113. Special Orders No. 6, Army of the Mississippi, Oct. 22, 1862, Huntington Library, San Marino, Calif.

114. McWhiney, *Braxton Bragg and Confederate Defeat,* 1: 329.

115. See, for example, the report of James A. Seddon, Confederate Secretary of War, *OR,* ser. 4, vol. 2: 285.

116. *OR,* vol. 16, pt. 1: 1087.

117. Wampler, Journal, Oct. 21–27, 1862. Dr. Clagett was listed on the rolls of "Disloyalists" maintained by the Union Army as "a violent and rabid Rebel." "Leesburg, Virginia: Statements Relative to Disloyalists There," Baker #839, Turner-Baker Papers, RG94, NA.

118. Col. Marcus J. Wright to Wampler, Oct. 28, 1862. It is quite possible that Wampler and Tyler enjoyed a friendship dating back to the 1850s, as both were Baltimore natives of approximately the same age who left that city to join the Southern cause. Tyler had reached the rank of brigadier general when he was killed in action in 1865.

119. Wampler, Journal, Oct. 28–Nov. 4, 1862.

120. *OR,* vol. 16, pt. 2: 982–83.

121. Cheatham to Wampler, Nov. 3, 1862.

122. *Chattanooga Daily Rebel,* Feb. 24, 1863.

123. Wampler, Journal, Nov. 1–6, 1862.

124. Ibid., Nov. 7–15, 1862.

125. Ibid., Nov. 17–27, 1862.

126. Special Orders No. 38, Army of the Mississippi, Nov. 15, 1862, Huntington Library, San Marino, Calif.

127. *OR,* vol. 20, pt. 2: 411.

128. Ibid., 412.

129. Ibid., 421.

130. McWhiney, *Braxton Bragg and Confederate Defeat,* 1: 280.

131. Special Orders 48, Headquarters, Department No. 2, Nov. 28, 1862, Wampler, Engineers, C.S.A., CMSR, NA.

132. Record Book of the Army of Tennessee, Dec. 3, 1862, Huntington Library, San Marino, Calif.

133. Wampler to Bragg, Dec. 1, 1862.

134. "Information received at Engineer Office, Murfreesboro Tenn. about entrenchments around Nashville," Dec. 17, 1862, Braxton Bragg Papers, William P. Palmer Collection, Western Reserve Historical Collection, Cleveland, Ohio.

135. Wampler, Journal, Nov. 28–Dec. 11, 1862.

136. Indeed, these functions were not unlike those which "Stonewall" Jackson assigned to his engineers in the storied Valley Campaign of 1862. Jedediah Hotchkiss was dispatched to guide a brigade into place at one point and to watch the Federals movements at another, while Lt. Keith Boswell set about the task of restoring a bridge needed to transport the infirm. Denied comprehensive engineer support in the Seven Days Campaign, Jackson's awareness of his environs, and subsequently his combat effectiveness, suffered severely. Robertson, *Stonewall Jackson,* 419, 427, 458, 488.

CHAPTER SEVEN: THE ENGINEER CORPS IN TENNESSEE

1. *OR,* vol. 20, pt. 2: 439; and McWhiney, *Braxton Bragg and Confederate Defeat,* 1: 344.

2. *OR,* vol. 20, pt. 2: 449.

3. Larry J. Daniel, *Soldiering in the Army of Tennessee: A Portrait of Life in a Confederate Army* (Chapel Hill: Univ. of North Carolina Press, 1991), 73–75.

4. Alfred Jay Bollet, M.D., clinical professor of medicine, Yale Univ. School of Medicine, to author, Oct. 29, 1996.

5. *OR,* vol. 20, pt. 2: 464.

6. Wampler, Journal, Dec. 11, 1862–Jan. 24, 1863.

7. Special Orders No. 76, Headquarters Department, No. 2, Dec. 28, 1862, Hun-

tington Library, San Marino, Calif.; Daniel, *Soldiering in the Army of Tennessee,* 77; and *OR,* vol. 23, pt. 2: 618.

8. Ball to Wampler, Jan. 21, 1863; J. R. Mayson to Wampler, Feb. 4, 1863; Capt. M. G. Galloway to Wampler, Jan. 30, 1863; and Wampler, Journal, Jan. 24–30, 1863.

9. "Report of Operations in the District of Tennessee River for the Month of January 1863," Miscellaneous Papers, 1862–1865, of the Engineer Department, RG 109, NA.

10. Wampler, Journal, Feb. 8, 1863.

11. Salvanus W. Steele, Engineers, C.S.A., CMSR, NA.

12. Edward B. Sayers, General and Staff Officers, C.S.A., CMSR, NA.

13. Henry N. Pharr, 1 Mounted Rifles, Arkansas, and Engineers, C.S.A., and 3 Confederate Engineer Troops, CMSR, NA.

14. John W. Green, General and Staff Officers, C.S.A., CMSR, NA.

15. George M. Helm, Engineers, C.S.A., CMSR, NA; and *Confederate Veteran* 3 (June 1895): 187.

16. John F. Steele, Engineers, C.S.A., CMSR, NA; and *Students of the University of Virginia: A Semi-Centennial Catalogue,* comp. Maximilian Schele de Vere (Baltimore: Charles Harvey & Co., 1878).

17. Henry C. Force, 5 Alabama Infantry and Engineers, C.S.A., CMSR, NA.; and Wampler, Journal, Nov. 10, 1862.

18. Robert P. Rowley, 4 Tennessee Infantry, Engineers, C.S.A., and 4 Confederate Engineer Troops, CMSR, NA.

19. Andrew H. Buchanan returned to Cumberland University after the war and served on its faculty for a total of forty-nine years before retiring in 1911. For twenty years, he was also employed during vacations in the triangulation of Tennessee by the Coast and Geodetic Survey, the successor organization to the U.S. Coast Survey. His career at the university had begun in 1854 as an assistant to Alexander P. Stewart, later a Confederate lieutenant general, in the Department of Mathematics and Engineering. A. H. Buchanan, Engineers, C.S.A., CMSR, NA; and *Confederate Veteran* 3 (May 1895): 148, and 19 (Sept. 1911): 421.

20. J. K. P. McFall, Engineers, C.S.A., CMSR, NA; *Confederate Veteran* 16 (Dec. 1908): 656; and Wampler, Journal, Oct. 30, 1862.

21. Conrad Meister, Sappers and Miners, C.S.A., CMSR, NA.

22. A. S. Darrow, 25 Louisiana Infantry, and Engineers, C.S.A., CMSR, NA.

23. Walter J. Morris, Engineers, C.S.A., CMSR, NA.

24. See, for example, Sayers to Gilmer, Aug. 3, 1862, Jeremy F. Gilmer Papers, Southern Historical Collection, Chapel Hill, N.C. Sayers reported from Chattanooga: "We have a very nice set of men now in the Corps. Only two of the commissioned officers cannot do anything as Engineers."

25. *OR,* vol. 23, pt. 2: 622, 829.

26. Ibid., 632–33.

27. McWhiney, *Braxton Bragg and Confederate Defeat*, 1: 389; Connelly, *Autumn of Glory*, 70–71; Arthur James Lyon Fremantle, *Three Months in the Southern States* (New York: Bradburn, 1864), 145; and Daniel H. Hill, "Chickamauga — The Great Battle of the West," *Battles and Leaders*, 3: 639.

28. William B. Feis, "The Deception of Braxton Bragg: The Tullahoma Campaign, June 23–July 4, 1863," *Blue and Gray Magazine* 10 (Oct.1992): 12.

29. "Report of Operations in the District of the Tennessee River during the Month of March 1863," Miscellaneous Papers, 1862–65, of the Engineer Department, RG 109, NA.

30. Wampler, Journal, Feb. 10–Mar. 4, 1863.

31. *Chattanooga Daily Rebel*, Feb. 24, 1863.

32. Matthews to Wampler, Mar. 5, 1863.

33. Special Orders No. 8, Mar. 13, 1863, Headquarters, Engineer Department, Army of Tennessee.

34. See, for example, the illustration by H. R. Hubner, entitled "Shelbyville: The Only Union Town of Tennessee," *Harper's Weekly* 6 (Oct. 18, 1862): 661.

35. The owner was related to both the former president and the Confederate lieutenant general with the same family name.

36. Wampler, "Report of Trip to Columbia," holographic MS, undated; and Brent to Presstman, Mar. 21, 1863, Braxton Bragg Papers, William P. Palmer Collection, Western Reserve Historical Society, Cleveland, Ohio.

37. J. Stoddard Johnston, Diary, Aug. 20, 1863, Military Papers, Filson Club, Louisville, Ky.; W. J. McMurray, *History of the Twentieth Tennessee Regiment Volunteer Infantry, C.S.A.* (Nashville, Tenn.: Publication Committee, 1904), 250; George Brent, Diary, Apr. 10, 1863, Braxton Bragg Papers, William P. Palmer Collection, Western Reserve Historical Society, Cleveland, Ohio; and William C. Davis, *Breckinridge: Statesman, Soldier, Symbol* (Baton Rouge: Louisiana State Univ. Press), 364.

38. Joseph E. Johnston, *Narrative of Military Operations, Directed, During the Late War Between the States* (New York: D. Appleton and Company, 1874), 163–64; and Brent, Diary, Mar. 18–19, 1863.

39. *OR*, vol. 23, pt. 2: 760–61. Bragg's chief of staff expressed similar reservations about the value of these defensive positions. "The Engineers are busy in strengthening the field works around Tullahoma. Gen. Bragg has never shown much confidence in them, Murfreesboro for example. Gen. Johnston has imparted this increased activity. But these works will amount to nothing." Brent, Diary, Apr. 12, 1863.

40. Williams was nine years younger than Wampler and Presstman. The reference to "Col. Williams alias Orton" in Wampler's journal refers to the colonel's recent name change from William Orton Williams to Lawrence Williams Orton. Whatever his name, he was the great-great-grandson of Martha Washington and a cousin of Gen. Robert E. Lee's wife. In April 1863, the newly

appointed colonel was commanding a cavalry brigade. Williams and an accomplice (his cousin), 2nd Lt. Walter Gibson "Gip" Peter, were apprehended in June 1863, after passing through the lines, wearing Federal uniforms, and posing as inspectors general from Washington, D.C. The twosome reportedly gathered information on the number of available troops, cannon, small arms, ammunition, and commissary stores on hand at Fort Granger. They had nerve enough to accept cigars from the commander and ask for a loan of fifty dollars in cash. When confronted, the imposters acknowledged their true identities and were executed after a "drumhead court-martial." William T. Crawford to W. J. Isaacs, June 27, 1909, Spy Data, Confederate Collection, Tennessee State Library and Archives; *OR,* vol. 23, pt. 2: 397–98, 415–16, and 424–27; Lawrence Williams Orton, General and Staff Officers, C.S.A., CMSR, NA; and W. G. Peter, Capt. Tobin's Co., Light Artillery (Memphis Light) (Tennessee), C.S.A., CMSR, NA.

41. William M. Robinson Jr., "The Confederate Engineers," *The Military Engineer* 22 (July–Aug. 1930): 302.

42. Matthews, *Statutes at Large,* 60.

43. Gilmer to his wife, Oct. 12, 1862, Jeremy F. Gilmer Papers, Southern Historical Collection, Chapel Hill, N.C.

44. Gilmer to Lee, Johnston, Beauregard, Bragg, and Buckner, February 6, 1863, Letters and Telegrams Sent by the Engineer Bureau of the Confederate War Department, 1861–1864, M628, RG 109, NA.

45. Gilmer to Beauregard, Feb. 17, 1863, Letters and Telegrams Sent by the Engineer Bureau of the Confederate War Department, 1861–1864, M628, RG 109, NA.

46. It is interesting that Presstman did not receive an endorsement from Bragg as well, quite possibly a reflection on the relationship of the incumbent chief engineer with his irascible commanding general.

47. Wampler to Bragg, Feb. 21, 1863.

48. Wampler to Beauregard, May 23, 1863.

49. Wampler to Gilmer, June 25, 1863.

50. Maj. Henry A. Peyton to Wampler, June 11, 1863.

51. Maj. A. S. Rives, Assistant Chief Engineer, to Lt. J. F. Steele, June 8, 1863, Letters and Telegrams Sent by the Engineer Bureau of the Confederate War Department, 1861–1864, M628, RG 109, NA.

52. S. W. Presstman to Wampler, June 23, 1863; and Rives to Nocquet, Jan. 26, 1863.

53. Matthews, *Statutes at Large,* 98–99.

54. William M. Robinson Jr., "The Confederate Engineers," *The Military Engineer* 22 (Sept.–Oct. 1930), 410–11.

55. Gilmer to Polk, May 22, 1863, Letters and Telegrams Sent by the Engineer Bureau of the Confederate War Department, 1861–1864, M628, RG 109, NA; and *OR,* vol. 23, pt. 2: 819.

56. Gilmer to Wampler, Jan. 13, 1863, and July 14, 1863, Letters and Telegrams Sent by the Engineer Bureau of the Confederate War Department, 1861–1864, M628, RG 109, NA; and Wampler to Gilmer, Feb. 15, 1863, J. M. Wampler, Engineers, C.S.A., CMSR, NA.

57. Cummings would be discharged from active service later in April for wounds received at Perryville and Stones River. Pleasant J. Cummings, 33 Tennessee Infantry, C.S.A., CMSR, NA.

58. Wampler, Journal, Apr. 8–21, 1863.

59. *OR,* vol. 23, pt. 2: 248, 256–58.

60. Ibid., pt. 1: 274–75.

61. Wampler, Journal, Apr. 21–22, 1863.

62. Special Orders No. 20, Apr. 27, 1863, Headquarters, Engineer Department, Army of Tennessee.

63. Thomas S. Newcomb, 3 Confederate Engineer Troops, CMSR, NA.

64. Special Orders No. 20, Apr. 27, 1863, Headquarters, Engineer Department, Army of Tennessee.

65. Wampler, Journal, Apr. 27–May 6, 1863.

66. *OR,* vol. 23, pt. 2: 807.

67. Gilmer to Presstman, May 7, 1863, Letters and Telegrams Sent by the Engineer Bureau of the Confederate War Department, 1861–1864, M628, RG 109, NA.

68. Hartje, *Van Dorn,* 308–13; and I. N. Rainey, "Experiences of I. N. Rainey in the Confederate Army," Confederate Collection, Tennessee State Library and Archives.

69. At the same time Wampler had lost none of his interest in the design of the Confederate flag, as he had sketched the new national banner, adopted on May 1, for a lady visiting Bragg's new chief of staff, Brig. Gen. W. W. Mackall, a fellow Marylander.

70. Wampler, Journal, May 6–21, 1863.

71. *OR,* vol. 23, pt. 1: 566.

72. Ibid., pt. 2: 617, 862.

73. Wampler, Journal, May 25–27, 1863.

74. Ibid., May 28, 1863; and Fremantle, *Three Months,* 109–12.

75. James L. Nichols, *Confederate Engineers* (Tuscaloosa, Ala.: Confederate Publishing Company, 1957), 25, 35, 87.

76. *OR,* vol. 23, pt. 2: 929.

77. *OR,* vol. 52, pt. 2: 417.

78. Pickett to Wampler, June 15, 19, and 21, 1863.

79. Foster was another native Marylander who had done civil engineering before the war. At the outbreak of war, Foster had been granted a commission in the Provisional Army of Tennessee by Gov. Isham Harris. His extensive military experience included laying out and superintending the building of Forts Henry

and Donelson, and leading work parties that obstructed roads in advance of the enemy by felling trees and destroying bridges. His excellent reputation was earned, however, as a mapmaker. Wilbur F. Foster, Engineers, C.S.A., CMSR, NA.

80. For a complete discussion of southern mapmaking during the war, see James L. Nichols, "Confederate Map Supply," *The Military Engineer* 46 (Jan.–Feb. 1946): 28–32.

81. Gilmer to Presstman, July 22, 1863, Letters and Telegrams Sent by the Engineer Bureau of the Confederate War Department, 1861–1864, M628, RG 109, NA.

82. As another example of the shortage of maps, Bragg used a map of the conflux of Tennessee, Alabama, and Georgia, drawn by E. G. Anstey, Meister's successor as draftsman for the engineer office, in conducting the Chickamauga campaign. *The Official Atlas of the Civil War* (New York: Thomas Yoseloff, 1958), plate 48-1.

83. Gilmer to Wampler, July 7 and 11, 1863, Letters and Telegrams Sent by the Engineer Bureau of the Confederate War Department, 1861–1864, M628, RG 109, NA; and Nichols, *Confederate Engineers*, 25.

84. Invoice, July 31, 1863, Wampler, Engineers, C.S.A., CMSR, NA.; and Rives to Harris, June 13, 1863, Letters and Telegrams Sent by the Engineer Bureau of the Confederate War Department, 1861–1864, M628, RG 109, NA. It is likely that Wampler received volumes of Mahan's classic reprinted in Richmond in 1862, rather than the original 1836 edition published in New York City. Henry L. Jackson, *First Regiment Engineer Troops P.A.C.S.: Robert E. Lee's Combat Engineers* (Louisa, Va.: R.A.E. Design and Publishing, 1998), 24.

85. Gilmer to Wampler, June 17, 1863.

86. Wampler, Journal, June 20–24, 1863.

87. J. Fraise Richard, "Mrs. E. K. Newsom," *Confederate Veteran* 6 (Apr. 1898): 162–63; and J. Fraise Richard, *The Florence Nightingale of the Southern Army: Experiences of Mrs. Ella K. Newsom, Confederate Nurse in the Great War of 1861–65* (New York: Broadway Publishing Co., 1914), 43.

88. *OR*, ser. 4, vol. 1: 368–72, 879–80; and Cox to Wampler, June 26, 1863.

89. Presstman to Wampler, June 23, 1863; and Gilmer to Presstman and Greene, June 29, 1863, Letters and Telegrams Sent by the Engineer Bureau of the Confederate War Department, 1861–1864, M628, RG 109, NA.

90. *OR*, ser. 4, vol. 2: 260.

91. Gilmer to Nocquet and Presstman, June 17 and 19, 1863, Letters and Telegrams Sent by the Engineer Bureau of the Confederate War Department, 1861–1864, M628, RG 109, NA.

92. John G. Mann, General and Staff Officers, C.S.A., CMSR, NA.

93. Felix R. R. Smith, Engineers, C.S.A., CMSR, NA.

94. Gilmer to Presstman, July 13 and 22, 1863, and to Nocquet, July 31, 1863,

Letters and Telegrams Sent by the Engineer Bureau of the Confederate War Department, 1861–1864, M628, RG 109, NA.

95. General Orders No. 90, June 28, 1863, Adjutant and Inspector General's Office, Richmond, Va., Jeremy F. Gilmer Papers, Southern Historical Collection, Chapel Hill, N.C.

96. *OR,* vol. 23, pt. 1, 585.

97. Gilmer to Nocquet, Oct. 7, 1862, Letters and Telegrams Sent by the Engineer Bureau of the Confederate War Department, 1861–1864, M628, RG 109, NA; *OR,* vol. 16, pt. 2: 877–78; vol. 23, pt. 1: 622–24; pt. 2: 797, 830, 874, 891, and 893–95; Captain H. W. Walter, Assistant Adjutant General, Army of Tennessee, to Presstman, July 1, 1863, Braxton Bragg Papers, William P. Palmer Collection, Western Reserve Historical Society, Cleveland, Ohio; and Stanley F. Horn, *The Army of Tennessee* (Norman: Univ. of Oklahoma Press, 1952), 460.

98. Patrick Abbazia, *The Chickamauga Campaign: December 1862–November 1863* (New York: Combined Books, 1988), 18.

99. Wampler, Journal, June 30, 1863.

100. Wampler to Jackson, June 28, 1863.

101. Wampler, Journal, June 29–July 3, 1863.

102. James Nocquet, "Design for a Pontoon Train," Jeremy F. Gilmer Papers, Southern Historical Collection, Chapel Hill, N.C.

103. The U.S. Army had tested and examined field bridging in use by the French, Russian, and Austrian armies, using the criteria of mobility, ferrying, and bridging capacity, and agreed with Gilmer's assessment. The superior flexibility of canvas boats was acknowledged at war's end. Its success as employed by the Western army, made canvas the material of choice in the advance or for fast-moving cavalry. Canvas boats were not resistant to ice and driftwood, suitable for ferrying troops, or durable enough to carry an entire army with its cavalry, trains, and artillery, in addition to endless columns of men. Thus, a combination of wood and canvas pontoons was decided upon as the ideal equipage for the U.S. Army. Despite continuous study, this same complement remained with the U.S. Corps of Engineers when the nation entered the Great War in 1917. For a comprehensive treatment of pontoon bridging by the Union army and for fifty years thereafter, see M. J. McDonough and P. S. Bond, "Use and Development of the Ponton Equipage in the United States Army, with Special Reference to the Civil War," *Professional Memoirs, Corps of Engineers* 6 (Nov.–Dec. 1914): 692–58.

104. Gilmer to Nocquet, Jan. 7 and Feb. 13, 1863, Letters and Telegrams Sent by the Engineer Bureau of the Confederate War Department, 1861–1864, M628, RG 109, NA.

105. Wampler, Journal, Mar. 5, 1863.

106. John Berrien Lindsley, ed., *The Military Annals of Tennessee: Confederate* (Nashville: J. M. Lindsley & Co., 1886), 819; William W. Carnes, Capt. Marshall's Co. Artillery (Steuben Artillery) (Tenn.), C.S.A., CMSR, NA.; and *OR,* vol. 23, pt. 2: 897.

107. *OR,* vol. 52, pt. 2: 417.

108. Wampler, Journal, July 3–6, 1863; and Bell Irvin Wiley, ed., *Fourteen Hundred and 91 Days in the Confederate Army* (Jackson, Tenn.: McCowat-Mercer Press, 1954), 137.

109. Wampler to Jackson, July 6, 1863; *OR,* vol. 23, pt. 1: 626–27; pt. 2: 898–900, 902; Capt. H. W. Walter to Brig. Gen. Nathan Bedford Forrest, July 5, 1863, Braxton Bragg Papers, William P. Palmer Collection, Western Reserve Historical Society, Cleveland, Ohio; and Wampler, Journal, July 12, 1863.

110. Wampler, Journal, June 28, July 1, 7–9, 1863; Wampler, pass, June 29, 1863; Wampler to Capt. S. A. Morens, Assistant Adjutant General, District of Tennessee River, July 1, 1863; Maj. R. H. Whiteley to Brig. Gen. J. K. Jackson, July 3, 1863; and William Thompson, 2nd Battalion, Georgia Sharp Shooters, C.S.A., CMSR, NA.

111. Wampler, [Orders], July 16, 1863, Headquarters, Engineer Department, District of Tennessee River.

112. Wampler, Journal, July 9–22, 1863; and Henry Campbell Bugler, Diary, 75, Chickamauga and Chattanooga National Military Park.

113. A contrary point of view is presented by Thomas Connelly, who contends that Bragg had finally come to the realization that a concentration of his army with that of Johnston's was necessary to strike at the Federals before they completed preparations for an assault against Chattanooga. See Connelly, *Autumn of Glory,* 146–47.

Chapter Eight: Ten Days at Charleston

1. Col. J. F. Gilmer to J. M. Wampler, July 25, 1863.

2. *OR,* vol. 23, pt. 2: 909; and James Lee McDonough and James Pickett Jones, *War So Terrible: Sherman and Atlanta* (New York: W. W. Norton, 1987), 82.

3. *OR,* vol. 23, pt. 2: 910.

4. Wampler, Journal, July 26–27 and Aug. 4, 1863.

5. *OR,* vol. 28, pt. 2: 233.

6. Fremantle, *Three Months,* 179–80, 186; and Charles Girard, *A Visit to the Confederate States of America in 1863* (Tuscaloosa, Ala.: Confederate Publishing Company, 1962), 51.

7. John F. Marszalek, ed., *The Diary of Miss Emma Holmes, 1861–1866* (Baton Rouge: Louisiana State Univ. Press, 1979), 278–90.

8. Quincy A. Gillmore, "The Army Before Charleston in 1863," *Battles and Leaders,* 4: 55.

9. Wise, *Gate of Hell,* 117.

10. John B. Patrick, Journal, Aug. 14–15, 1863, South Caroliniana Library, Univ. of South Carolina.

11. For a comprehensive compilation of state-of-the-art technology of the classification, firing mechanisms, methods of detonation, observation, effects, and place-

ment of torpedoes during the Civil War, see Viktor Ernst Karl Rudolf von Scheliha, *A Treatise on Coast Defence* (London: E. & F. N. Spon, 1868), 219–97. Von Scheliha served as a lieutenant colonel in the Confederate Corps of Engineers, P.A.C.S., and chief engineer of the Department of the Gulf of Mexico.

12. *OR,* vol. 28, pt. 2: 221.

13. Ibid., 205.

14. P. G. T. Beauregard, "Defense of Charleston, South Carolina," *North American Review* 354 (May 1886): 429.

15. Echols to Maj. Martin J. Ford, July 31, 1863, Press Copies of Letters Sent By Major William H. Echols, Chief Engineer, Department of South Carolina, Georgia, and Florida, July 1863–February 1864, chap. 3, vol. 14, RG 109, NA.

16. United Daughters of the Confederacy, South Carolina Division, *South Carolina Women in the Confederacy* (Columbia: State Company, 1907), 2: 18.

17. Harris to Gov. M. L. Bonham, Feb. 13, 1863, Gen. P. G. T. Beauregard Papers, 1862–1864, Entry 116, RG 109, NA.

18. Press Copies of Letters Sent By Major William H. Echols, chief engineer, Department of South Carolina, Georgia, and Florida, July 1863–Feb. 1864, chap. 3, vol. 14, RG 109, NA.

19. Harris to his wife, Aug. 14, 1863, David Bullock Harris Papers, Special Collections Library, Duke Univ.

20. While the orders specified relief of Tennent, his subsequent report of his tour of duty at Battery Gregg indicated that he was relieved by Lt. Alexander Gillon on August 11. Presumably Stewart, in turn, relieved the more junior Gillon the following evening. *OR,* vol. 28, pt. 1: 509.

21. Marszalek, *Diary of Miss Emma Holmes,* 279.

22. Robert C. Gilchrist, "The Confederate Defence of Morris Island," *Charleston Yearbook, 1884* (Charleston: News and Courier Press, 1884), 355–56.

23. Johnson Hagood, *Memoirs of the War of Secession* (Columbia: State Company, 1910), 185.

24. Beauregard, "Defense of Charleston," 22; and Wise, *Gate of Hell,* 15–17.

25. Gillmore, "The Army Before Charleston," 68. General Beauregard disputed this characterization, however, describing Battery Wagner as "an ordinary fieldwork with thick parapets, but with ditches of little depth." John Johnson, *The Defense of Charleston Harbor, Including Fort Sumter and the Adjacent Islands, 1863–1865* (Charleston, S.C.: Walker, Evans & Cogswell Co., 1890), 82.

26. "Pounder" referred to the weight of the projectile fired, whereas inches indicated its diameter and, of course, the size of the weapon's bore.

27. H. D. D. Twiggs, "The Defence of Battery Wagner," *Southern Historical Society Papers* 20 (Jan.–Dec. 1892): 171; and Charles H. Olmstead, "The Memoirs of Charles H. Olmstead, Part VIII," *Georgia Historical Quarterly* 44 (Sept. 1960): 313.

28. *OR,* vol. 28, pt. 1: 410–11; and Warren Ripley, *Artillery and Ammunition of the Civil War,* 4th ed., rev. (Charleston, S.C.: Battery Press, 1994), 45, 52, 64, 71, 183, 368.

29. Wise, *Gate of Hell,* 131–132, 177; P. G. T. Beauregard, "Visit to Morris Island & Sumter," handwritten notes, Aug. 3, 1863, Gen. P. G. T. Beauregard Papers, 1862–1864, Entry 116, RG 109, NA.

30. *OR,* vol. 28, pt. 2, 228; and Beauregard, "Visit to Morris Island & Sumter."

31. After the war, recollections varied as to the intervals at which the garrison was exchanged. Col. Charles H. Olmstead recalled seven or eight days as the maximum stint a body of troops could withstand the siege on Morris Island. Olmstead, "Memoirs," 311. Capt. S. A. Ashe, on the other hand, stated that troops were rotated every third night. S. A. Ashe, "Life at Fort Wagner," *Confederate Veteran* 35 (July 1927): 254.

32. Edmund H. Cummins, "The Signal Corps in the Confederate States Army," *Southern Historical Society Papers* 16 (1888) 104–5.

33. Gilchrist, "Confederate Defence of Morris Island," 382.

34. Beauregard, "Visit to Morris Island & Sumter."

35. Patrick, Journal, Aug. 5, 1863.

36. John Harleston, "Battery Wagner on Morris Island 1863," *South Carolina Historical Magazine* 57 (Jan. 1956): 5–6; Paul Hamilton Hayne, "The Defense of Fort Wagner," *Southern Bivouac* 1 (Mar. 1886): 606–7; and John E. Florance Jr., "Morris Island: Victory or Blunder?" *South Carolina Historical Magazine* 55 (July 1964): 150.

37. Gilchrist, "Confederate Defence of Morris Island," 377; and Theodore A. Honour, personal letter, Aug. 3, 1863, South Caroliniana Library, Univ. of South Carolina.

38. Twiggs, "The Defence of Battery Wagner," 175; and Charles H. Olmstead, "Reminiscences of Services in Charleston Harbor," *Southern Historical Society Papers* 11 (Apr.–May 1883): 164–65.

39. Ellison Capers, *South Carolina,* vol. 5: *Confederate Military History* (Atlanta: Confederate Publishing Company, 1899), 244.

40. Wise, *Gate of Hell,* 120, 139–44.

41. James Burke, *Connections* (Boston: Little, Brown, 1978), 271.

42. Gilchrist, "Confederate Defence of Morris Island," 388; Patrick, Journal, Aug. 12, 1863; and Hagood, *Memoirs of the War of Secession,* 151.

43. William H. Roberts, "The Neglected Ironclad: A Design and Constructional Analysis of the *U.S.S. New Ironsides,*" *Warship International,* 26 (June 1989): 110–11.

44. The monitor *Nahant* would join them on August 14.

45. Wise, *Gate of Hell,* 27–28, 93.

46. *OR,* vol. 28, pt. 1: 21.

47. Wampler, Journal, Aug. 12, 1863; *OR*, vol. 28, pt. 1: 495; and *Charleston Daily Courier,* Aug. 13, 1863.

48. *OR*, vol. 28, pt. 1: 462; and Echols to Mr. Seabrook, Aug. 16, 17, 1863, Press Copies of Letters Sent By Major William H. Echols, Chief Engineer, Department of South Carolina, Georgia, and Florida, July 1863–Feb. 1864, chap. 3, vol. 14, RG 109, NA.

49. *OR*, vol. 28, pt. 2: 276.

50. Ibid., pt. 1: 411.

51. Ibid., 465–66; and *ORN*, ser. 1, vol. 14: 449.

52. *OR*, vol. 28, pt. 1: 459–60.

53. Ibid., 466.

54. Johnson, *Defense of Charleston Harbor,* 148.

55. Echols to Capt. J. W. Gregorie, Aug. 1, 1863, and Thomas Taylor to Lt. Stiles, Aug. 2, 1863, Press Copies of Letters Sent By Major William H. Echols, Chief Engineer, Department of South Carolina, Georgia, and Florida, July 1863– Feb. 1864, chap. 3, vol. 14, RG 109, NA.

56. P. G. T. Beauregard, "Memorandum of Orders," Aug. 8, 1863, Gen. P. G. T. Beauregard Papers, 1862–64, Entry 116, RG 109, NA; and *OR*, vol. 28, pt. 1: 409–10.

57. A lighthearted account of the Yankees enjoying the South Carolina surf is found in Anita Palladino, ed., *Diary of a Yankee Engineer: The Civil War Story of John H. Westervelt, Engineer, 1st New York Volunteer Engineer Corps* (New York: Fordham Univ. Press, 1997), 11–12.

58. *ORN*, ser. 1, vol. 14: 442.

59. Hagood, *Memoirs of the War of Secession,* 152.

60. *OR*, vol. 28, pt. 1: 387.

61. Wampler, Journal, Aug. 13, 1863.

62. *ORN*, ser. 1, vol. 14: 441–42; *OR*, vol. 28, pt. 1: 387; and Hagood, *Memoirs of the War of Secession,* 152.

63. Wampler, Journal, Aug. 14, 1863.

64. *ORN*, ser. 1, vol. 14: 442.

65. *OR*, vol. 28, pt. 1: 555.

66. Ibid., 515–16.

67. Ibid., 467, 533.

68. Wampler, Journal, Aug. 15, 1863.

69. *OR*, vol. 28, pt. 1: 388.

70. Ibid., 467–68.

71. Ibid., 516.

72. This practice would subsequently be formalized by an offer published by the departmental headquarters of "a fair price per pound to soldiers and negroes at Gregg, Wagner, and Sumter for all balls, shells, old iron, etc." *OR*, vol. 28,

pt. 2: 340. A call had been sent to private citizens a month earlier. P. G. T. Beauregard, notes, Aug. 3, 1863, Gen. P. G. T. Beauregard Papers, 1862–1864, Entry 116, RG 109, NA.

73. Wampler, Journal, Aug. 16, 1863; and *OR,* vol. 28, pt. 1: 469.
74. *ORN,* ser. 1, vol. 14: 452–83.
75. Ashe, "Life at Fort Wagner," 254.
76. *OR,* vol. 28, pt. 1: 517–18; and Twiggs, "The Defence of Battery Wagner," 171, 175.
77. Wise, *Gate of Hell,* 85, 93.
78. Olmstead, "Reminiscences," 120, 163.
79. Gilchrist, "Confederate Defence of Morris Island," 34; Ashe, "Life at Fort Wagner"; and *OR,* vol. 28, pt. 1: 84.
80. *ORN,* ser. 1, vol. 14: 457.
81. *Charleston Daily Courier,* Aug. 18, 1863.
82. Charles S. Hill and G. Thomas Cox first entered the Confederate army as members of the National Rifles, "a veritable society corps," recruited in Georgetown and Washington City. Also serving as a lieutenant in this unique unit was Edmund H. Cummins, another of Wampler's colleagues in the West. There is no evidence, however, that Wampler had any connection with the National Rifles in 1861, although it is quite possible that, living in and around Washington in the late 1840s and 1850s, he knew one or more of these men, his contemporaries in age, if traveling in a faster social set. See T. C. De Leon, *Belles, Beaux and Brains of the 60's* (New York: G. W. Dillingham Company, 1909), 320–22.

Epilogue

1. *OR,* vol. 27, pt. 2: 314–15.
2. Wise, *Gate of Hell,* 212–18.
3. R. G. H. Kean, Chief of Bureau of War, Dispatch, Jan. 12, 1864.
4. Kate Wampler untitled reminiscence, undated.
5. Rable, *Civil Wars,* 26–27.
6. Thomas Jordan to Kate Wampler, July 7 [year unstated].
7. City of Charleston, South Carolina, *Journal of Council, 1892–1895,* 343–44. Georgia H. Strong to Kate Wampler, Oct. 19 [year unstated, but, from its content, probably written in 1894 or 1895].
8. Wampler, Journal, June 13, 1850.
9. Ibid., July 9, 1850, and Feb. 22, 1851.
10. Maj. Gen. J. F. Gilmer to Bragg, Nov. 24, 1863, Braxton Bragg Papers, William P. Palmer Collection, Western Reserve Historical Society, Cleveland, Ohio.
11. Stephen W. Presstman, 3 Confederate Engineer Troops, CMSR, NA; A. L. Rives to Presstman, Nov. 19, 1863, Letters and Telegrams Sent by the Engineer

Bureau of the Confederate War Department, 1861–1864, M628, RG 109, NA; and *Alexandria Gazette,* Feb. 10 and 11, 1865.

12. Edward B. Sayers, General and Staff Officers, C.S.A., CMSR, NA; and *OR,* vol.30, pt. 1: 782.

13. Conrad Meister, Lieutenant Flynn's Company, Sappers and Miners, C.S.A., CMSR, NA.

14. James Nocquet, Engineers, C.S.A., CMSR, NA; and Connelly, *Autumn of Glory,* 25.

15. Will T. Martin, "Letter to General Bragg," *Southern Historical Society Papers* 11 (Apr.–May 1883): 204; Lt. Col. David Urquhart, [Statement], Nov. 21, 1863, Braxton Bragg Papers, William P. Palmer Collection, Western Reserve Historical Society, Cleveland, Ohio; and *OR,* vol. 30, pt. 2: 29, 294–97, 301, 311.

16. Connelly, *Autumn of Glory,* 183; Gilmer to Gen. Samuel Cooper, Oct. 7, 1864, James Nocquet, Engineers, C.S.A., CMSR, NA; and Rives to Gilmer, Oct. 31 and Nov. 17, 1863, and to Brig. Gen. Danville Leadbetter, Nov. 16 and 24, 1863, Letters and Telegrams Sent by the Engineer Bureau of the Confederate War Department, 1861–1864, M628, RG 109, NA.

17. Francois L. J. Thysseus, Engineers, C.S.A., CMSR, NA.; and *OR,* vol. 8: 812–13.

18. David Kahn, *The Codebreakers: The Story of Secret Writing* (New York: Macmillan, 1967), 216–17.

19. The Masonic Cipher, found in the advanced degree of Royal Arch Mason, grouped the twenty-six letters of the alphabet by pairs within the nine sectors of what today is known as a pound sign or tit-tac-toe mark (and in the cryptology of that day was referred to as the "pigpen cipher"), plus the four areas created by an "X." Each letter was represented by its border or dividing line in the pound sign or X, wherever the letter fell in order of succession, with the two inhabitants distinguishable by the inclusion or exclusion of a dot within the cipher. Thus the letters A and B were each represented by a backwards L, with a dot in the center denoting the second letter. Similarly, C and D were shown as a rigid U, with a dot inside in the case of D. E and F used a conventional L with a dot for the consonant, etc. Wampler's code employed similar kinds of symbols, plus other characters of his own creation, e.g., an S and a comma-like marking drawn in various positions to denote different letters. It is therefore accurate to state that while Wampler's secret writing appears to have been based in part on the Masonic Code, it was not a replica of that or any other pattern of ciphers known to be in use at the time of the war. By avoiding the use of Arabic numerals or the Roman alphabet, Wampler conformed to the popular conception that the encoded entry was somehow more secure, less vulnerable to being deciphered.

20. Andrew Hickenlooper, "Our Volunteer Engineers," *Sketches of War History, 1861–1865: Papers Read Before the Ohio Commandery of the Military Order of the*

Loyal Legion of the United States, ed. R. Hunter (Cincinnati: Robert Clarke & Co., 1890), 3: 305–6; Gilmer to Maj. William S. Bassinger, June 15, 1863, Confederate Engineer Department Records, Record Group 109, NA; and O. E. Hunt, "Engineer Corps of the Federal Army," *The Photographic History of the Civil War,* ed. Francis Trevelyan Miller, vol. 5: *Forts and Artillery* (New York: Review of Reviews Co., 1911), 226.

21. Ted Phillips, "The City of the Silent," unpublished MS, 1995, South Carolina Historical Society.

Bibliography

PRIMARY SOURCES

Manuscripts

American Philosophical Society, Philadelphia, Pennsylvania
 Alexander Dallas Bache Collection
Thomas Balch Library, Leesburg, Virginia
Baltimore City Archives
 RG 13, S. 1, Law Department
 RG 16, S. 1, City Council
 RG 19, S. 1, Health Department
 RG 25, S. 1, Water Works
Inez A. Brown
 Wampler Family Papers
Chickamauga–Chattanooga National Military Park
 Henry Campbell Bugler Papers
Cumberland Gap National Historical Park
 Civil War— Letters
John E. Divine, Estate of
 Civil War Collection
East Baton Rouge [Louisiana] Parish, Clerk of Court Archives
Duke University, Special Collections Library
David Bullock Harris Papers
Filson Club Historical Society, Louisville, Kentucky
 J. Stoddard Johnston Papers
 Military Papers
Historical Society of Pennsylvania
 Simon Gratz Collection
Henry E. Huntington Library, San Marino, California
 Brock Collection
 Civil War Collection
 William Jones Rhees Papers
 Charles Shaw Papers

Louisa Hutchison
        Sarah E. Linton Papers
George G. Kundahl
        Alfred Jay Bollet, M.D. Letter
        Harry Hunter Letter
        Adelaide Wampler Kundahl Letter
        Emory Alex Morgan Letters
        John Morris Wampler Papers
        Catharine Nugent Cummings Wampler Papers
Library of Congress
        P. G. T. Beauregard Papers
        Ward Family of Richmond County, Va., Papers
Loudoun County, Virginia, Clerk of the Circuit Court
Maryland Historical Society
        Dielman-Hayward Files
Maryland State Archives
        Baltimore City Superior Court, Court Papers
        Baltimore County Administration Accounts
        Baltimore County Guardian Accounts
        Maryland State Papers, Scharf Collection
Museum of the Confederacy
National Archives and Records Administration
        RG 15. Records of the Veterans Administration
        RG 23. Records of the Coast and Geodetic Survey
        RG 77. Records of the Office of the Chief of Engineers
        RG 94. Records of the Adjutant General's Office
        RG 109. War Department Collection of Confederate Records
South Carolina Department of Archives and History
South Carolina Historical Society
        John White Gregorie Notebook
South Caroliniana Library, University of South Carolina
        Frederick L. Childs Letters
        Theodore A. Honour Papers
        John B. Patrick Diary
Southern Historical Collection, University of North Carolina
        Samuel A. Agnew Papers
        Jeremy F. Gilmer Papers
Tennessee State Library and Archives
        George Thompson Blakemore Papers
        Benjamin Franklin Cheatham Papers
        Confederate Collection
        L. Virginia French Papers
        Joseph R. Mothershead Papers

    I. N. Rainey Papers
    Spy Data
    Tennessee Historical Society Miscellaneous Files
    Marcus Joseph Wright Papers
U. S. Military History Institute
    Alexander R. Chamberlin Papers
    Civil War Times Illustrated Collection
    James P. Coburn Papers
    Avery Harris Papers
    Harrisburg Civil War Round Table Collection
    Daniel Harvey Hill Papers
    Robert Hubbard Letters
    Jay Luvaas Collection
    Michael Winey Collection
Virginia State Archives
    Berkeley Family Papers
    Pension Applications
Mrs. Thomas N. Wampler
    John Morris Wampler Papers
    Catharine Nugent Cummings Wampler Papers
Western Reserve Historical Society, Cleveland, Ohio
    William P Palmer Collection

Newspapers

Alexandria (Va.) Gazette. 1865.
Baltimore American. 1831.
Baltimore Gazette and Daily Advertiser. 1827.
Baltimore Weekly Dispatch. 1859.
(Bardstown) Kentucky Standard. 1987.
Boston Courier. 1850.
Charleston Daily Courier. 1863.
Charleston Mercury. 1863.
Chattanooga Daily Rebel. 1863.
Chicago Times. 1862.
(Cincinnati) Daily Commercial. 1862.
Cincinnati Daily Enquirer. 1862.
(Leesburg, Va.) Democratic Mirror. 1860–62.
(Leesburg, Va.) Washingtonian. 1861.
(Louisville) Daily Democrat. 1862.
(Louisville) Daily Evening News. 1862.
Louisville Daily Journal. 1862.
Loudoun (Va.) Times Mirror. 1976–77, 1985.

New York Daily Tribune. 1862.
New York Times. 1853, 1862.
Richmond Times-Dispatch. 1904.
Salem (Mass.) Gazette. 1850.
(Washington City) Daily National Intelligencer. 1846.
(Washington, D. C.) Sunday Star. 1918.

Books

Alexander, Edward Porter. *Military Memoirs of a Confederate.* New York: Charles Scribner's Sons, 1907.

Blackford, W. W. *War Years with Jeb Stuart.* New York: Charles Scribner's Sons, 1945.

Burke, Benjamin Franklin. *Letters of Pvt. Benjamin F. Burke: Written While in the Terry's Texas Rangers, 1861–1864.* Compiled by Jessie Burke Heard. Texas: n.p., 1965.

Chambers, William. *Sketch of the Life of Gen. T. J. Chambers of Texas.* Galveston: Galveston News Office, 1853.

Dahlgren, Madeleine Vinton. *Memoir of John A. Dahlgren.* New York: Charles L. Webster and Co., 1891.

Daniel, Frederick S. *Richmond Howitzers in the War: Four Years Campaigning with the Army of Northern Virginia.* Richmond: 1891.

de Lemartine, Alphonse. *Raphael; or Pages of the Book of Life at Twenty.* New York: Harper & Brothers, 1849.

De Leon, T. C. *Belles, Beaux and Brains of the 60's.* New York: G. W. Dillingham Company, 1909.

Dickens, Charles. *American Notes.* London: Oxford Univ. Press, 1957.

Early, Jubal A. *Autobiographical Sketch and Narrative of the War Between the States.* Philadelphia: J. B. Lippincott Company, 1912.

Estvan, B. *War Pictures from the South.* New York: D. Appleton and Company, 1863.

Freemasons, M. W. Grand Lodge of Free and Accepted Masons of the District of Columbia. *Reprint of the Proceedings of the Free and Accepted Masons of the District of Columbia, 1850 to 1862.* Washington, D.C.: John F. Sheivy, 1903.

Fremantle, Arthur James Lyon. *Three Months in the Southern States.* New York: Bradburn, 1864.

Frobel, Anne S. *The Civil War Diary of Anne S. Frobel.* McLean, Va.: EPM Publications, 1992.

Garcia, Celine Fremaux. *Celine: Remembering Louisiana, 1850–1871.* Edited by Patrick J. Geary. Athens: Univ. of Georgia Press, 1987.

Girard, Charles. *A Visit to the Confederate States of America in 1863.* Tuscaloosa, Ala.: Confederate Publishing Company, 1962.

Goodhart, Briscoe. *History of the Independent Loudoun Virginia Rangers, 1862–65.* Washington, D.C.: Press of McGill & Wallace, 1896.

Graber, Henry W. *The Life of H. W. Graber: A Terry Texas Ranger, 1861–1865; Sixty-two Years in Texas.* N.p.: H. W. Graber, 1916.

Hagood, Johnson. *Memoirs of the War of Secession*. Columbia: State Company, 1910.

Harrison, Mrs. Burton [née Constance Cary]. *Recollections Grave and Gay*. New York: Charles Scribner's Sons, 1911.

Holmes, Oliver Wendell, Jr. *Touched With Fire: Civil War Letters and Diary of Oliver Wendell Holmes, Jr., 1861–1864*. Cambridge, Mass.: Harvard Univ. Press, 1946.

Hunter, Alexander. *The Women of the Debatable Land*. Washington, D.C.: Corden Publishing Company, 1912.

Hunton, Eppa. *Autobiography of Eppa Hunton*. Richmond, Va.: William Byrd Press, 1933.

Ingraham, J. H. *The Throne of David*. Boston: Roberts Brothers, 1871.

Janney, Samuel M. *Memoirs*. Philadelphia: Friends' Book Association, 1881.

Jeffries, C. C. *Terry's Rangers*. New York: Vantage Press, 1961.

Johnson, John. *The Defense of Charleston Harbor, Including Fort Sumter and the Adjacent Islands, 1863–1865*. Charleston, S.C.: Walker, Evans & Cogswell Co., 1890.

Johnston, Joseph E. *Narrative of Military Operations, Directed, During the Late War Between the States*. New York: D. Appleton and Company, 1874.

Kirkley, Joseph W. *Itinerary of the Army of the Potomac and Co-Operating Forces in the Gettysburg Campaign, June and July, 1863*. Washington, D.C.: U.S. Adjutant General's Office, 1886.

Liddell, St. John Richardson. *Liddell's Record: St. John Richardson Liddell, Brigadier General, CSA, Staff Officer and Brigade Commander, Army of Tennessee*. Edited by Nathaniel C. Hughes. Dayton, Ohio: Morningside, 1985.

Mahan, Dennis Hart. *A Complete Treatise on Field Fortification, with the General Outlines of the Principles*. New York: Wiley and Long, 1836.

Manigault, Edward. *Siege Train; The Journal of a Confederate Artilleryman in the Defense of Charleston*. Edited by Warren Ripley. Columbia: Univ. of South Carolina Press, 1986.

Marszalek, John F., ed. *The Diary of Miss Emma Holmes, 1861–1866*. Baton Rouge: Louisiana State Univ. Press, 1979.

Martin, Joseph. *A New and Comprehensive Gazetteer of Virginia, and the District of Columbia*. Charlottesville, Va.: Moseley & Tompkins, Printers, 1835.

Mercer, Margaret. *Popular Lectures on Ethics, or Moral Obligation: For the Use of Schools*. Petersburg, Va.: Edmund & Julian C. Ruffin, 1841.

Morris, Caspar. *Memoir of Miss Margaret Mercer*. 2nd ed., rev. Philadelphia: Lindsay & Blakiston, 1848.

Mosby, John S. *The Memoirs of Colonel John S. Mosby*. Edited by Charles Wells Russell. Boston: Little, Brown, and Company, 1917.

Myers, Frank M. *The Comanches: A History of White's Battalion, Virginia Cavalry*. Baltimore: Kelly, Piet & Co., 1871.

The Official Atlas of the Civil War. New York: Thomas Yoseloff, 1958.

Palladino, Anita, ed. *Diary of a Yankee Engineer: The Civil War Story of John H. Westervelt, Engineer, 1st New York Volunteer Engineer Corps*. New York: Fordham Univ. Press, 1997.

Pratt, Willis W., ed. *Galveston Island Or, A Few Months Off the Coast of Texas: The Journal of Francis C. Sheridan, 1839–1840*. Austin: Univ. of Texas Press, 1954.

Ripley, Roswell S. *Correspondence Relating to Fortification of Morris Island*. New York: J. J. Coulon, 1878.

Roman, Alfred. *The Military Operations of General Beauregard*. 2 vols. New York: Da Capo Press, 1994.

Scheliha, Viktor Ernst Karl Rudolf von. *A Treatise on Coast Defence*. London: E. & F. N. Spon, 1868.

Scott, John. *Partisan Life with Col. John S. Mosby*. New York: Harper & Brothers, 1867.

Shotwell, Randolph Abbott. *The Papers of Randolph Abbott Shotwell*. 2 vols. Raleigh: North Carolina Historical Commission, 1929.

Smith, Robert D. *Confederate Diary of Robert D. Smith*. Columbia, Tenn.: United Daughters of the Confederacy, 1975.

Sorrel, G. Moxley. *Recollections of a Confederate Staff Officer*. New York: Bantam Books, 1992.

Taylor, Richard. *Destruction and Reconstruction, Personal Experiences of the Late War*. New York: Longman, Green and Co., 1955.

Taylor, Yardley. *Memoir of Loudon [sic] County, Virginia*. Leesburg: Thomas Reynolds, 1853.

Toney, Marcus B. *The Privations of a Private*. Nashville, Tenn.: Privately printed, 1905.

Tower, R. Lockwood, ed. *A Carolinian Goes to War: The Civil War Narrative of Arthur Middleton Manigault, Brigadier General, C.S.A.* Columbia: Univ. of South Carolina Press, 1983.

United Daughters of the Confederacy, South Carolina Division. *South Carolina Women in the Confederacy*. 2 vols. Columbia: State Company, 1907.

Wainwright, Charles S. , *Personal Journals, 1861–1865*. New York: Harcourt, Brace, and World, 1962.

Watkins, Sam R. *"Co. Aytch": A Side Show of the Big Show*. New York: Collier Books, 1962.

Welton, J. Michael, ed. *"My Heart Is So Rebellious": The Caldwell Letters, 1861–1865*. Warrenton, Va.: Fauquier National Bank, 1991.

White, Elijah V. *History of the Battle of Ball's Bluff*. Leesburg, Va.: Washingtonian Print, 1904.

Williams, Alpheus S. *From the Cannon's Mouth: The Civil War Letters of General Alpheus S. Williams*. Edited by Milo M. Quaife. Detroit: Wayne State Univ. Press and the Detroit Historical Society, 1959.

Williamson, James J. *Mosby's Rangers: A Record of the Operation of the Forty–Third Battalion of Virginia Cavalry from its Organization to the Surrender*. 2nd ed. New York: Sturgis & Welton Company, 1909.

Womack, J. J. *The Civil War Diary of Capt. J. J. Womack*. McMinnville, Tenn.: Womack Printing Company, 1961.

Wynne, Lewis N., and Robert A. Taylor, ed. *This War So Horrible: The Civil War Diary of Hiram Smith Williams.* Tuscaloosa: Univ. of Alabama Press, 1993.

Articles

Alexander, Edward Porter. "The Battle of Bull Run." *Scribner's Magazine* 41 (Jan. 1907): 80–94.

Ashe, S. A. "Life at Fort Wagner." *Confederate Veteran* 35 (July 1927): 254–56.

Beauregard, P. G. T. "The Defense of Charleston." In *Battles and Leaders of the Civil War.* 4: 1–23. New York: Century Company, 1884.

———. "Defense of Charleston, South Carolina." *North American Review* 354 (May 1886): 419–36.

———. "The First Battle of Bull Run." In *Battles and Leaders of the Civil War.* 1: 196–227. New York: Century Company, 1884.

Carnes, W. W. "Artillery at the Battle of Perryville, Ky." *Confederate Veteran* 33 (Jan. 1925): 8–9.

Cheek, Christen Ashby, ed. "Memoirs of Mrs. E. B. Patterson: A Perspective on Danville During the Civil War." *Register of the Kentucky Historical Society* 92 (Autumn 1994): 347–99.

Cummins, Edmund H. "The Signal Corps in the Confederate States Army." *Southern Historical Society Papers* 16 (1888): 93–107.

Duke, Basil W. "Bragg's Campaign in Kentucky, 1862." *Southern Bivouac* 1 (Aug. 1885): 161–67; (Sept. 1885): 232–40.

Elmore, Albert Rhett. "Incidents of Service with the Charleston Light Dragoons." *Confederate Veteran* 24 (Dec. 1916): 538–43.

Finley, Luke W. "The Battle of Perryville." *Southern Historical Society Papers* 30 (1902): 238–50.

Gilbert, C. C. "Bragg's Campaign in Kentucky, 1862." *Southern Bivouac* 1 (Oct. 1885): 296–301; (Nov. 1885): 336–42; (Dec. 1885): 430–36; (Jan. 1886): 465–77; (Feb. 1886): 550–56.

Gilchrist, Robert C. "The Confederate Defence of Morris Island." In *Charleston Yearbook, 1884.* Charleston: News and Courier Press, 1884, 350–402.

Gillmore, Quincy A. "The Army Before Charleston in 1863." In *Battles and Leaders of the Civil War.* 4: 52–71. New York: Century Company, 1884.

Gould, Benjamin Apthorp. "Address in Commemoration of Alexander Dallas Bache." *Proceedings of the American Association for the Advancement of Science* 17 (1868): 1–47.

Harleston, John. "Battery Wagner on Morris Island 1863." *South Carolina Historical Magazine* 57 (Jan. 1956): 1–13.

Hayne, Paul Hamilton. "The Defense of Fort Wagner." *Southern Bivouac* 1 (Mar. 1886): 599–608.

Henry, Joseph. "Memoir of Alexander Dallas Bache, 1806–1867." *National Academy of Sciences, Biographical Memoirs* 1 (1869): 181–205.

Hickenlooper, Andrew. "Our Volunteer Engineers." In *Sketches of War History, 1861–1865: Papers Read Before the Ohio Commandery of the Military Order of the Loyal Legion of the United States*. Edited by R. Hunter. Cincinnati: Robert Clarke & Co., 1890, 3: 301–18.

Hill, Daniel H. "Chickamauga—The Great Battle of the West." In *Battles and Leaders of the Civil War*. 3: 638–62. New York: Century Company, 1884.

Hunt, O. E. "Engineer Corps of the Federal Army." In *The Photographic History of the Civil War*. 5: 219–54. New York: Review of Reviews Co., 1911.

Hunter, R. W. "Men of Virginia at Ball's Bluff." *Southern Historical Society Papers* 34 (1906): 254–74.

Johnson, E. Polk. "Some Generals I Have Known." *Southern Bivouac* 1 (July 1885): 120–22.

Martin, Will T. "Letter to General Bragg." *Southern Historical Society Papers* 11 (Apr.–May 1883): 203–6.

"The Murder of General Nelson." *Harper's Weekly* 6 (Oct. 18, 1862): 671.

Olmstead, Charles H. "The Memoirs of Charles H. Olmstead, Part VIII." *Georgia Historical Quarterly* 44 (Sept. 1960): 313.

———. "Reminiscences of Services in Charleston Harbor." *Southern Historical Society Papers* 11 (Feb.–Mar. 1883): 118–25; (Apr.–May 1883): 158–71.

Ripley, Roswell S. "Charleston and Its Defences." In *Charleston Yearbook, 1885*. Charleston: News and Courier Press, 1885, 347–58.

Rives, Jeannie Tree. "Old Families and Houses—Greenleaf's Point." *Records of the Columbia Historical Society, Washington, D.C.* 5 (1902): 54–63.

Ruggles, Daniel. "The Battle of Farmington, Tennessee [*sic*]." *Southern Historical Society Papers* 7 (July 1879): 330–33.

Sellman, Mrs. John P. "Experiences of a War-Time Girl." *Confederate Veteran* 35 (Jan. 1927): 19–20.

"Shelbyville: The Only Union Town in Tennessee." *Harper's Weekly* 6 (Oct. 18, 1862): 661.

Smith, William. "Reminiscences of the First Battle of Manassas." *Southern Historical Society Papers* 10 (Oct.–Nov. 1882): 433–44.

Steely, Will Frank, and Orville W. Taylor, eds. "Bragg's Kentucky Campaign: A Confederate Soldier's Account." *Register of the Kentucky Historical Society* 57 (Jan. 1959): 49–53.

Strother, David Hunter. "Personal Recollections of the War." *Harper's New Monthly Magazine* 33 (Sept. 1866): 409–28.

Talcott, T. M. R. "Reminiscences of the Confederate Engineer Service." In *The Photographic History of the Civil War*. 5: 255–73. New York: Review of Reviews Co., 1911.

Twiggs, H. D. D. "The Defence of Battery Wagner." *Southern Historical Society Papers* 20 (Jan.–Dec. 1892): 166–83.

———. "Defence of Battery Wagner, July 18th, 1863." *In Addresses Delivered Before the*

Confederate Survivors' Association in Augusta, Georgia, April 26th, 1892. Augusta, Ga.: Chronicle Publishing Company, 1892.

————. "Perilous Adventure at Battery Wagner." *Confederate Veteran* 12 (Mar. 1904): 104–6.

Urquhart, David. "Bragg's Advance and Retreat." In *Battles and Leaders of the Civil War.* 3: 600–609. New York: Century Company, 1884.

Wheeler, Joseph. "Bragg's Invasion of Kentucky." In *Battles and Leaders of the Civil War.* 3: 1–25. New York: Century Company, 1884.

Witherspoon, Jean. "Woman's Part in the Confederate War." *The Lost Cause,* 8 (Feb. 1903): 105–9.

Wright, J. M. "A Glimpse of Perryville," *Southern Bivouac* 1 (Aug. 1885): 129–34.

Public Documents

Bache, Alexander Dallas. *Reports of the Superintendent of the Coast Survey.* Ex. Doc. No. 6, 30th Cong., 1st Sess., 1847; Ex. Doc. No. 1, 30th Cong., 2nd Sess., 1848; Ex. Doc. No. 5, 31st Cong., 1st Sess., 1849; Ex. Doc. No. 12, 31st Cong., 2nd Sess., 1850; Ex. Doc. No. 3, 32nd Cong., 1st Sess., 1851; and Ex. Doc. No. 58, 32nd Cong., 2nd Sess., 1852.

Baltimore City Directory. 1856–60.

Cairo and Fulton Railroad Company. *Proceedings of the Board of Directors of the Cairo and Fulton Railroad, and the Report of the Chief Engineer Upon the Preliminary Surveys.* Little Rock: True Democrat Office, 1854.

————. *Rail Road Reports.* 1856.

Covington and Ohio Railroad. *Report of the Chief Engineer.* Richmond, Va.: 1854.

Laws and Acts of Incorporation Relating to the Covington and Ohio Railroad. Richmond: James E. Goode, 1867.

Maryland Institute for the Promotion of the Mechanic Arts. *Annual Report of the Board of Managers and Treasurer.* Baltimore: Samuel Sands Mills. 1857–58, 1859.

Matthews, James M., ed. *The Statutes at Large of the Provisional Government of the Confederate States of America.* Richmond: R. M. Smith, 1864.

Meigs, Montgomery C. "The surveys, plans, and estimates for supplying the cities of Washington and Georgetown with water." Ex. Doc. No. 48, 32nd Cong., 2nd Sess., 1853.

Provisional and Permanent Constitutions of the Confederate States. Richmond: Tyler, Wise, Allegre and Smith, 1861.

Provisional and Permanent Constitutions, Together with the Acts and Resolutions of the First Session of the Provisional Congress of the Confederate States. Montgomery, Ala.: Shorter & Reid, 1861.

The Public Statutes at Large of the United States of America. Vol. 2. Boston: Charles C. Little and James Brown, 1845.

Students of the University of Virginia: A Semi-Centennial Catalogue. Compiled by Maximilian Schele de Vere. Baltimore: Charles Harvey & Co., 1878.

U.S. Adjutant General's Office. *Itinerary of the Army of the Potomac and Co-operating Forces in the Gettysburg Campaign, June and July 1863.* Washington, D.C.: U.S. Government Printing Office, 1886.

U.S. Bureau of the Census. *Census of the United States.* 1830, 1840, 1850, 1860.

U.S. Patent Office. Letters Patent No. 20,908, dated July 13, 1858; and No. 27,399, dated Mar. 6, 1860.

War of the Rebellion: Official Records of the Union and Confederate Armies in the War of the Rebellion. 128 vols. Washington, D.C.: U.S. Government Printing Office, 1901.

War of the Rebellion: Official Records of the Union and Confederate Navies in the War of the Rebellion. 31 vols. Washington, D.C.: U.S. Government Printing Office, 1902.

Washington District Corps of Engineers. *History of the Washington Aqueduct.* Washington, D.C.: U.S. Government Printing Office, 1953.

Woods' Baltimore City Directory. 1858–78.

Wraight, A. Joseph, and Elliott B. Roberts. *The Coast and Geodetic Survey 1807–1957: 150 Years of History.* Washington, D.C.: U.S. Government Printing Office, 1957.

Unpublished Material

Berkeley, Edmund. "War Reminiscences and Others of a Son of the Old Dominion, 1824–1917." In the estate of John Divine, Leesburg, Virginia.

"A Brief History of the Parish Church of Saint David, Belmont (Within the Bounds of Old Cameron Parish), Ashburn, Virginia." Saint David's Episcopal Church, Ashburn, Virginia.

Di Zerega, Philip. "History of Secondary Education in Loudoun County, Virginia." M.A. thesis, Univ. of Virginia, 1948.

Dulaney, Ida. "The Diary of Mrs. Ida Dulaney, Oakley Plantation, Upperville, Va." In the estate of John Divine, Leesburg, Virginia.

Ellzey, Mason Graham. "The Cause We Lost and the Land We Love." In the estate of John Divine, Leesburg, Virginia.

Friend, Llerena Beaufort. "The Life of Thomas Jefferson Chambers." M.A. thesis, Univ. of Texas, 1928.

Hickin, Patricia P. "Antislavery in Virginia, 1831–1861." Ph.D. diss., Univ. of Virginia, 1968.

Johnson, A. B. "Union Army on Way to Gettysburg." Typewritten MS, 1963. In the estate of John Divine, Leesburg, Virginia.

Johnson, Ruth Loden. "A History of Tupelo." M.A. thesis, Mississippi State College [Univ.], 1951.

Kelly, Frances King. "The Gifted One: A Brief Biography of Margaret Mercer, 1791–1846, Educator, Emancipator and Heaven's Advocate." Typewritten MS, Saint David's Episcopal Church, Ashburn, Virginia.

Lilley, David A. "Mapping in North America, 1775 to 1865, Emphasizing Union Military Topography in the Civil War." Master's thesis, George Mason Univ., 1982.

Marsh, Helen Hirst. "Water Mills of Loudoun County." Typewritten MS, 1973. Thomas Balch Library, Leesburg, Virginia.

Phillips, Ted. "The City of the Silent." Typewritten MS, 1995. South Carolina Historical Society.

Secondary Materials

Books

Abbazia, Patrick. *The Chickamauga Campaign: December 1862–November 1863.* New York: Combined Books, 1988.

Ash, Stephen V. *When the Yankees Came.* Chapel Hill: Univ. of North Carolina Press, 1995.

Bearss, Edwin C. *First Manassas Battlefield Map Study.* Lynchburg, Va.: H. E. Howard, 1991.

Black, Robert C., III. *The Railroads of the Confederacy.* Chapel Hill: Univ. of North Carolina Press, 1952.

Boney, F. N. *John Letcher of Virginia: The Story of Virginia's Civil War Governor.* University, Ala.: Univ. of Alabama Press, 1966.

Bradshaw, Timothy E., Jr. *Battery Wagner: The Siege, the Men Who Fought, and the Casualties.* Columbia, S.C.: Palmetto Historical Works, 1993.

Bridges, Hal. *Lee's Maverick General: Daniel Harvey Hill.* New York: McGraw-Hill, 1961.

Bruce, Robert V. *The Launching of Modern American Science, 1846–1876.* Ithaca, N.Y.: Cornell Univ. Press, 1987.

Burke, James *Connections.* Boston: Little, Brown, 1978.

Burton, E. Milby. *The Siege of Charleston, 1861–1865.* Columbia: Univ. of South Carolina Press, 1970.

Capers, Ellison. *South Carolina.* Vol. 5: *Confederate Military History.* Atlanta: Confederate Publishing Company, 1899.

Catton, Bruce. *Terrible Swift Sword.* Garden City, N.Y.: Doubleday, 1963.

Claiborne, John Francis Hamtramck. *Mississippi, as a Province, Territory, and State, with Biographies and Notices of Eminent Citizens.* Vol. 1. Jackson, Miss.: Power and Barksdale, 1880.

Clinton, Catherine. *The Plantation Mistress: Woman's World in the Old South.* New York: Pantheon Books, 1982.

———. *Tara Revisited: Women, War, and the Plantation Legend.* New York: Abbeville Press, 1995.

Clinton, Catherine, and Nina Siber, eds. *Divided Houses: Gender and the Civil War.* New York: Oxford Univ. Press, 1992.

Connelly, Thomas Lawrence. *Army of the Heartland: The Army of Tennessee, 1861–1862.* Baton Rouge: Louisiana State Univ. Press, 1967.

————. *Autumn of Glory: The Army of Tennessee, 1862–1865*. Baton Rouge: Louisiana State Univ. Press, 1971.

Crouch, Richard E. *"Rough-Riding Scout": The Story of John W. Mobberly, Loudoun's Own Civil War Guerrilla Hero*. Arlington, Va.: Elden Editions, 1994.

Crute, Joseph H., Jr. *Confederate Staff Officers, 1861–1865*. Powhatan, Va.: Derwent Books, 1982.

Daniel, Larry J. *Soldiering in the Army of Tennessee: A Portrait of Life in a Confederate Army*. Chapel Hill: Univ. of North Carolina Press, 1992.

Davis, William C. *Battle at Bull Run: A History of the First Major Campaign of the Civil War*. Baton Rouge: Louisiana State Univ. Press, 1981.

————. *Breckinridge: Statesman, Soldier, Symbol*. Baton Rouge: Louisiana State Univ. Press.

————. *The Orphan Brigade: The Kentucky Confederates Who Couldn't Go Home*. Garden City, N.Y.: Doubleday, 1980.

Divine, John. *8th Virginia Infantry*. Lynchburg, Va.: H. E. Howard, 1983.

————. *35th Battalion Virginia Cavalry*. 2nd ed. Lynchburg, Va.: H. E. Howard, 1985.

Divine, John, Wilbur C. Hall, Marshall Andrews, and Penelope M. Osburn. *Loudoun County and the Civil War: A History and Guide*. Loudoun County, Va.: Civil War Centennial Commission, 1961.

Dyer, Brainerd. *Zachary Taylor*. New York: Barnes & Noble, 1967.

Dyer, John P. *"Fightin' Joe" Wheeler*. University, La.: Louisiana State Univ. Press, 1941.

Evans, W. A. *Who's Who in Monroe County Cemeteries*. Aberdeen, Miss.: Mother Monroe Publishing Company, 1979.

Faust, Drew Gilpin. *Mothers of Invention: Women of the Slaveholding South in the American Civil War*. Chapel Hill: Univ. of North Carolina Press, 1996.

Freeman, Douglas Southall. *R. E. Lee*. 4 vols. New York: Charles Scribner's Sons, 1934.

Hafendorfer, Kenneth A. *Perryville: Battle for Kentucky*. Utica, Ky.: McDowell Publications, 1981.

————. *They Died by Twos and Tens: The Confederate Cavalry in the Kentucky Campaign of 1862*. Louisville, Ky.: KH Press, 1995.

Hall, Clayton Colman, ed. *Baltimore: Its History and Its People*. Vol. I: *History*. New York: Lewis Historical Publishing Company, 1912.

Hallock, Judith Lee. *Braxton Bragg and Confederate Defeat*. Vol. 2. Tuscaloosa: Univ. of Alabama Press, 1991.

Hartje, Robert G. *Van Dorn: The Life and Times of a Confederate General*. Nashville, Tenn.: Vanderbilt Univ. Press, 1967.

Hartzler, Daniel D. *Marylanders in the Confederacy*. Westminster, Md.: Family Line Publications, 1986.

Head, James W. *History and Comprehensive Description of Loudoun County Virginia*. [Leesburg:] Park View Press, 1908.

Hennessy, John. *The First Battle of Manassas: An End to Innocence, July 18–21, 1861*. Lynchburg, Va.: H. E. Howard, 1989.

History of Baltimore, Maryland from Its Founding as a Town to the Current Year, 1729–1893. Baltimore: S. B. Nelson, 1893.

Holien, Kim Bernard. *Battle at Ball's Bluff.* Orange, Va.: Moss Publications, 1985.

Horn, Stanley F. *The Army of Tennessee.* Norman: Univ. of Oklahoma Press, 1952.

Hughes, Nathaniel Cheairs, Jr. *General William J. Hardee: Old Reliable.* Baton Rouge: Louisiana State Univ. Press, 1965.

Jackson, Henry L. *First Regiment Engineer Troops P.A.C.S.: Robert E. Lee's Combat Engineers.* Louisa, Va.: R.A.E. Design and Publishing, 1998.

Johnson, Allen, and Dumas Malone, eds. *Dictionary of American Biography.* 14 vols. New York: Charles Scribner's Sons, 1958.

Kahn, David. *The Codebreakers: The Story of Secret Writing.* New York: Macmillan Company, 1967.

Keen, Hugh C., and Horace Mewborn. *43rd Battalion Virginia Cavalry, Mosby's Command.* 2nd ed. Lynchburg, Va.: H. E. Howard, 1993.

Lindsley, John Berrien, ed. *The Military Annals of Tennessee: Confederate.* Nashville: J. M. Lindsley & Co., 1886.

Long, E. B. *The Civil War Day by Day: An Almanac, 1861–1865.* New York: Da Capo Press, 1971.

Losson, Christopher. *Tennessee's Forgotten Warriors: Frank Cheatham and His Confederate Division.* Knoxville: Univ. of Tennessee Press, 1989.

Massey, Mary Elizabeth. *Ersatz in the Confederacy: Shortages and Substitutes on the Southern Homefront.* Columbia: Univ. of South Carolina Press, 1952.

McDonough, James Lee. *Stones River—Bloody Winter in Tennessee.* Knoxville: Univ. of Tennessee Press, 1980.

———. *War in Kentucky: From Shiloh to Perryville.* Knoxville: Univ. of Tennessee Press, 1994.

McDonough, James Lee, and James Pickett Jones. *War So Terrible: Sherman and Atlanta.* New York: W. W. Norton, 1987.

McMurray, W. J. *History of the Twentieth Tennessee Regiment Volunteer Infantry, C.S.A.* Nashville, Tenn.: Publication Committee, 1904.

McMurry, Richard M. *Two Great Rebel Armies.* Chapel Hill: Univ. of North Carolina Press, 1989.

McPherson, James M. *Battle Cry of Freedom.* New York: Ballantine Books, 1989.

McWhiney, Grady. *Braxton Bragg and Confederate Defeat.* Vol. 1. Tuscaloosa: Univ. of Alabama Press, 1969.

Miller, William J. *Mapping for Stonewall: The Civil War Service of Jed Hotchkiss.* Washington, D.C.: Elliott and Clark Publishing, 1993.

Nevins, Allan. *Ordeal of the Union.* Vol. 1: *Fruits of Manifest Destiny, 1847–1852.* Vol. 2: *A House Dividing, 1852–1857.* New York: Charles Scribner's Sons, 1947.

Nichols, James L. *Confederate Engineers.* Tuscaloosa, Ala.: Confederate Publishing Company, 1957.

Odell, George C. D. *Annals of the New York Stage.* Vol. 5. New York: Columbia Univ. Press, 1931.

Odgers, Merle M. *Alexander Dallas Bache: Scientist and Educator, 1806–1867*. Philadelphia: Univ. of Pennsylvania Press, 1947.

Olson, Sherry H. *Baltimore: The Building of an American City*. Baltimore: Johns
Hopkins Univ. Press, 1980.

Parks, Joseph H. *General Leonidas Polk, C. S. A.: The Fighting Bishop*. Baton Rouge:
Louisiana State Univ. Press, 1962.

Phillips, D. L. *The Early History of the Cairo and Fulton Railroad in Arkansas*. Missouri Pacific Railroad Company, 1924.

Pleasants, Lucy Lee Pleasants. *Old Virginia Days and Ways*. Menasha, Wisc.: George
Banta Publishing Company, 1916.

Poland, Charles P., Jr. *From Frontier to Suburbia*. Marceline, Mo.: Walsworth Publishing Company, 1976.

Rable, George C. *Civil Wars: Women and the Crisis of Southern Nationalism*. Urbana:
Univ. of Illinois Press, 1989.

Richard, J. Fraise. *The Florence Nightingale of the Southern Army: Experiences of Mrs.
Ella K. Newson, Confederate Nurse in the Great War of 1861–65*. New York: Broadway Publishing Co., 1914.

Ripley, Warren. *Artillery and Ammunition of the Civil War*. 4th ed., rev. Charleston,
S.C.: Battery Press, 1994.

Robertson, James I., Jr. *Soldiers: Blue and Gray*. New York: Warner Books, 1991.

———. *Stonewall Jackson: The Man, the Soldier, the Legend*. New York: Macmillan,
1997.

Savage, Edward H. *Boston Events*. Boston: Tolman & White, 1884.

Saxon, A. H. *P. T. Barnum: The Legend and the Man*. New York: Columbia Univ.
Press, 1989.

Schildt, John W. *Roads to Gettysburg*. Parsons, W.Va.: McClain Printing Company,
1978.

Shenton, James P. *Robert John Walker: A Politician from Jackson to Lincoln*. New
York: Columbia Univ. Press, 1961.

Simms, Henry H. *The Rise of the Whigs in Virginia, 1824–1840*. Richmond, Va.:
William Byrd Press, 1929.

Slotten, Richard Hugh. *Patronage, Practice, and the Culture of American Science:
Alexander Dallas Bache and the U. S. Coast Survey*. New York: Cambridge Univ.
Press, 1994.

Stevenson, Brenda E. *Life in Black and White: Family and Community in the Slave
South*. New York: Oxford Univ. Press, 1996.

Stover, John F. *Iron Road to the West: American Railroads in the 1850s*. New York:
Columbia Univ. Press, 1978.

Thompson, Edwin Porter. *History of the Orphan Brigade*. Louisville, Ky.: L. N.
Thompson, 1898.

Trout, W. E., III. *The Goose Creek Scenic River Atlas*. Lexington, Va.: Virginia Canals
and Navigations Society, 1991.

Warner, Ezra J. *Generals in Blue: Lives of the Union Commanders.* Baton Rouge: Louisiana State Univ. Press, 1964.

———. *Generals in Gray: Lives of the Confederate Commanders.* Baton Rouge: Louisiana State Univ. Press, 1959.

Weigley, Russell F. *Quartermaster General of the Union Army: A Biography of M. C. Meigs.* New York: Columbia Univ. Press, 1959.

Weinert, Richard P., Jr. *The Confederate Regular Army.* Shippensburg, Pa.: White Mane, 1991.

Wertz, Mary Alice. *Marriages of Loudoun County, Virginia, 1757–1853.* Baltimore: Genealogical Publishing Co., 1985.

Wiley, Bell Irvin, ed. *Fourteen Hundred and 91 Days in the Confederate Army.* Jackson, Tenn.: McCowat–Mercer Press, 1954.

Williams, Harrison. *Legends of Loudoun.* Richmond, Va.: Garrett and Massie, 1938.

Williams, T. Harry. *P. G. T. Beauregard: Napoleon in Gray.* Baton Rouge: Louisiana State Univ. Press, 1955.

———. *With Beauregard in Mexico; The Mexican War Reminiscences of P. G. T. Beauregard.* Baton Rouge: Louisiana State Univ. Press, 1956.

Wills, Brian Steel. *A Battle from the Start: The Life of Nathan Bedford Forrest.* New York: Harper Collins, 1992.

Winsor, Justin, ed. *The Memorial History of Boston.* 4 vols. Boston: James R. Osgood and Company, 1881.

Wise, Stephen R. *Gate of Hell: Campaign for Charleston Harbor, 1863.* Columbia: Univ. of South Carolina Press, 1994.

Articles

"The Battle of Perryville." *Blue and Gray Magazine* 1 (Oct.–Nov. 1983): 21–44.

Bearss, Edwin C. "General Bragg Abandons Kentucky." *Register of the Kentucky State Historical Society* 59 (July 1961): 217–44.

Crowson, E. T. "Aftermath of Battle." *Virginia Cavalcade* 18 (Spring 1969): 31–40.

Divine, John. "Loudoun Christmas, 1861." *Loudoun Times-Mirror,* Dec. 26, 1985.

———. "The Passage of the Armies Through Loudoun: 1861–65." *Bulletin of the Loudoun County Historical Society* 2 (1960): 33–55.

Dyke, Linda F. "Henry Mercer's Mercer Ancestors: Plums on the Family Tree." *Mercer Mosaic* (Summer/Fall 1987): 63–74.

Ellis, Robert R. "The Confederate Corps of Engineers." *Military Engineer* 42 (Nov.–Dec. 1950): 444–47; 43 (Jan.–Feb. 1951): 36–40; (Mar.–Apr. 1951): 120–23: (May–June 1951): 187–90.

Feis, William B. "The Deception of Braxton Bragg: The Tullahoma Campaign, June 23–July 4, 1863." *Blue and Gray Magazine* 10 (Oct. 1992): 10–21, 46–53.

Florance, John E., Jr. "Morris Island: Victory or Blunder?" *South Carolina Historical Magazine* 55 (July 1964): 150.

Gruener, Claude Michael. "Rutherford B. Hayes's Horseback Ride Through Texas." *Southwestern Historical Quarterly* 68 (Jan. 1965): 352–60.

Holien, Kim Bernard. "The Battle of Ball's Bluff." *Blue and Gray Magazine* 7 (Feb. 1990): 9–18, 46–53.

McDonough, M. J., and P. S. Bond. "Use and Development of the Ponton Equipage in the United States Army, with Special Reference to the Civil War." *Professional Memoirs, Corps of Engineers* 6 (Nov.–Dec. 1914): 692–758.

Ness, George T., Jr. "Engineers of the Civil War." *Military Engineer* 44 (May–June 1952): 179–87.

Nichols, James L. "Confederate Engineer Odd Jobs." *Military Engineer* 103 (Jan.–Feb. 1961): 13–15.

———. "Confederate Map Supply." *Military Engineer* 46 (Jan.–Feb. 1954): 28–32.

Osburn, Penelope M. "Historic Leesburg Often Took Part in Great Events." *Virginia and the Virginia County* 7 (Jan. 1953): 16.

Quisenberry, A. C. "The Battle of Perryville." *Register of the Kentucky State Historical Society* 17 (Jan. 1919): 31–38.

Richard, J. Fraise. "Mrs. E. K. Newsom." *Confederate Veteran* 6 (Apr. 1898): 162–63.

Roberts, William H. "The Neglected Ironclad: A Design and Constructional Analysis of the *U.S.S. New Ironside*." *Warship International* 26 (June 1989): 109–33.

Robinson, William M., Jr. "The Confederate Engineers." *Military Engineer* 22 (July–Aug. 1930): 297–305; (Sept.–Oct. 1930): 410–19.

Scheel, Eugene M. "John Hough's Mill at Goose Creek's Lower Ford." *Loudoun Times-Mirror,* Sept. 29, 1977.

———. "Plantation into Village," *Loudoun Times-Mirror,* Apr. 1, 1976.

Shannon, J. Harry. "Margaret Mercer's Academy for Young Girls." *(Washington, D.C.) Sunday Star,* Dec. 22, 1918, 2.

———. "The Rambler Writes of Miss Margaret Mercer." *(Washington, D.C.) Sunday Star,* Dec. 15, 1918, 3.

———. "The Rambler Writes of the Old Belmont House," *(Washington, D.C.) Sunday Star,* Dec. 8, 1918.

———. "The Rambler Writes of the Old Mavin Mill." *(Washington, D.C.) Sunday Star,* Oct. 27, 1918, 3.

Trout, W. E., III. "The Goose Creek and Little River Navigation." *Virginia Cavalcade* 16 (Winter 1967): 31–34.

"United States Coast Survey." *American Journal of Education* 1 (Aug. 1855): 103–6.

Wooster, Ralph A. "Confederate Success at Perryville." *Register of the Kentucky State Historical Society* 59 (Oct. 1961): 318–23.

Index

Bragg, Braxton: appointment as army
	commander, 154; Army of Tennessee,
	185–86, 189, 193, 195, 201, 204, 218, 224–
	25; criticism of, 181, 186, 189, 204;
	Kentucky campaign, 163, 164, 165, 167–
	69, 172, 178, 181; Louisiana Board of
	Public Works, 144; Middle Tennessee,
	184, 185–87, 193, 214, 300; Mississippi,
	146, 152, 157; Perryville, 173, 174–75;
	personality, 186, 188, 201, 206, 301;
	recommendations, 206, 231, 301;
	strategy, 160–61, 167–68, 178, 205, 214,
	225, 229–30, 305
Breckinridge, John C., 76, 146, 181, 195, 265
Breech-loading weapons, 74–75
Brent, George W., 175, 185, 300
Bridgeport, Ala., 211–12, 214
Brown, John C., 220
Buchanan, Andrew H., 195, 199, 264, 299
Buckner, Simon Bolivar, 160, 164, 168, 175,
	218, 265, 266
Buell, Don Carlos, 159, 168, 171, 173–74,
	175, 177, 178, 203–4
Bull Run, battle of. *See* First Manassas,
	battle of
Burnt Bridge. *See* Leesburg Turnpike,
	Goose Creek Bridge

Cairo & Fulton Railroad, 63–64
Camp Berkeley, Va., 89, 92
Camp Burt, Va., 100–101
Camp Carolina, Va., 97, 100
Camp Dick Robinson, Ky., 169, 178, 179, 296
Camp Evans, Va. 97
Camp Hunton, Va., 97
Camp Johnston, Va., 92, 96
Camp Taylor, Va., 113
Campbell, Edward F., 65, 66
Carnes, William W., 227–28
Catskill, USS, xx, 243, 248, 249, 250
Cavalry employment, 81, 95, 98, 99, 110,
	130, 150–51, 152–53, 162, 163–64, 165, 168,
	169, 170, 171, 172, 179, 182, 202, 208,
	210–11, 216, 217, 241
Centreville, Va., encampment, 102–6, 112,
	267

Chambers, Thomas Jefferson, 43–44
Charleston, S.C., 233–34, 236, 250
Charleston Harbor, 235, 257
Chattanooga, Tenn., 160, 218–19, 221–22, 229
Cheatham, Benjamin Franklin: Kentucky
	campaign, 160, 161, 162, 164, 168, 175,
	178; Middle Tennessee, 183, 184, 204;
	Perryville, 173, 174, 175, 177, 178, 296
Chesapeake & Ohio Canal, 81
Church, Nelson B., 170
Civil engineering, 67–68
Clagett, Thomas H., 182, 297
Clagett, Thomas H., Jr., 153, 295
Cleburne, Patrick, 146, 175, 181, 216
Cocke, Philip St. George, 82, 87–88, 101,
	102, 104, 113
Columbia, Tenn., 203–4
Cooper, Samuel, 81
Corinth, Miss., 144
Corps of Engineers, C.S.: bureau, 142, 193,
	205, 206, 208, 215, 218–19, 220, 221, 223,
	224, 225; engineer troops, 206–8, 223–
	24; establishment, 142–44, 205; maps,
	187, 199–200, 219–20, 221, 224, 303;
	regular army, 82; uniform, 222–23
Corps of Engineers, U.S., 124, 142, 193, 220,
	292, 308
Corps of Topographical Engineers, U.S.,
	142, 177, 219
Covington & Ohio Railroad, 69
Cowan (Tenn.) tunnel, 184, 226
Cox, G. Thomas, 223, 252–53, 255, 309
Craven, Tunis A. M., 42, 53
Crittenden, Thomas L., 171, 174
Cryptography, 266–68, 310
Cumberland Gap, Ky., 180
Cumberland Plateau, Tenn., 163, 183
Cummings, Catharine Nugent. *See*
	Wampler, Catharine Nugent Cummings
Cummings, Pleasant J., 209–10
Cutts, Richard D., 20, 25, 27, 35, 53

Dahlgren, John, xx, 248, 249, 250
Dan Smith, USS, 246
Dana, James Dwight, 60
Darrow, Amos S., 197, 265

Confederate Engineer was designed and typeset on a Macintosh computer system using PageMaker software. The text and titles are set in Garamond. This book was designed and composed by Ellen Beeler and manufactured by Thomson-Shore, Inc. The recycled paper used in this book is designed for an effective life of at least three hundred years.